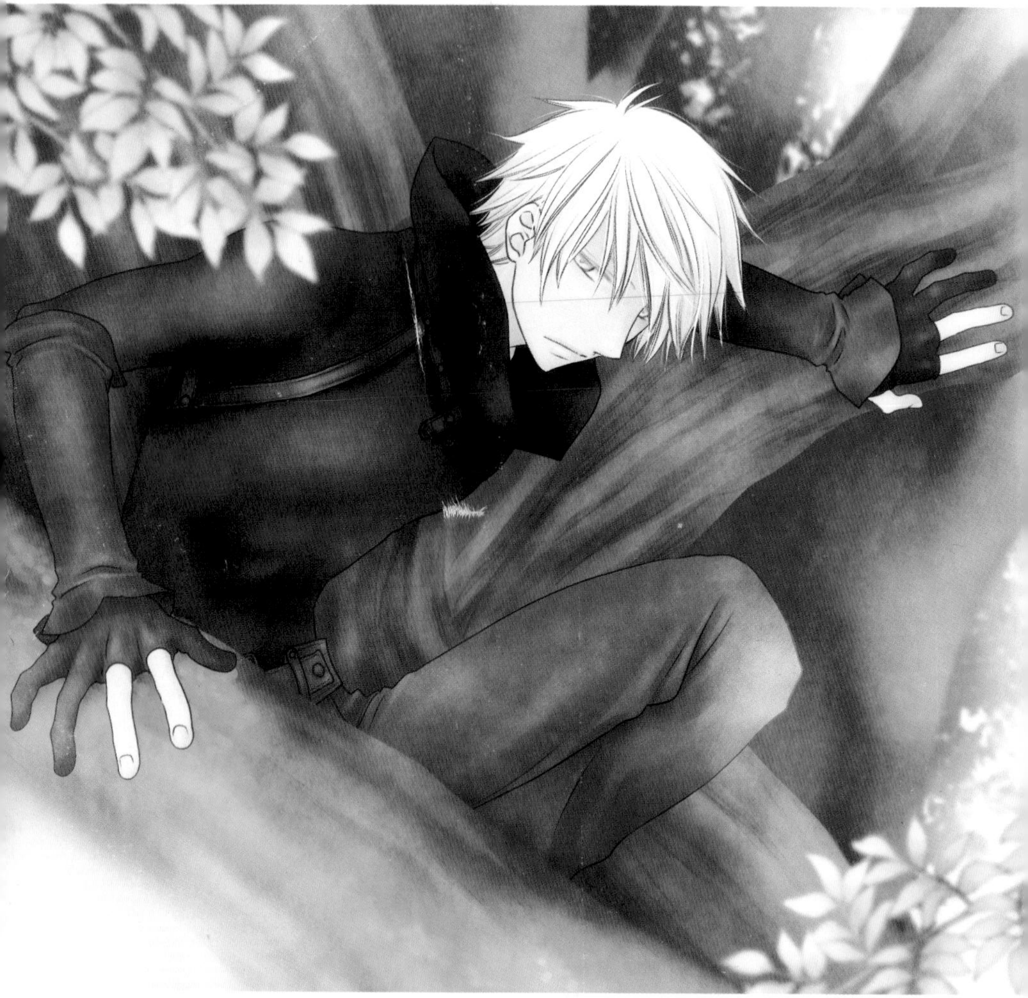

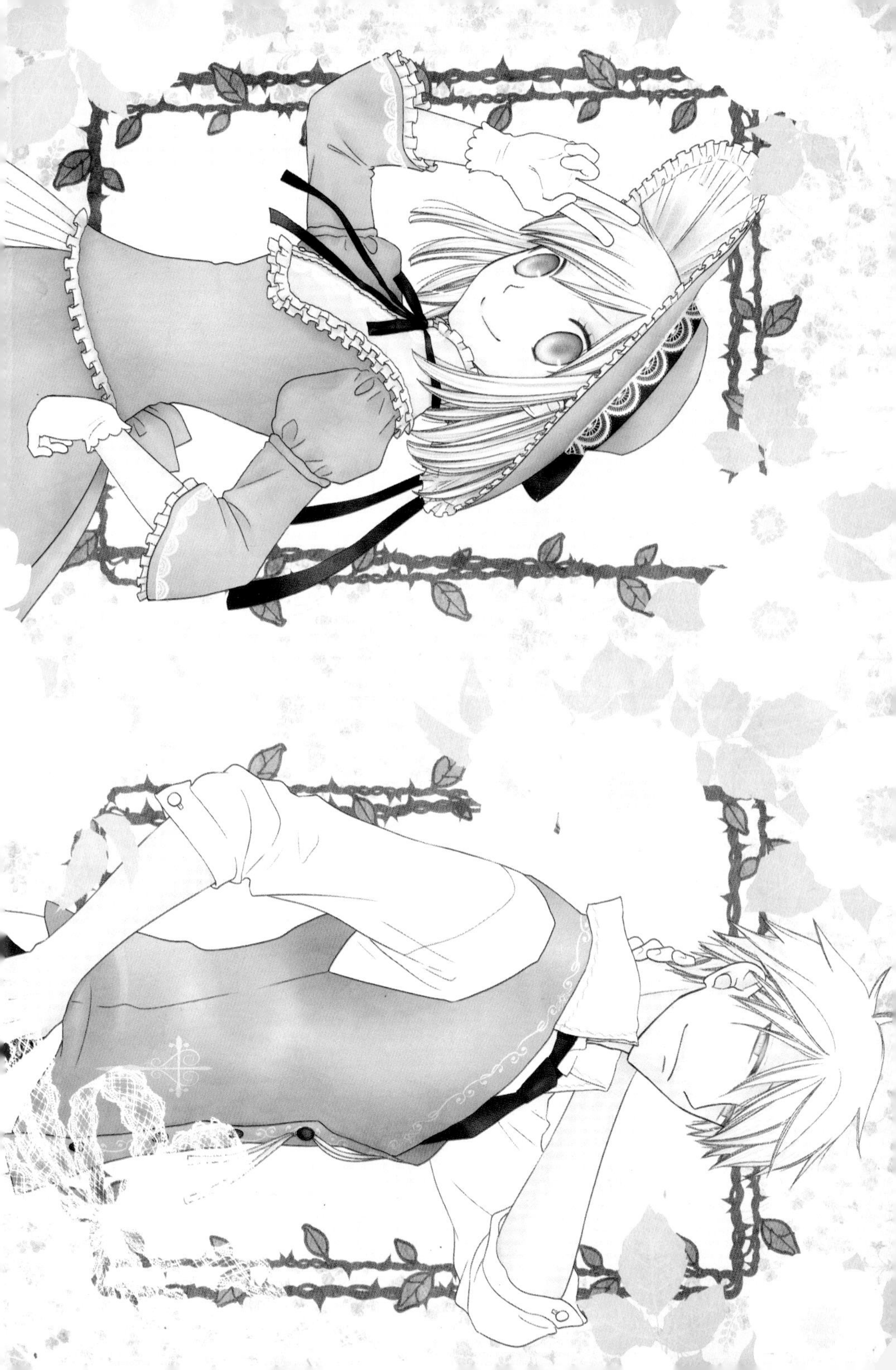

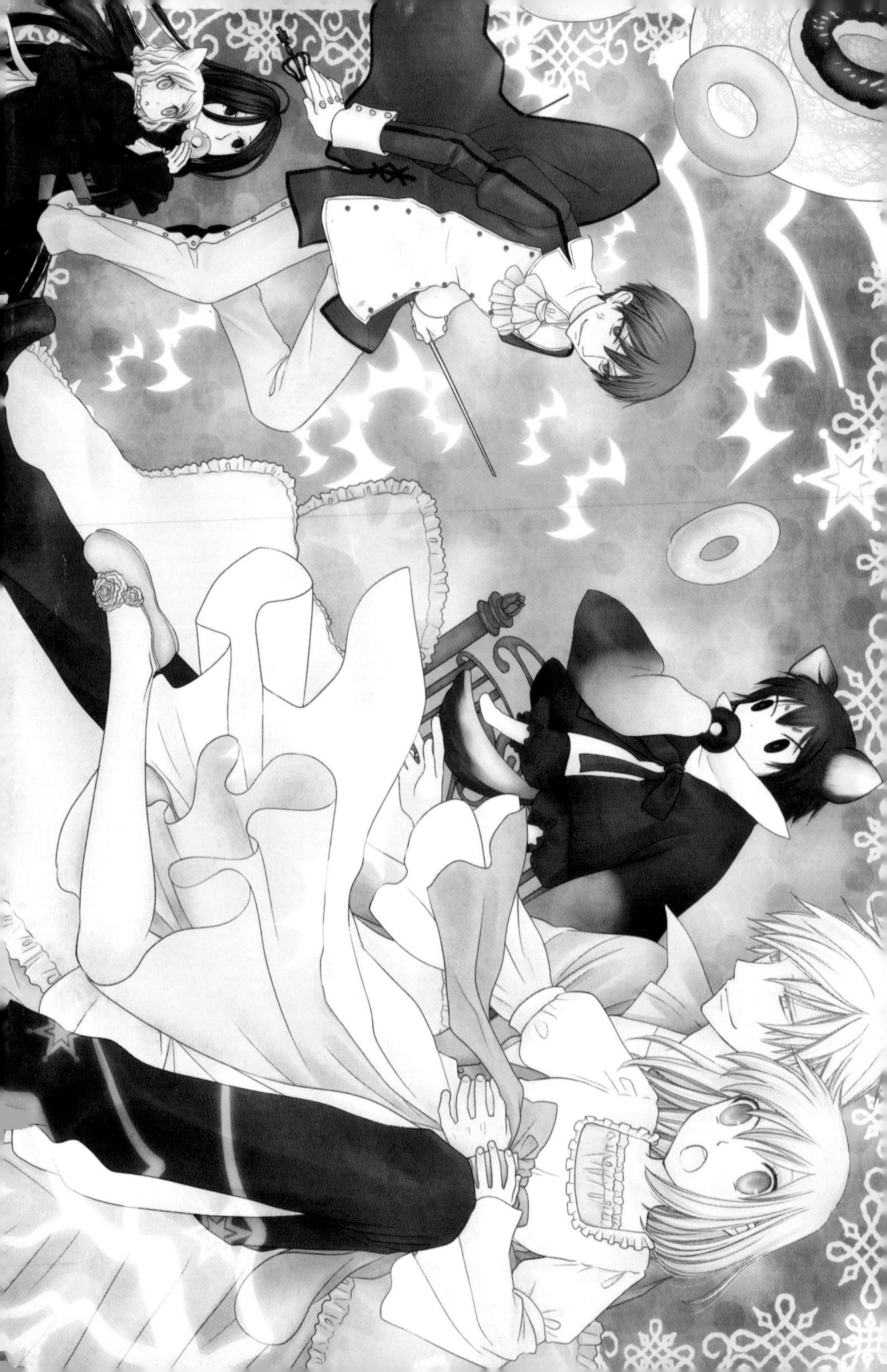

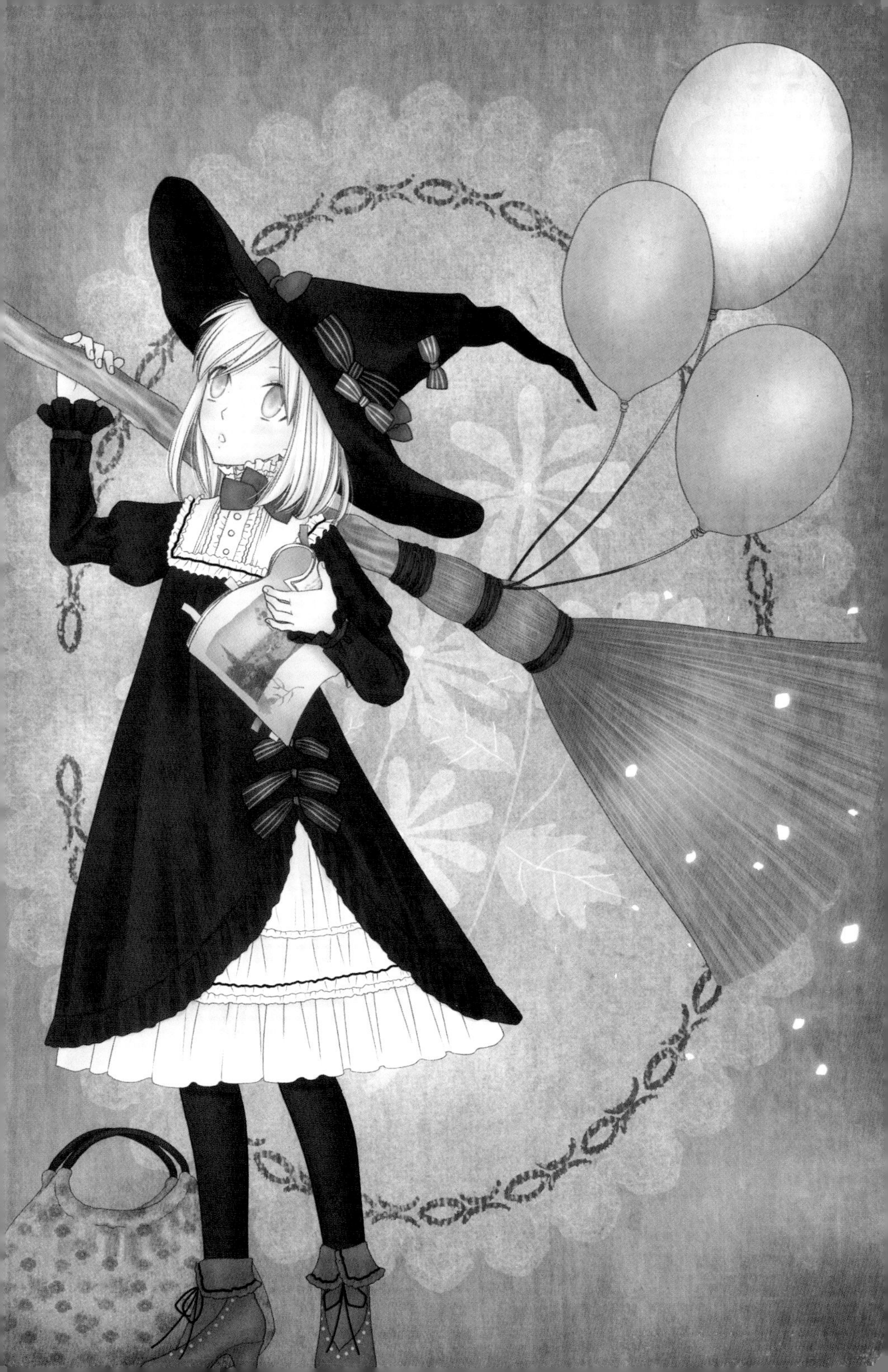

Liselotte & Witch's Forest

4

NATSUKI TAKAYA

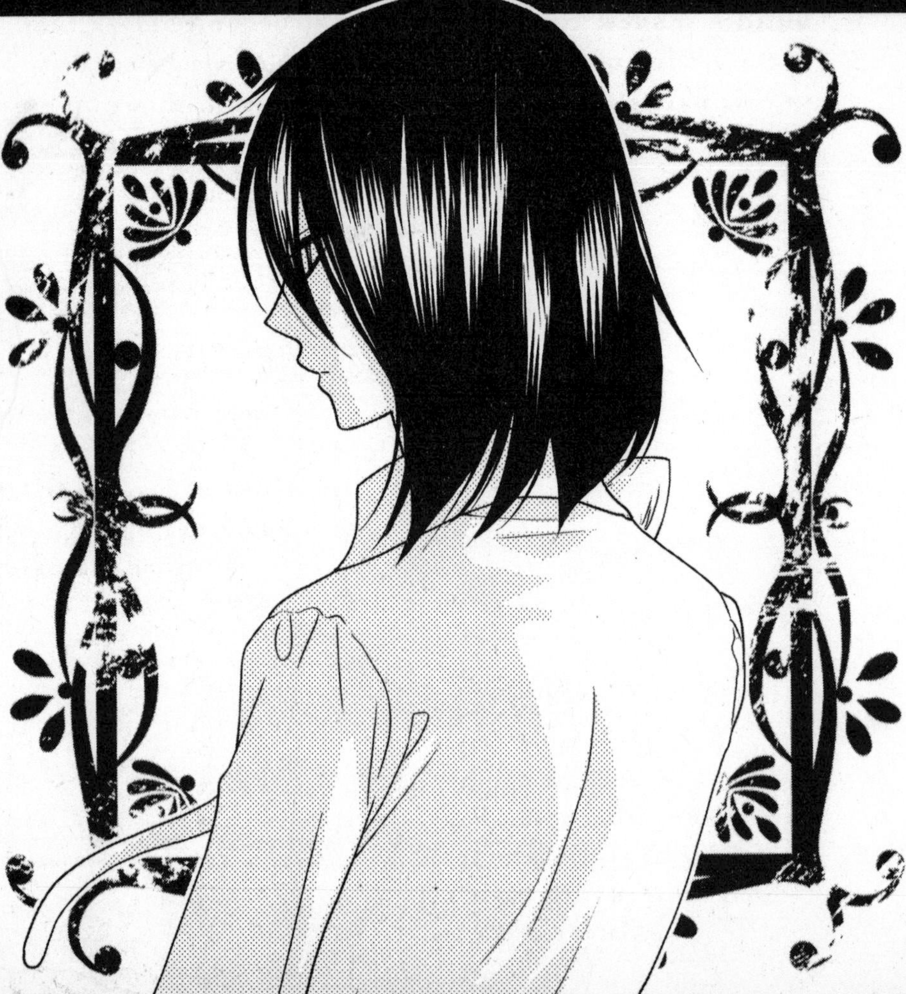

Liselotte & Witch's Forest

Natsuki Takaya

SUMMARY

Liselotte, the daughter of a feudal lord, is exiled to the frontier area east of the east of the east. She begins living her new life near a forest that is also a den of witches and soon meets a living wooden puppet, Engetsu, a familiar, Yomi, and even the witches of the forest themselves. They build a modest life together, but it becomes clear that someone is not happy about Liselotte moving next door to this particular forest. Now, new trouble shows up in front of them...!

CHARACTER INTRODUCTION

LISELOTTE BERENK

The daughter of a feudal lord. Framed for treason and imprisoned. Finally exiled to the frontier by her older brother, Richard.

ENGETSU

Lise-sama's old friend Enrich. Became a puppet after losing his human body. Saved by the Eiche tree, which subsequently stole his memories of Lise.

YOMI

The witch Vartelinde's familiar. Although, Hilde said, "But Vartelinde-sama is no longer with us...,"!?

ALTO

Lise-sama's servant. Caring but prone to worrying. The elder twin.

ANNA

Lise-sama's servant. Sharp-tongued and ever-smiling. The younger twin.

VERGUE

Witch who lives deep in the forest. Hot-tempered. Uses magic that animates turnip-headed scarecrows.

MYRTE

Hilde's familiar.

HILDE

Witch who lived deep in the forest. Currently lives at Lise-sama's house. Crybaby. Specialty is "twig transport" magic.

THE EICHE TREE

Great tree near Liselotte's house. The spirit of this tree lent its power to save Engetsu.

WILHEL

Assassin who was paid to murder Liselotte. Acquainted with Enrich...?

RICHARD

Lise-sama's older brother. Receives periodic reports about Lise-sama from Erwin, who is posted in the east.

Liselotte & Witch's Forest

VOLUME 4

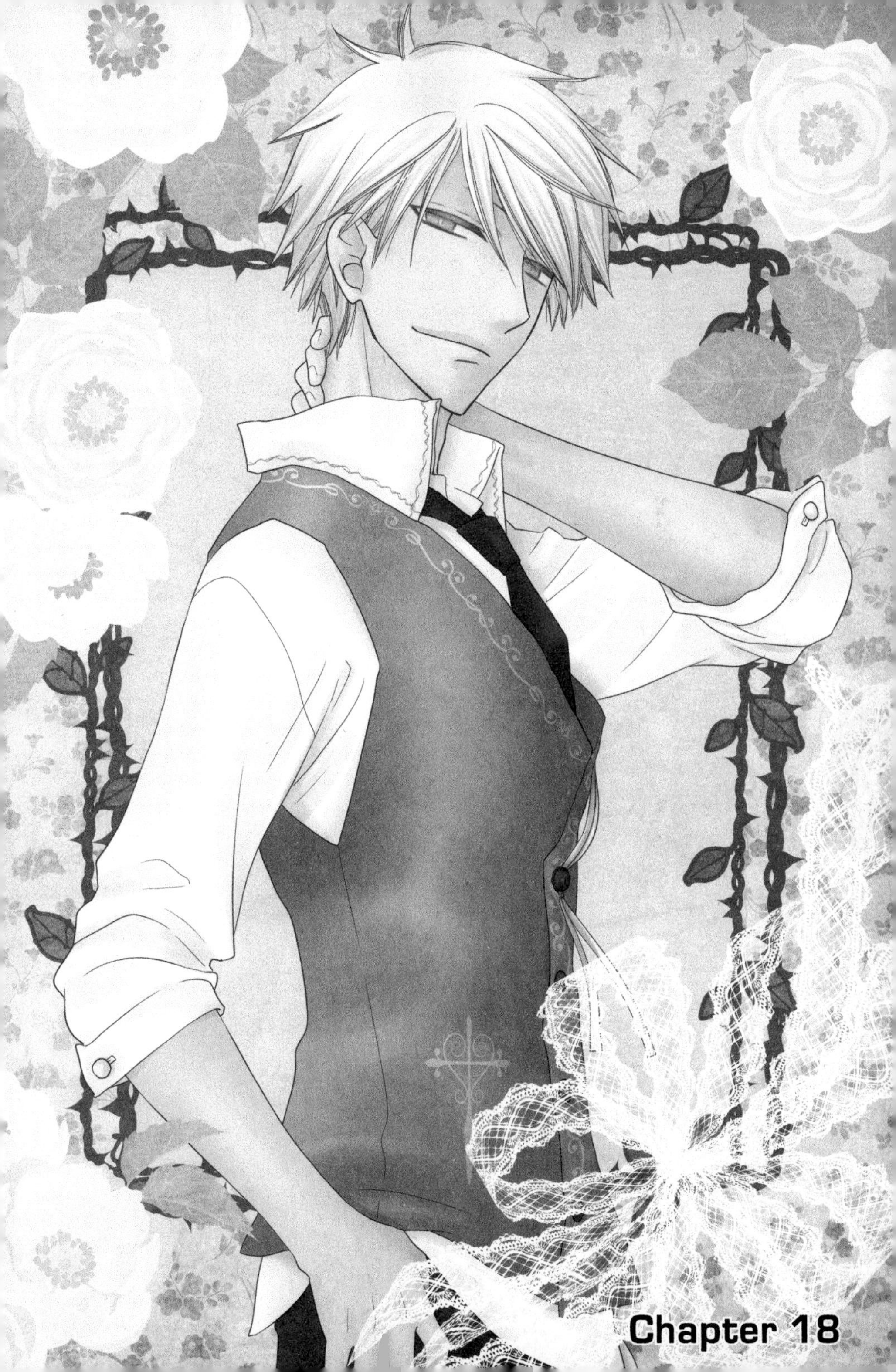

Chapter 18

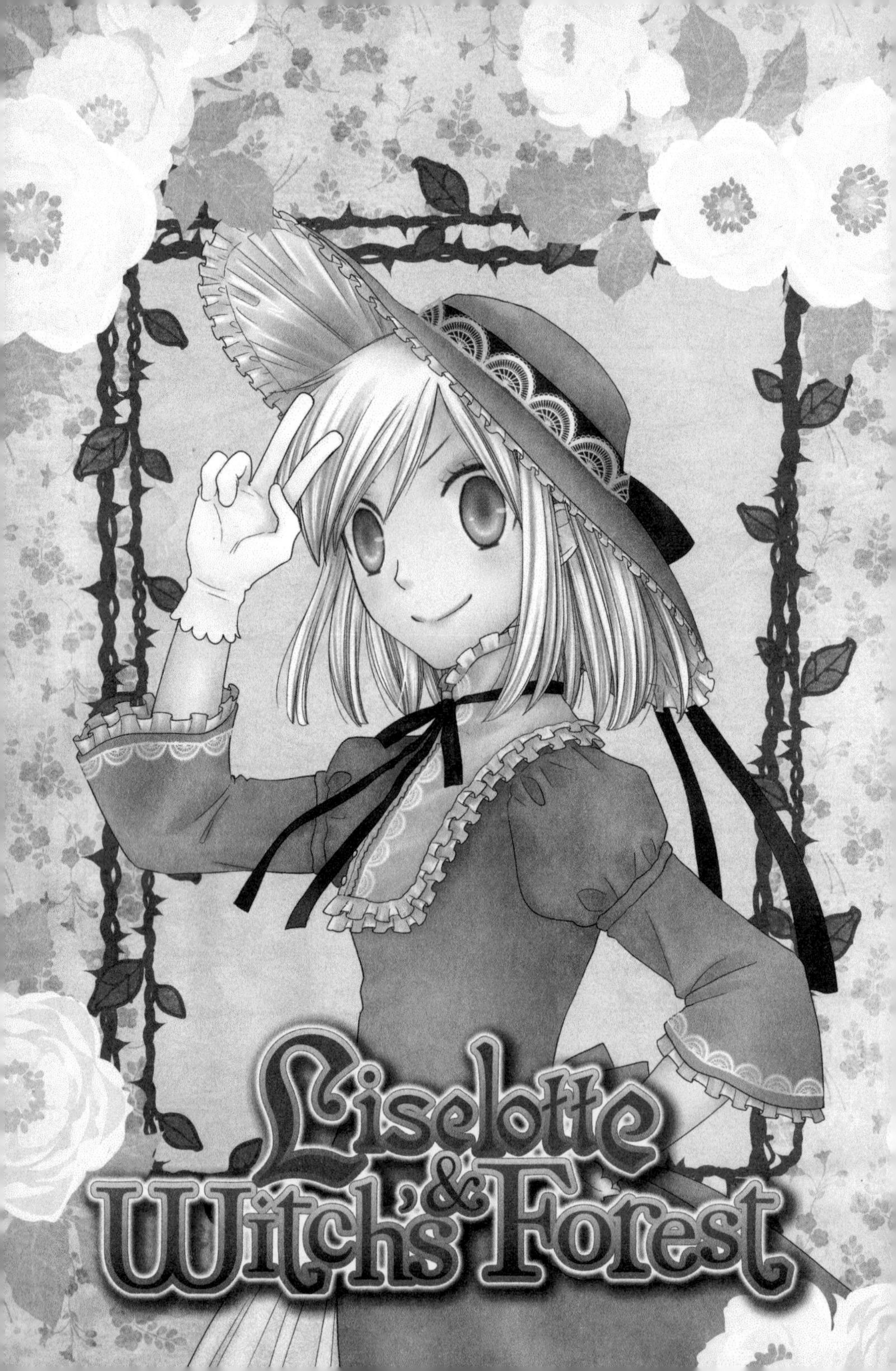
Liselotte & Witch's Forest

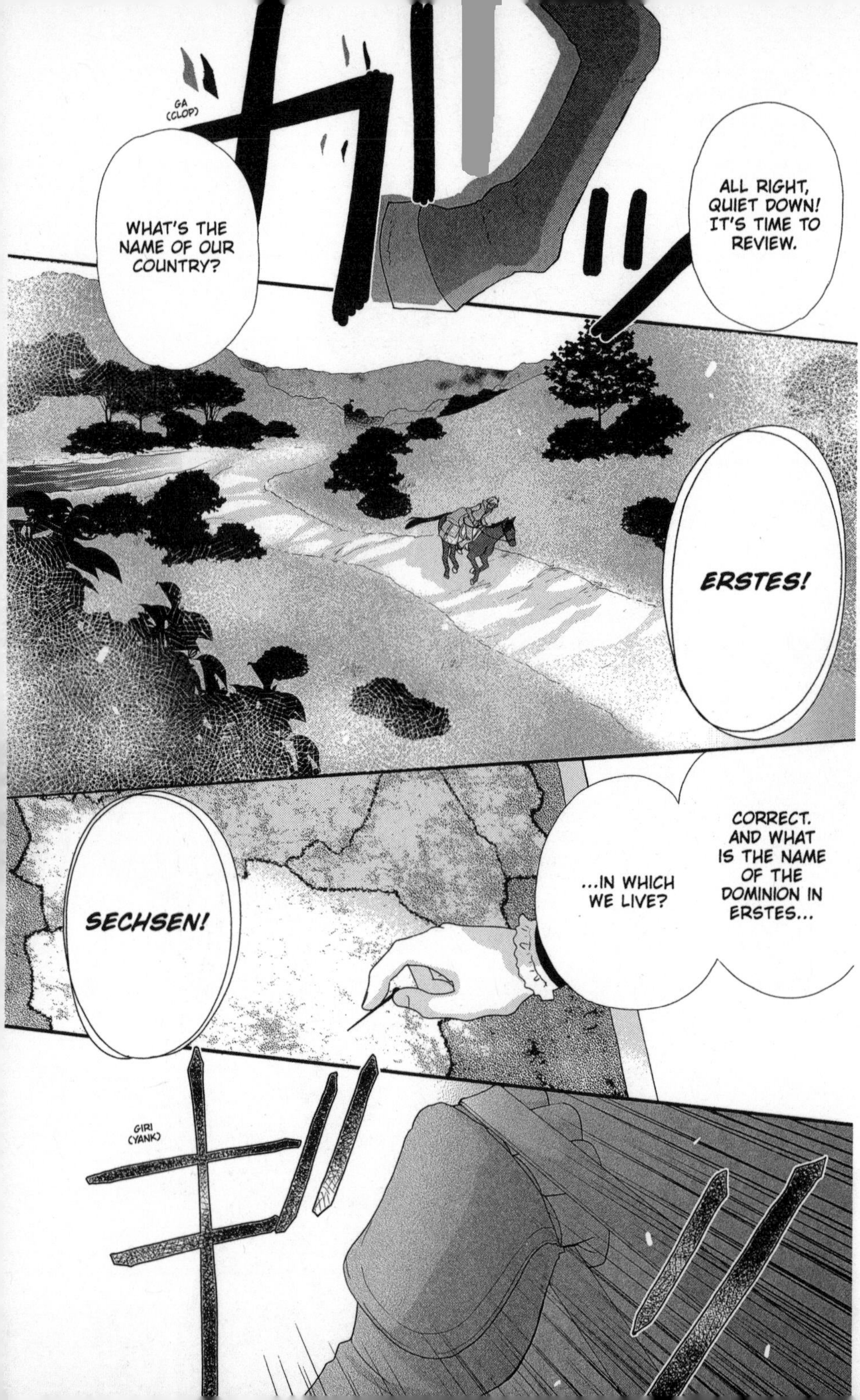
ALL RIGHT, QUIET DOWN! IT'S TIME TO REVIEW.
GA (CLOP)
WHAT'S THE NAME OF OUR COUNTRY?
ERSTES!
CORRECT. AND WHAT IS THE NAME OF THE DOMINION IN ERSTES...
...IN WHICH WE LIVE?
SECHSEN!
GIRI (YANK)

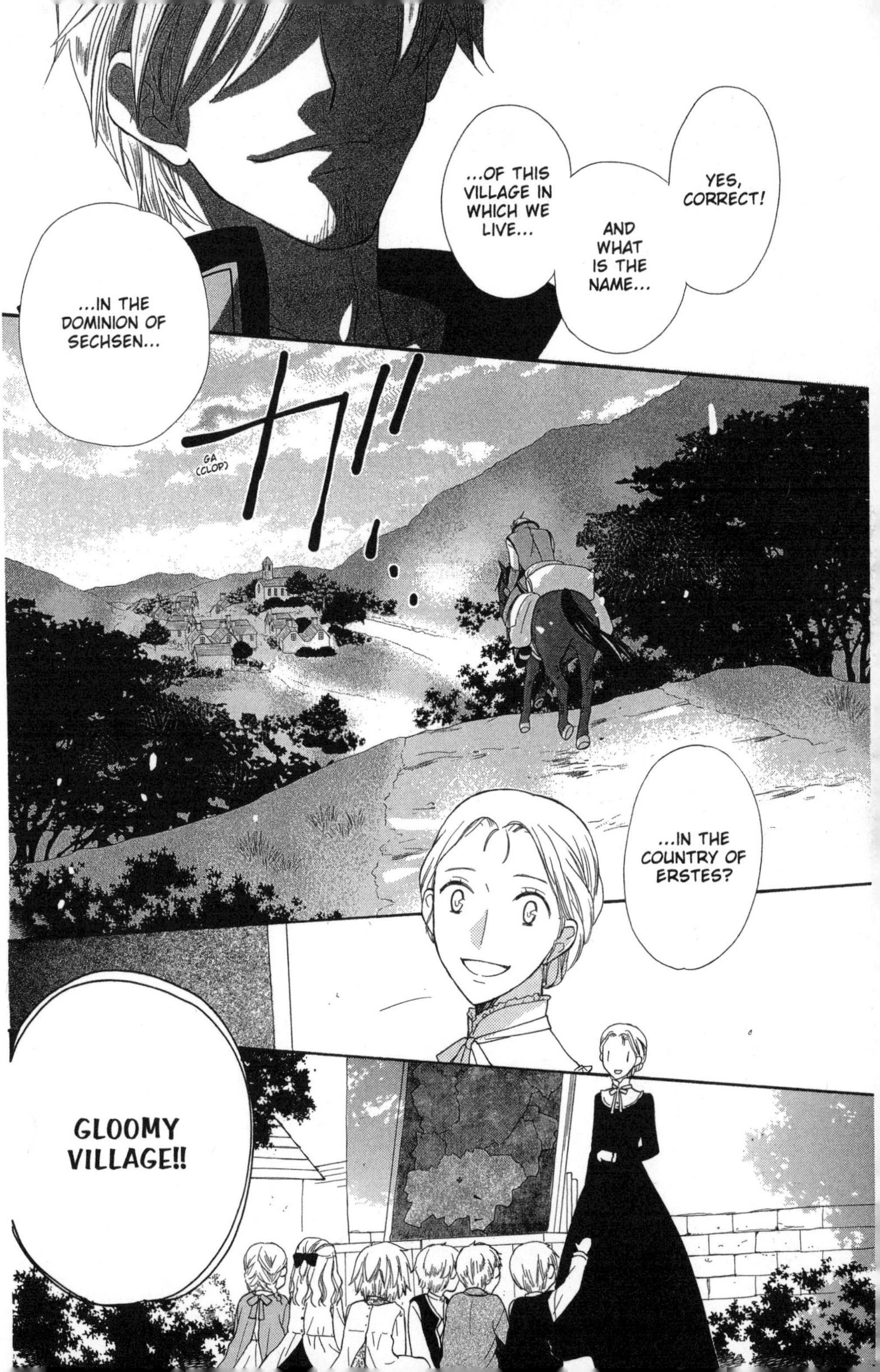
YES, CORRECT!
AND WHAT IS THE NAME...
...OF THIS VILLAGE IN WHICH WE LIVE...
...IN THE DOMINION OF SECHSEN...
GA (CLOP)
...IN THE COUNTRY OF ERSTES?
GLOOMY VILLAGE!!

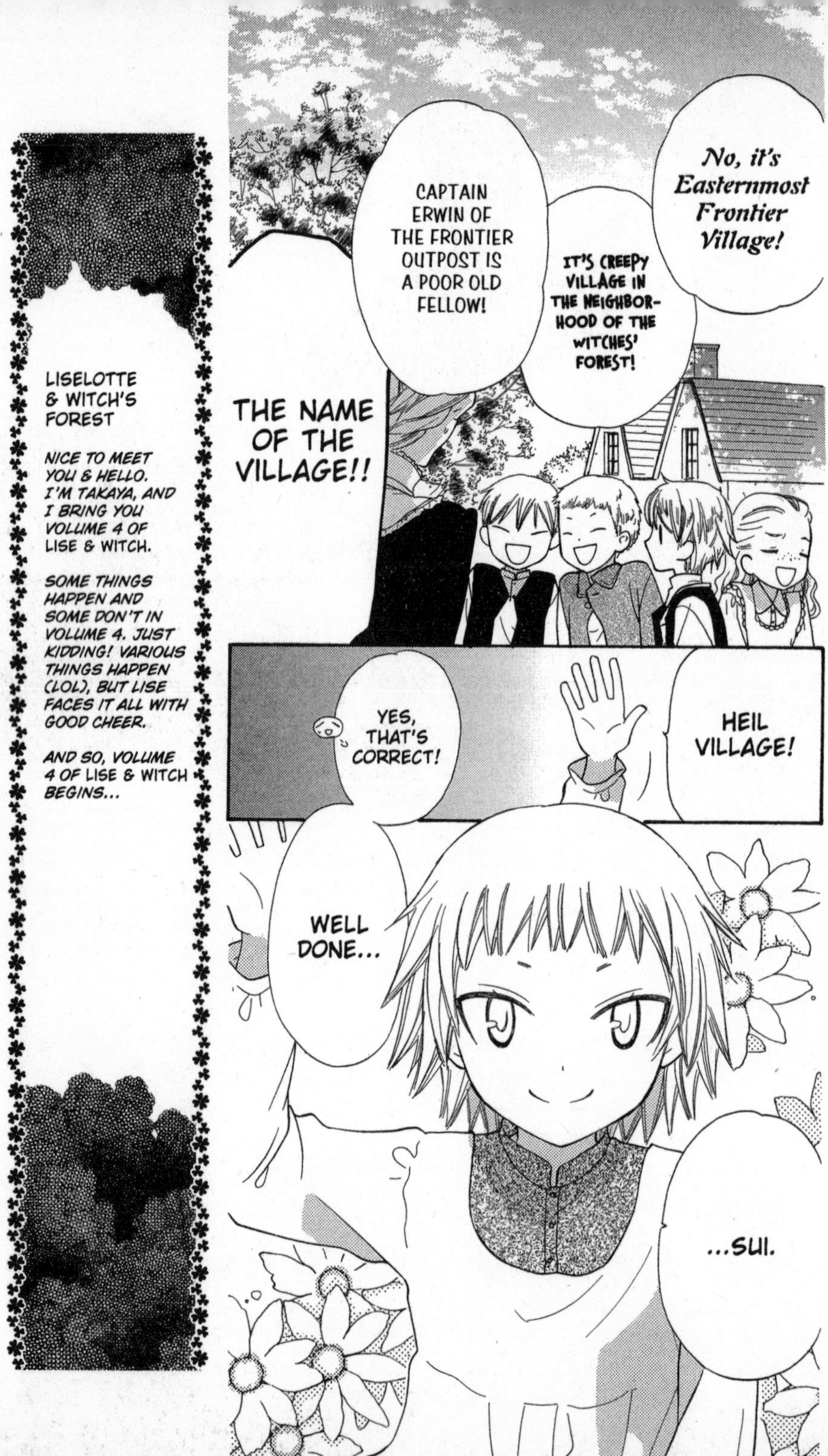
No, it's Easternmost Frontier Village!
IT'S CREEPY VILLAGE IN THE NEIGHBOR-HOOD OF THE WITCHES' FOREST!
CAPTAIN ERWIN OF THE FRONTIER OUTPOST IS A POOR OLD FELLOW!
THE NAME OF THE VILLAGE!!
HEIL VILLAGE!
YES, THAT'S CORRECT!
WELL DONE...
...SUI.

LISELOTTE & WITCH'S FOREST

NICE TO MEET YOU & HELLO. I'M TAKAYA, AND I BRING YOU VOLUME 4 OF LISE & WITCH.

SOME THINGS HAPPEN AND SOME DON'T IN VOLUME 4. JUST KIDDING! VARIOUS THINGS HAPPEN (LOL), BUT LISE FACES IT ALL WITH GOOD CHEER.

AND SO, VOLUME 4 OF LISE & WITCH BEGINS...

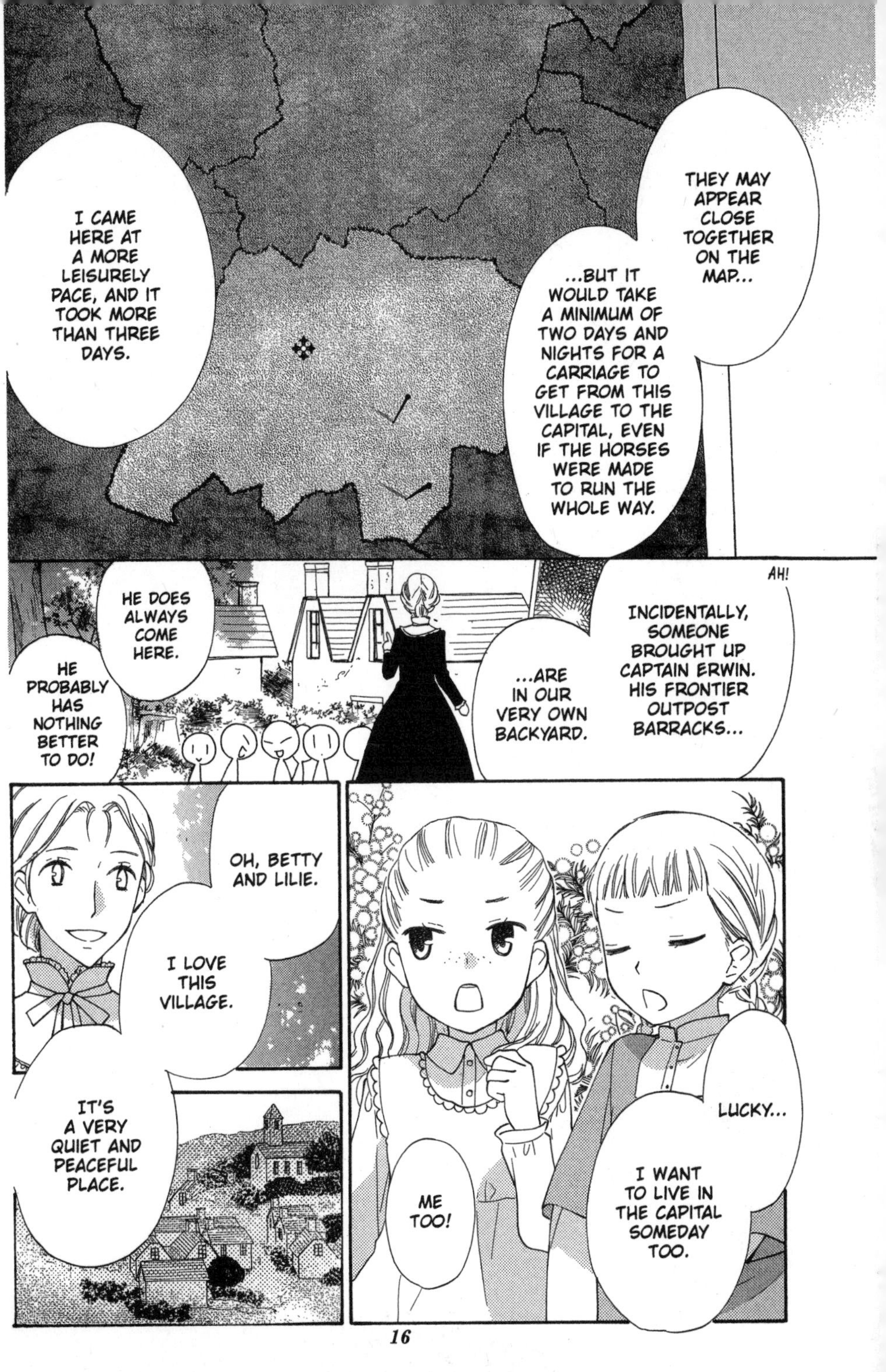
THEY MAY APPEAR CLOSE TOGETHER ON THE MAP...
...BUT IT WOULD TAKE A MINIMUM OF TWO DAYS AND NIGHTS FOR A CARRIAGE TO GET FROM THIS VILLAGE TO THE CAPITAL, EVEN IF THE HORSES WERE MADE TO RUN THE WHOLE WAY.
I CAME HERE AT A MORE LEISURELY PACE, AND IT TOOK MORE THAN THREE DAYS.
AH!
INCIDENTALLY, SOMEONE BROUGHT UP CAPTAIN ERWIN. HIS FRONTIER OUTPOST BARRACKS...
...ARE IN OUR VERY OWN BACKYARD.
HE DOES ALWAYS COME HERE.
HE PROBABLY HAS NOTHING BETTER TO DO!
LUCKY...
I WANT TO LIVE IN THE CAPITAL SOMEDAY TOO.
ME TOO!
OH, BETTY AND LILIE.
I LOVE THIS VILLAGE.
IT'S A VERY QUIET AND PEACEFUL PLACE.

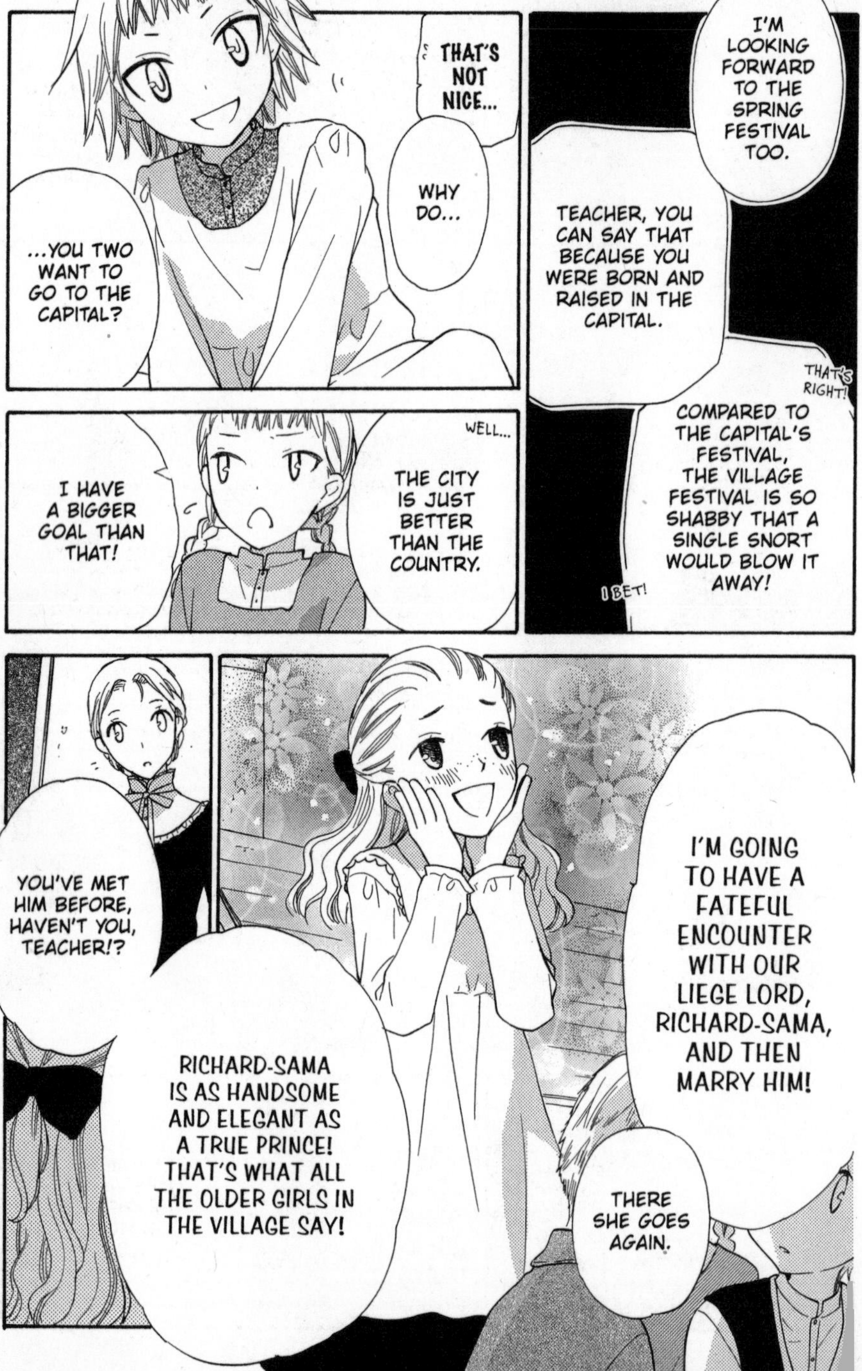
I'M LOOKING FORWARD TO THE SPRING FESTIVAL TOO.
TEACHER, YOU CAN SAY THAT BECAUSE YOU WERE BORN AND RAISED IN THE CAPITAL.
THAT'S RIGHT!
COMPARED TO THE CAPITAL'S FESTIVAL, THE VILLAGE FESTIVAL IS SO SHABBY THAT A SINGLE SNORT WOULD BLOW IT AWAY!
I BET!
THAT'S NOT NICE...
WHY DO...
...YOU TWO WANT TO GO TO THE CAPITAL?
WELL...
THE CITY IS JUST BETTER THAN THE COUNTRY.
I HAVE A BIGGER GOAL THAN THAT!
I'M GOING TO HAVE A FATEFUL ENCOUNTER WITH OUR LIEGE LORD, RICHARD-SAMA, AND THEN MARRY HIM!
THERE SHE GOES AGAIN.
RICHARD-SAMA IS AS HANDSOME AND ELEGANT AS A TRUE PRINCE! THAT'S WHAT ALL THE OLDER GIRLS IN THE VILLAGE SAY!
YOU'VE MET HIM BEFORE, HAVEN'T YOU, TEACHER!?

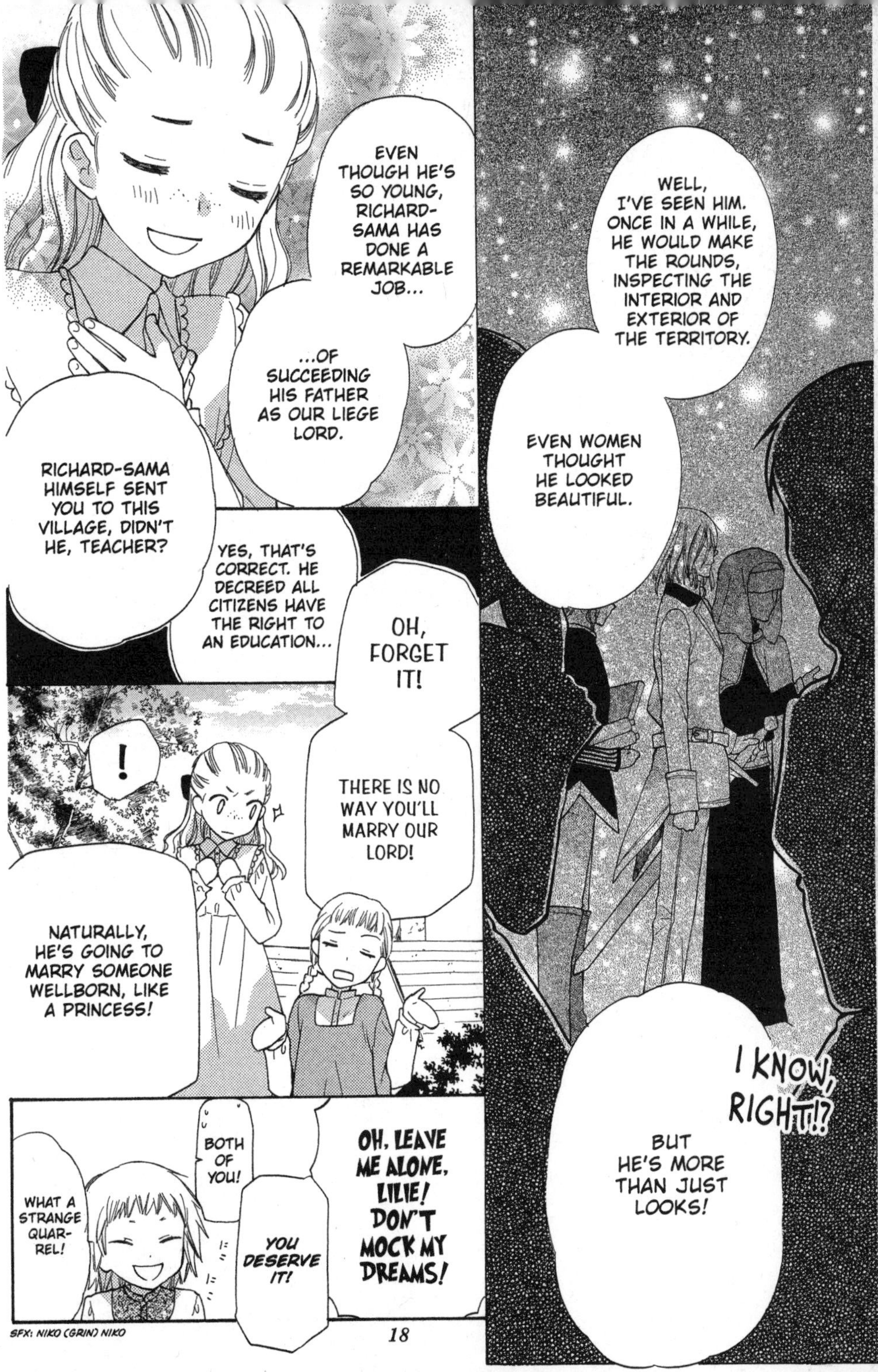
WELL, I'VE SEEN HIM. ONCE IN A WHILE, HE WOULD MAKE THE ROUNDS, INSPECTING THE INTERIOR AND EXTERIOR OF THE TERRITORY.
EVEN WOMEN THOUGHT HE LOOKED BEAUTIFUL.
I KNOW, RIGHT!?
BUT HE'S MORE THAN JUST LOOKS!
EVEN THOUGH HE'S SO YOUNG, RICHARD-SAMA HAS DONE A REMARKABLE JOB...
...OF SUCCEEDING HIS FATHER AS OUR LIEGE LORD.
RICHARD-SAMA HIMSELF SENT YOU TO THIS VILLAGE, DIDN'T HE, TEACHER?
YES, THAT'S CORRECT. HE DECREED ALL CITIZENS HAVE THE RIGHT TO AN EDUCATION...
OH, FORGET IT!
THERE IS NO WAY YOU'LL MARRY OUR LORD!
!
NATURALLY, HE'S GOING TO MARRY SOMEONE WELLBORN, LIKE A PRINCESS!
OH. LEAVE ME ALONE, LILIE! DON'T MOCK MY DREAMS!
YOU DESERVE IT!
BOTH OF YOU!
WHAT A STRANGE QUARREL!

SFX: NIKO (GRIN) NIKO

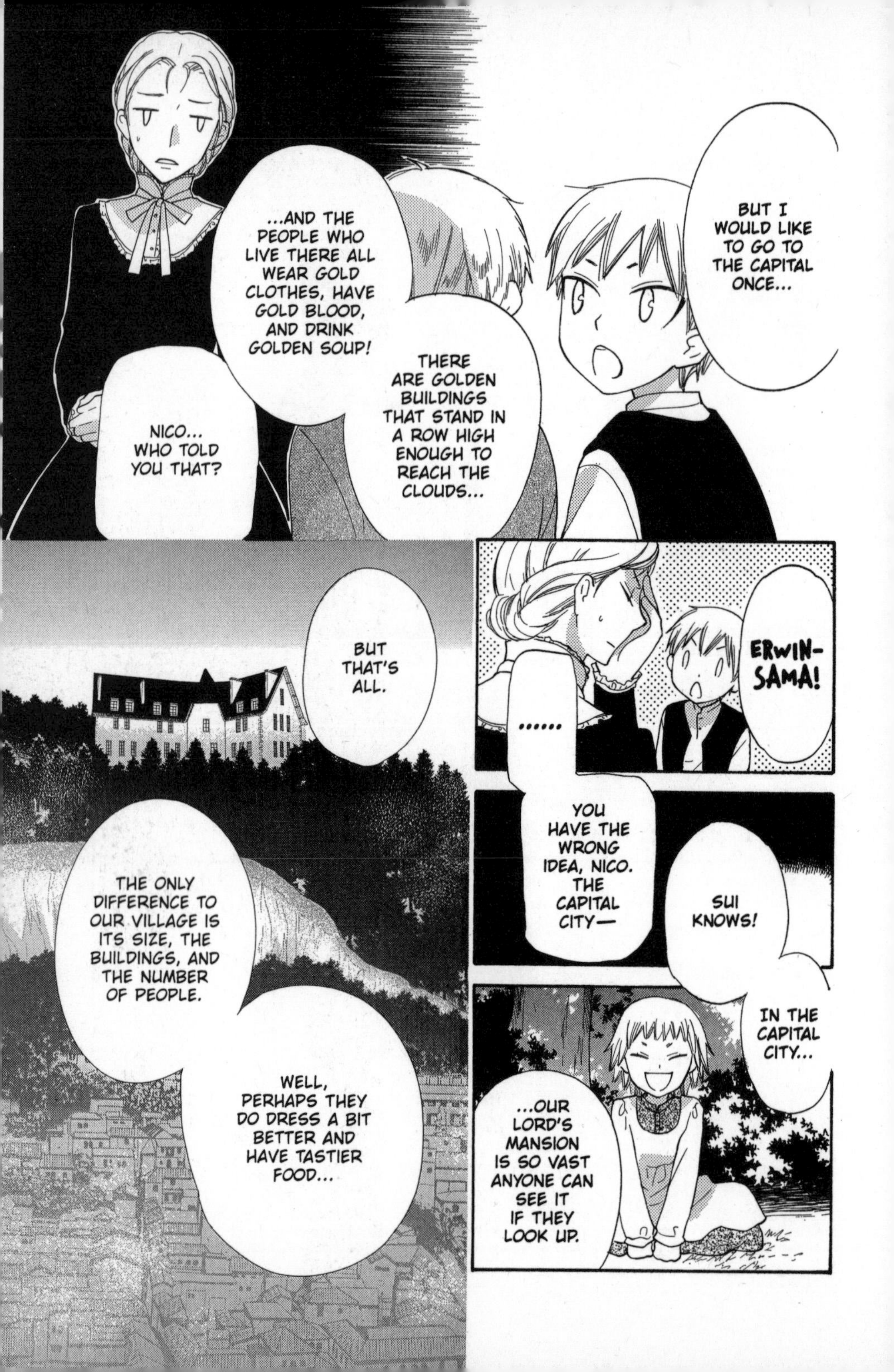

BUT I WOULD LIKE TO GO TO THE CAPITAL ONCE...
THERE ARE GOLDEN BUILDINGS THAT STAND IN A ROW HIGH ENOUGH TO REACH THE CLOUDS...
...AND THE PEOPLE WHO LIVE THERE ALL WEAR GOLD CLOTHES, HAVE GOLD BLOOD, AND DRINK GOLDEN SOUP!
NICO... WHO TOLD YOU THAT?
ERWIN-SAMA!
......
YOU HAVE THE WRONG IDEA, NICO. THE CAPITAL CITY—
SUI KNOWS!
IN THE CAPITAL CITY...
...OUR LORD'S MANSION IS SO VAST ANYONE CAN SEE IT IF THEY LOOK UP.
BUT THAT'S ALL.
THE ONLY DIFFERENCE TO OUR VILLAGE IS ITS SIZE, THE BUILDINGS, AND THE NUMBER OF PEOPLE.
WELL, PERHAPS THEY DO DRESS A BIT BETTER AND HAVE TASTIER FOOD...

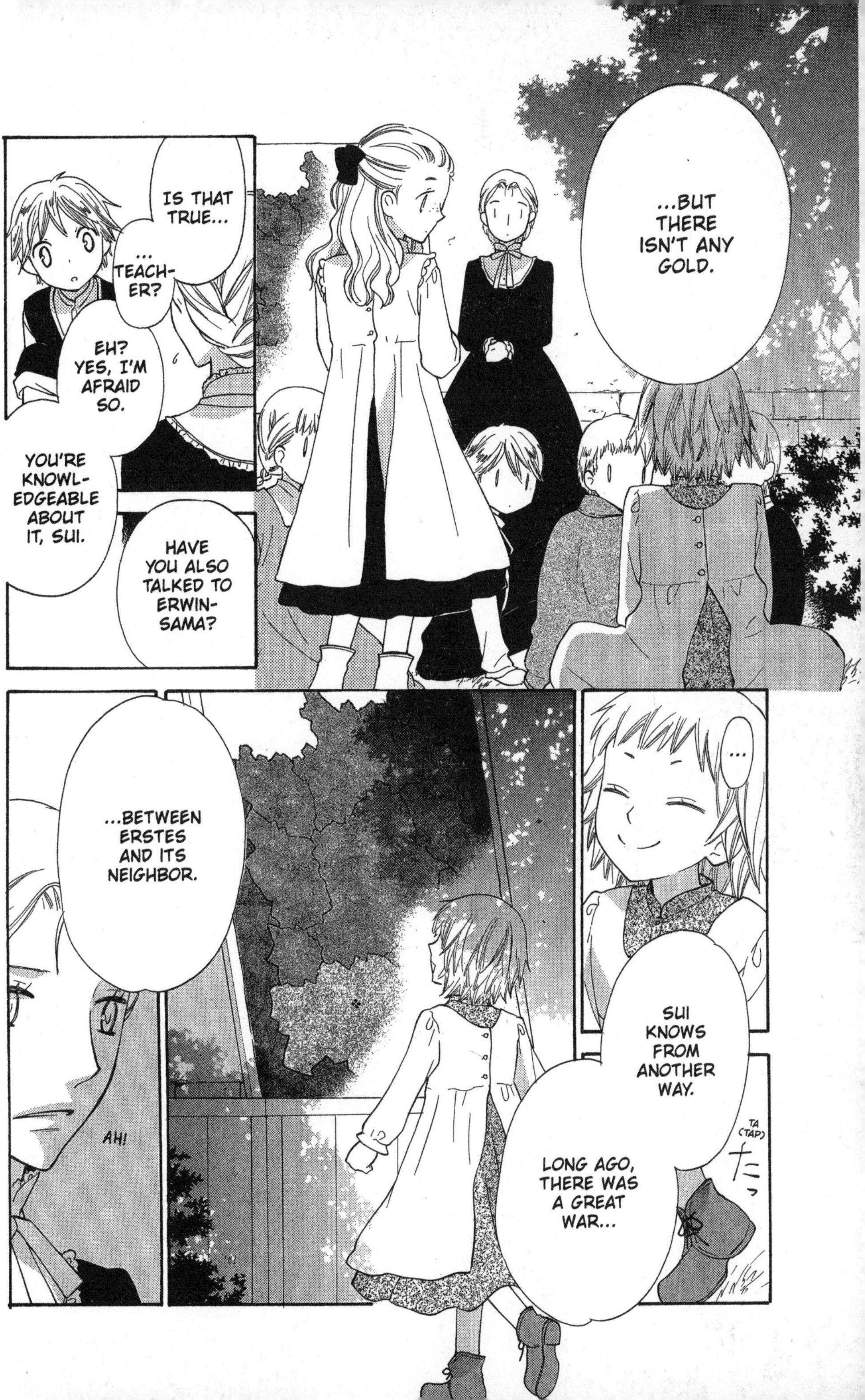
...BUT THERE ISN'T ANY GOLD.
IS THAT TRUE...
...TEACHER?
EH? YES, I'M AFRAID SO.
YOU'RE KNOWL-EDGEABLE ABOUT IT, SUI.
HAVE YOU ALSO TALKED TO ERWIN-SAMA?
...
SUI KNOWS FROM ANOTHER WAY.
TA (TAP)
LONG AGO, THERE WAS A GREAT WAR...
...BETWEEN ERSTES AND ITS NEIGHBOR.
AH!

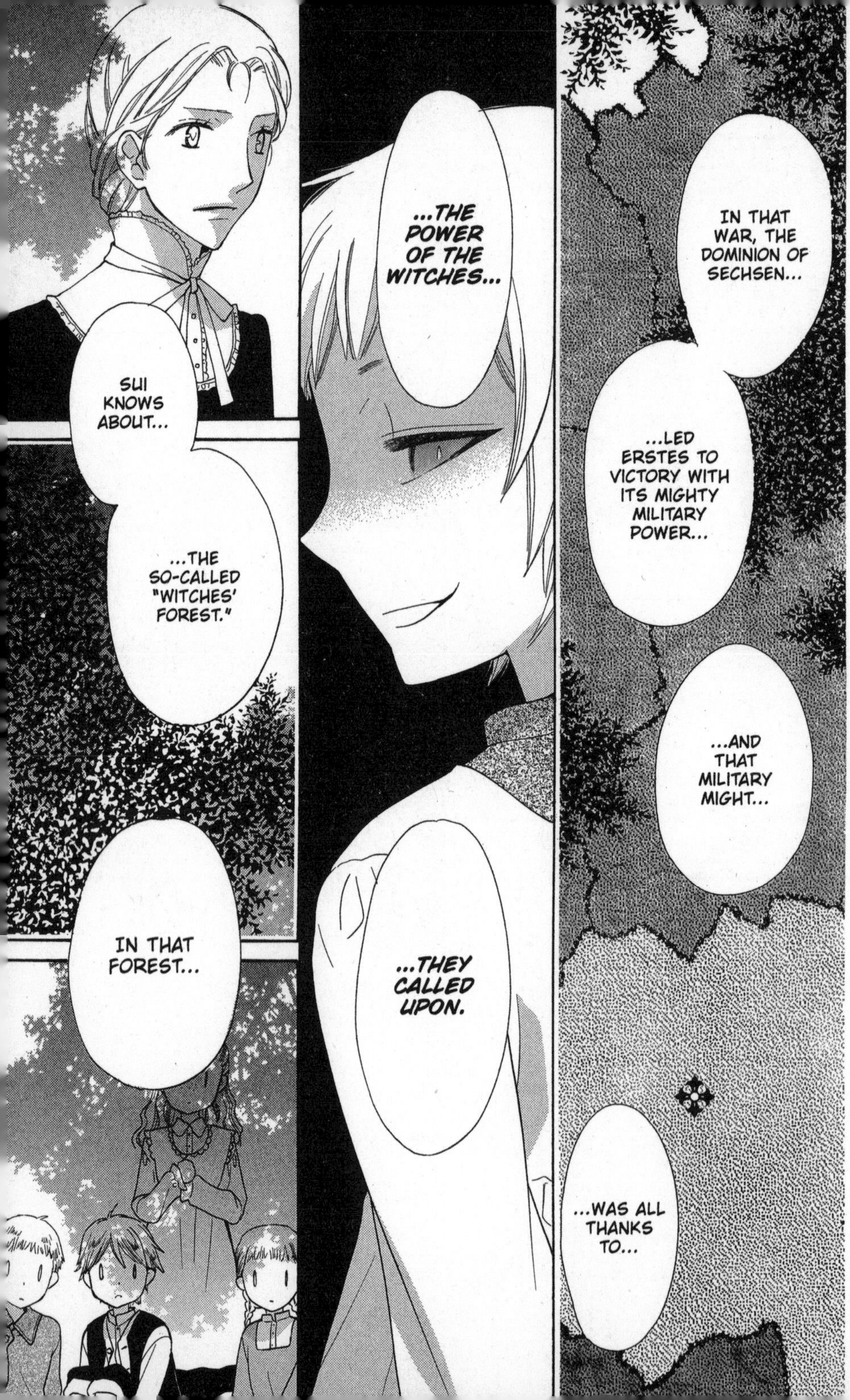
IN THAT WAR, THE DOMINION OF SECHSEN...
...LED ERSTES TO VICTORY WITH ITS MIGHTY MILITARY POWER...
...AND THAT MILITARY MIGHT...
...WAS ALL THANKS TO...
...THE POWER OF THE WITCHES...
...THEY CALLED UPON.
SUI KNOWS ABOUT...
...THE SO-CALLED "WITCHES' FOREST."
IN THAT FOREST...

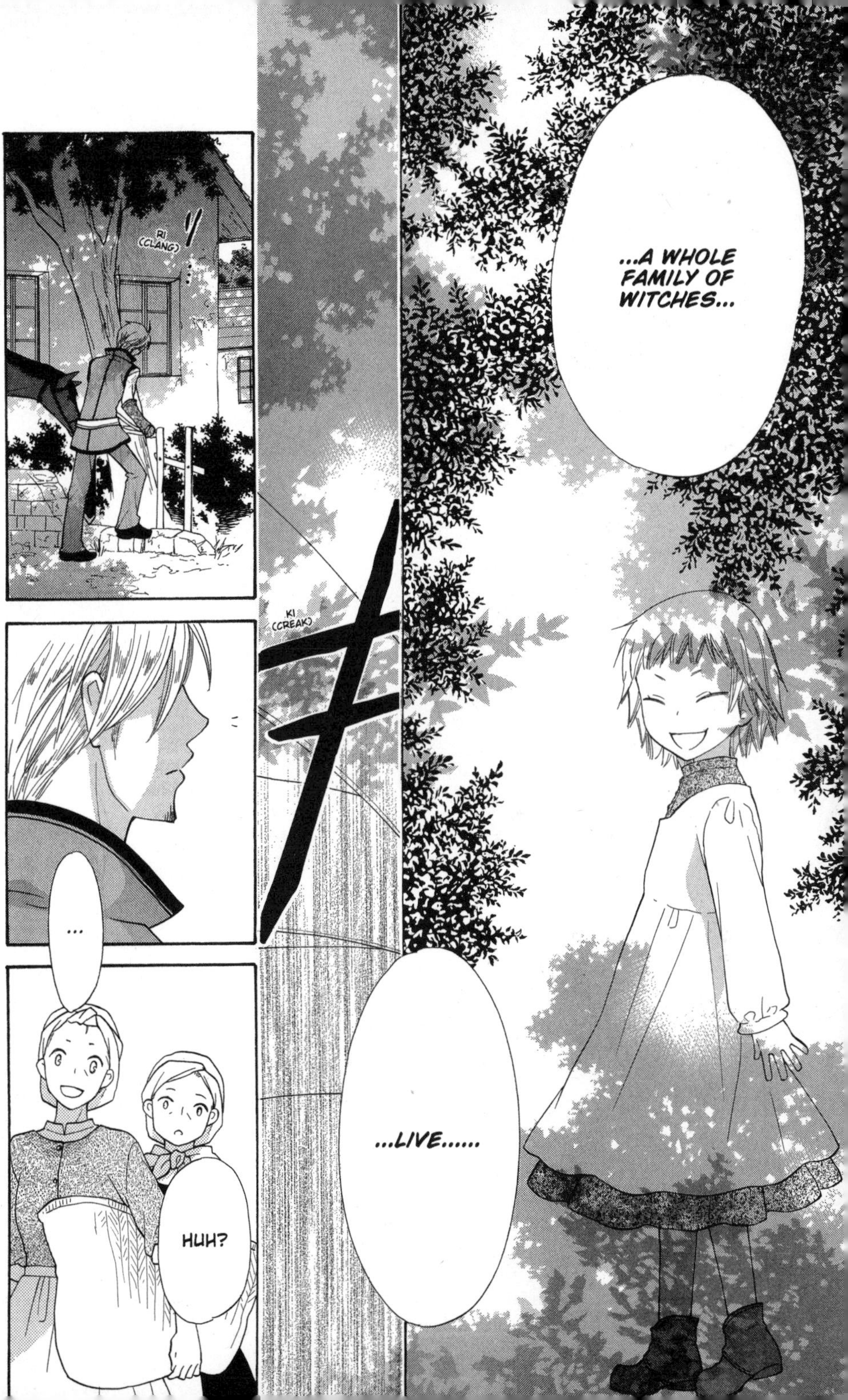
...A WHOLE FAMILY OF WITCHES...
...LIVE......
KI (CREAK)
RI (CLANG)
...
HUH?

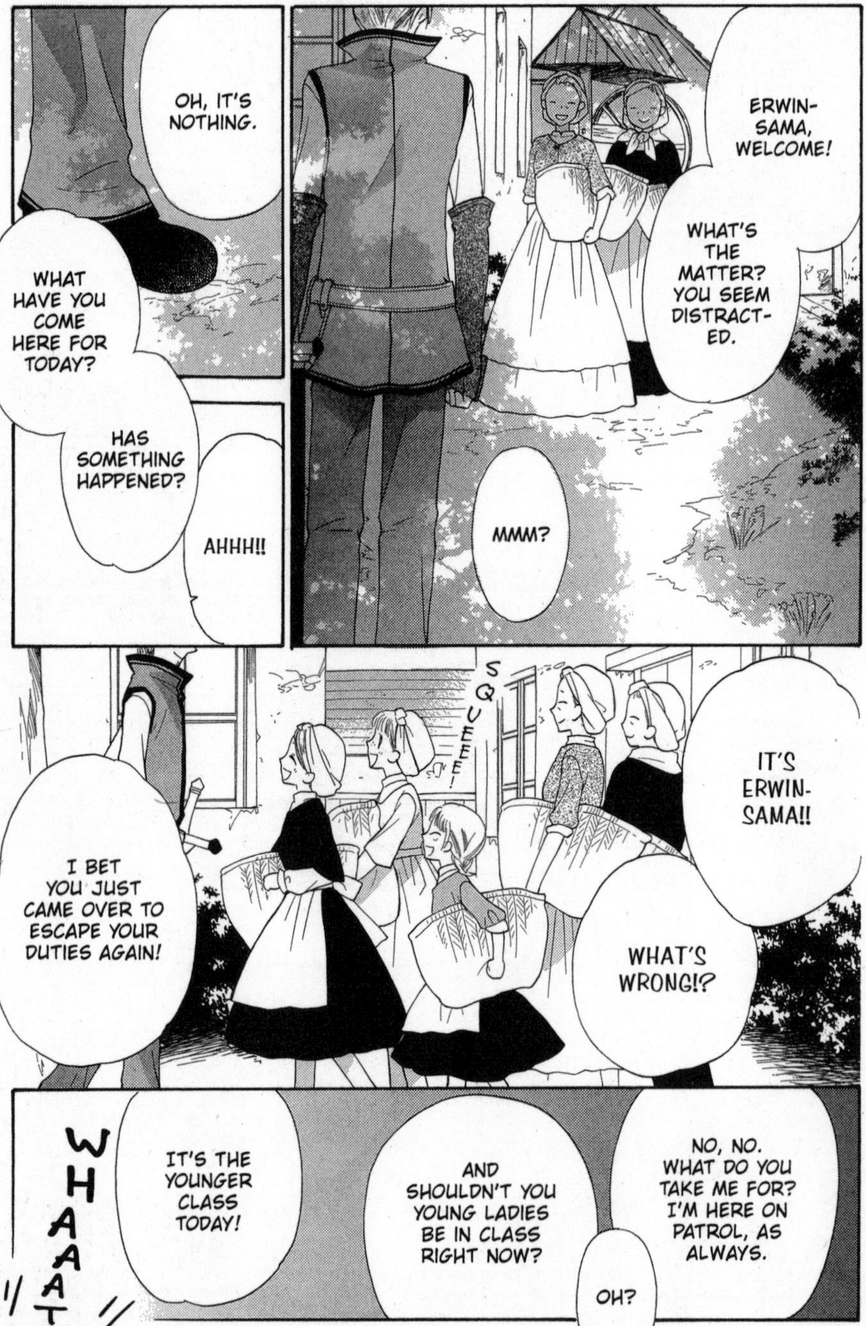

ERWIN-SAMA, WELCOME!
WHAT'S THE MATTER? YOU SEEM DISTRACT-ED.
MMM?
OH, IT'S NOTHING.
WHAT HAVE YOU COME HERE FOR TODAY?
HAS SOMETHING HAPPENED?
AHHH!!
SQUEEEE!
IT'S ERWIN-SAMA!!
WHAT'S WRONG!?
I BET YOU JUST CAME OVER TO ESCAPE YOUR DUTIES AGAIN!
NO, NO. WHAT DO YOU TAKE ME FOR? I'M HERE ON PATROL, AS ALWAYS.
OH?
AND SHOULDN'T YOU YOUNG LADIES BE IN CLASS RIGHT NOW?
IT'S THE YOUNGER CLASS TODAY!
WHAAAAT!?
HEE HEE!

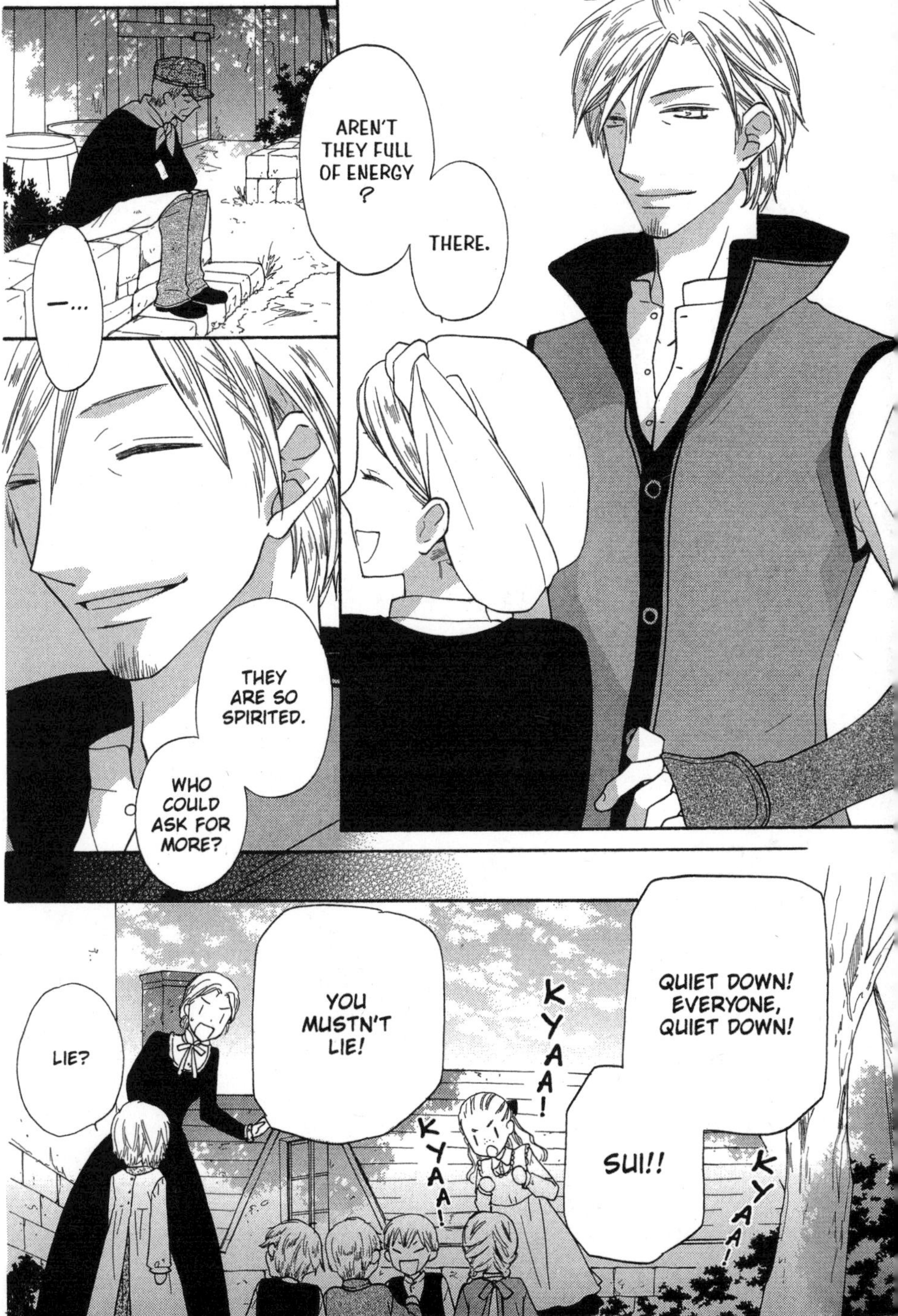
AREN'T THEY FULL OF ENERGY?
THERE.
—...
THEY ARE SO SPIRITED.
WHO COULD ASK FOR MORE?
QUIET DOWN! EVERYONE, QUIET DOWN!
KYAA!
SUI!!
KYAA!
KYAA!
YOU MUSTN'T LIE!
LIE?

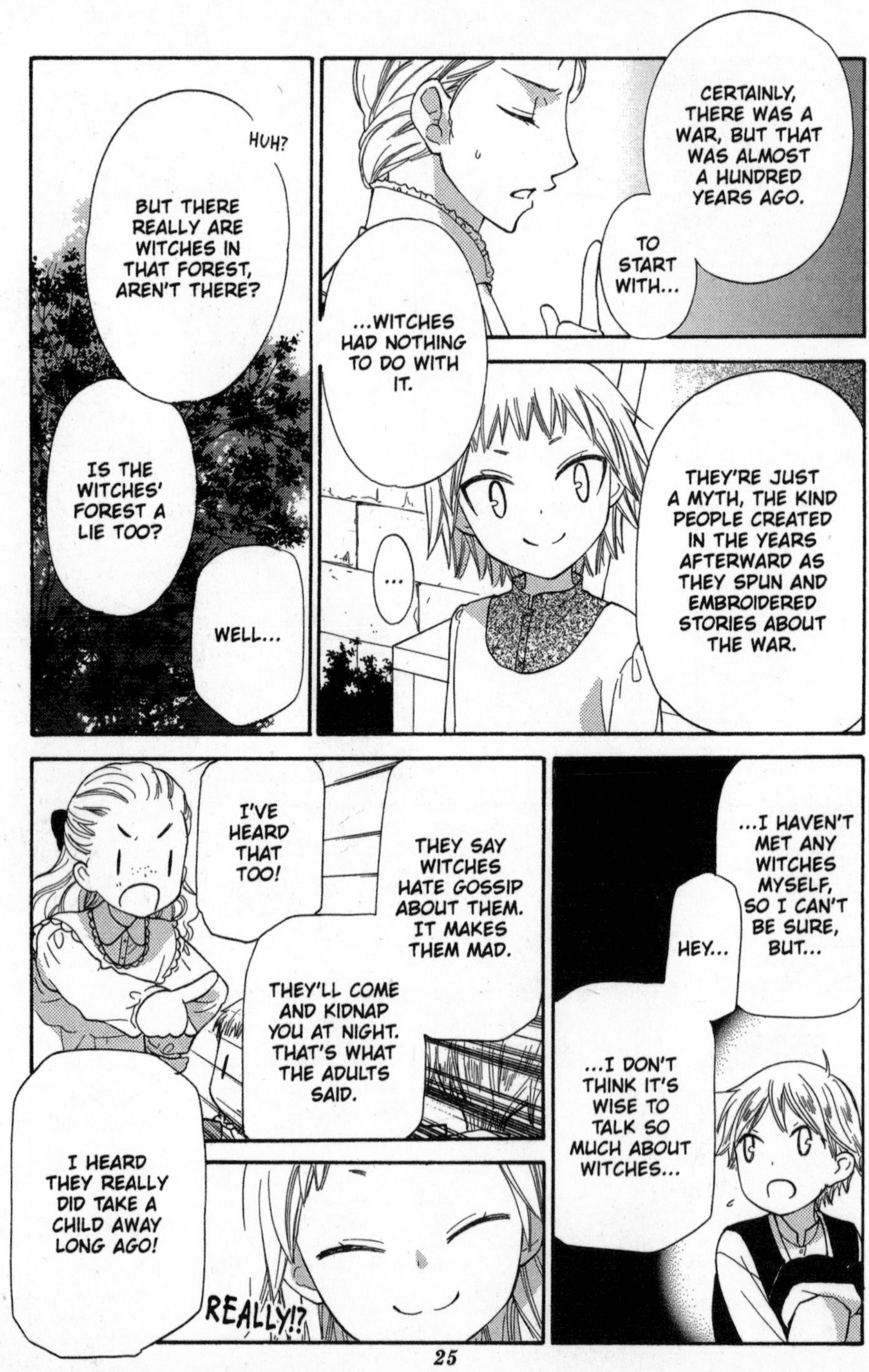
CERTAINLY, THERE WAS A WAR, BUT THAT WAS ALMOST A HUNDRED YEARS AGO.
TO START WITH...
...WITCHES HAD NOTHING TO DO WITH IT.
THEY'RE JUST A MYTH, THE KIND PEOPLE CREATED IN THE YEARS AFTERWARD AS THEY SPUN AND EMBROIDERED STORIES ABOUT THE WAR.
...
HUH?
BUT THERE REALLY ARE WITCHES IN THAT FOREST, AREN'T THERE?
IS THE WITCHES' FOREST A LIE TOO?
WELL...
...I HAVEN'T MET ANY WITCHES MYSELF, SO I CAN'T BE SURE, BUT...
HEY...
...I DON'T THINK IT'S WISE TO TALK SO MUCH ABOUT WITCHES...
I'VE HEARD THAT TOO!
THEY SAY WITCHES HATE GOSSIP ABOUT THEM. IT MAKES THEM MAD.
THEY'LL COME AND KIDNAP YOU AT NIGHT. THAT'S WHAT THE ADULTS SAID.
I HEARD THEY REALLY DID TAKE A CHILD AWAY LONG AGO!
REALLY!?

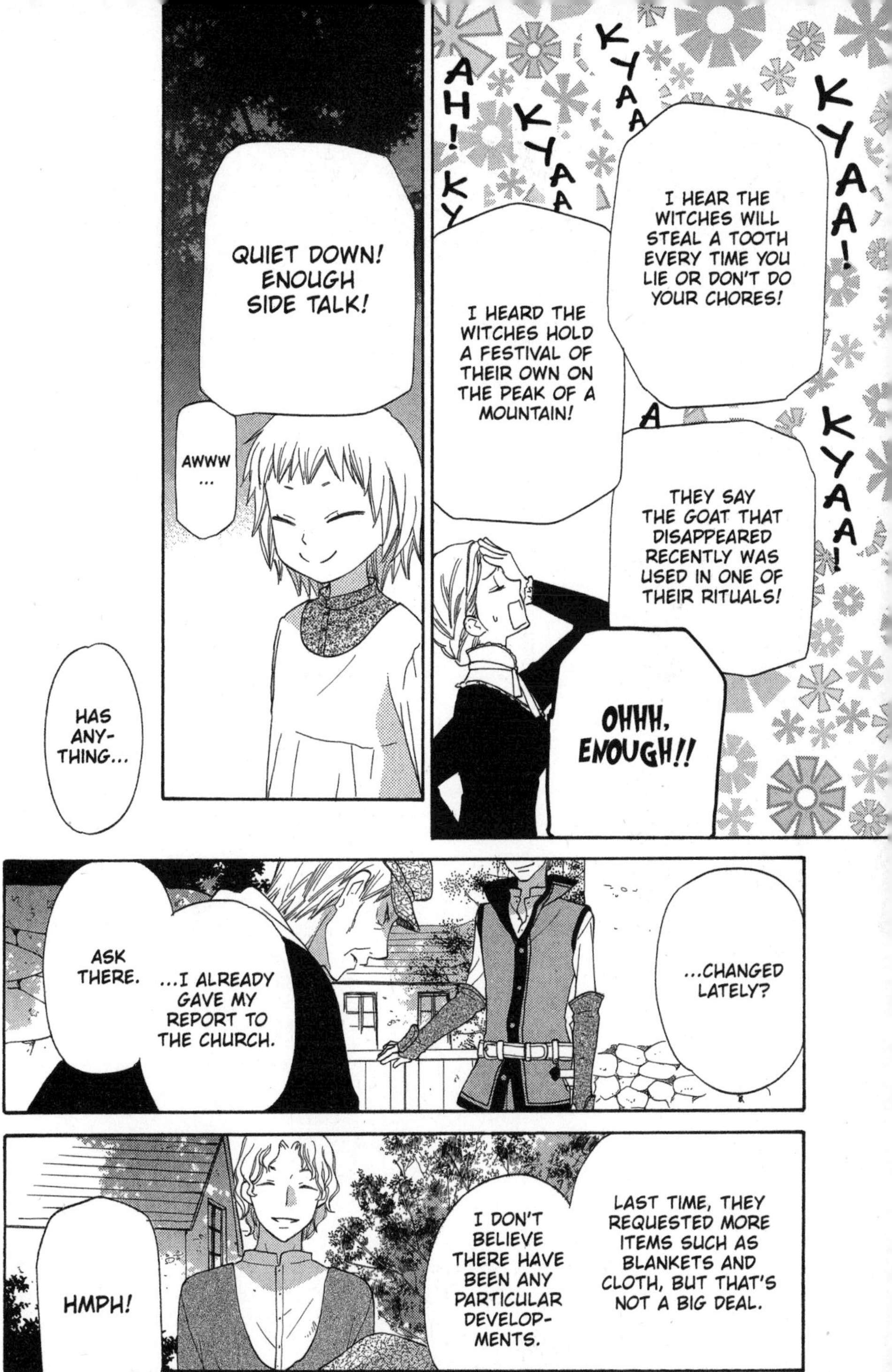
KYAAA!
KYAAA
KYAA
AH! KY
I HEAR THE WITCHES WILL STEAL A TOOTH EVERY TIME YOU LIE OR DON'T DO YOUR CHORES!
I HEARD THE WITCHES HOLD A FESTIVAL OF THEIR OWN ON THE PEAK OF A MOUNTAIN!
A
KYAAA!
THEY SAY THE GOAT THAT DISAPPEARED RECENTLY WAS USED IN ONE OF THEIR RITUALS!
OHHH, ENOUGH!!
QUIET DOWN! ENOUGH SIDE TALK!
AWWW...
HAS ANY-THING...
...CHANGED LATELY?
...I ALREADY GAVE MY REPORT TO THE CHURCH.
ASK THERE.
LAST TIME, THEY REQUESTED MORE ITEMS SUCH AS BLANKETS AND CLOTH, BUT THAT'S NOT A BIG DEAL.
I DON'T BELIEVE THERE HAVE BEEN ANY PARTICULAR DEVELOP-MENTS.
HMPH!

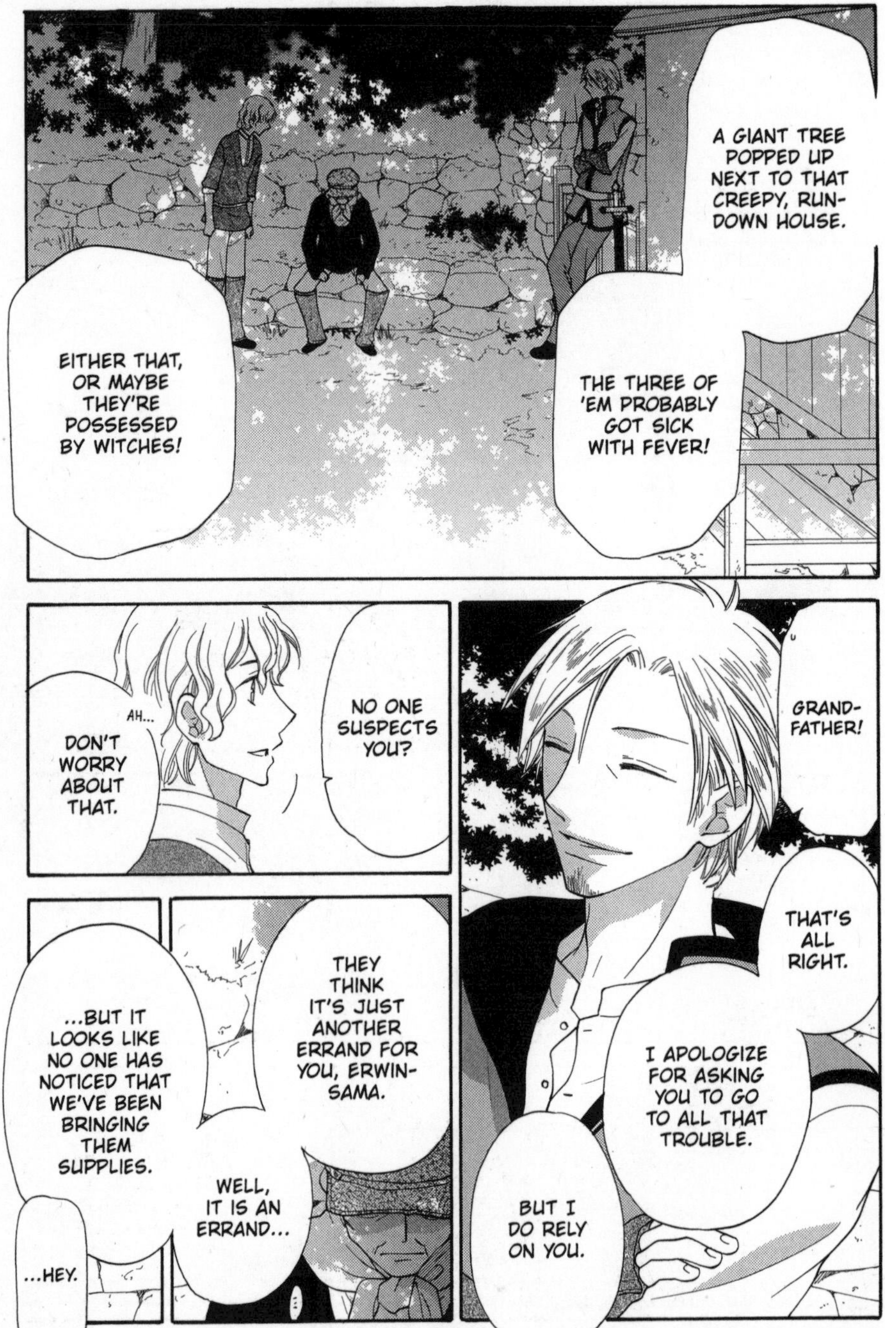
A GIANT TREE POPPED UP NEXT TO THAT CREEPY, RUN-DOWN HOUSE.
THE THREE OF 'EM PROBABLY GOT SICK WITH FEVER!
EITHER THAT, OR MAYBE THEY'RE POSSESSED BY WITCHES!
GRAND-FATHER!
THAT'S ALL RIGHT.
I APOLOGIZE FOR ASKING YOU TO GO TO ALL THAT TROUBLE.
BUT I DO RELY ON YOU.
NO ONE SUSPECTS YOU?
AH...
DON'T WORRY ABOUT THAT.
THEY THINK IT'S JUST ANOTHER ERRAND FOR YOU, ERWIN-SAMA.
WELL, IT IS AN ERRAND...
...
...BUT IT LOOKS LIKE NO ONE HAS NOTICED THAT WE'VE BEEN BRINGING THEM SUPPLIES.
...HEY.

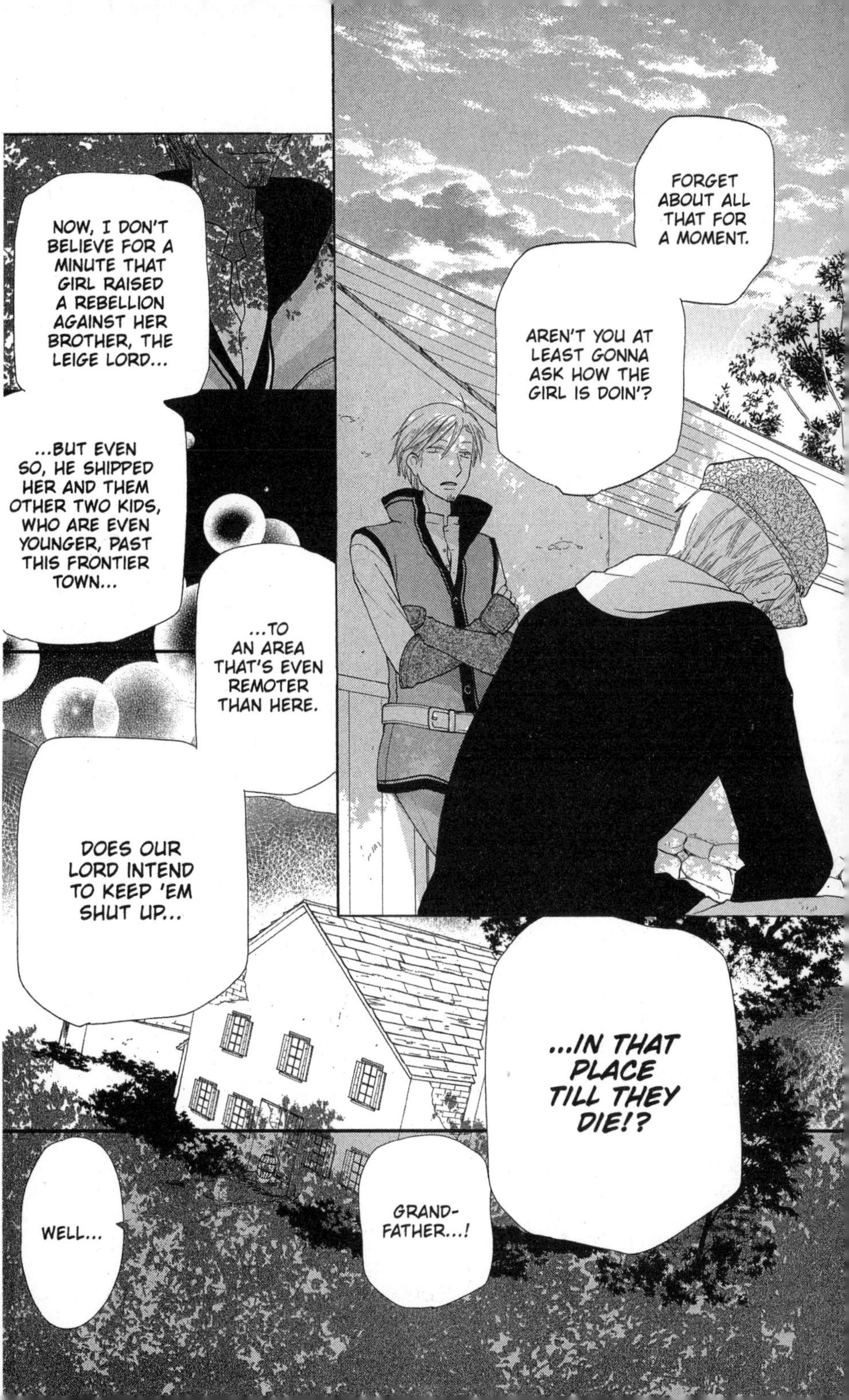
FORGET ABOUT ALL THAT FOR A MOMENT.
AREN'T YOU AT LEAST GONNA ASK HOW THE GIRL IS DOIN'?
NOW, I DON'T BELIEVE FOR A MINUTE THAT GIRL RAISED A REBELLION AGAINST HER BROTHER, THE LEIGE LORD...
...BUT EVEN SO, HE SHIPPED HER AND THEM OTHER TWO KIDS, WHO ARE EVEN YOUNGER, PAST THIS FRONTIER TOWN...
...TO AN AREA THAT'S EVEN REMOTER THAN HERE.
DOES OUR LORD INTEND TO KEEP 'EM SHUT UP...
...IN THAT PLACE TILL THEY DIE!?
GRAND-FATHER...!
WELL...

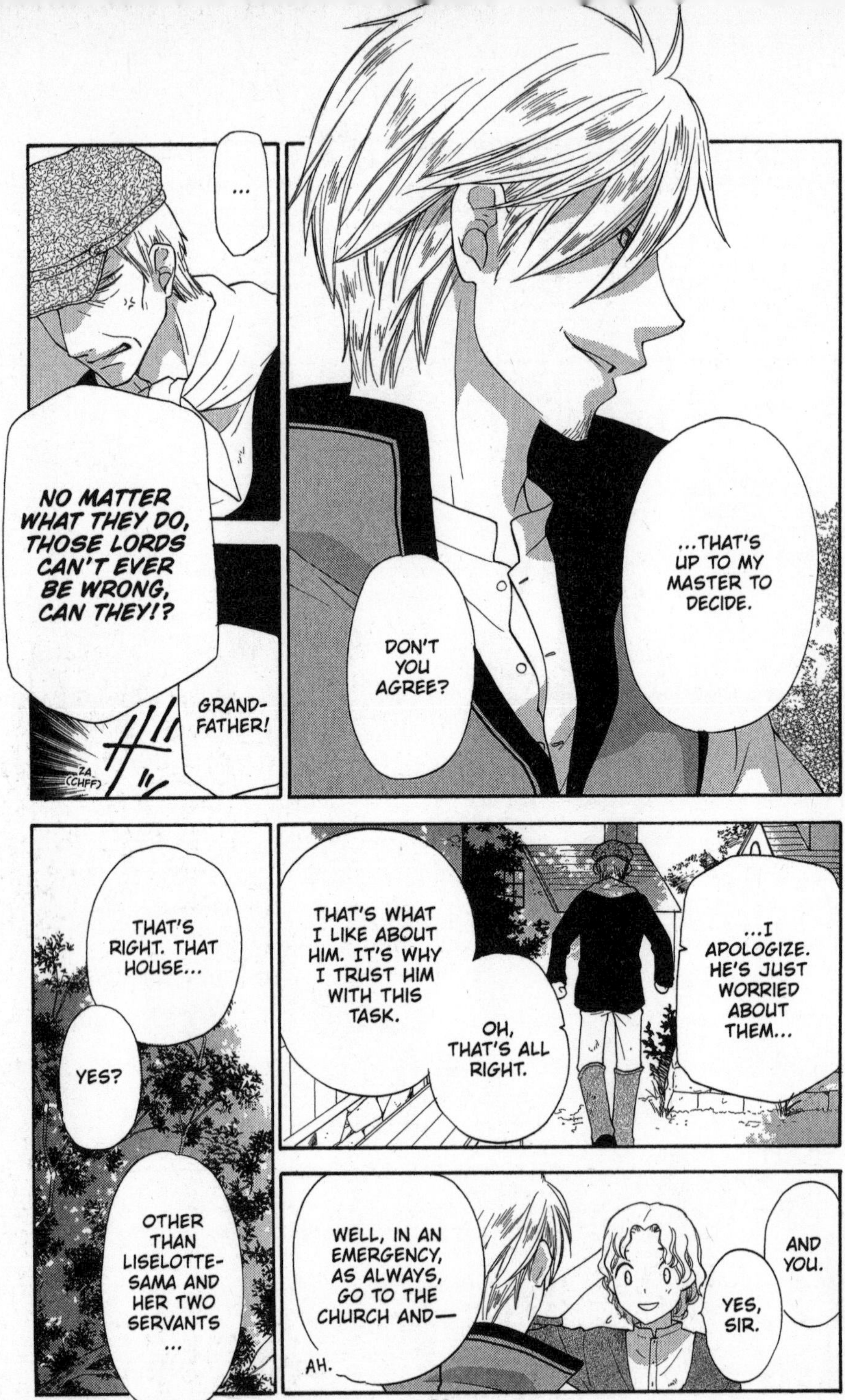
...THAT'S UP TO MY MASTER TO DECIDE.
DON'T YOU AGREE?
...
NO MATTER WHAT THEY DO, THOSE LORDS CAN'T EVER BE WRONG, CAN THEY!?
GRAND-FATHER!
ZA (CHFF)
...I APOLOGIZE. HE'S JUST WORRIED ABOUT THEM...
OH, THAT'S ALL RIGHT.
THAT'S WHAT I LIKE ABOUT HIM. IT'S WHY I TRUST HIM WITH THIS TASK.
AND YOU.
YES, SIR.
WELL, IN AN EMERGENCY, AS ALWAYS, GO TO THE CHURCH AND—
AH.
THAT'S RIGHT. THAT HOUSE...
YES?
OTHER THAN LISELOTTE-SAMA AND HER TWO SERVANTS ...

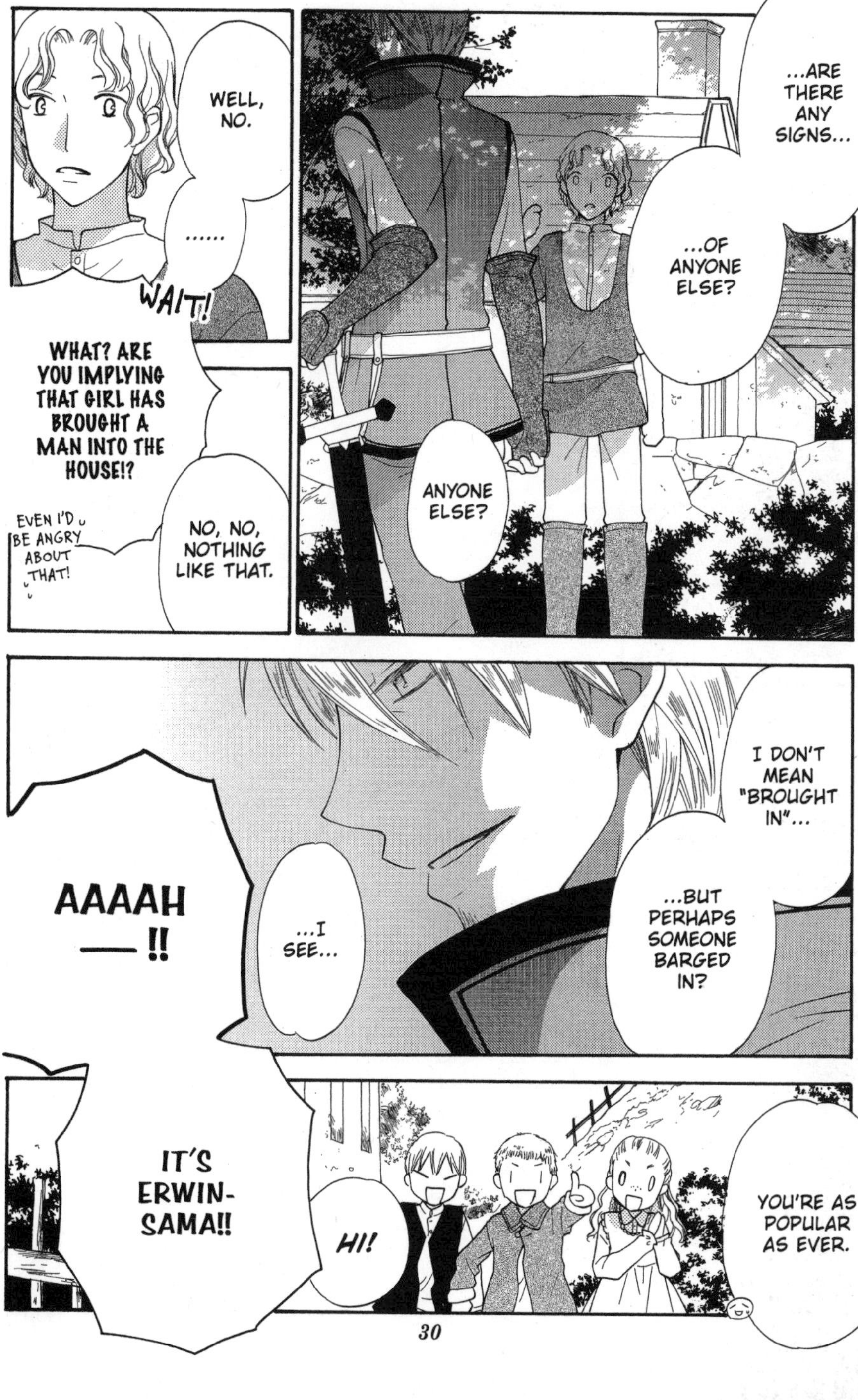
...ARE THERE ANY SIGNS...
...OF ANYONE ELSE?
ANYONE ELSE?
WELL, NO.
......
WAIT!
WHAT? ARE YOU IMPLYING THAT GIRL HAS BROUGHT A MAN INTO THE HOUSE!?
NO, NO, NOTHING LIKE THAT.
EVEN I'D BE ANGRY ABOUT THAT!
I DON'T MEAN "BROUGHT IN"...
...BUT PERHAPS SOMEONE BARGED IN?
...I SEE...
AAAAH—!!
YOU'RE AS POPULAR AS EVER.
HI!
IT'S ERWIN-SAMA!!

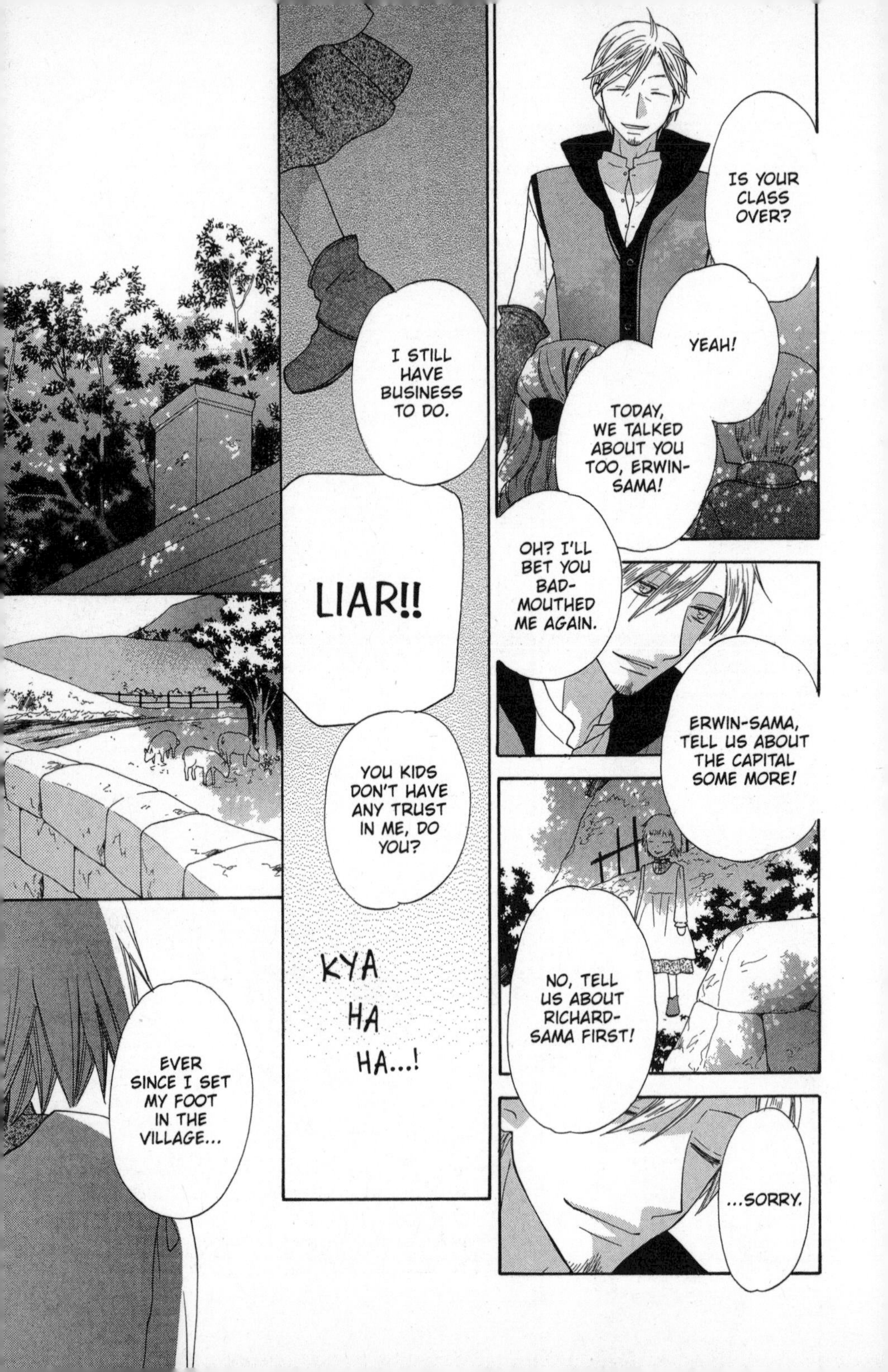
IS YOUR CLASS OVER?
YEAH!
TODAY, WE TALKED ABOUT YOU TOO, ERWIN-SAMA!
OH? I'LL BET YOU BAD-MOUTHED ME AGAIN.
ERWIN-SAMA, TELL US ABOUT THE CAPITAL SOME MORE!
NO, TELL US ABOUT RICHARD-SAMA FIRST!
...SORRY.
I STILL HAVE BUSINESS TO DO.
LIAR!!
YOU KIDS DON'T HAVE ANY TRUST IN ME, DO YOU?
KYA HA HA...!
EVER SINCE I SET MY FOOT IN THE VILLAGE...

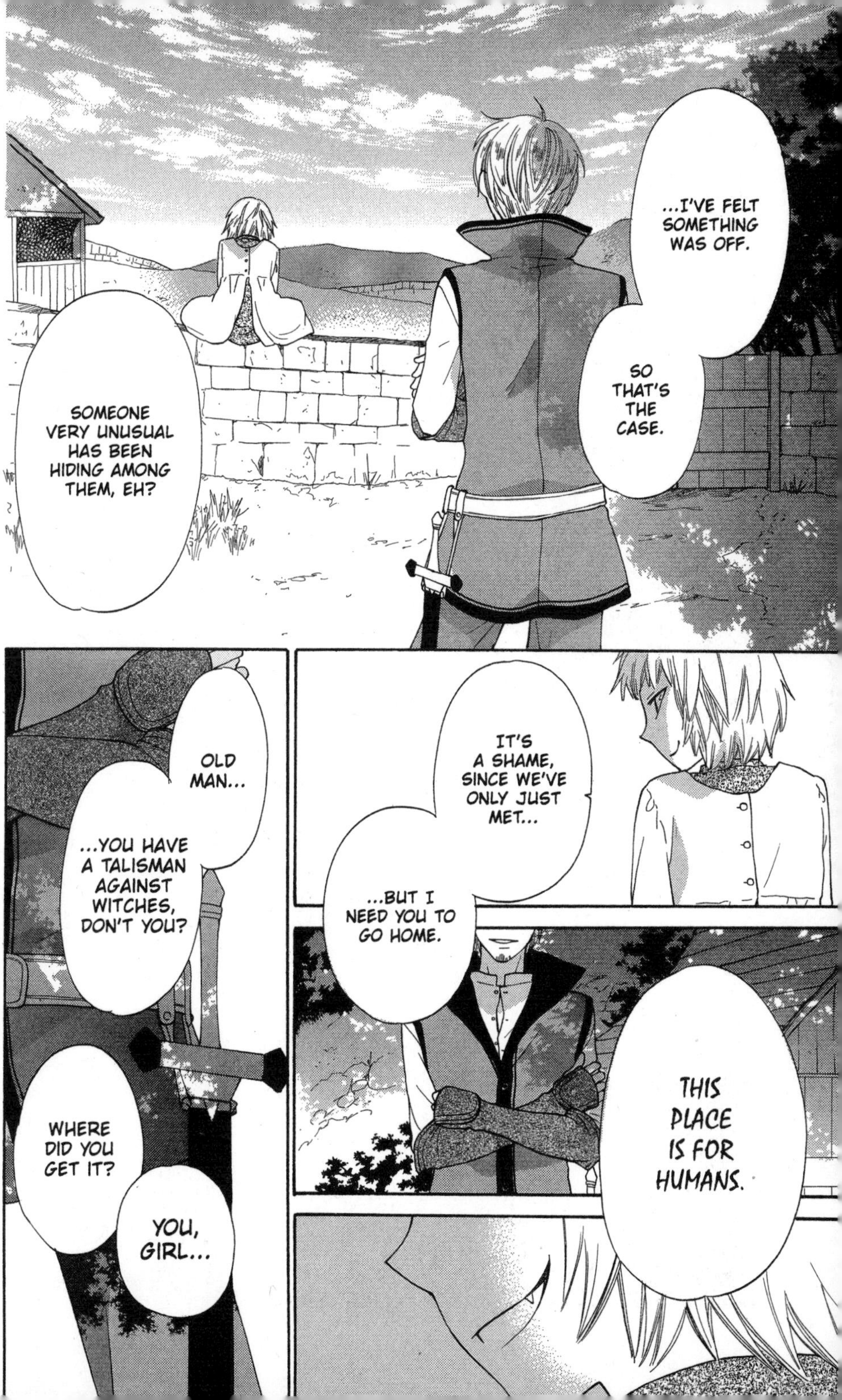
...I'VE FELT SOMETHING WAS OFF.
SO THAT'S THE CASE.
SOMEONE VERY UNUSUAL HAS BEEN HIDING AMONG THEM, EH?
IT'S A SHAME, SINCE WE'VE ONLY JUST MET...
...BUT I NEED YOU TO GO HOME.
THIS PLACE IS FOR HUMANS.
OLD MAN...
...YOU HAVE A TALISMAN AGAINST WITCHES, DON'T YOU?
WHERE DID YOU GET IT?
YOU, GIRL...

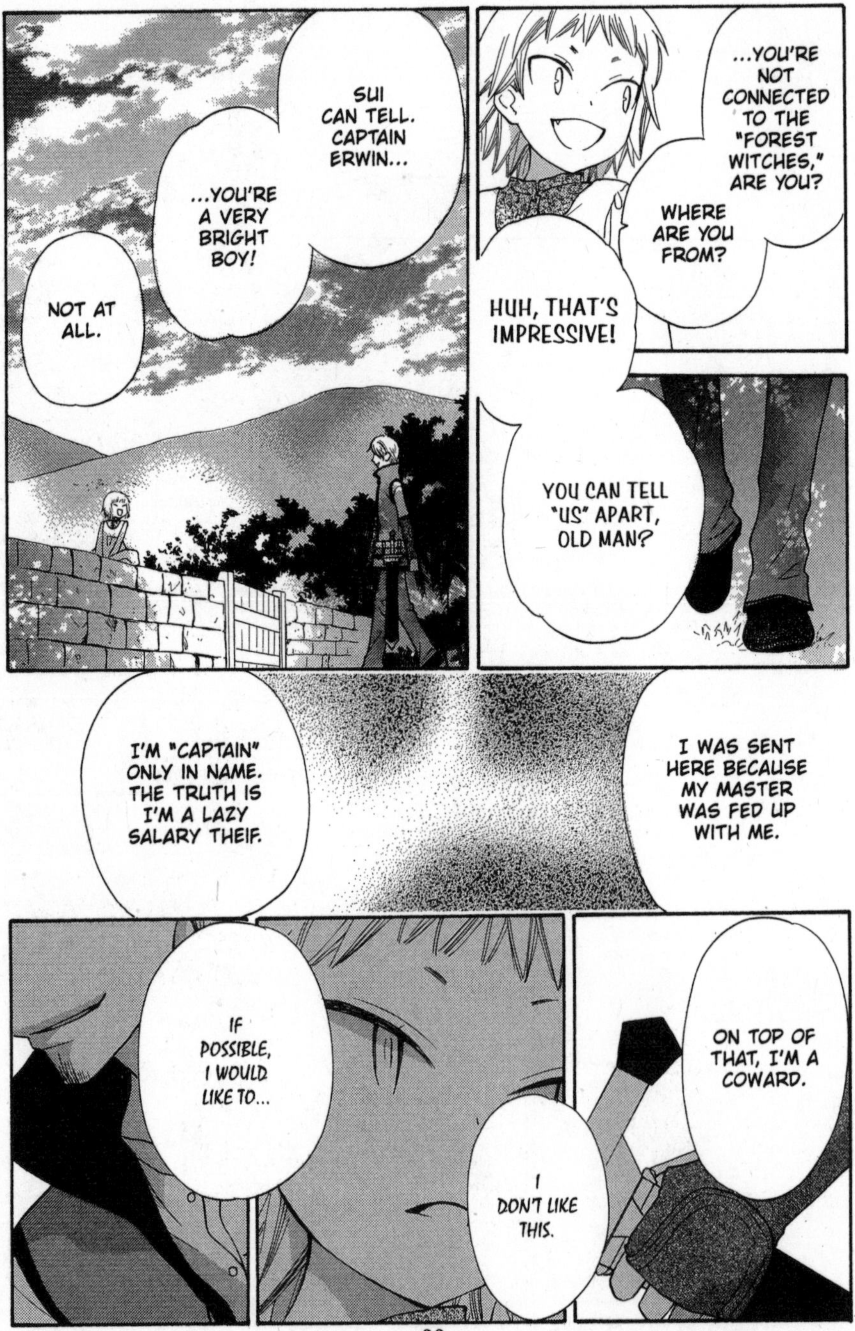
...YOU'RE NOT CONNECTED TO THE "FOREST WITCHES," ARE YOU?
WHERE ARE YOU FROM?
HUH, THAT'S IMPRESSIVE!
YOU CAN TELL "US" APART, OLD MAN?
SUI CAN TELL. CAPTAIN ERWIN...
...YOU'RE A VERY BRIGHT BOY!
NOT AT ALL.
I WAS SENT HERE BECAUSE MY MASTER WAS FED UP WITH ME.
I'M "CAPTAIN" ONLY IN NAME. THE TRUTH IS I'M A LAZY SALARY THEIF.
ON TOP OF THAT, I'M A COWARD.
IF POSSIBLE, I WOULD LIKE TO...
I DON'T LIKE THIS.

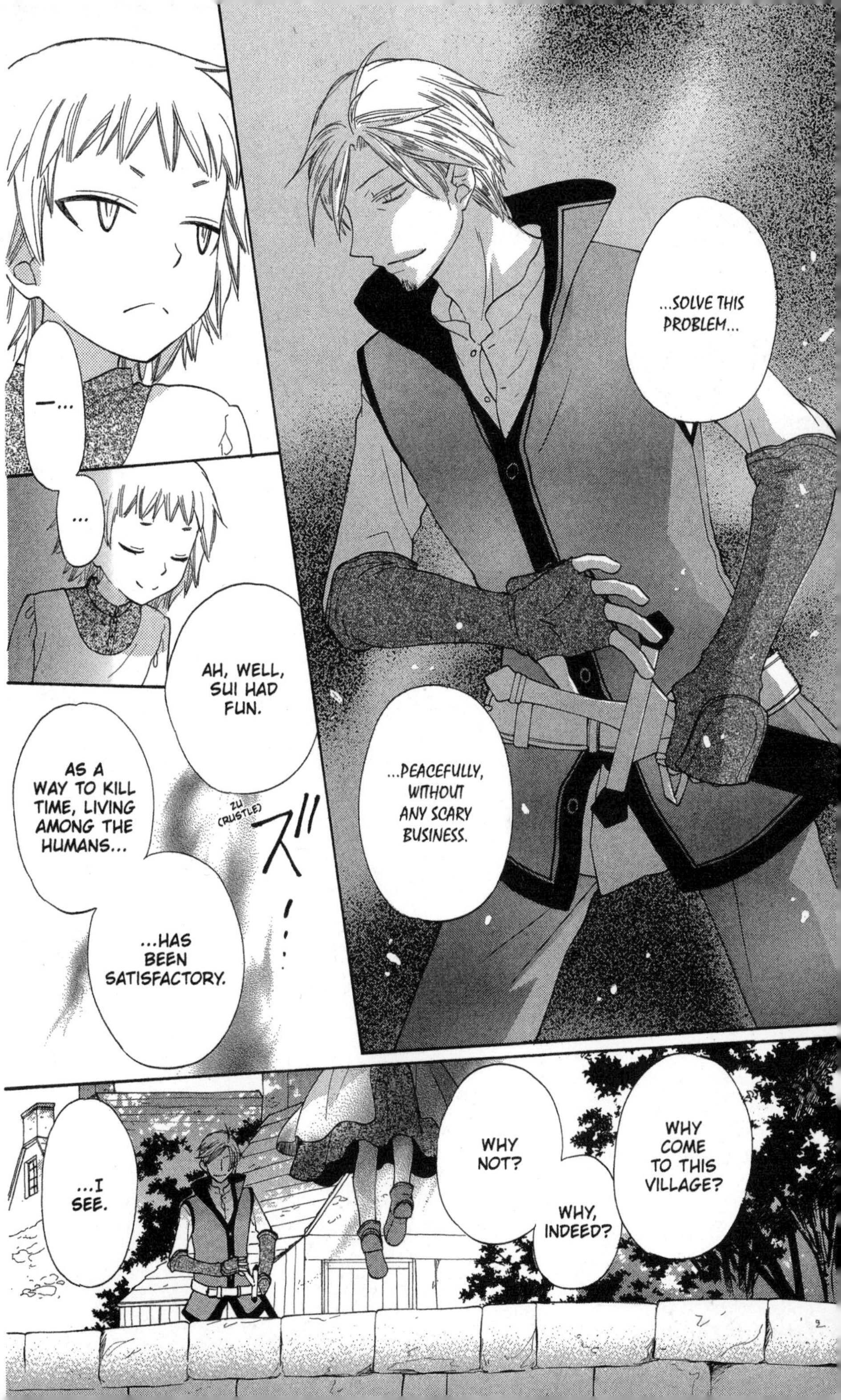
...SOLVE THIS PROBLEM...
...PEACEFULLY, WITHOUT ANY SCARY BUSINESS.
—...
...
AH, WELL, SUI HAD FUN.
AS A WAY TO KILL TIME, LIVING AMONG THE HUMANS...
ZU (RUSTLE)
...HAS BEEN SATISFACTORY.
WHY COME TO THIS VILLAGE?
WHY, INDEED?
WHY NOT?
...I SEE.

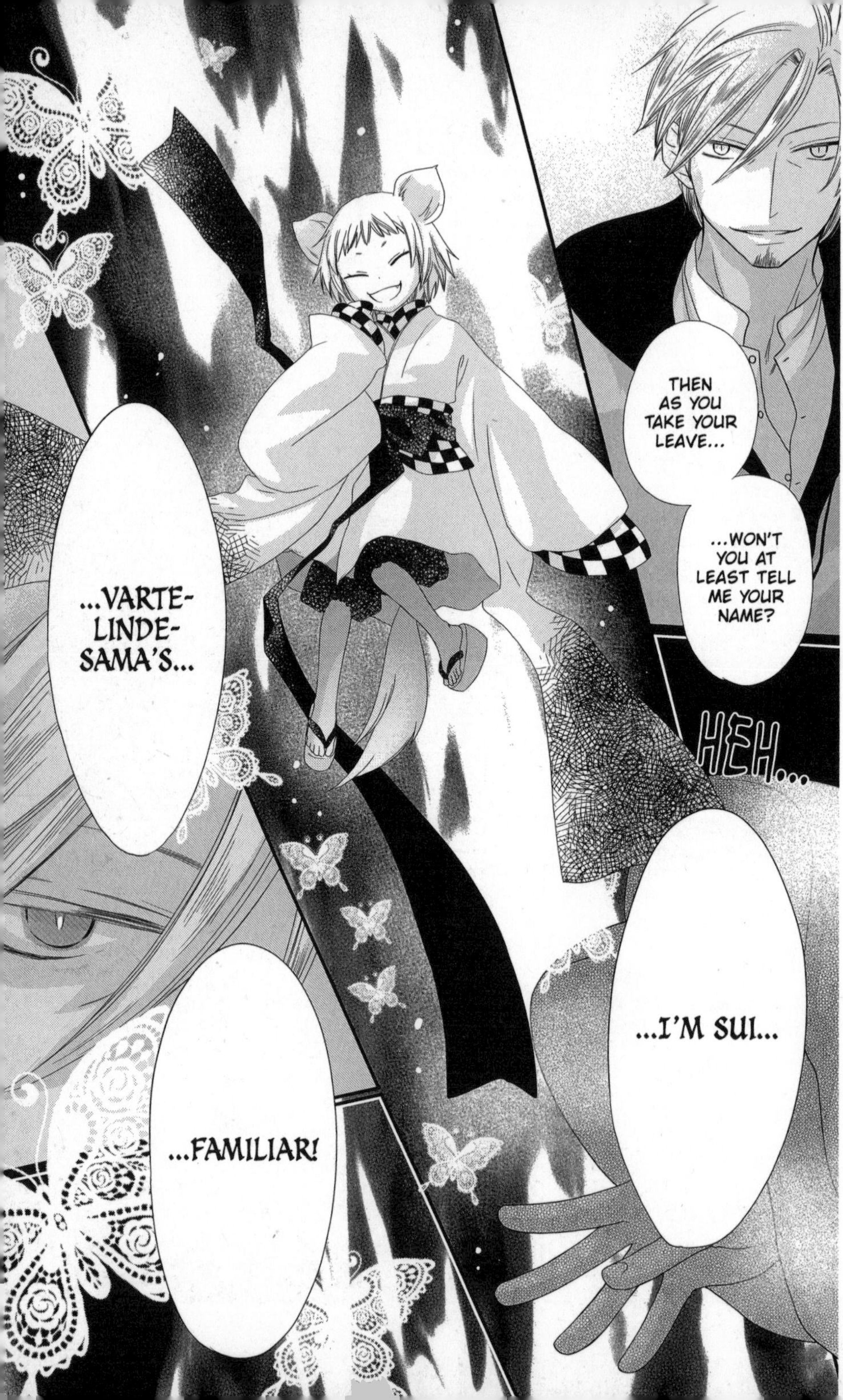
THEN AS YOU TAKE YOUR LEAVE...
...WON'T YOU AT LEAST TELL ME YOUR NAME?
HEH...
...I'M SUI...
...VARTE-LINDE-SAMA'S...
...FAMILIAR!

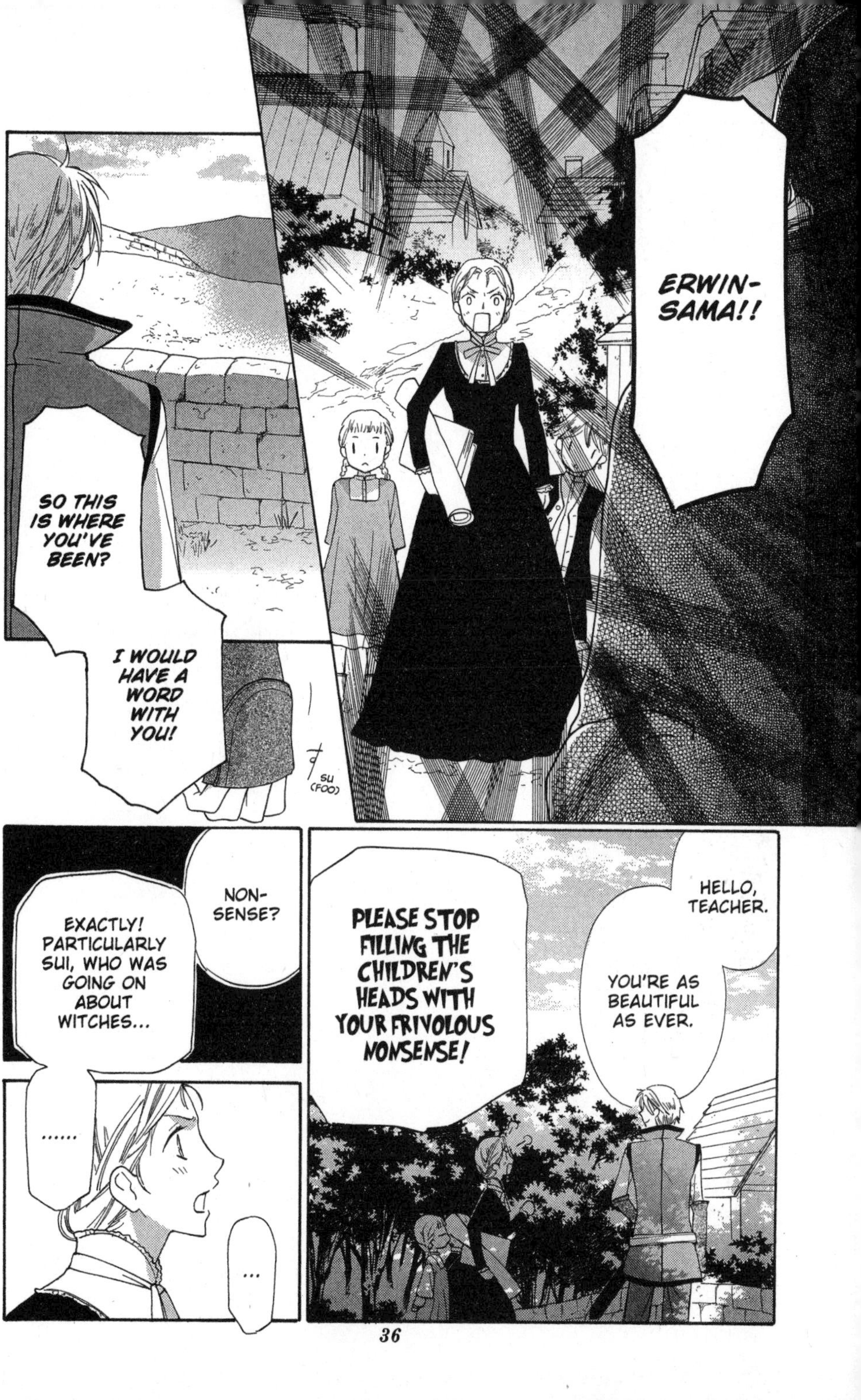
ERWIN-SAMA!!
SU (FOO)
SO THIS IS WHERE YOU'VE BEEN?
I WOULD HAVE A WORD WITH YOU!
HELLO, TEACHER.
YOU'RE AS BEAUTIFUL AS EVER.
PLEASE STOP FILLING THE CHILDREN'S HEADS WITH YOUR FRIVOLOUS NONSENSE!
NON-SENSE?
EXACTLY! PARTICULARLY SUI, WHO WAS GOING ON ABOUT WITCHES...
......
...

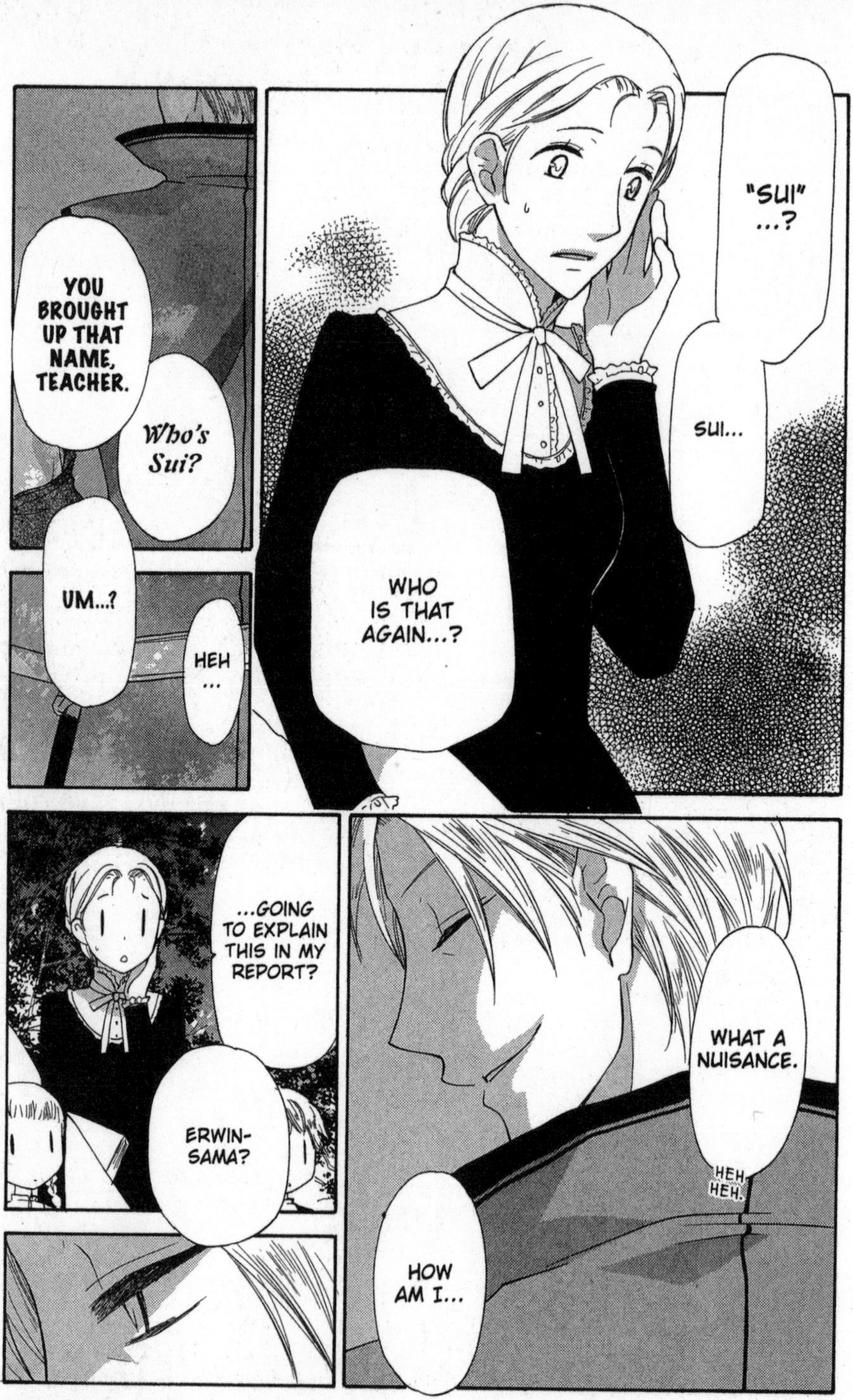
"SUI" ...?
SUI...
WHO IS THAT AGAIN...?
YOU BROUGHT UP THAT NAME, TEACHER.
Who's Sui?
UM...?
HEH ...
WHAT A NUISANCE.
HEH HEH.
HOW AM I...
...GOING TO EXPLAIN THIS IN MY REPORT?
ERWIN-SAMA?

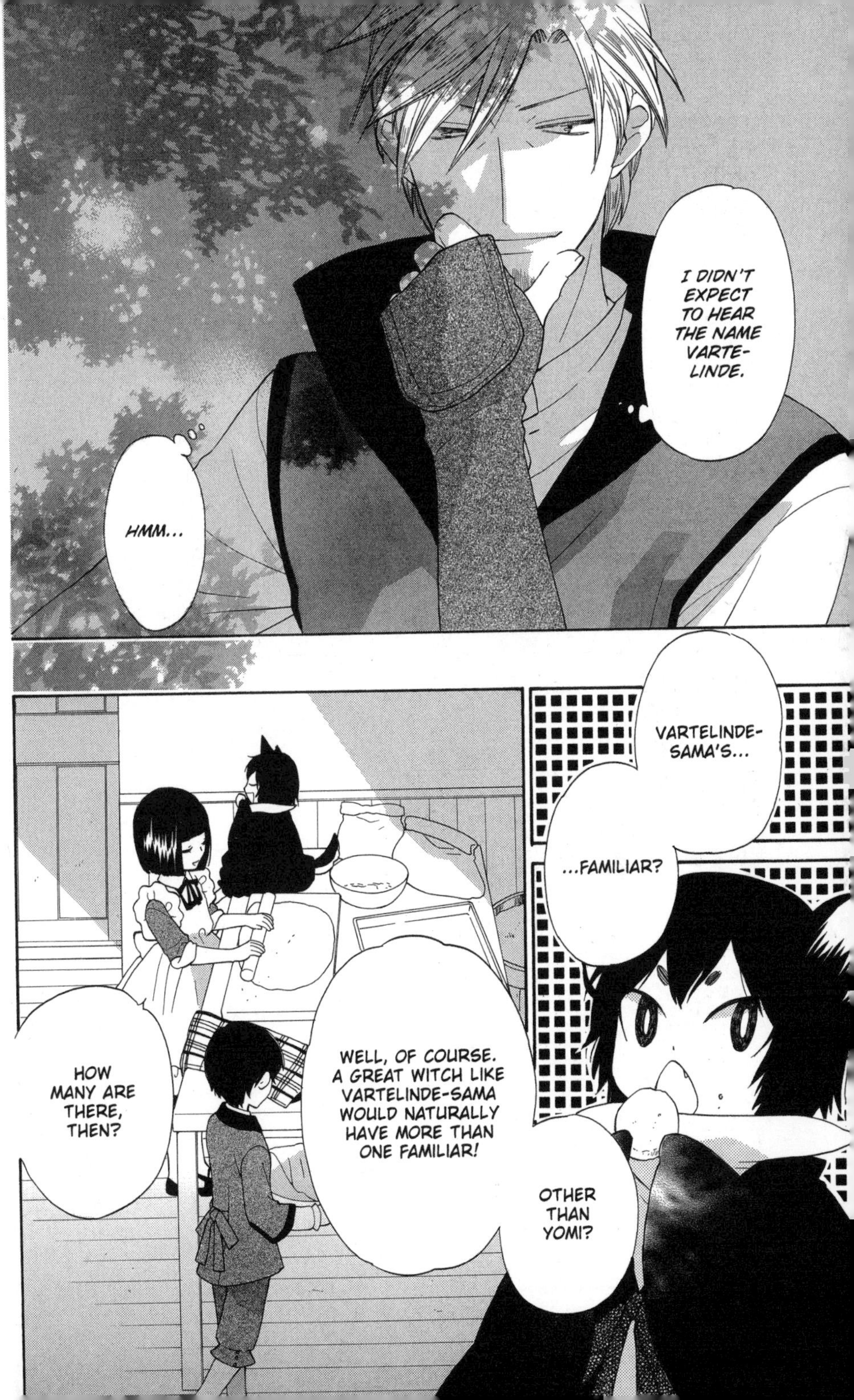
I DIDN'T EXPECT TO HEAR THE NAME VARTE-LINDE.
HMM...
VARTELINDE-SAMA'S...
...FAMILIAR?
OTHER THAN YOMI?
WELL, OF COURSE. A GREAT WITCH LIKE VARTELINDE-SAMA WOULD NATURALLY HAVE MORE THAN ONE FAMILIAR!
HOW MANY ARE THERE, THEN?

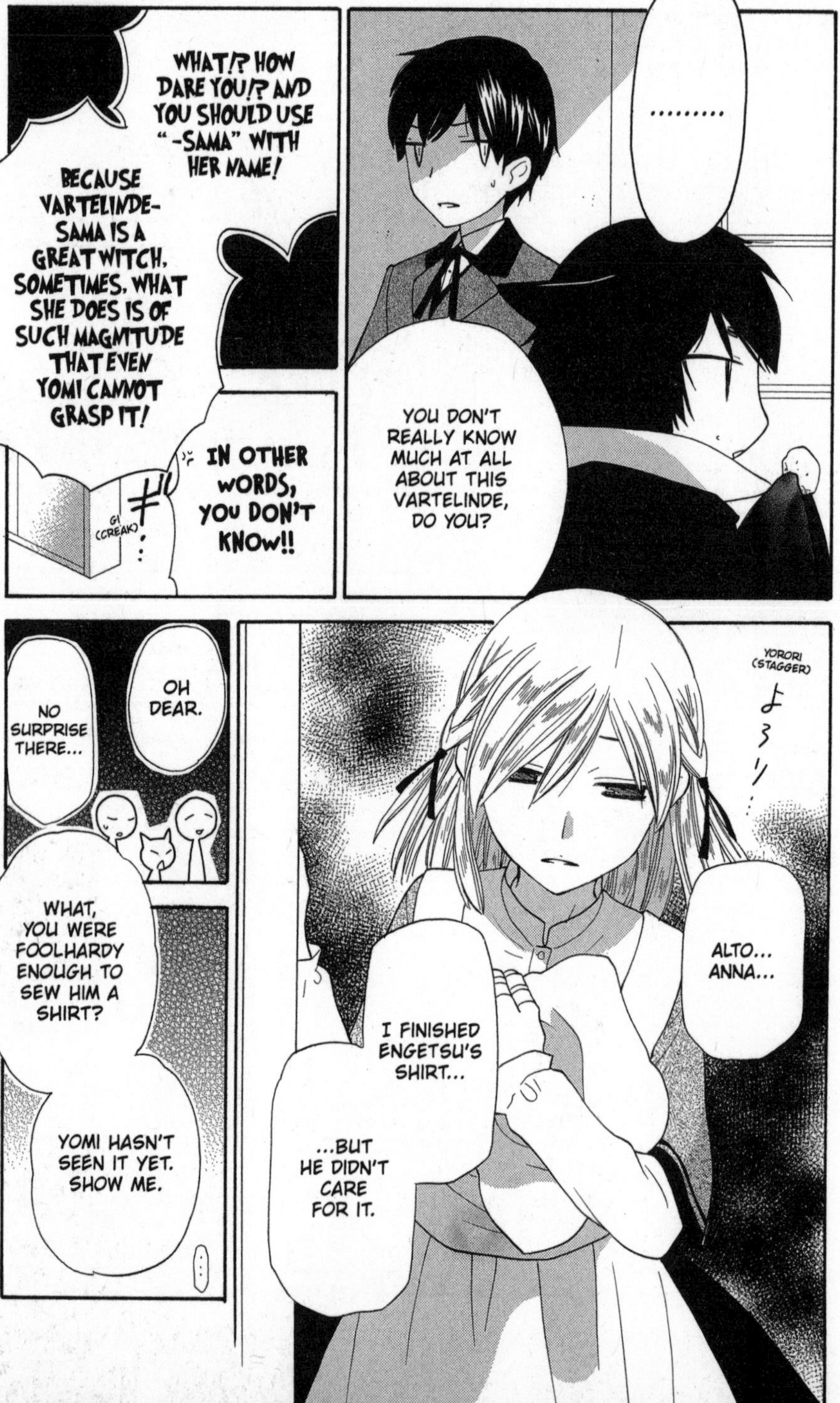
....
YOU DON'T REALLY KNOW MUCH AT ALL ABOUT THIS VARTELINDE, DO YOU?
WHAT!? HOW DARE YOU!? AND YOU SHOULD USE "-SAMA" WITH HER NAME!
BECAUSE VARTELINDE-SAMA IS A GREAT WITCH, SOMETIMES, WHAT SHE DOES IS OF SUCH MAGNITUDE THAT EVEN YOMI CANNOT GRASP IT!
IN OTHER WORDS, YOU DON'T KNOW!!
GI (CREAK)
YORORI (STAGGER)
よろり…
ALTO... ANNA...
I FINISHED ENGETSU'S SHIRT...
...BUT HE DIDN'T CARE FOR IT.
OH DEAR.
NO SURPRISE THERE...
WHAT, YOU WERE FOOLHARDY ENOUGH TO SEW HIM A SHIRT?
YOMI HASN'T SEEN IT YET. SHOW ME.
...

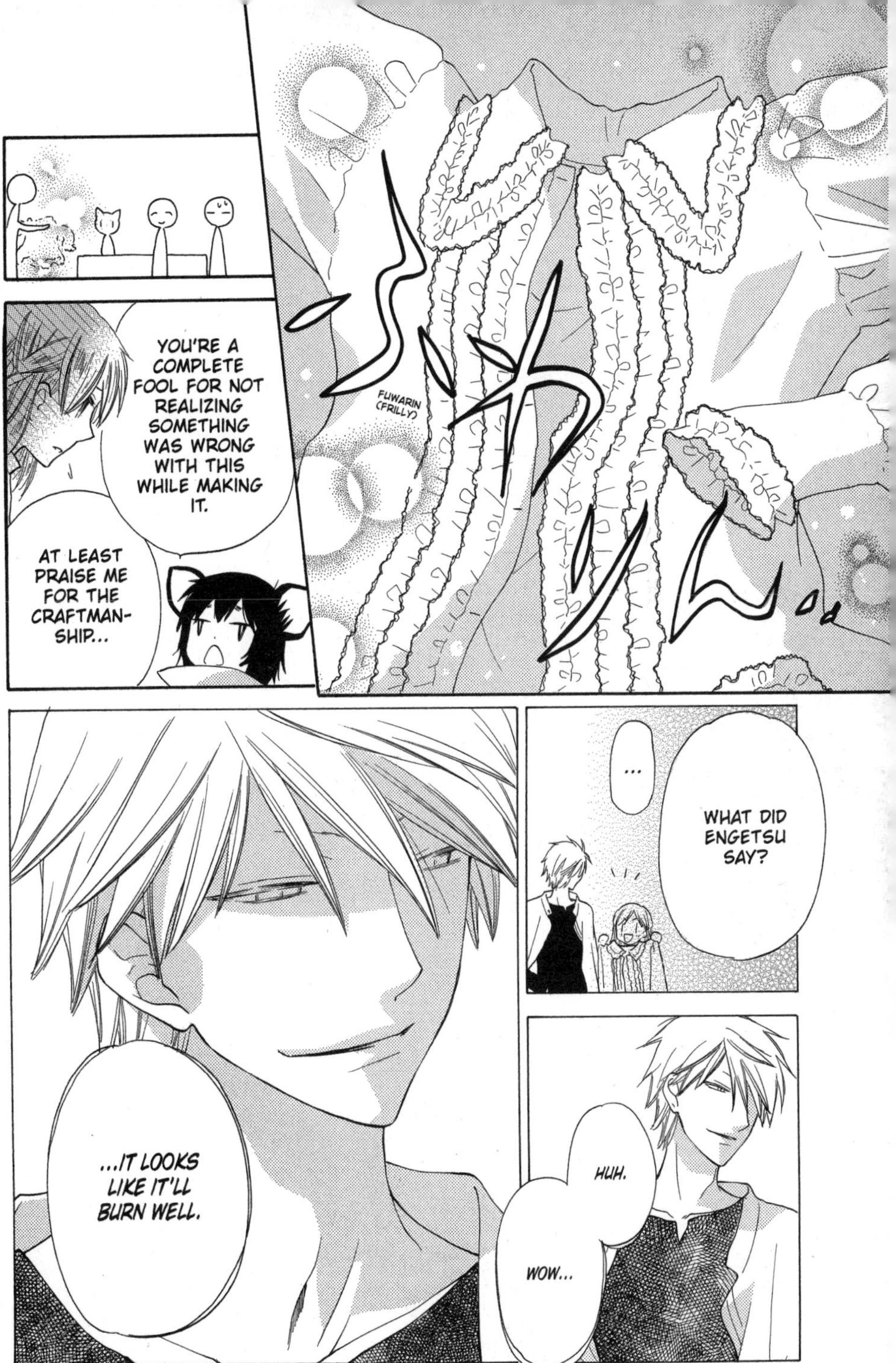

FUWARIN (FRILLY)
YOU'RE A COMPLETE FOOL FOR NOT REALIZING SOMETHING WAS WRONG WITH THIS WHILE MAKING IT.
AT LEAST PRAISE ME FOR THE CRAFTMAN-SHIP...
...
WHAT DID ENGETSU SAY?
HUH.
WOW...
...IT LOOKS LIKE IT'LL BURN WELL.

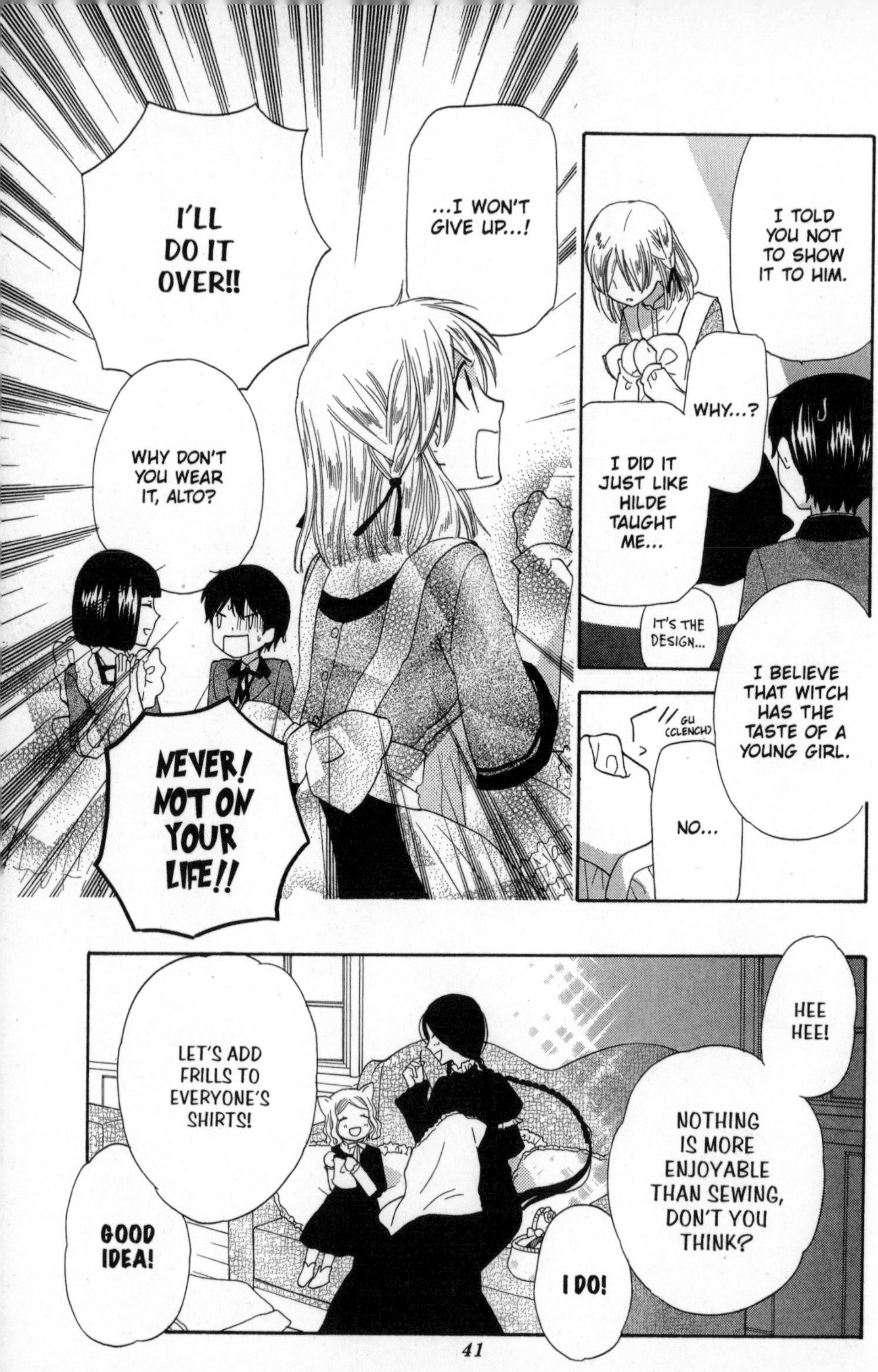
I TOLD YOU NOT TO SHOW IT TO HIM.
WHY...?
I DID IT JUST LIKE HILDE TAUGHT ME...
IT'S THE DESIGN...
I BELIEVE THAT WITCH HAS THE TASTE OF A YOUNG GIRL.
GU (CLENCH)
NO...
...I WON'T GIVE UP...!
I'LL DO IT OVER!!
WHY DON'T YOU WEAR IT, ALTO?
NEVER! NOT ON YOUR LIFE!!
HEE HEE!
NOTHING IS MORE ENJOYABLE THAN SEWING, DON'T YOU THINK?
I DO!
LET'S ADD FRILLS TO EVERYONE'S SHIRTS!
GOOD IDEA!

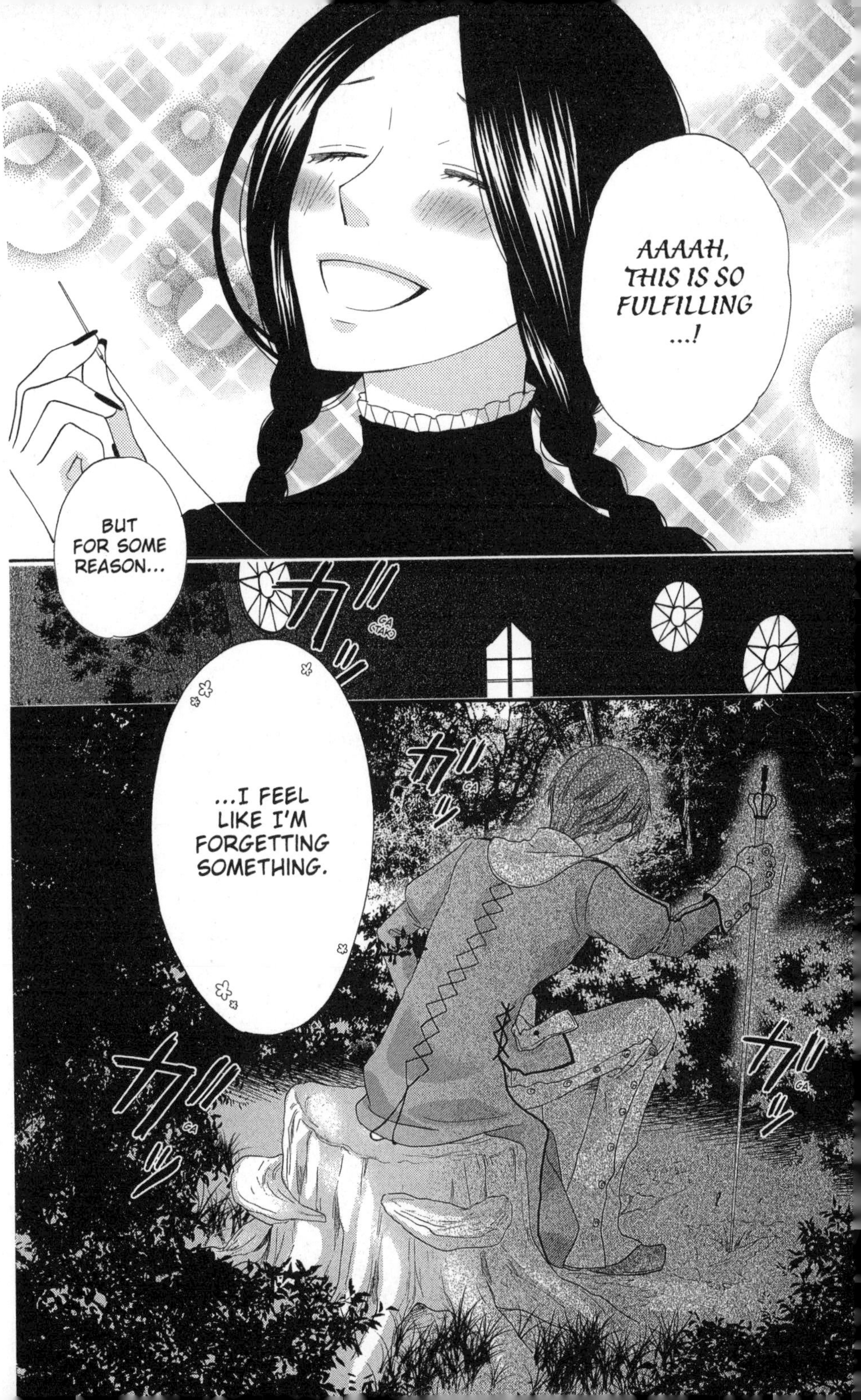

AAAAH, THIS IS SO FULFILLING ...!
BUT FOR SOME REASON...
GA GTAK
GA
GA
...I FEEL LIKE I'M FORGETTING SOMETHING.
GA

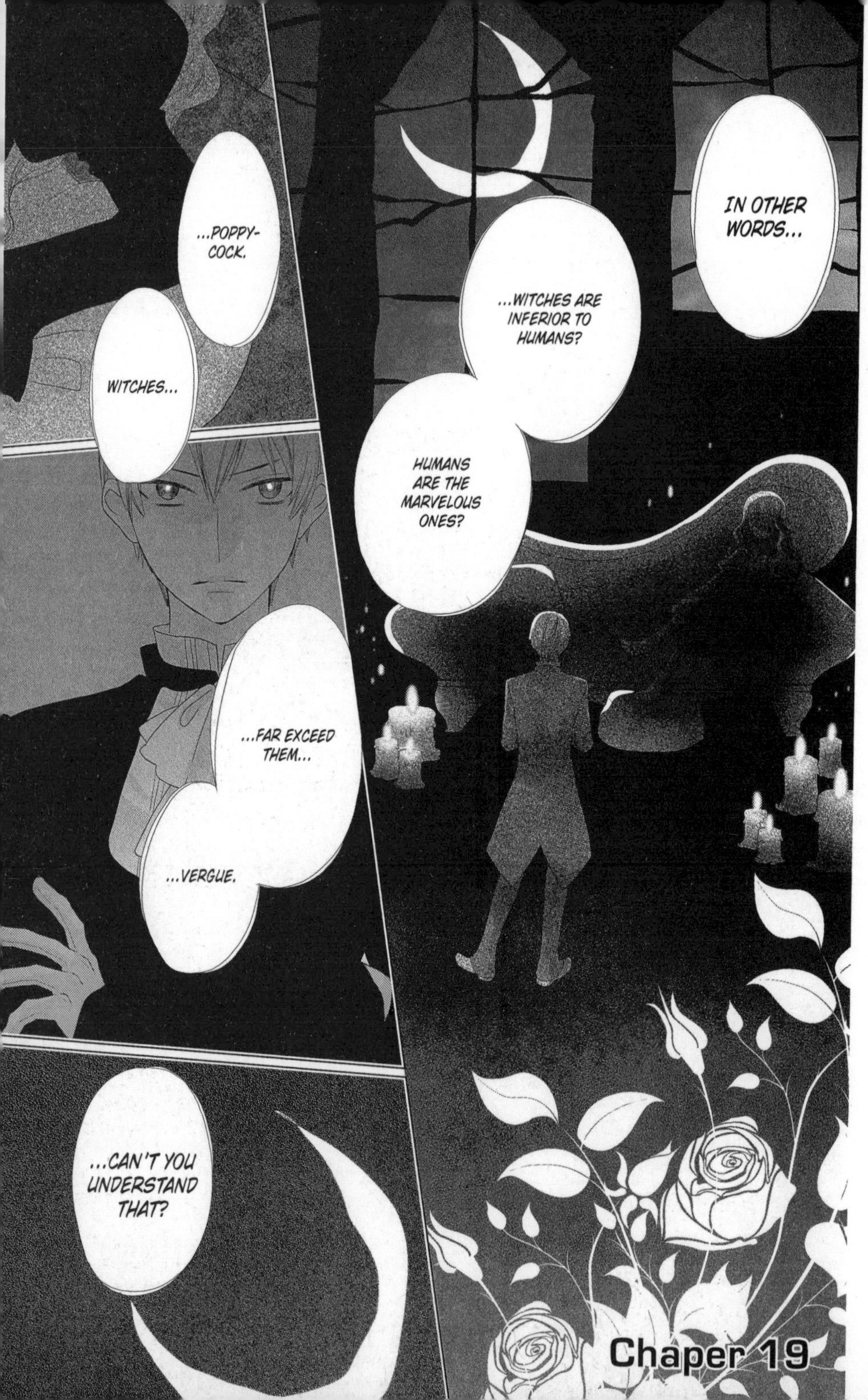
IN OTHER WORDS...
...WITCHES ARE INFERIOR TO HUMANS?
HUMANS ARE THE MARVELOUS ONES?
Chaper 19
...POPPY-COCK.
WITCHES...
...FAR EXCEED THEM...
...VERGUE.
...CAN'T YOU UNDERSTAND THAT?

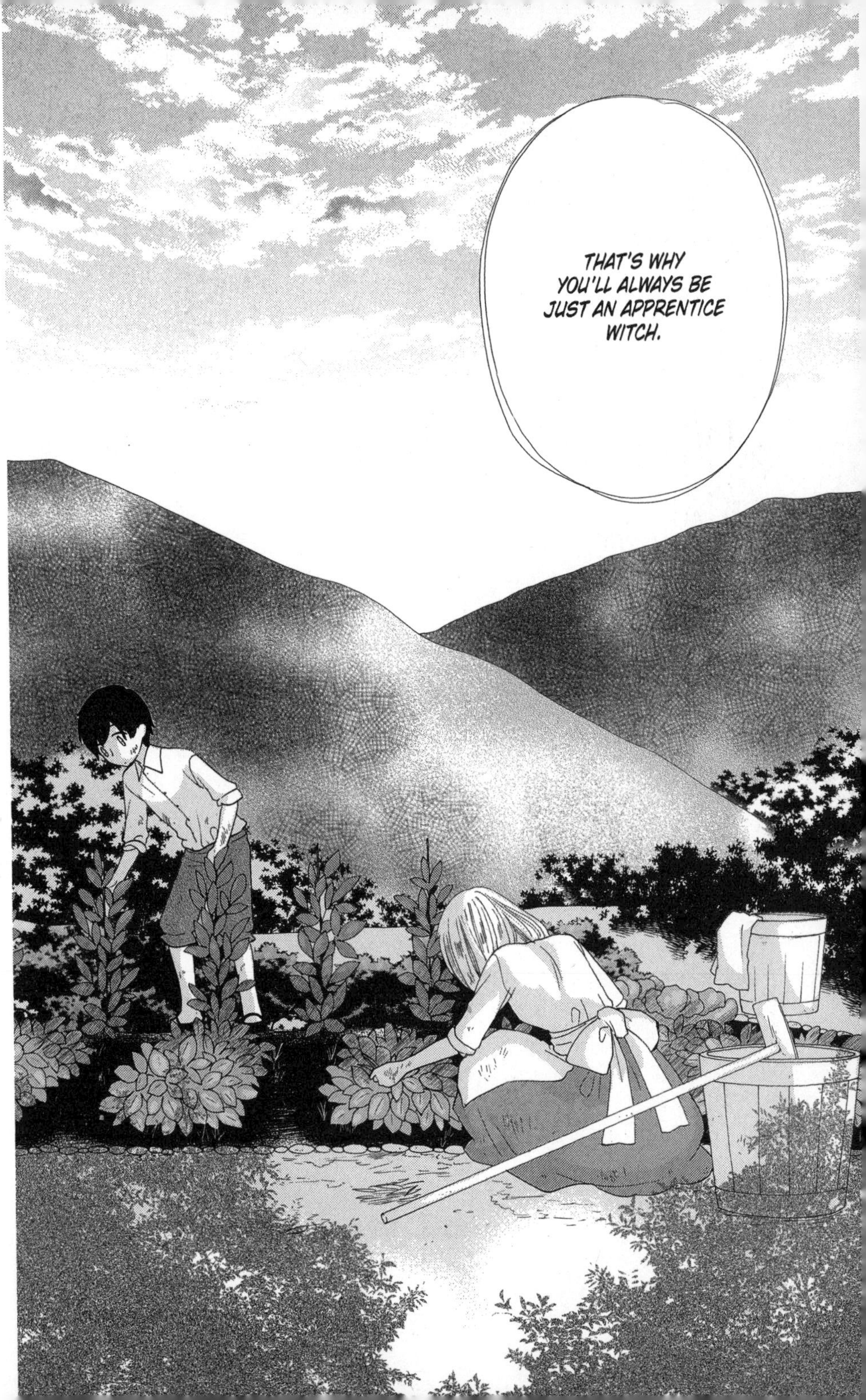
THAT'S WHY YOU'LL ALWAYS BE JUST AN APPRENTICE WITCH.

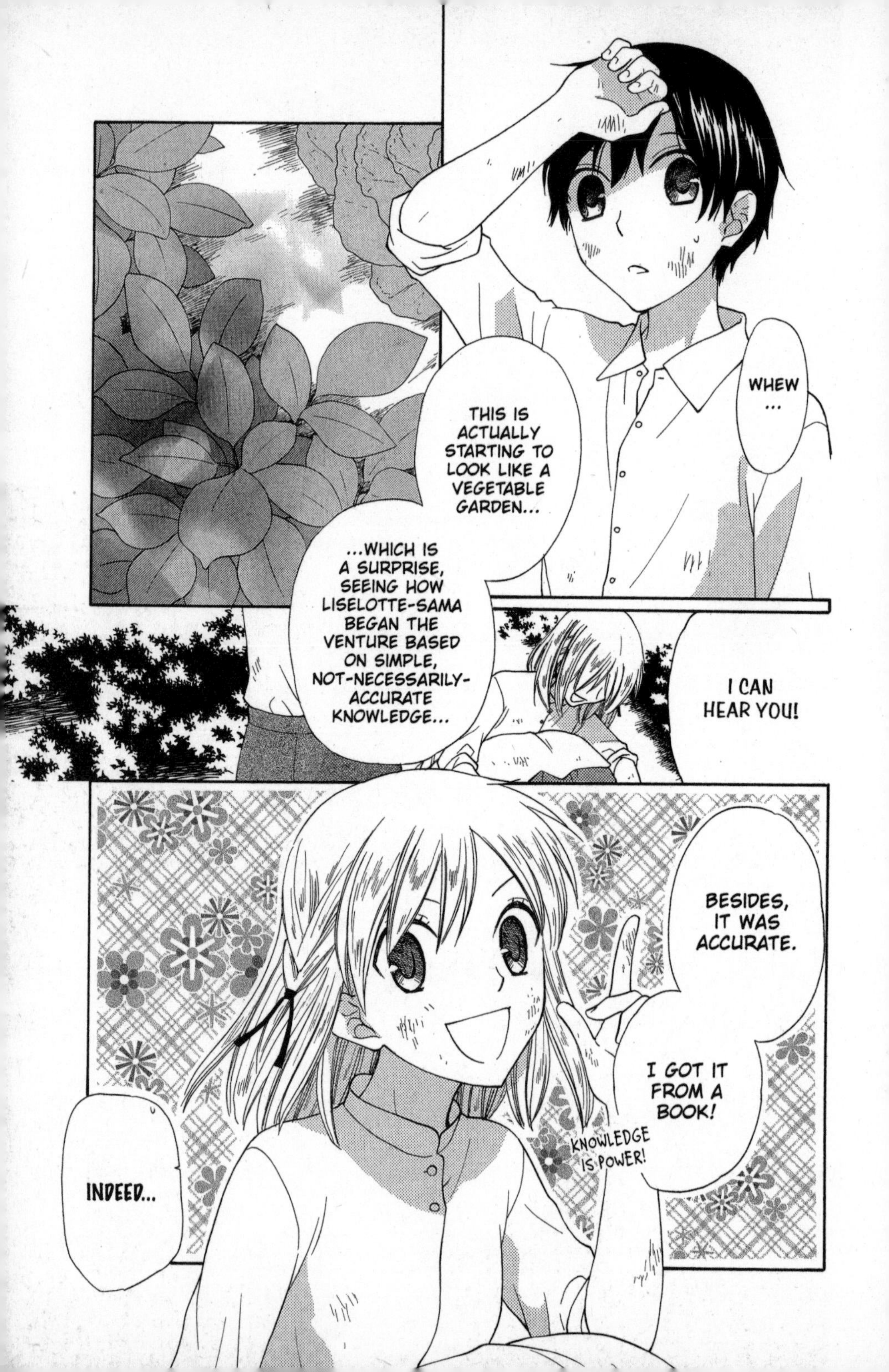
WHEW...
THIS IS ACTUALLY STARTING TO LOOK LIKE A VEGETABLE GARDEN...
...WHICH IS A SURPRISE, SEEING HOW LISELOTTE-SAMA BEGAN THE VENTURE BASED ON SIMPLE, NOT-NECESSARILY-ACCURATE KNOWLEDGE...
I CAN HEAR YOU!
BESIDES, IT WAS ACCURATE.
I GOT IT FROM A BOOK!
KNOWLEDGE IS POWER!
INDEED...

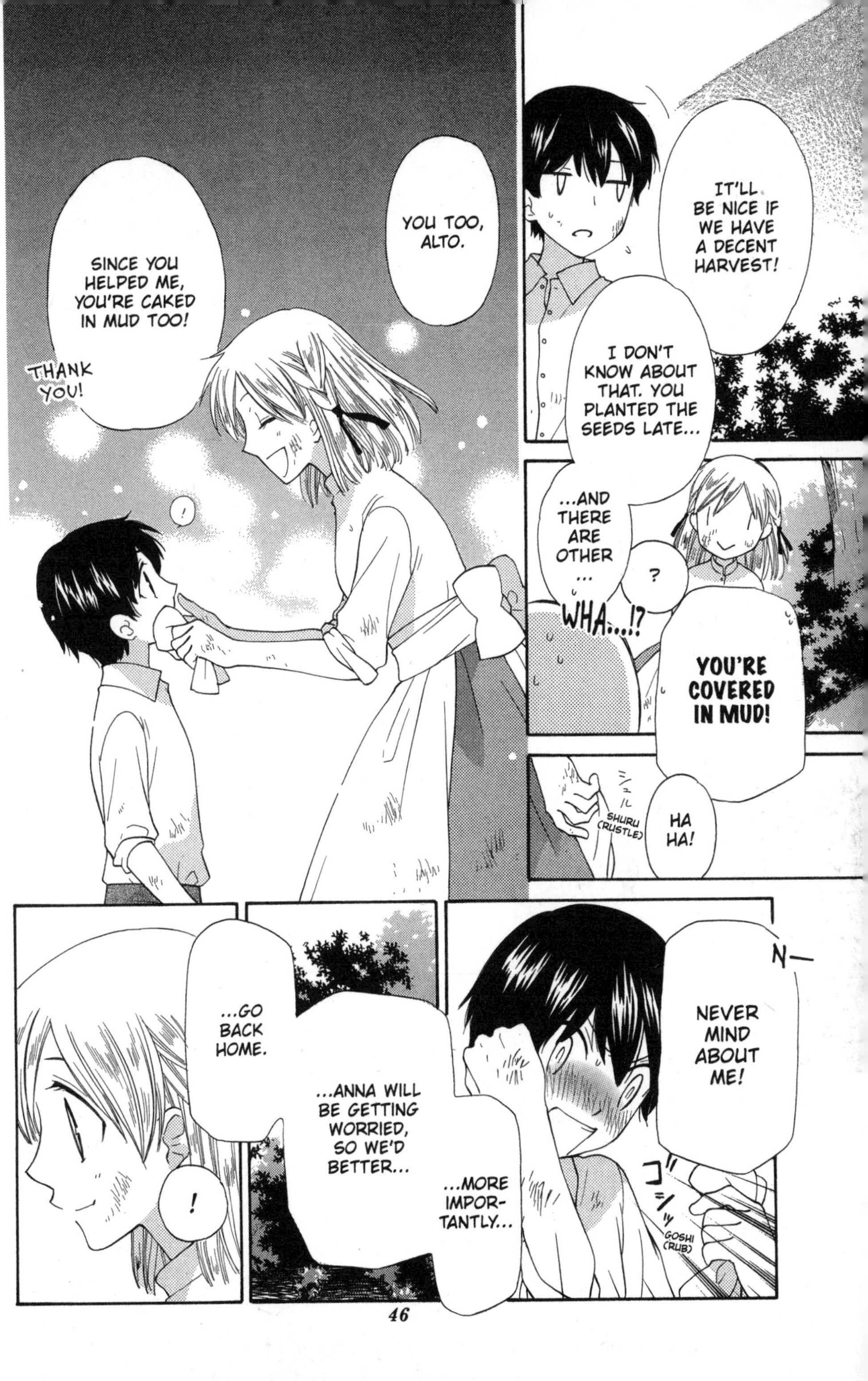
IT'LL BE NICE IF WE HAVE A DECENT HARVEST!
I DON'T KNOW ABOUT THAT. YOU PLANTED THE SEEDS LATE...
...AND THERE ARE OTHER ...
?
WHA...!?
YOU'RE COVERED IN MUD!
SHURU (RUSTLE)
HA HA!
YOU TOO, ALTO.
SINCE YOU HELPED ME, YOU'RE CAKED IN MUD TOO!
THANK YOU!
!
N—
NEVER MIND ABOUT ME!
GOSHI (RUB)
...MORE IMPORTANTLY...
...ANNA WILL BE GETTING WORRIED, SO WE'D BETTER...
...GO BACK HOME.
!

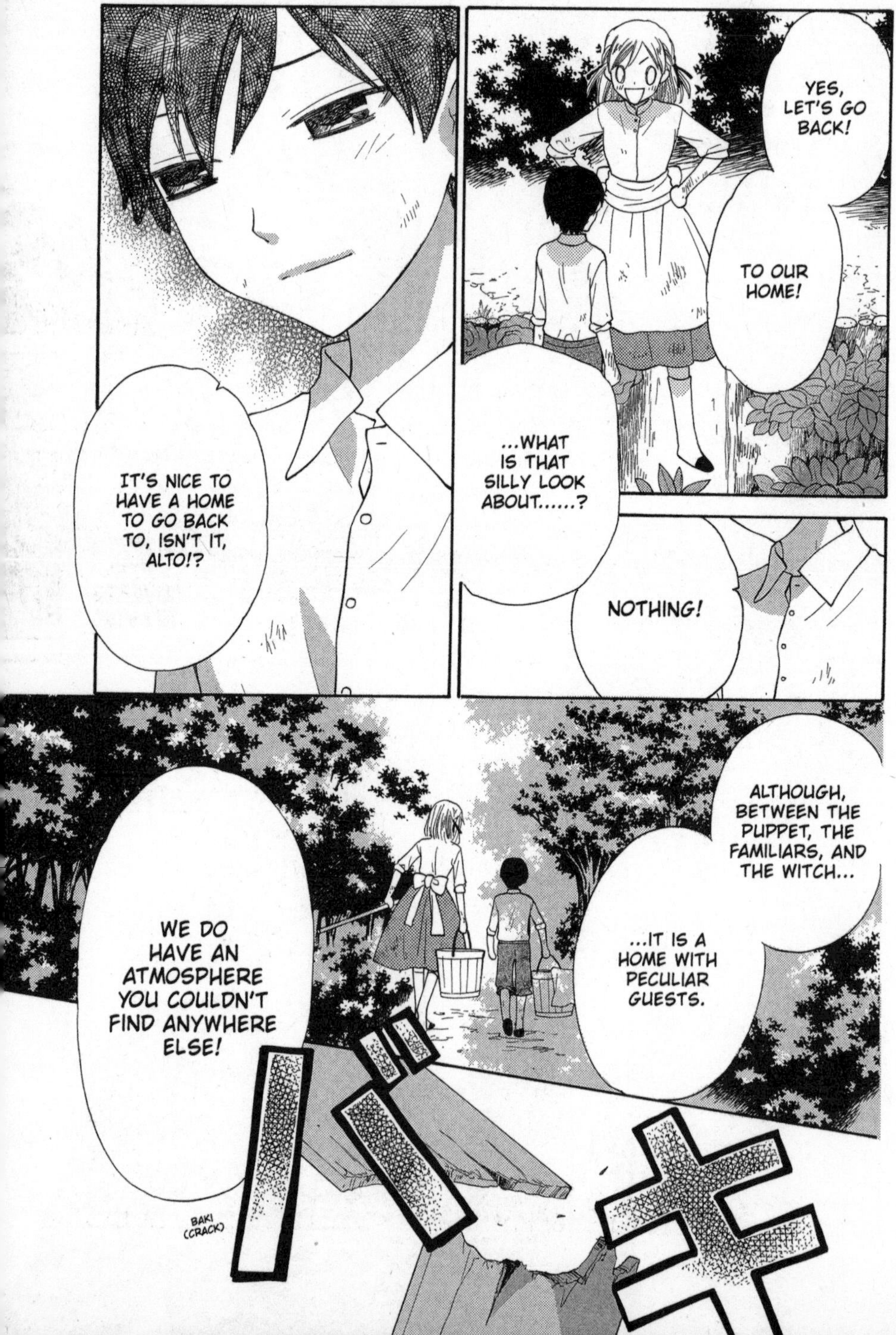
YES, LET'S GO BACK!
TO OUR HOME!
...WHAT IS THAT SILLY LOOK ABOUT......?
NOTHING!
IT'S NICE TO HAVE A HOME TO GO BACK TO, ISN'T IT, ALTO!?
ALTHOUGH, BETWEEN THE PUPPET, THE FAMILIARS, AND THE WITCH...
...IT IS A HOME WITH PECULIAR GUESTS.
WE DO HAVE AN ATMOSPHERE YOU COULDN'T FIND ANYWHERE ELSE!
BAKI (CRACK)

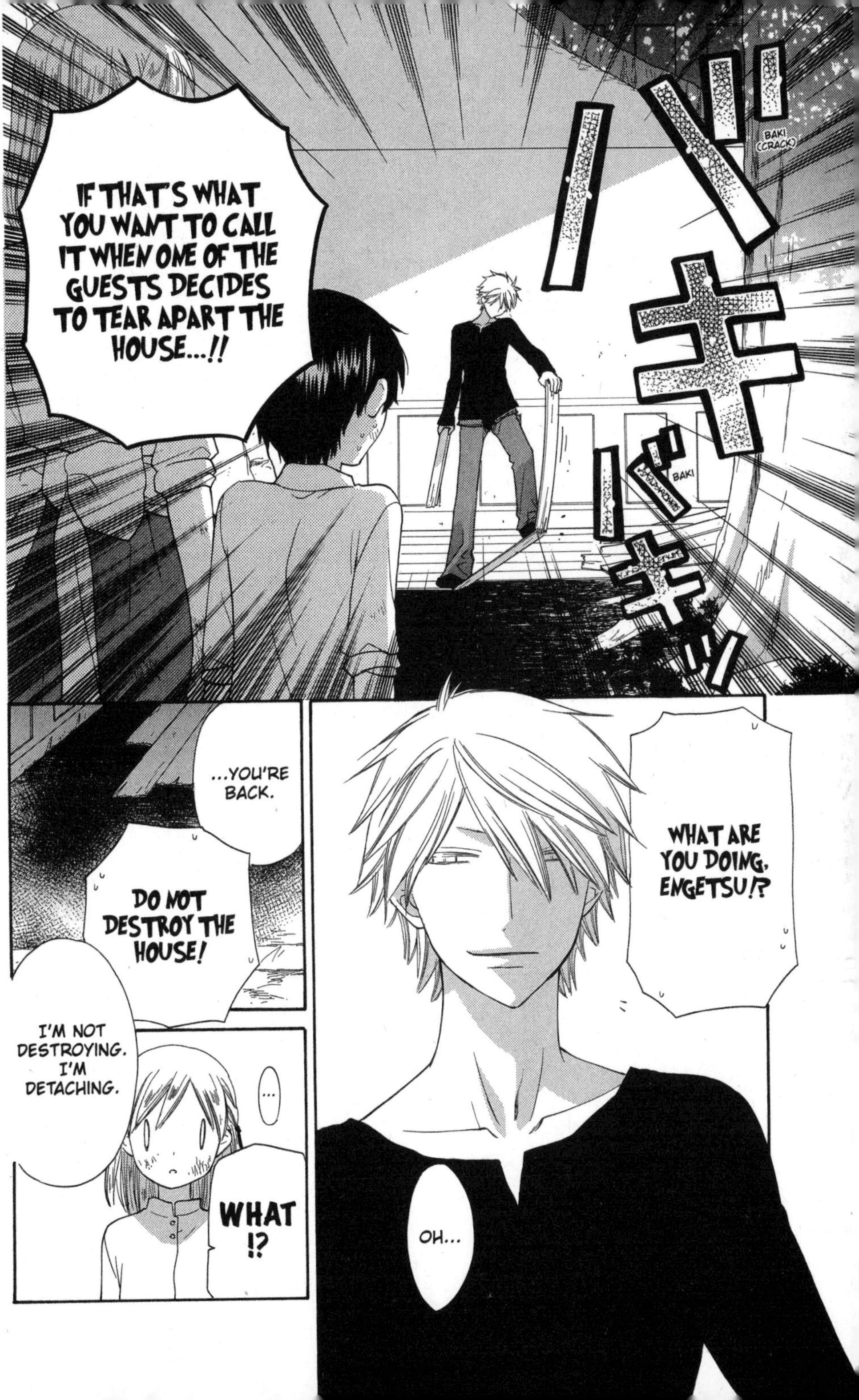
BAKI (CRACK)
BAKI
IF THAT'S WHAT YOU WANT TO CALL IT WHEN ONE OF THE GUESTS DECIDES TO TEAR APART THE HOUSE...!!
WHAT ARE YOU DOING, ENGETSU!?
...YOU'RE BACK.
DO NOT DESTROY THE HOUSE!
OH...
I'M NOT DESTROYING. I'M DETACHING.
...
WHAT!?

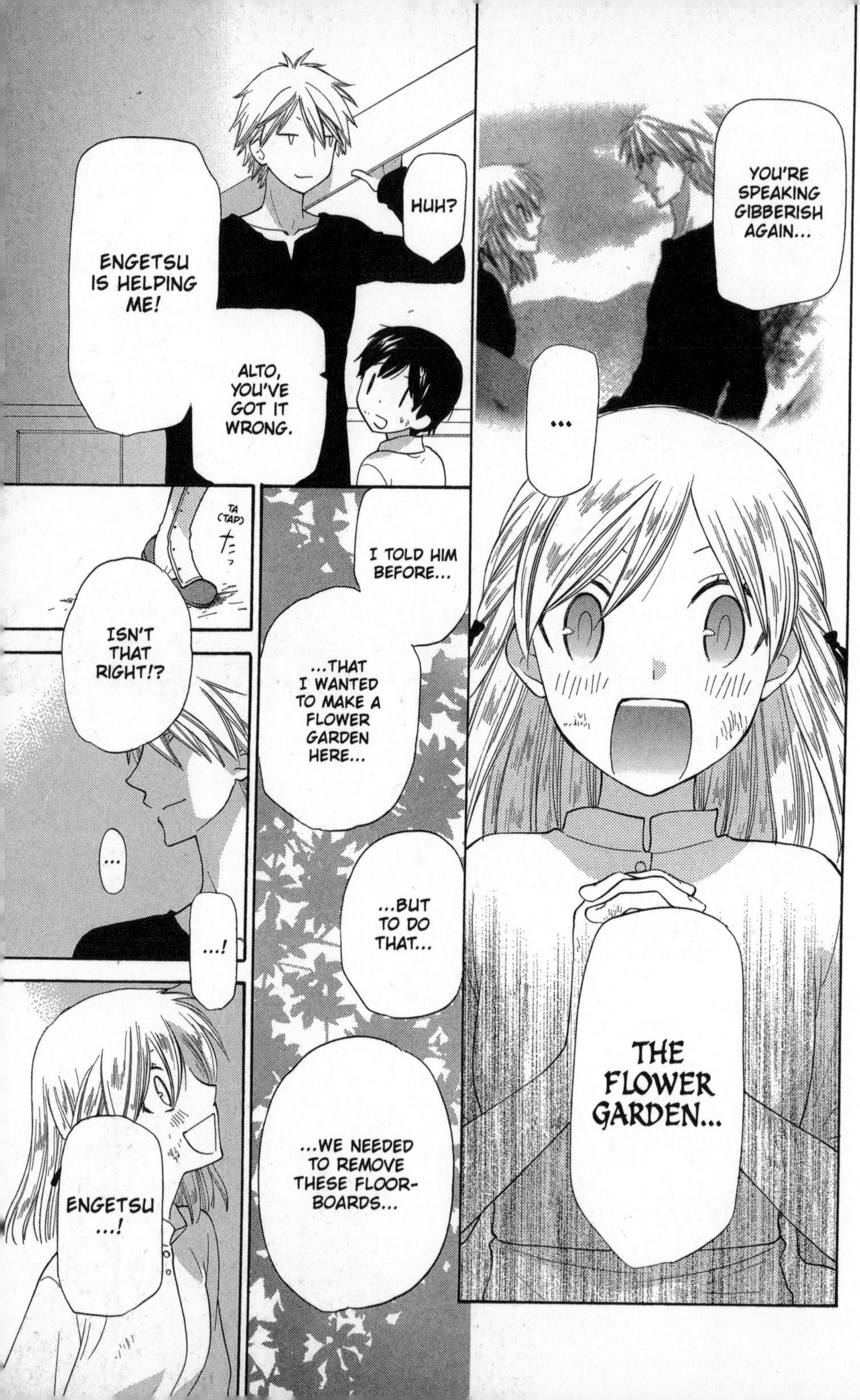
YOU'RE SPEAKING GIBBERISH AGAIN...
...
THE FLOWER GARDEN...
HUH?
ENGETSU IS HELPING ME!
ALTO, YOU'VE GOT IT WRONG.
I TOLD HIM BEFORE...
...THAT I WANTED TO MAKE A FLOWER GARDEN HERE...
...BUT TO DO THAT...
...WE NEEDED TO REMOVE THESE FLOOR-BOARDS...
TA (TAP)
ISN'T THAT RIGHT!?
...
...!
ENGETSU ...!

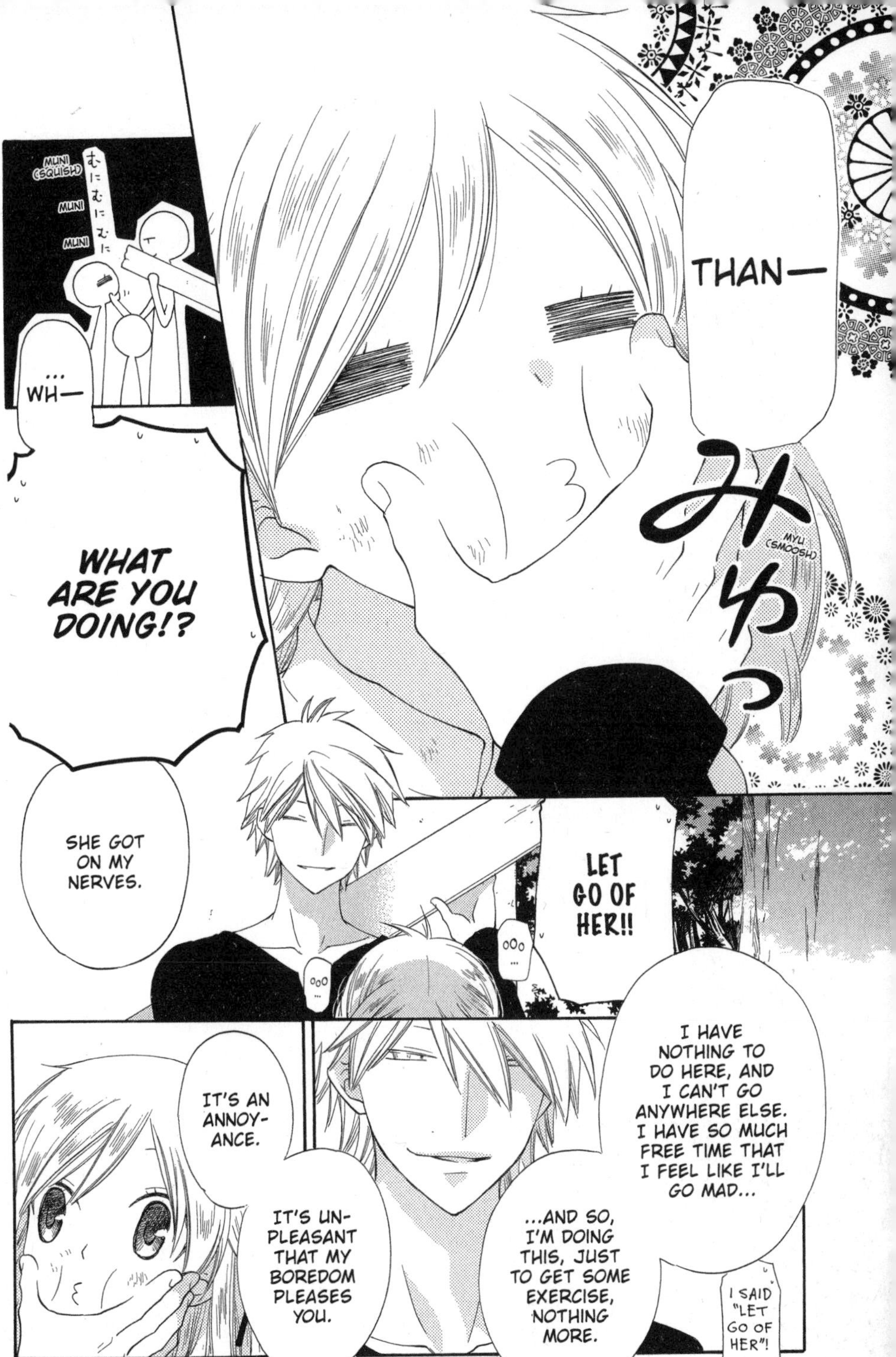
THAN—
みゅっ
MYU (SMOOSH)
むにむにむに
MUNI (SQUISH)
MUNI
MUNI
... WH—
WHAT ARE YOU DOING!?
SHE GOT ON MY NERVES.
LET GO OF HER!!
I HAVE NOTHING TO DO HERE, AND I CAN'T GO ANYWHERE ELSE. I HAVE SO MUCH FREE TIME THAT I FEEL LIKE I'LL GO MAD...
...AND SO, I'M DOING THIS, JUST TO GET SOME EXERCISE, NOTHING MORE.
I SAID "LET GO OF HER"!
IT'S AN ANNOY-ANCE.
IT'S UN-PLEASANT THAT MY BOREDOM PLEASES YOU.

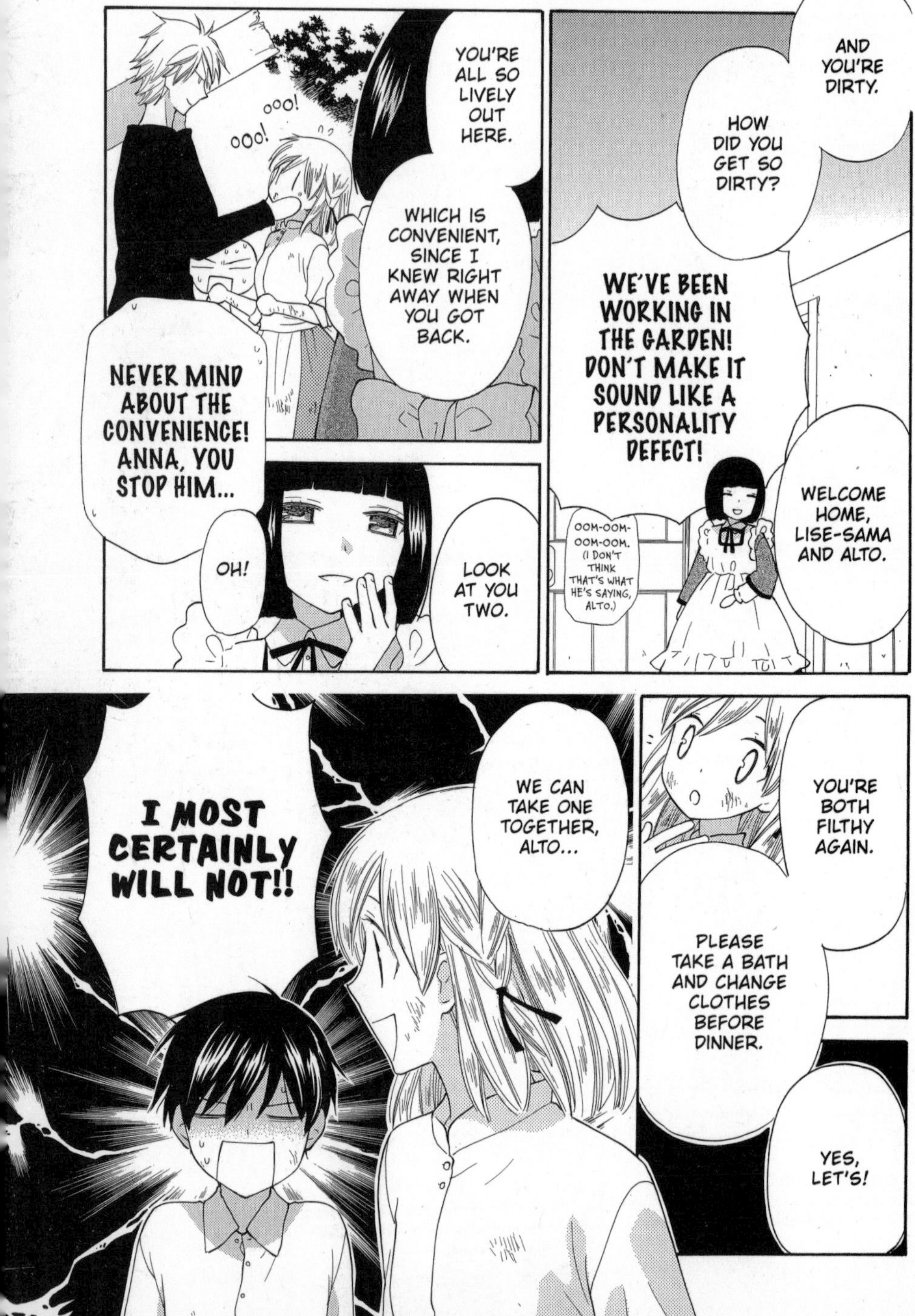
AND YOU'RE DIRTY.
HOW DID YOU GET SO DIRTY?
WELCOME HOME, LISE-SAMA AND ALTO.
WE'VE BEEN WORKING IN THE GARDEN! DON'T MAKE IT SOUND LIKE A PERSONALITY DEFECT!
OOM-OOM-OOM-OOM. (I DON'T THINK THAT'S WHAT HE'S SAYING, ALTO.)
YOU'RE ALL SO LIVELY OUT HERE.
WHICH IS CONVENIENT, SINCE I KNEW RIGHT AWAY WHEN YOU GOT BACK.
OOO!
OOO!
NEVER MIND ABOUT THE CONVENIENCE! ANNA, YOU STOP HIM...
LOOK AT YOU TWO.
OH!
YOU'RE BOTH FILTHY AGAIN.
PLEASE TAKE A BATH AND CHANGE CLOTHES BEFORE DINNER.
YES, LET'S!
WE CAN TAKE ONE TOGETHER, ALTO...
I MOST CERTAINLY WILL NOT!!

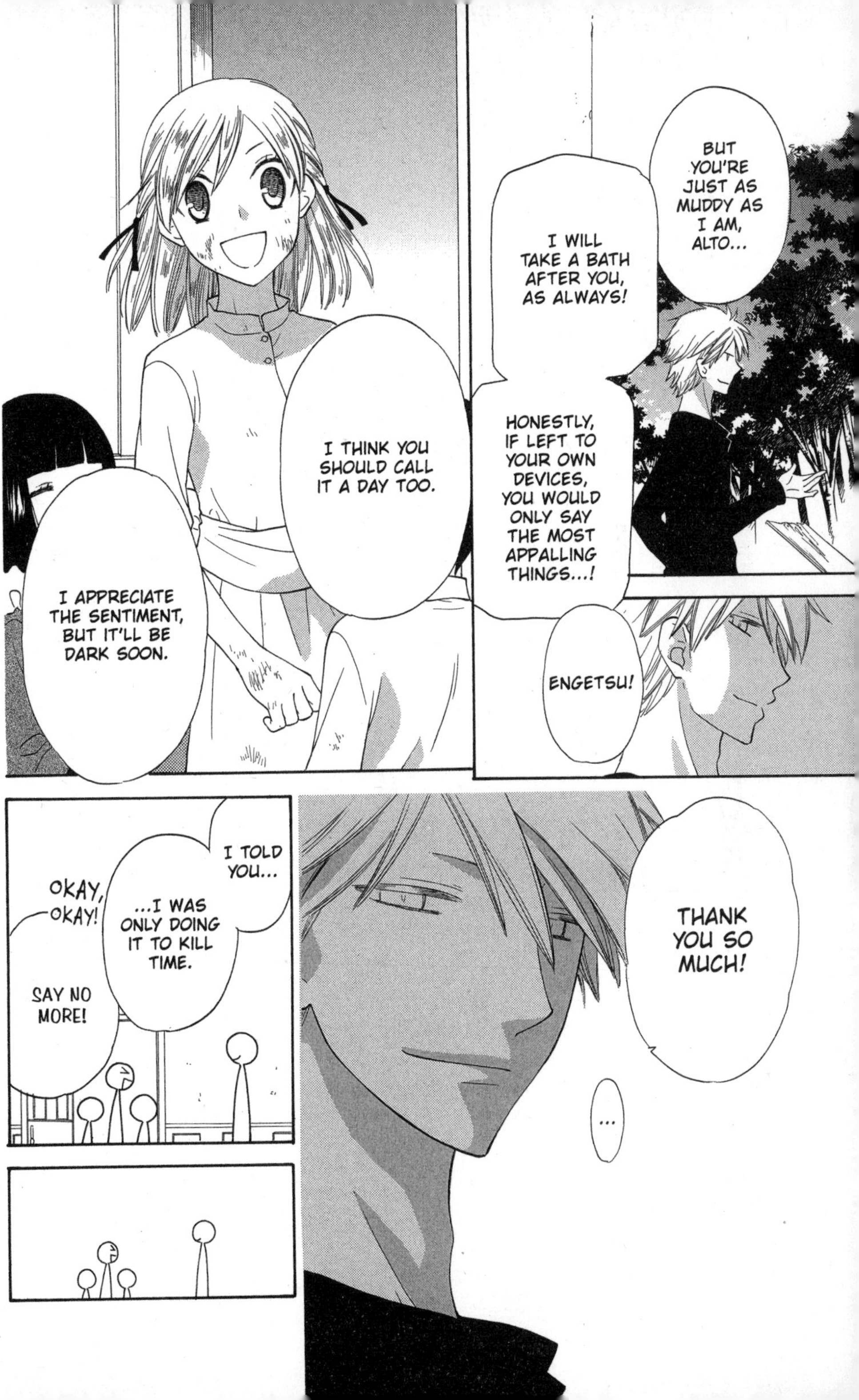
BUT YOU'RE JUST AS MUDDY AS I AM, ALTO...
I WILL TAKE A BATH AFTER YOU, AS ALWAYS!
HONESTLY, IF LEFT TO YOUR OWN DEVICES, YOU WOULD ONLY SAY THE MOST APPALLING THINGS...!
ENGETSU!
I THINK YOU SHOULD CALL IT A DAY TOO.
I APPRECIATE THE SENTIMENT, BUT IT'LL BE DARK SOON.
THANK YOU SO MUCH!
...
I TOLD YOU...
...I WAS ONLY DOING IT TO KILL TIME.
OKAY, OKAY!
SAY NO MORE!

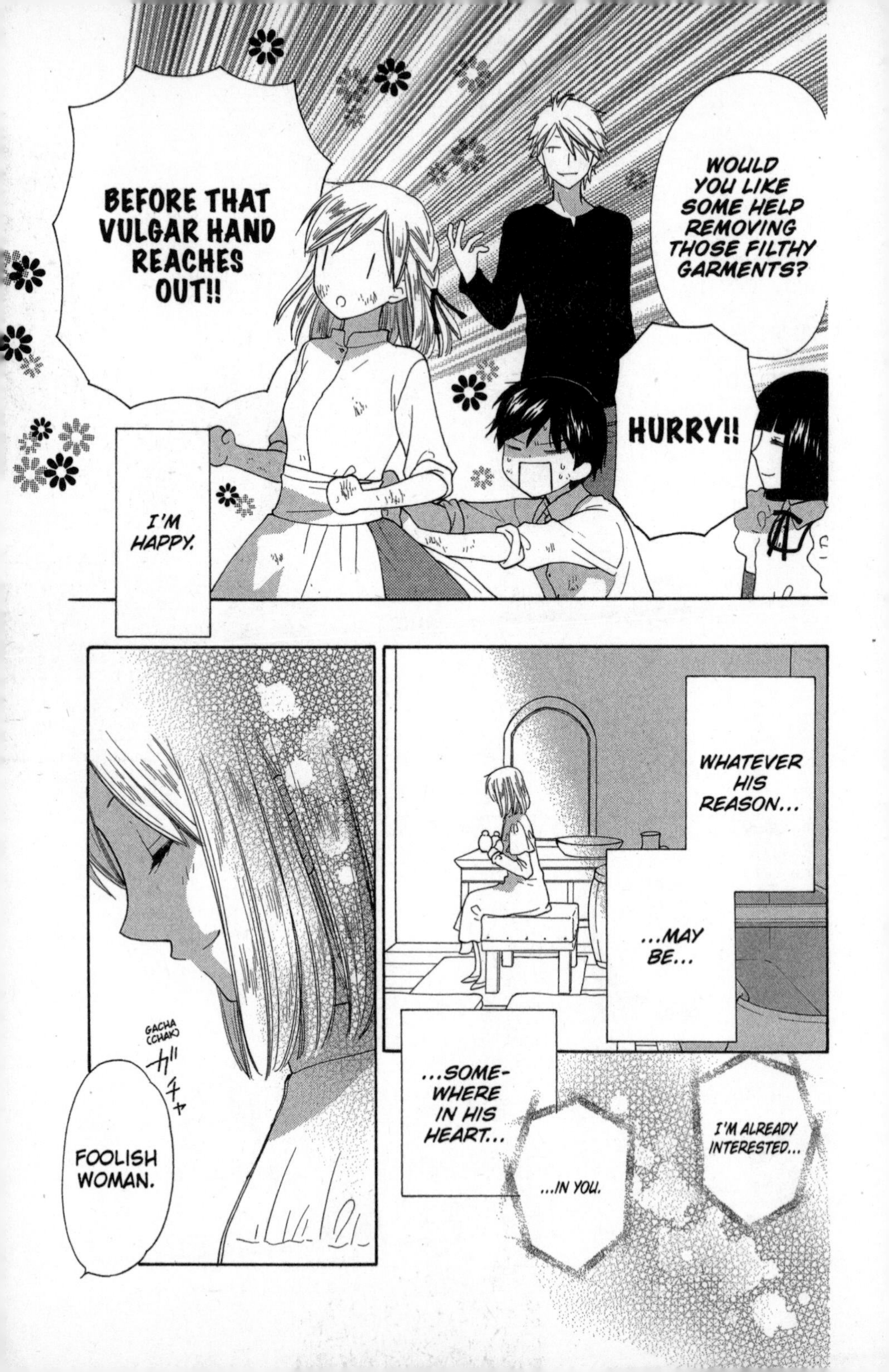
WOULD YOU LIKE SOME HELP REMOVING THOSE FILTHY GARMENTS?
HURRY!!
BEFORE THAT VULGAR HAND REACHES OUT!!
I'M HAPPY.
WHATEVER HIS REASON...
...MAY BE...
...SOME-WHERE IN HIS HEART...
I'M ALREADY INTERESTED...
...IN YOU.
GACHA (CHAK)
ガチャ
FOOLISH WOMAN.

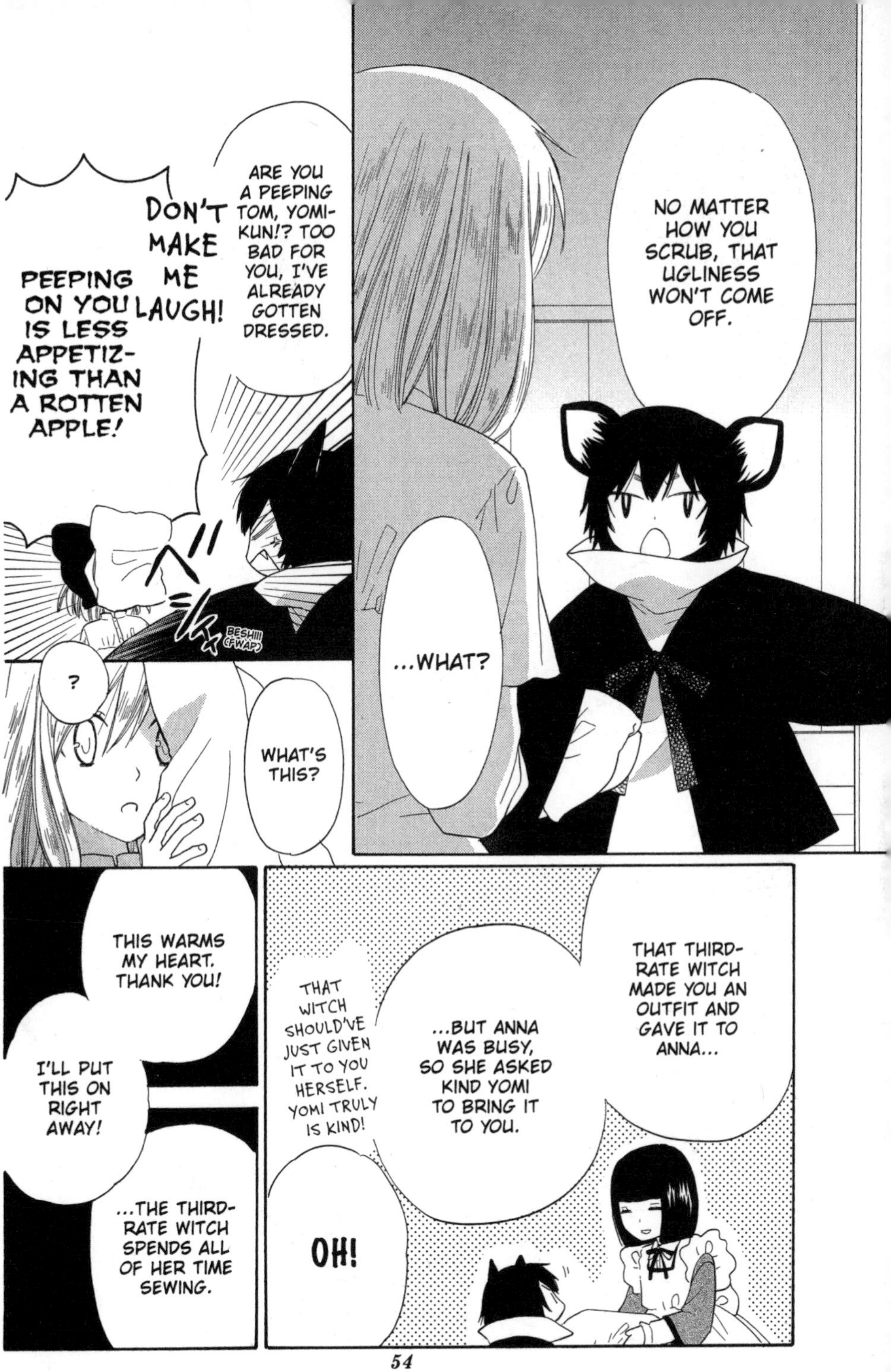
NO MATTER HOW YOU SCRUB, THAT UGLINESS WON'T COME OFF.
...WHAT?
ARE YOU A PEEPING TOM, YOMI-KUN!? TOO BAD FOR YOU, I'VE ALREADY GOTTEN DRESSED.
DON'T MAKE ME LAUGH!
PEEPING ON YOU IS LESS APPETIZ-ING THAN A ROTTEN APPLE!
BESHIII (FWAP)
WHAT'S THIS?
?
THAT THIRD-RATE WITCH MADE YOU AN OUTFIT AND GAVE IT TO ANNA...
...BUT ANNA WAS BUSY, SO SHE ASKED KIND YOMI TO BRING IT TO YOU.
THAT WITCH SHOULD'VE JUST GIVEN IT TO YOU HERSELF. YOMI TRULY IS KIND!
OH!
THIS WARMS MY HEART. THANK YOU!
I'LL PUT THIS ON RIGHT AWAY!
...THE THIRD-RATE WITCH SPENDS ALL OF HER TIME SEWING.

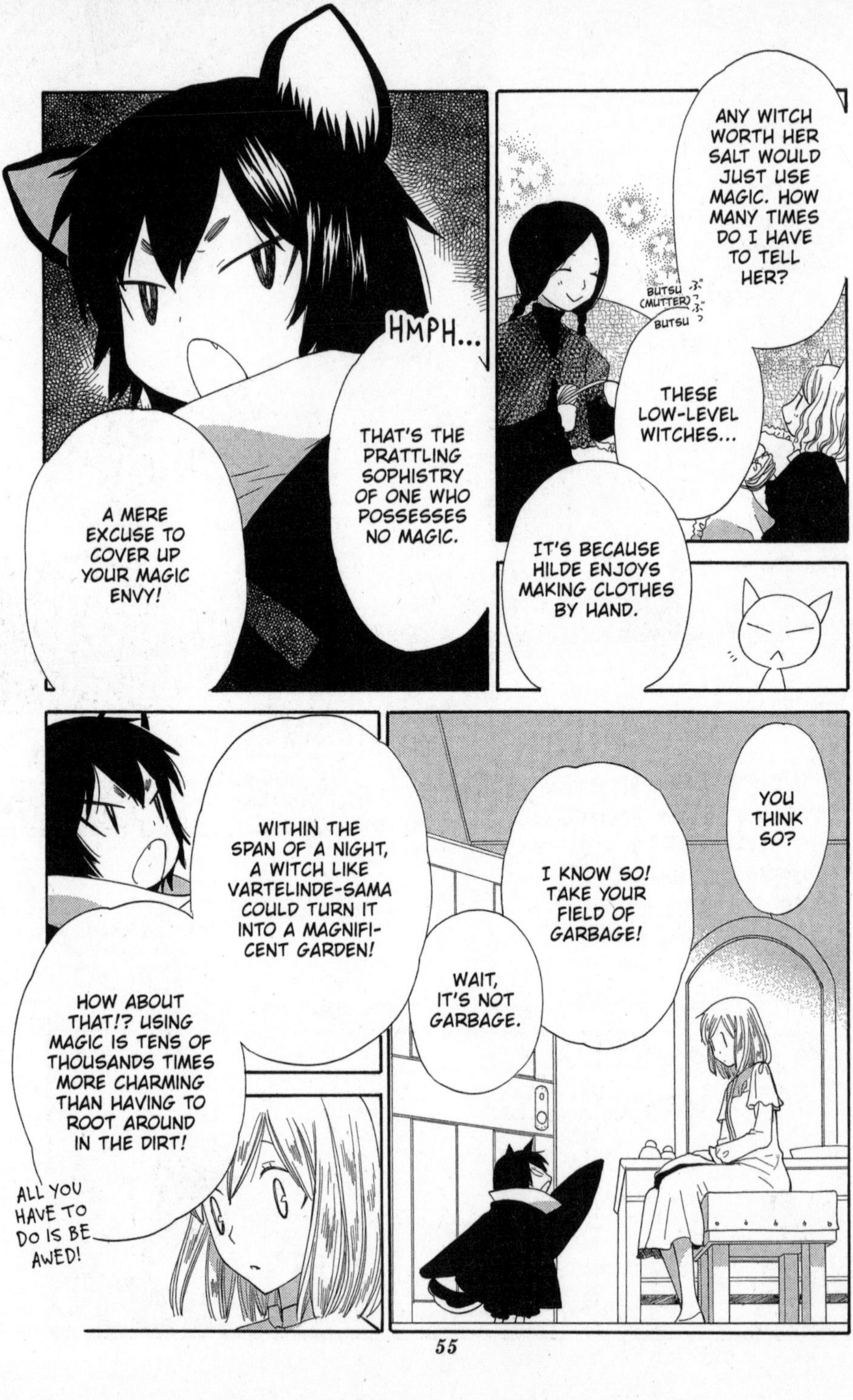
ANY WITCH WORTH HER SALT WOULD JUST USE MAGIC. HOW MANY TIMES DO I HAVE TO TELL HER?
BUTSU (MUTTER) BUTSU
THESE LOW-LEVEL WITCHES...
IT'S BECAUSE HILDE ENJOYS MAKING CLOTHES BY HAND.
HMPH...
THAT'S THE PRATTLING SOPHISTRY OF ONE WHO POSSESSES NO MAGIC.
A MERE EXCUSE TO COVER UP YOUR MAGIC ENVY!
YOU THINK SO?
I KNOW SO! TAKE YOUR FIELD OF GARBAGE!
WAIT, IT'S NOT GARBAGE.
WITHIN THE SPAN OF A NIGHT, A WITCH LIKE VARTELINDE-SAMA COULD TURN IT INTO A MAGNIFICENT GARDEN!
HOW ABOUT THAT!? USING MAGIC IS TENS OF THOUSANDS TIMES MORE CHARMING THAN HAVING TO ROOT AROUND IN THE DIRT!
ALL YOU HAVE TO DO IS BE AWED!

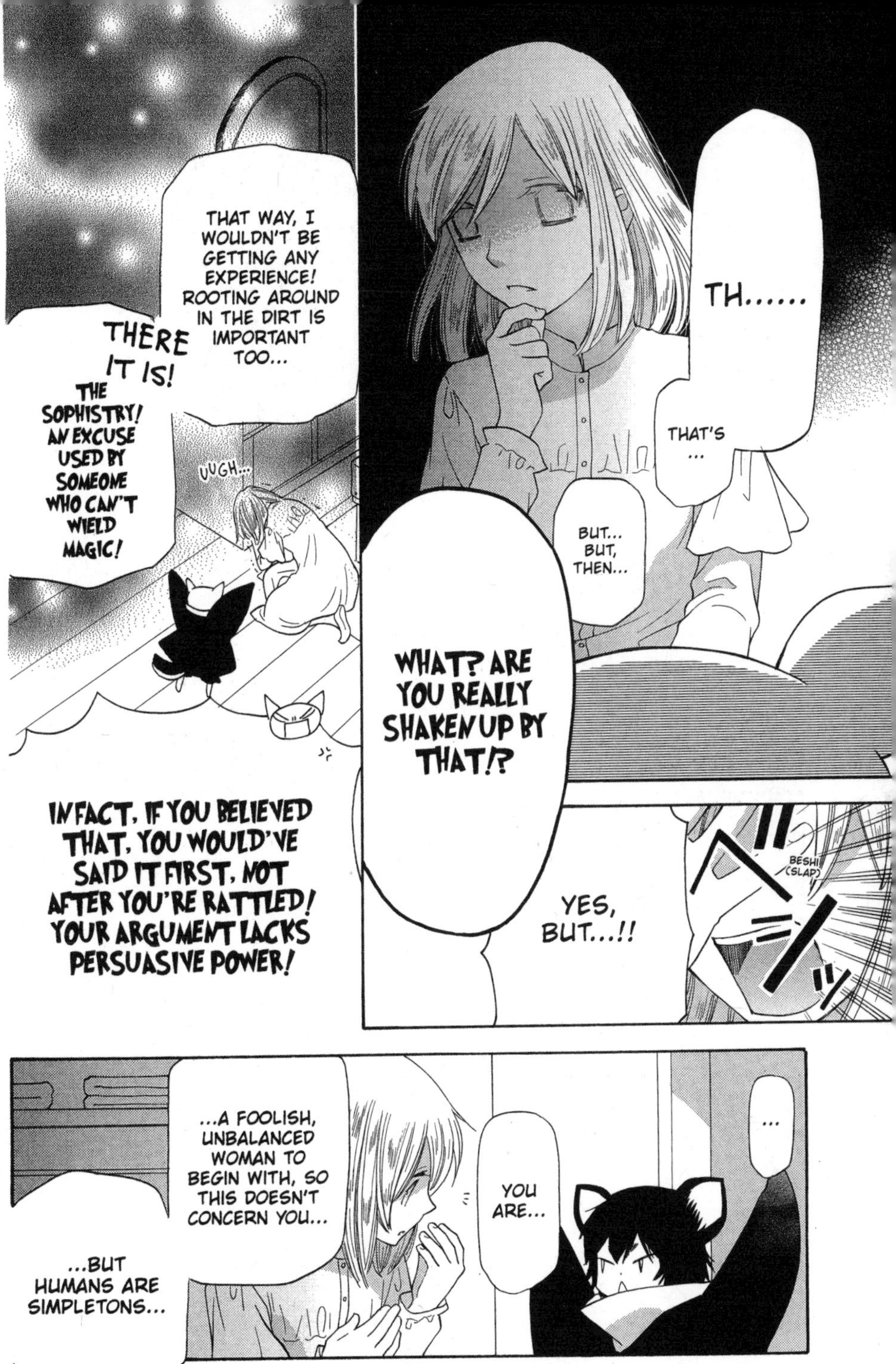
TH......
THAT'S ...
BUT... BUT, THEN...
THAT WAY, I WOULDN'T BE GETTING ANY EXPERIENCE! ROOTING AROUND IN THE DIRT IS IMPORTANT TOO...
THERE IT IS!
THE SOPHISTRY! AN EXCUSE USED BY SOMEONE WHO CAN'T WIELD MAGIC!
UUGH...
WHAT? ARE YOU REALLY SHAKEN UP BY THAT!?
YES, BUT...!!
BESHI (SLAP)
IN FACT, IF YOU BELIEVED THAT, YOU WOULD'VE SAID IT FIRST, NOT AFTER YOU'RE RATTLED! YOUR ARGUMENT LACKS PERSUASIVE POWER!
...
YOU ARE...
...A FOOLISH, UNBALANCED WOMAN TO BEGIN WITH, SO THIS DOESN'T CONCERN YOU...
...BUT HUMANS ARE SIMPLETONS...

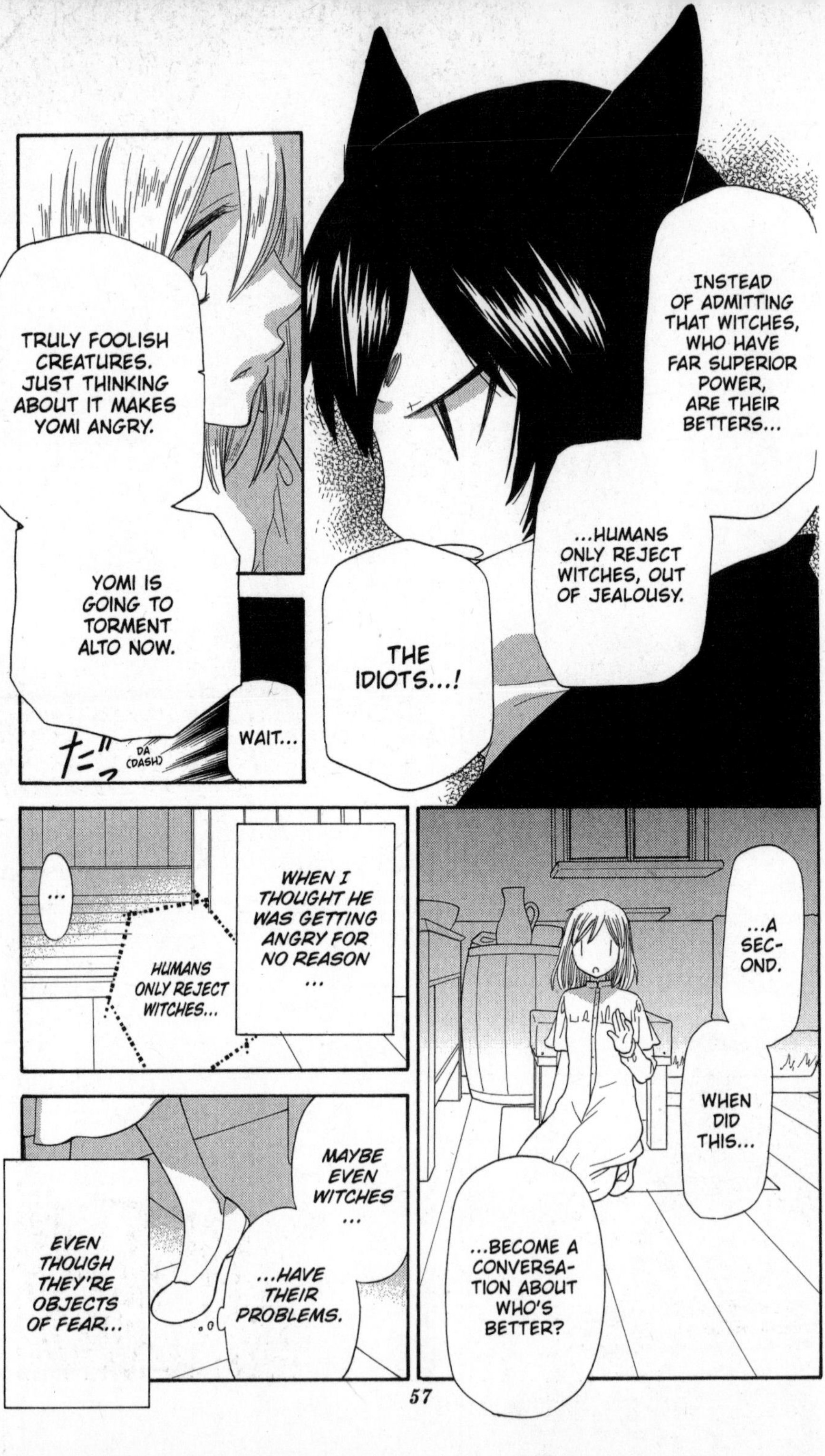
INSTEAD OF ADMITTING THAT WITCHES, WHO HAVE FAR SUPERIOR POWER, ARE THEIR BETTERS...
...HUMANS ONLY REJECT WITCHES, OUT OF JEALOUSY.
THE IDIOTS...!
TRULY FOOLISH CREATURES. JUST THINKING ABOUT IT MAKES YOMI ANGRY.
YOMI IS GOING TO TORMENT ALTO NOW.
WAIT...
DA (DASH)
...A SEC-OND.
WHEN DID THIS...
...BECOME A CONVERSA-TION ABOUT WHO'S BETTER?
WHEN I THOUGHT HE WAS GETTING ANGRY FOR NO REASON...
HUMANS ONLY REJECT WITCHES...
...
MAYBE EVEN WITCHES...
...HAVE THEIR PROBLEMS.
EVEN THOUGH THEY'RE OBJECTS OF FEAR...

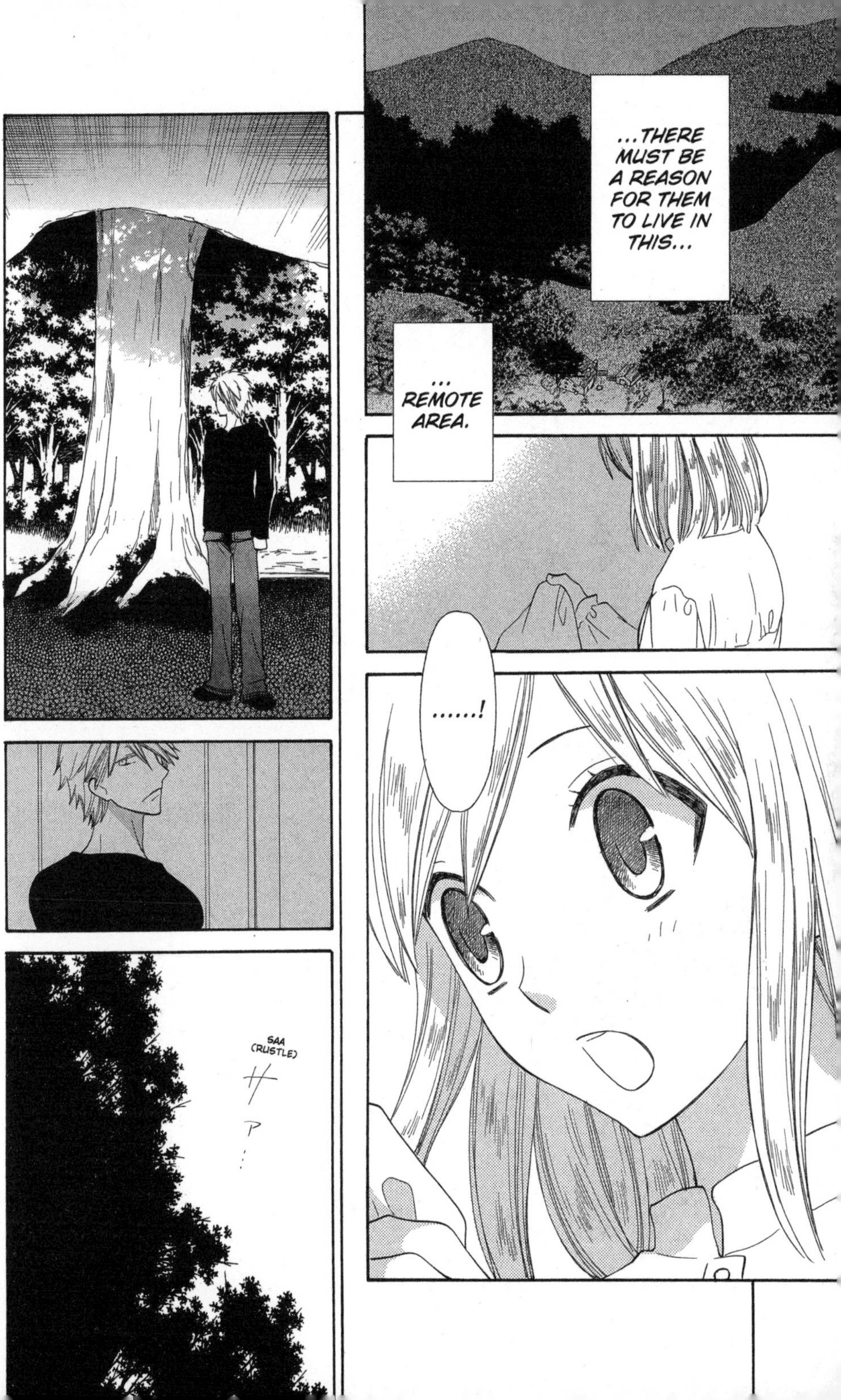
...THERE MUST BE A REASON FOR THEM TO LIVE IN THIS...
...REMOTE AREA.
......!
SAA (RUSTLE)
サァ…

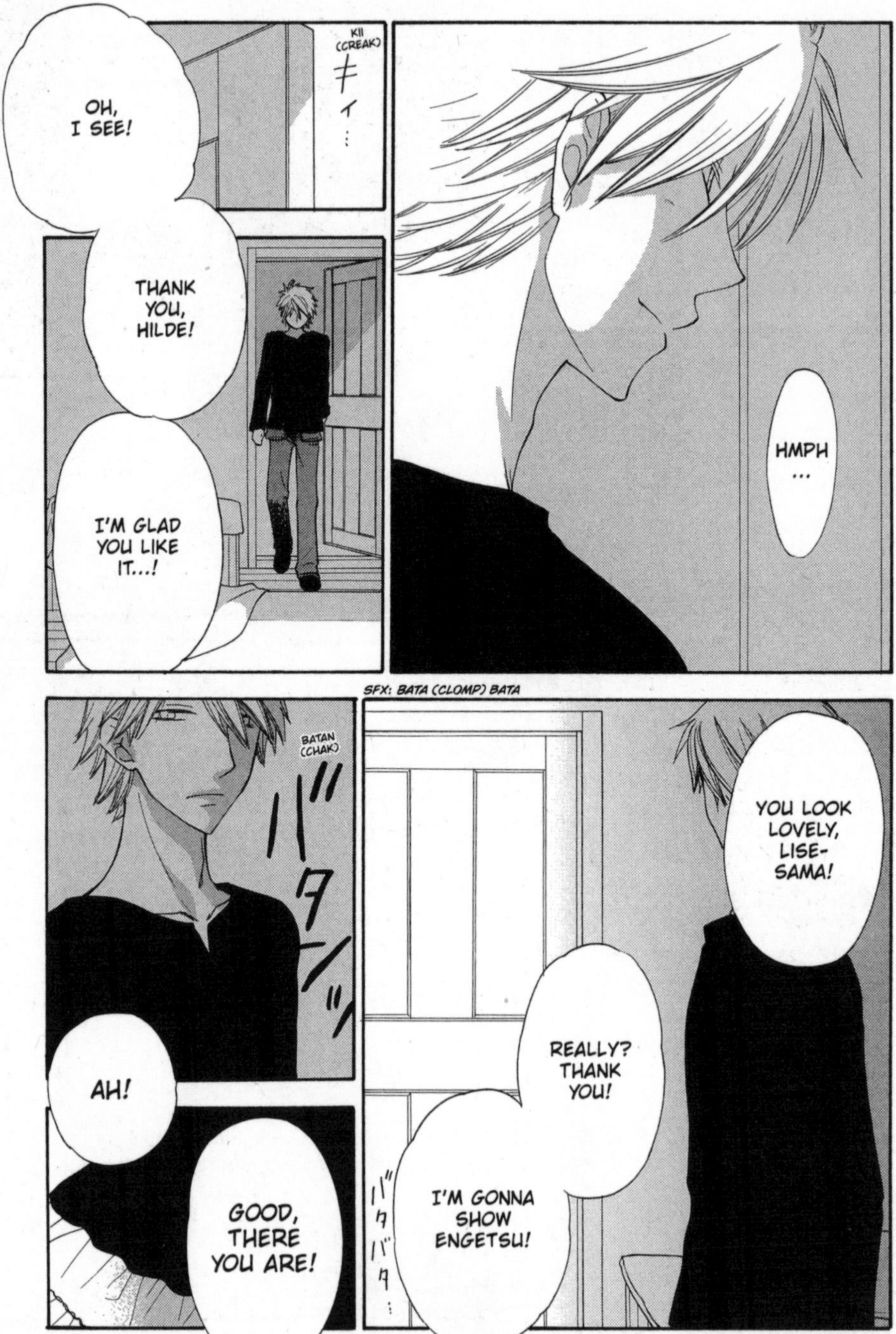
HMPH ...
KII (CREAK)
OH, I SEE!
THANK YOU, HILDE!
I'M GLAD YOU LIKE IT...!
SFX: BATA (CLOMP) BATA
YOU LOOK LOVELY, LISE-SAMA!
REALLY? THANK YOU!
I'M GONNA SHOW ENGETSU!
BATAN (CHAK)
AH!
GOOD, THERE YOU ARE!

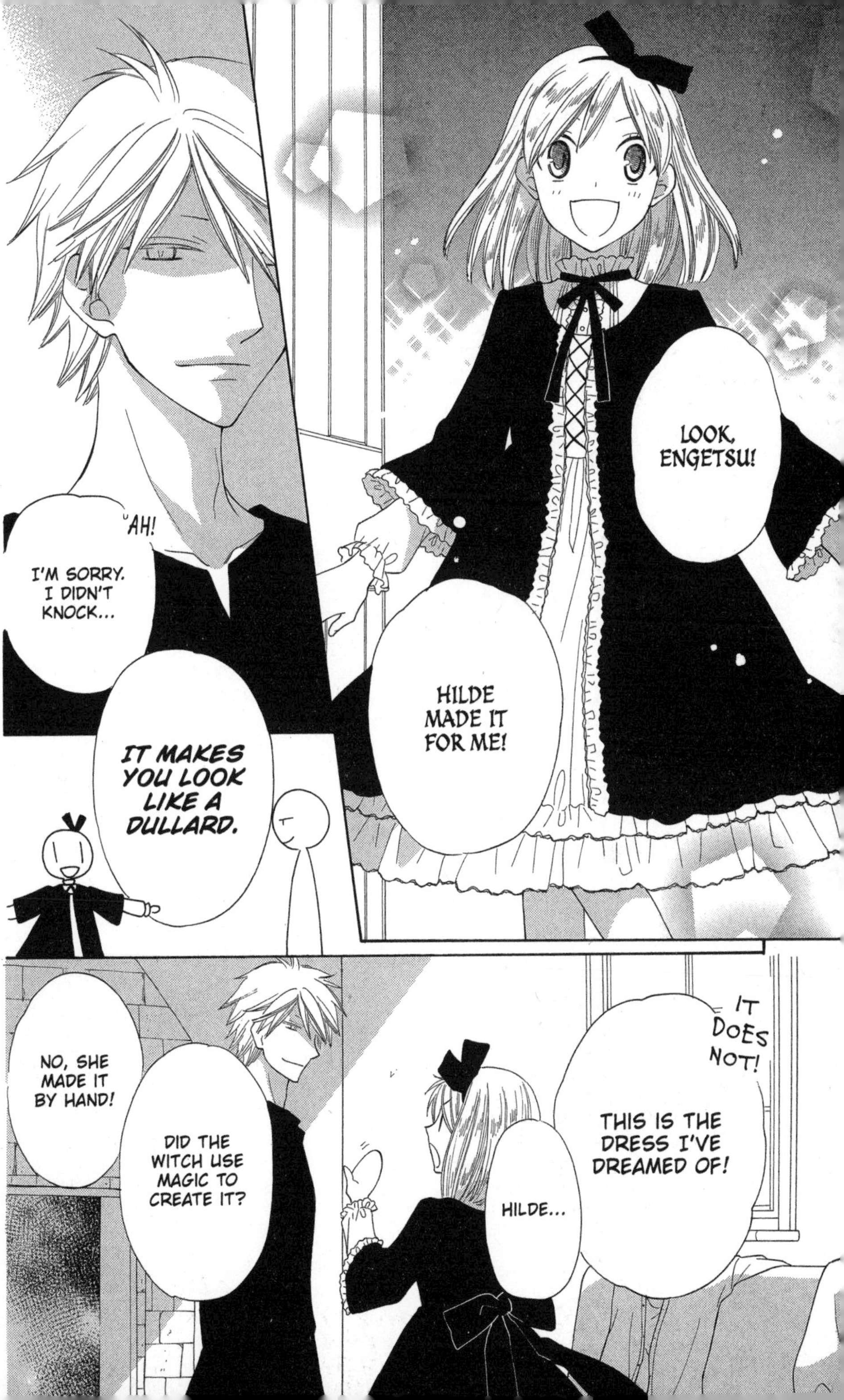
LOOK, ENGETSU!
HILDE MADE IT FOR ME!
AH!
I'M SORRY. I DIDN'T KNOCK...
IT MAKES YOU LOOK LIKE A DULLARD.
IT DOES NOT!
THIS IS THE DRESS I'VE DREAMED OF!
HILDE...
DID THE WITCH USE MAGIC TO CREATE IT?
NO, SHE MADE IT BY HAND!

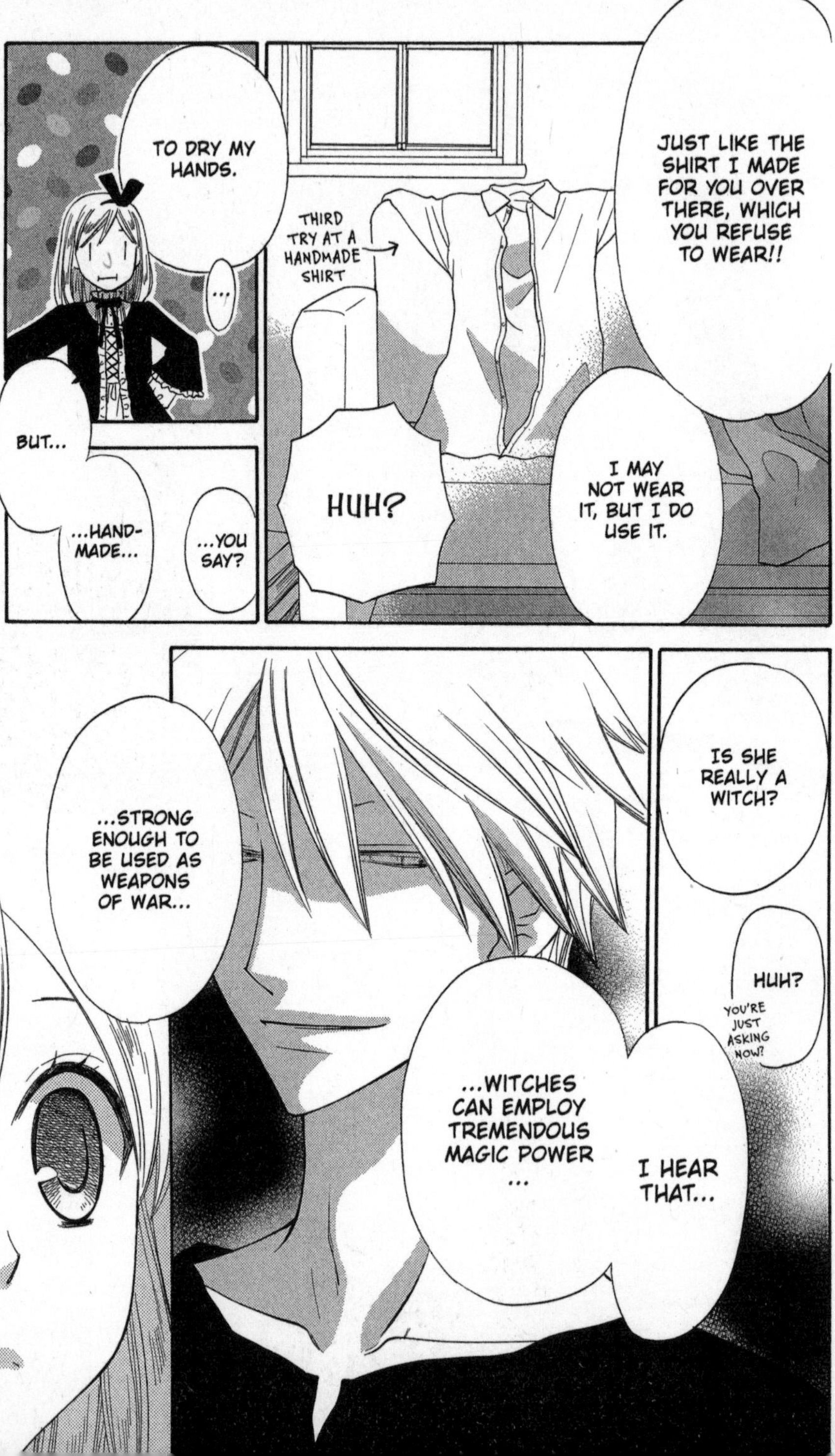
JUST LIKE THE SHIRT I MADE FOR YOU OVER THERE, WHICH YOU REFUSE TO WEAR!!
THIRD TRY AT A HANDMADE SHIRT
I MAY NOT WEAR IT, BUT I DO USE IT.
HUH?
TO DRY MY HANDS.
...
BUT...
...HAND-MADE...
...YOU SAY?
IS SHE REALLY A WITCH?
HUH?
YOU'RE JUST ASKING NOW?
I HEAR THAT...
...WITCHES CAN EMPLOY TREMENDOUS MAGIC POWER ...
...STRONG ENOUGH TO BE USED AS WEAPONS OF WAR...

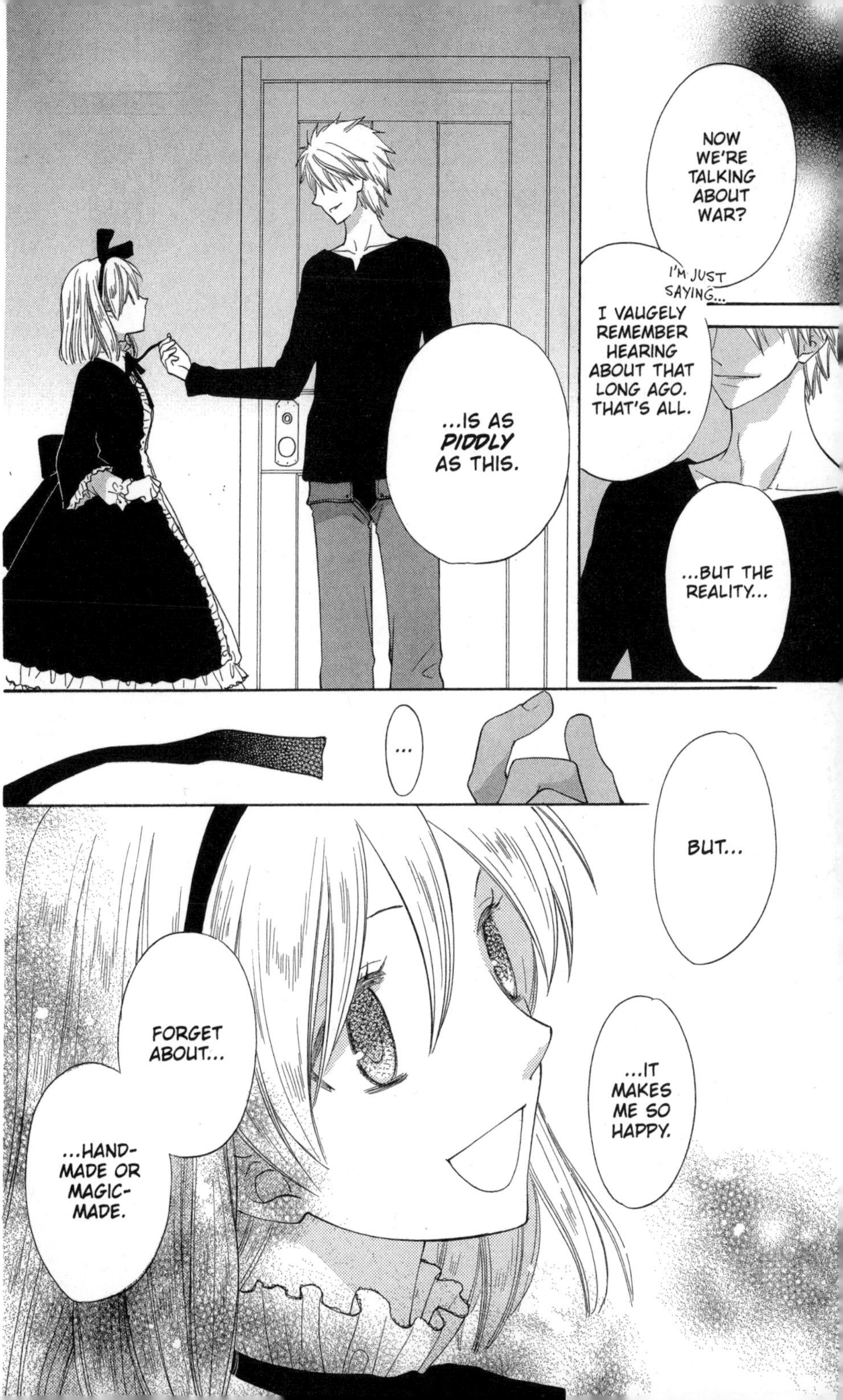
NOW WE'RE TALKING ABOUT WAR?
I'M JUST SAYING...
I VAUGELY REMEMBER HEARING ABOUT THAT LONG AGO. THAT'S ALL.
...BUT THE REALITY...
...IS AS PIDDLY AS THIS.
...
BUT...
...IT MAKES ME SO HAPPY.
FORGET ABOUT...
...HAND-MADE OR MAGIC-MADE.

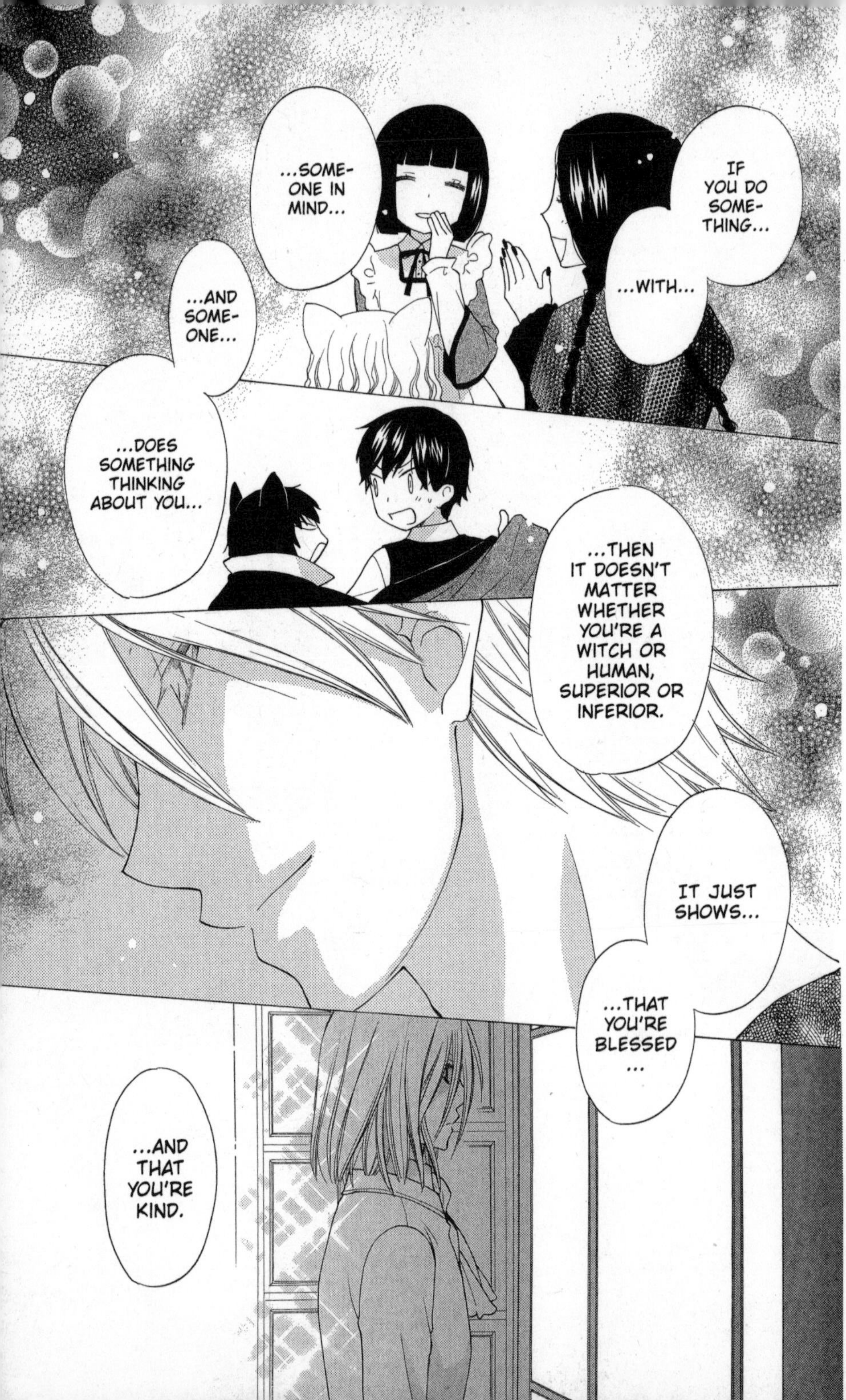
IF YOU DO SOME-THING...
...WITH...
...SOME-ONE IN MIND...
...AND SOME-ONE...
...DOES SOMETHING THINKING ABOUT YOU...
...THEN IT DOESN'T MATTER WHETHER YOU'RE A WITCH OR HUMAN, SUPERIOR OR INFERIOR.
IT JUST SHOWS...
...THAT YOU'RE BLESSED ...
...AND THAT YOU'RE KIND.

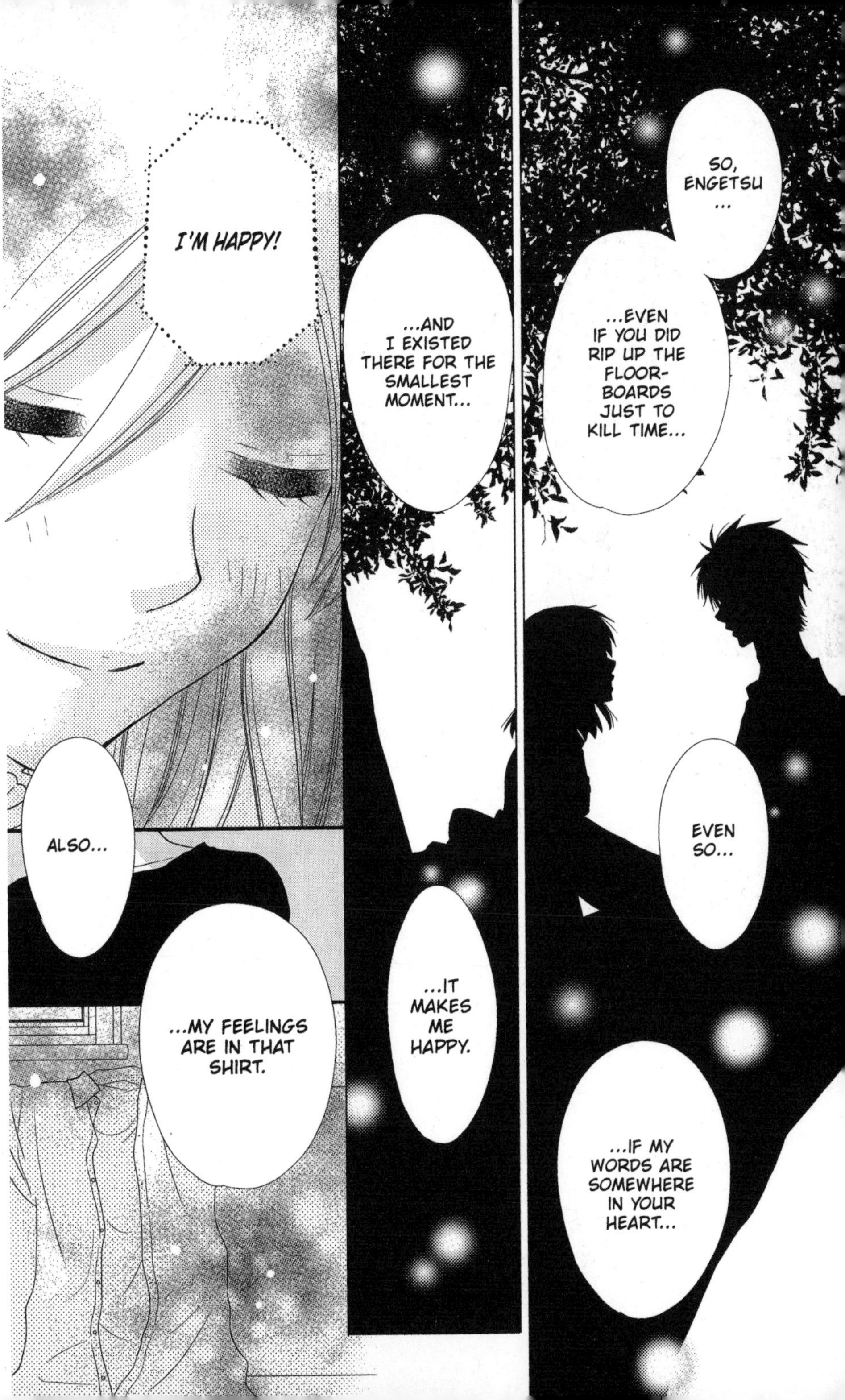
SO, ENGETSU...
...EVEN IF YOU DID RIP UP THE FLOOR-BOARDS JUST TO KILL TIME...
EVEN SO...
...IF MY WORDS ARE SOMEWHERE IN YOUR HEART...
...AND I EXISTED THERE FOR THE SMALLEST MOMENT...
...IT MAKES ME HAPPY.
I'M HAPPY!
ALSO...
...MY FEELINGS ARE IN THAT SHIRT.

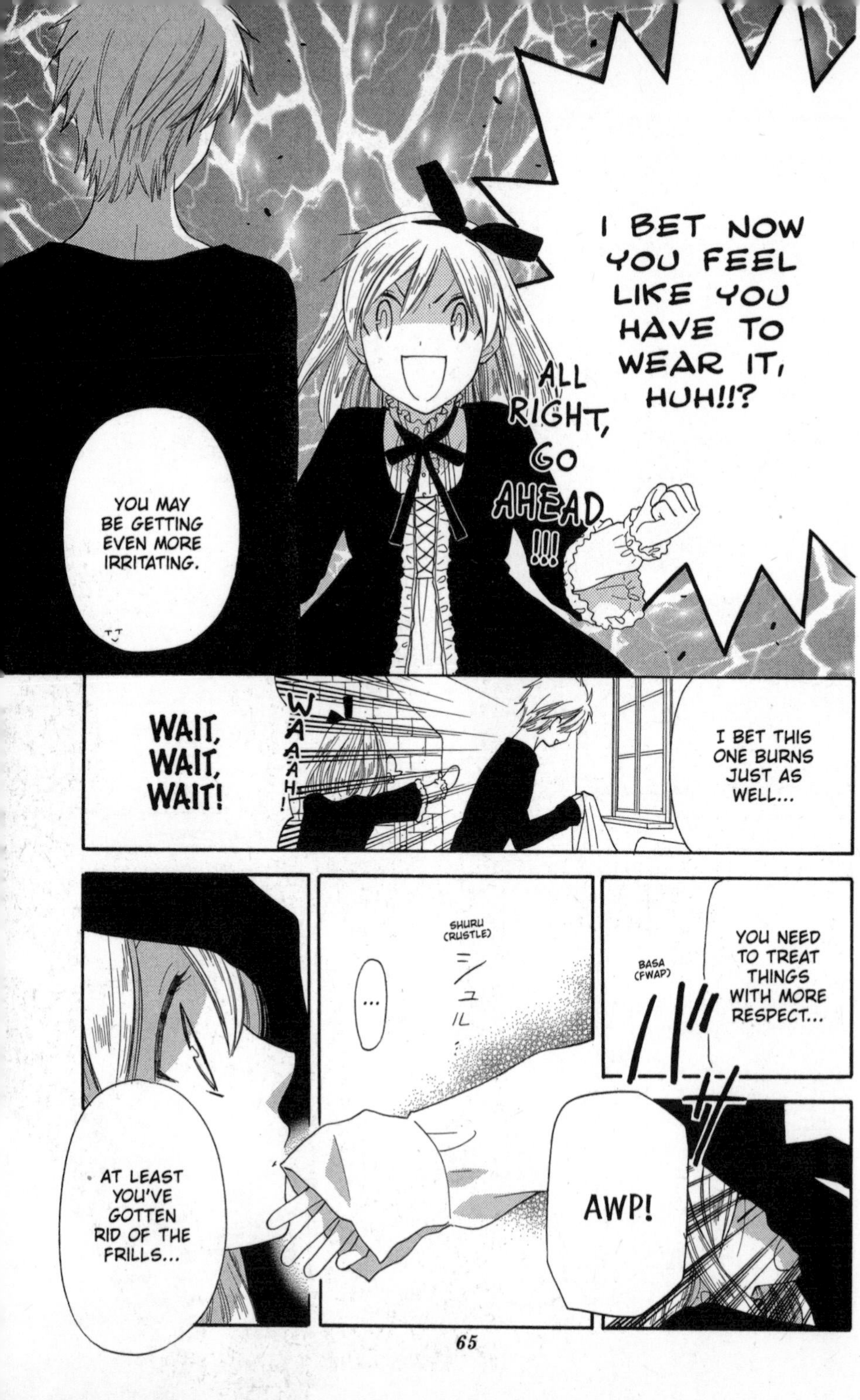
I BET NOW YOU FEEL LIKE YOU HAVE TO WEAR IT, HUH!!?
ALL RIGHT, GO AHEAD!!!
YOU MAY BE GETTING EVEN MORE IRRITATING.
I BET THIS ONE BURNS JUST AS WELL...
WAAAAH!
WAIT, WAIT, WAIT!
YOU NEED TO TREAT THINGS WITH MORE RESPECT...
BASA (FWAP)
AWP!
SHURU (RUSTLE)
シュル
...
AT LEAST YOU'VE GOTTEN RID OF THE FRILLS...

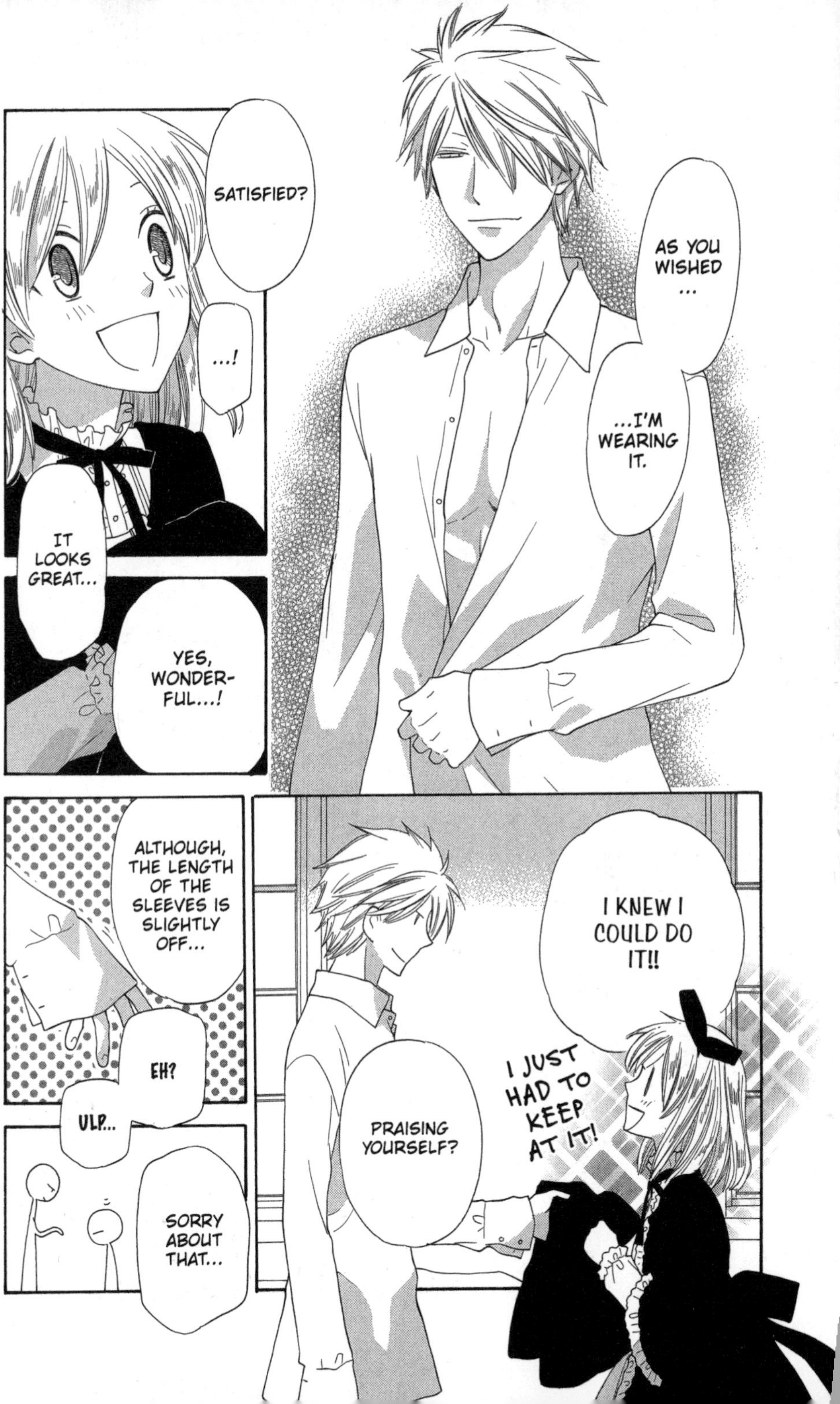
AS YOU WISHED ...
...I'M WEARING IT.
SATISFIED?
...!
IT LOOKS GREAT...
YES, WONDER-FUL...!
I KNEW I COULD DO IT!!
I JUST HAD TO KEEP AT IT!
PRAISING YOURSELF?
ALTHOUGH, THE LENGTH OF THE SLEEVES IS SLIGHTLY OFF...
EH?
ULP...
SORRY ABOUT THAT...

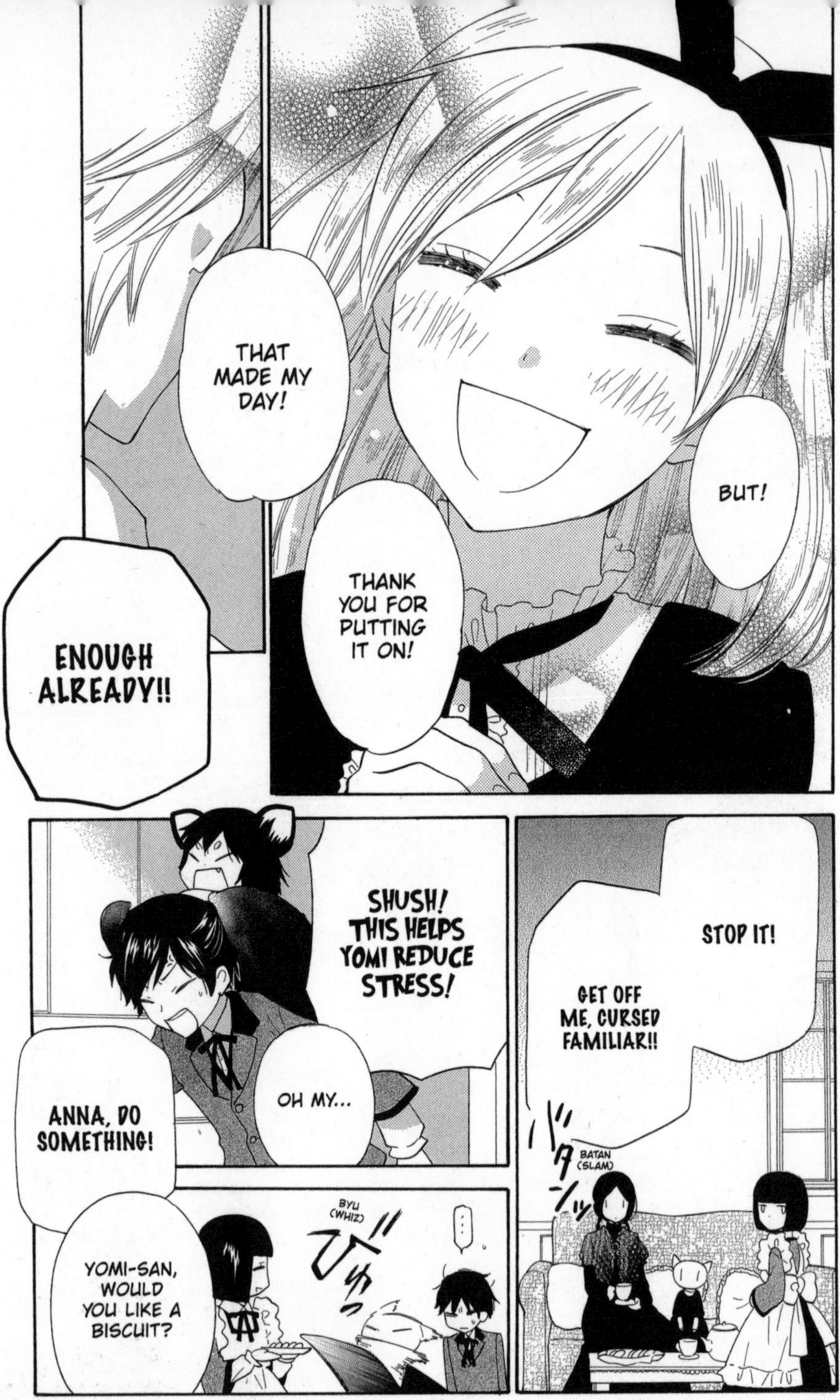
BUT!
THANK YOU FOR PUTTING IT ON!
THAT MADE MY DAY!
ENOUGH ALREADY!!
STOP IT!
GET OFF ME, CURSED FAMILIAR!!
BATAN (SLAM)
SHUSH! THIS HELPS YOMI REDUCE STRESS!
OH MY...
ANNA, DO SOMETHING!
BYU (WHIZ)
...
YOMI-SAN, WOULD YOU LIKE A BISCUIT?

...AH.
WHERE IS LISELOTTE-SAMA?
IN ENGETSU-SAN'S ROOM.
HUH?
DOKI (THUMP)
DOKI DOKI
THEN... THEY'RE ALONE?
YOU'RE SULKING AGAIN, YOU WORRYWART.
WHA ...!?
I AM NOT! IT'S NOT THAT...
...
IT FEELS LIKE ENGETSU...
...HAS BEEN MUCH RUDER TO LISELOTTE-SAMA RECENTLY.
OH, ALTO...
HE'S NOT, ACTUALLY. IT'S OKAY.
IT'S JUST...
......

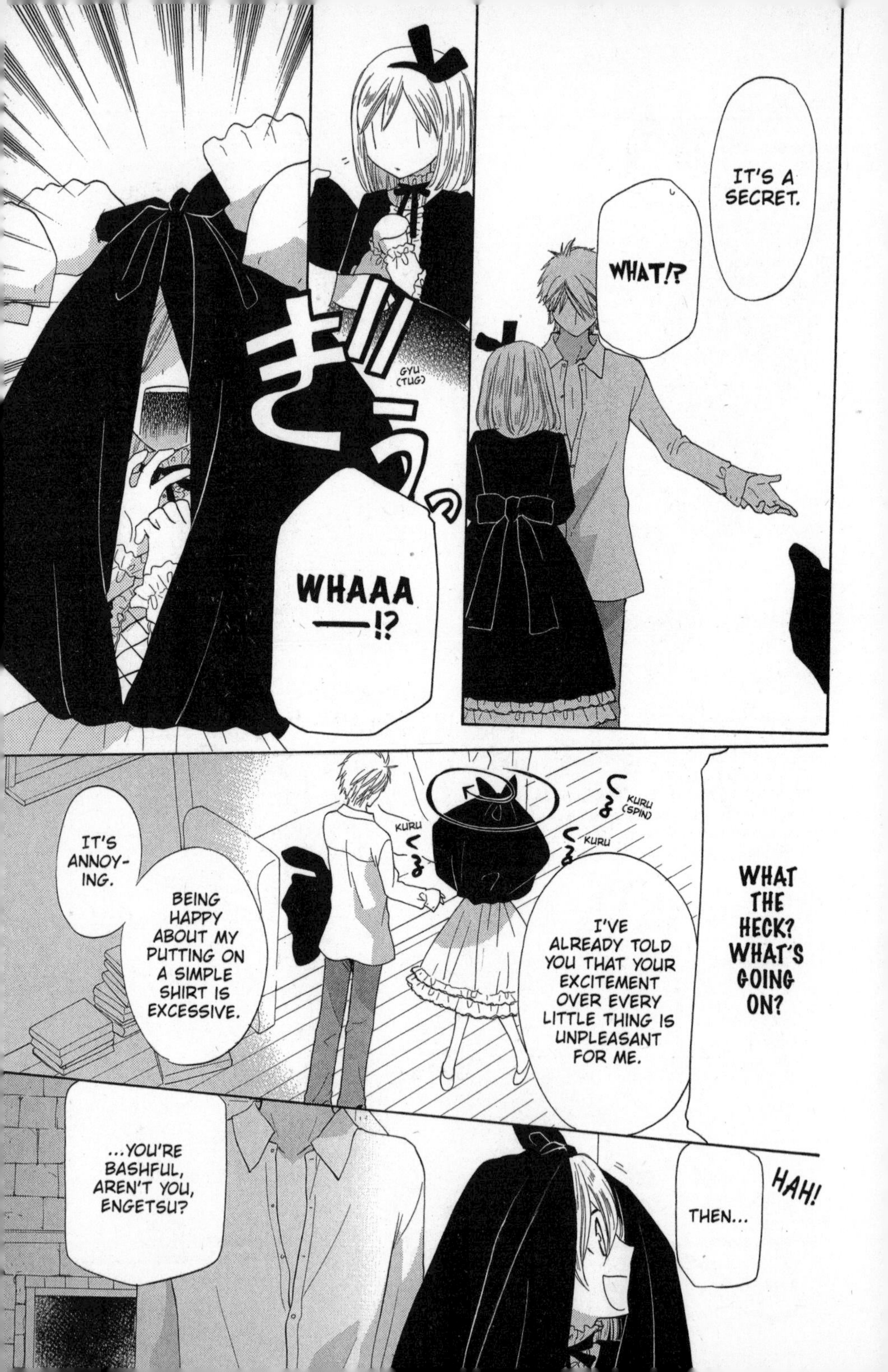

IT'S A SECRET.
WHAT!?
WHAAA—!?
GYU (TUG)
WHAT THE HECK? WHAT'S GOING ON?
KURU (SPIN)
KURU
KURU
I'VE ALREADY TOLD YOU THAT YOUR EXCITEMENT OVER EVERY LITTLE THING IS UNPLEASANT FOR ME.
IT'S ANNOY-ING.
BEING HAPPY ABOUT MY PUTTING ON A SIMPLE SHIRT IS EXCESSIVE.
HAH!
THEN...
...YOU'RE BASHFUL, AREN'T YOU, ENGETSU?

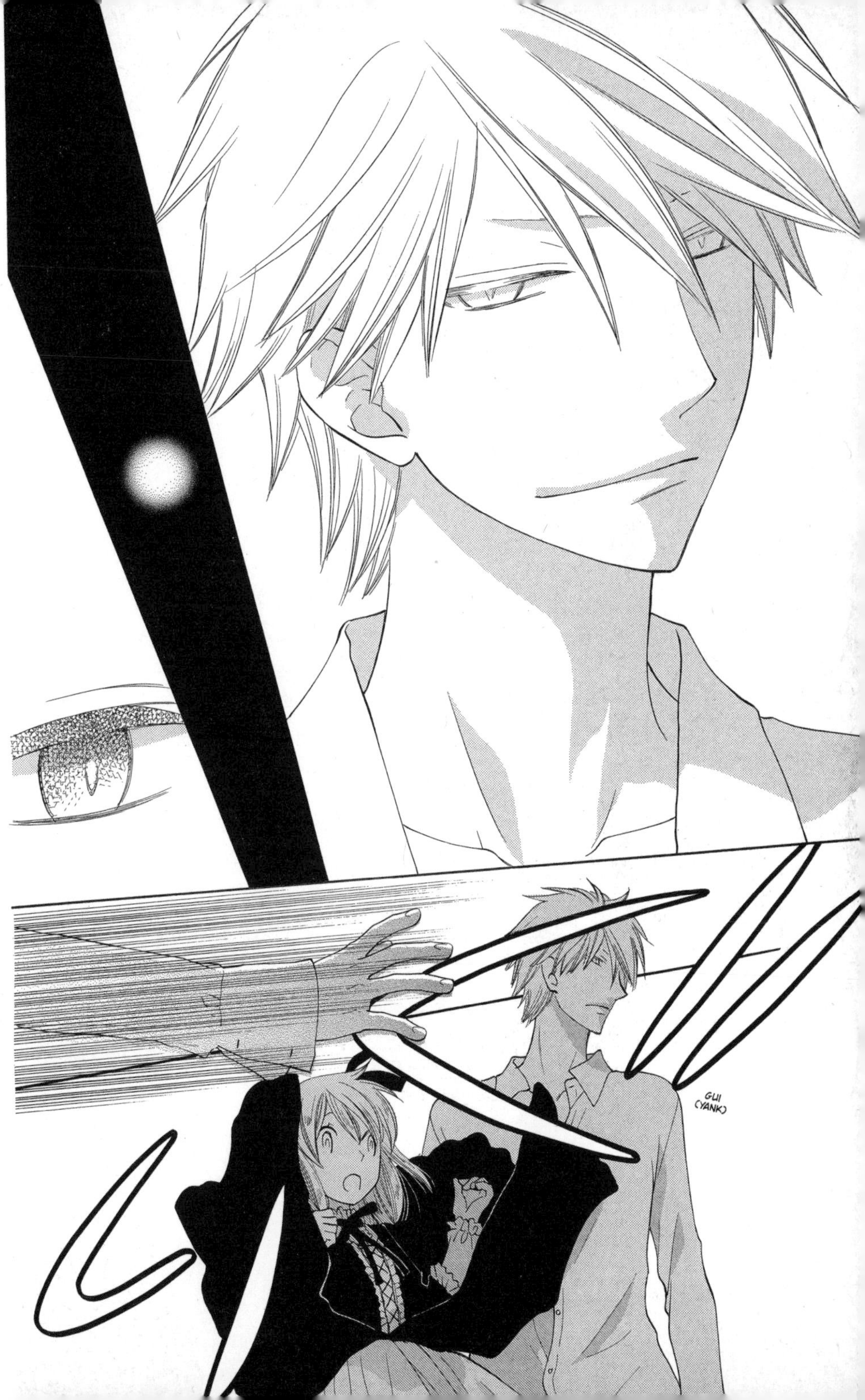
GUI
(YANK)

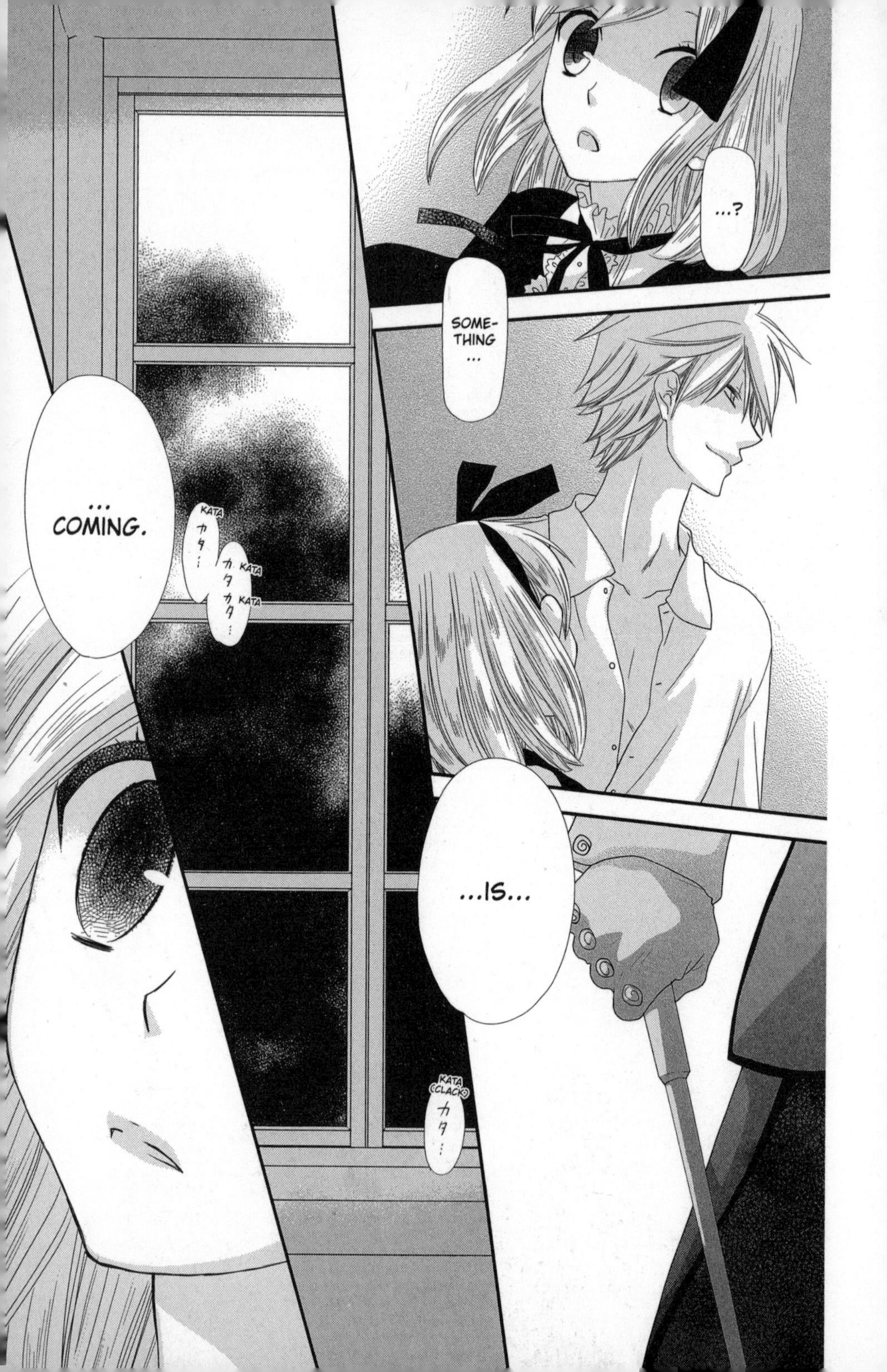
...?
SOME-THING...
...IS...
KATA (CLACK) カタ…
...COMING.
KATA カタ…
KATA KATA カタカタ…

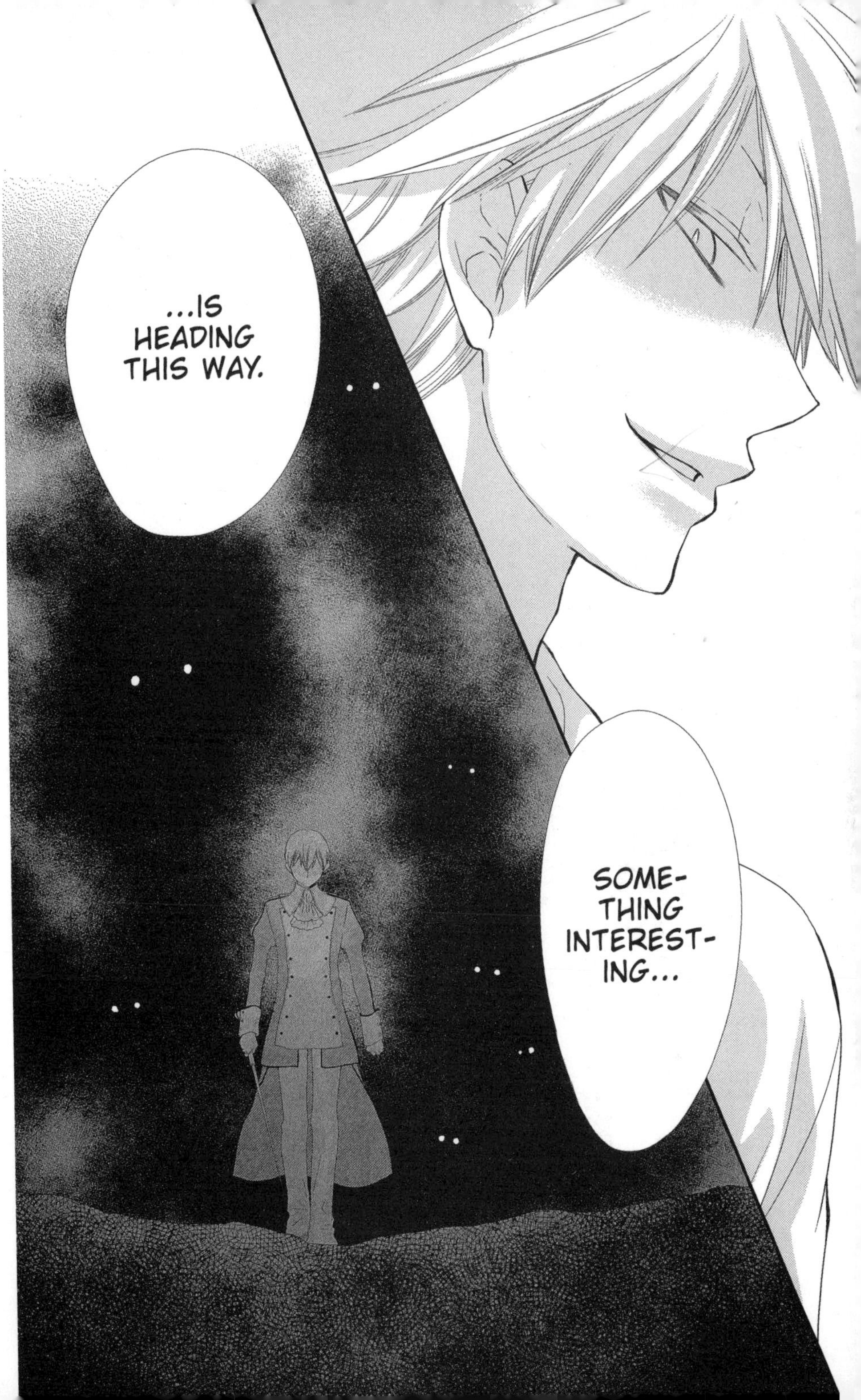
SOME-THING INTEREST-ING...
...IS HEADING THIS WAY.

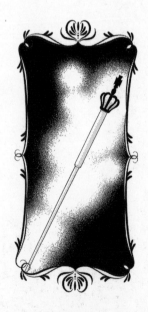

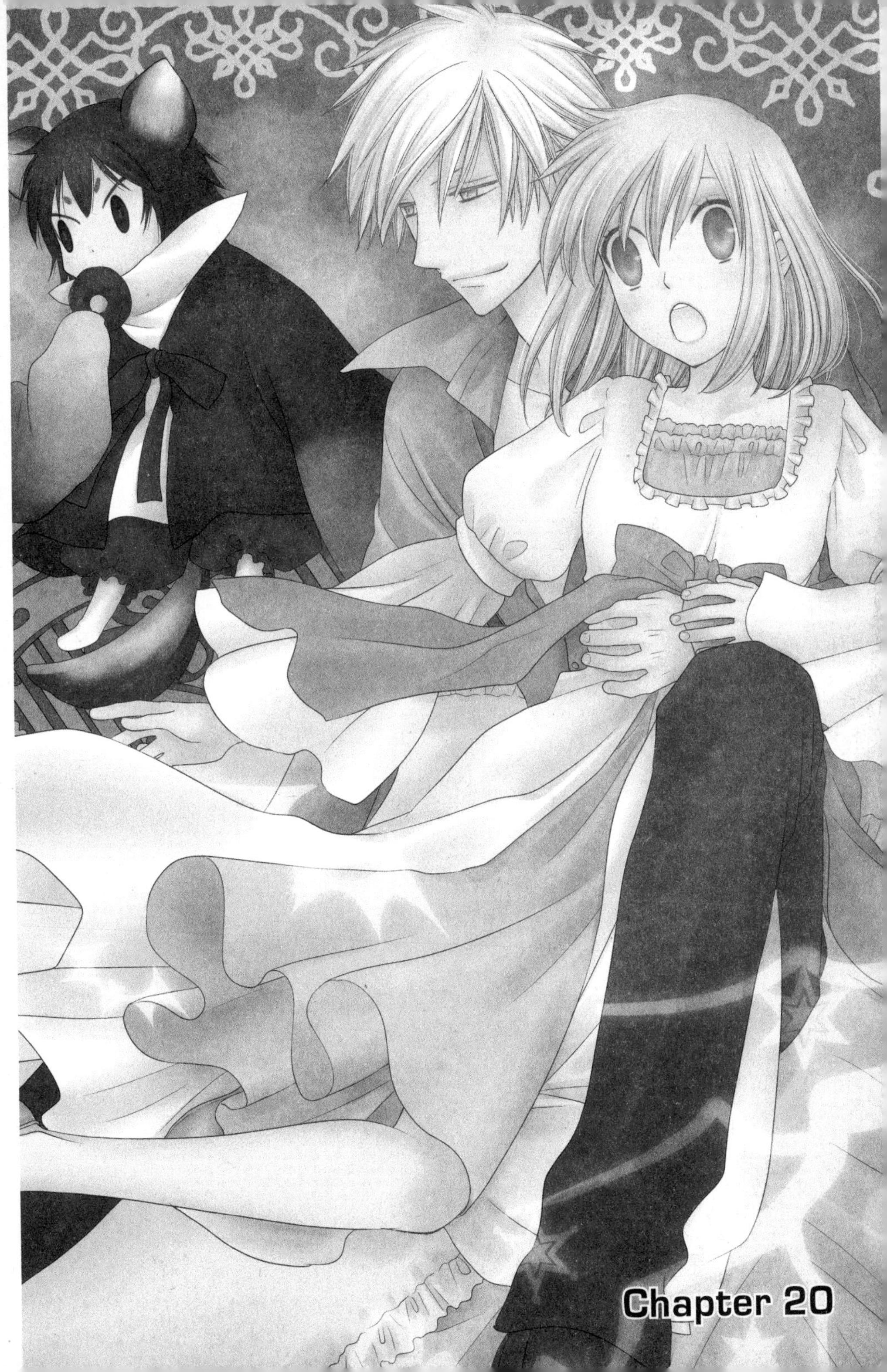
Chapter 20

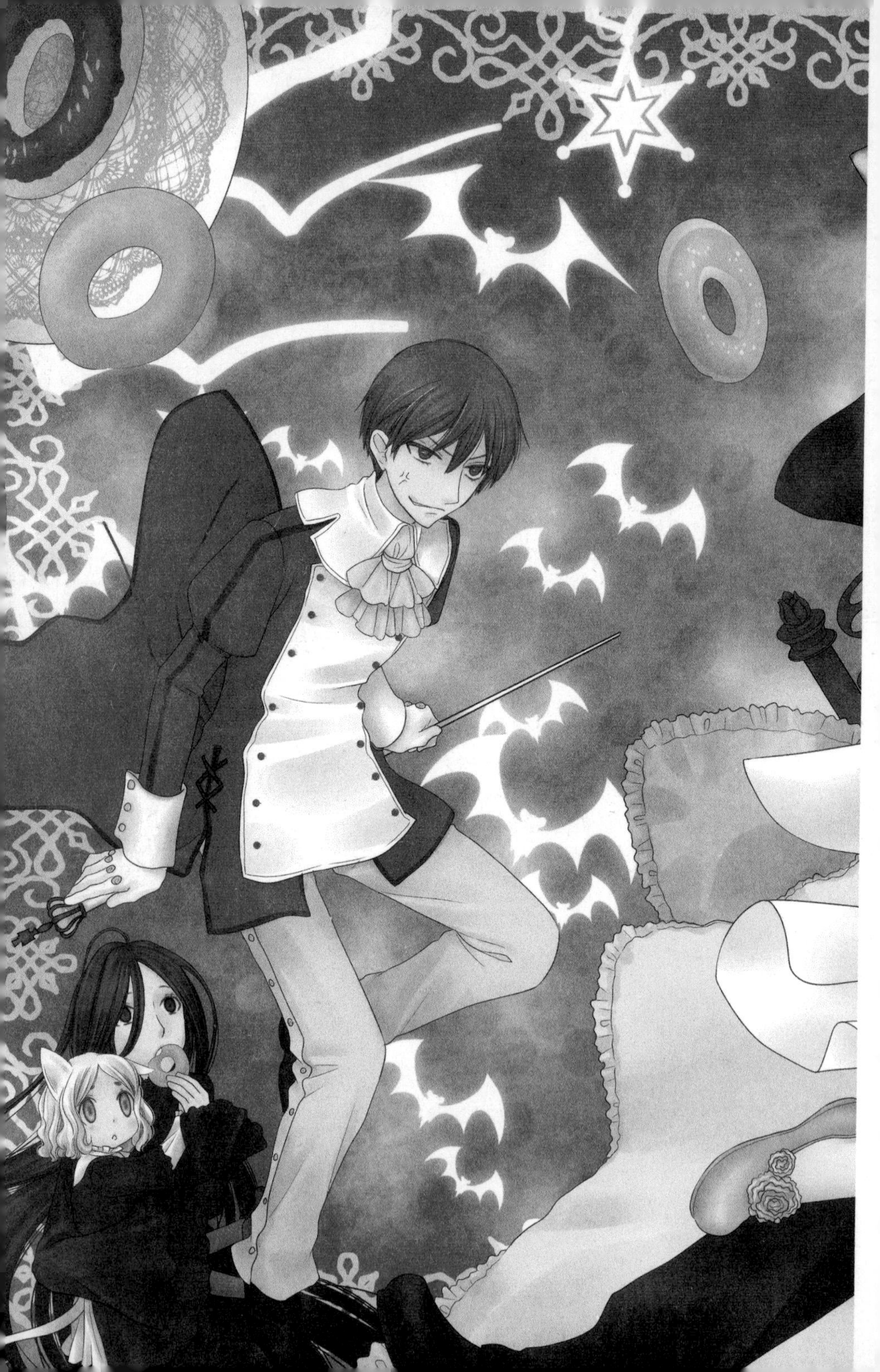

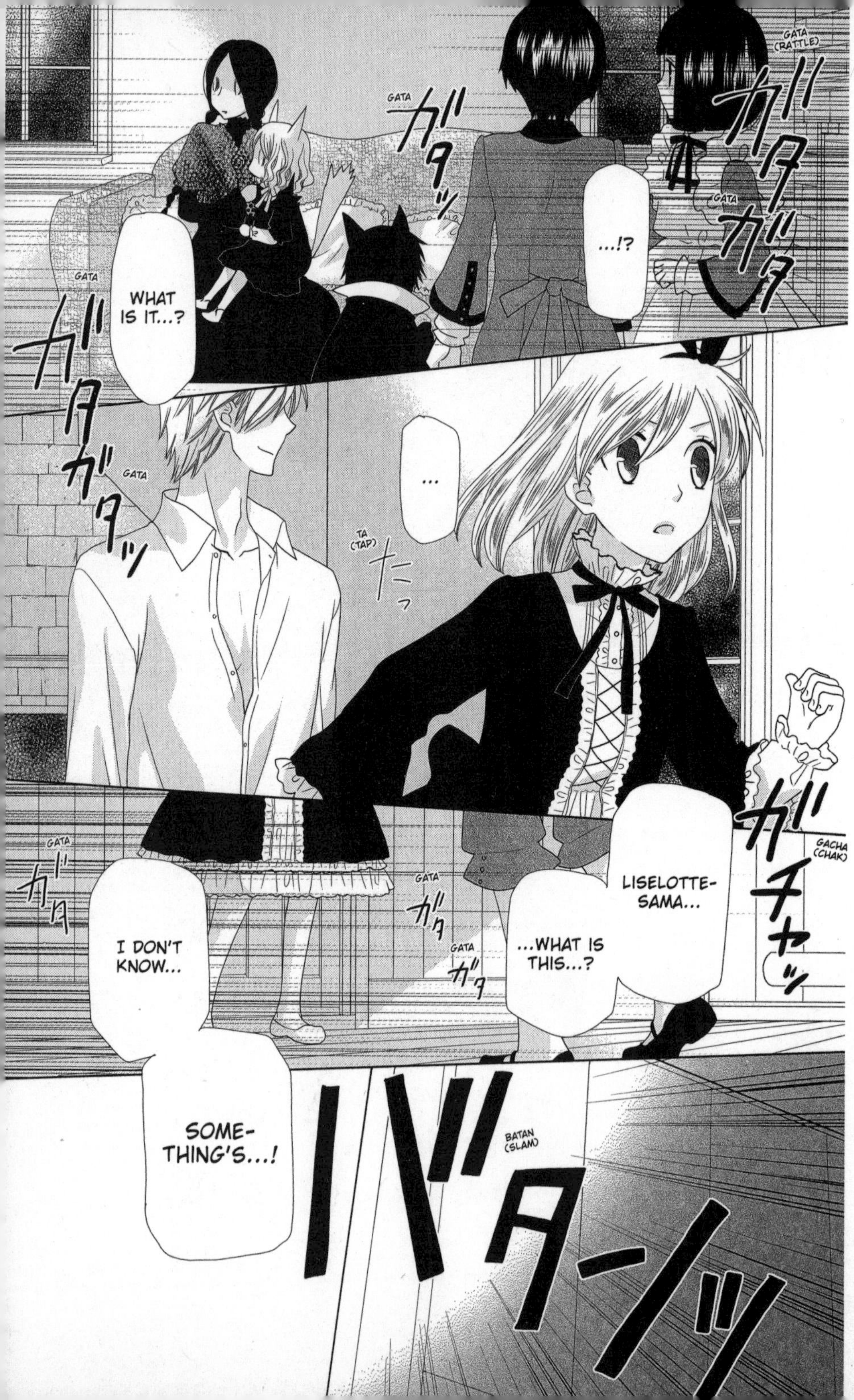
GATA (RATTLE)
GATA
...!?
GATA
WHAT IS IT...?
GATA
GATA
...
TA (TAP)
GACHA (CHAK)
LISELOTTE-SAMA...
...WHAT IS THIS...?
GATA
GATA
I DON'T KNOW...
GATA
SOME-THING'S...!
BATAN (SLAM)

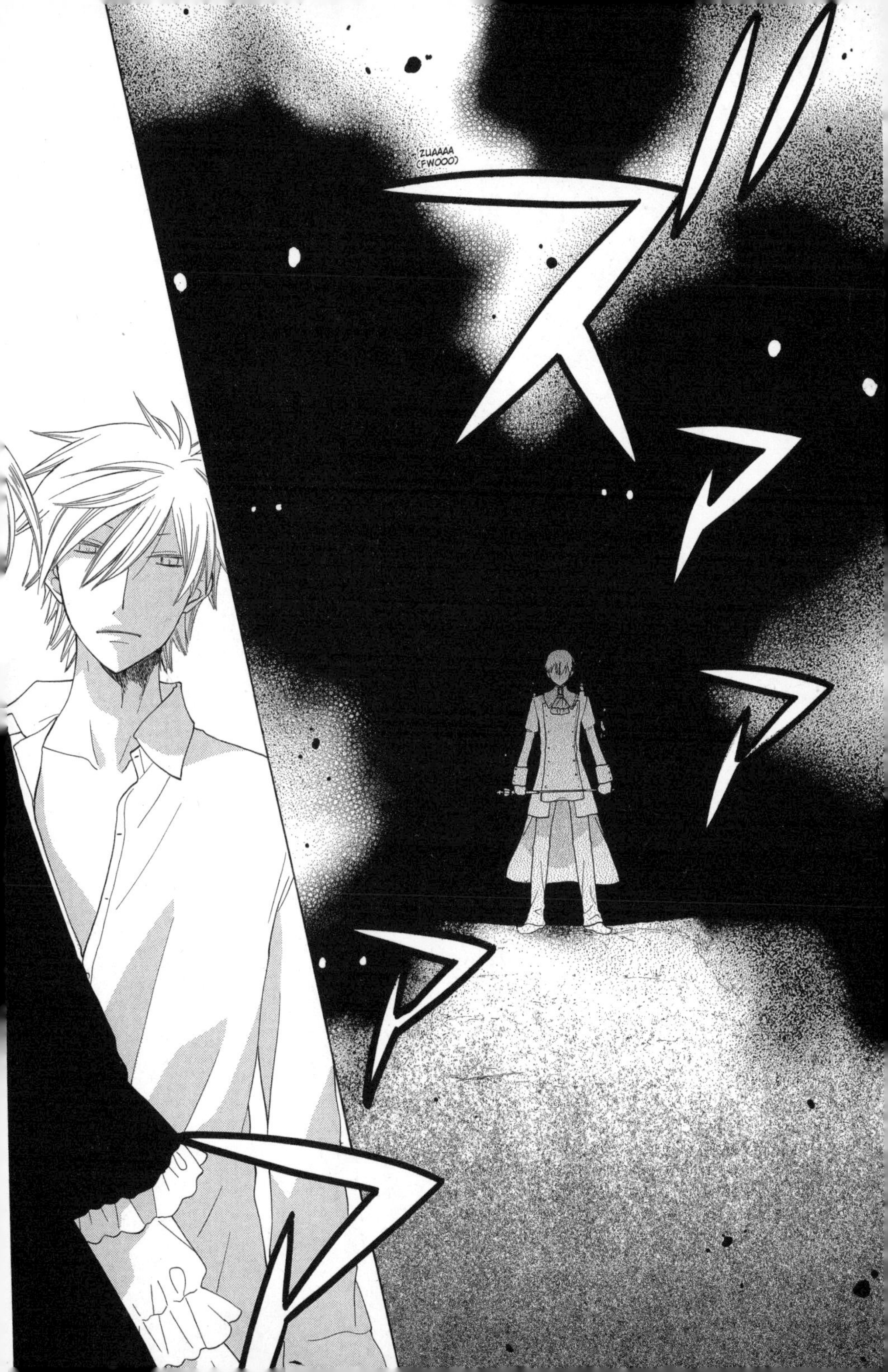
ZUAAAA
(FWOOO)

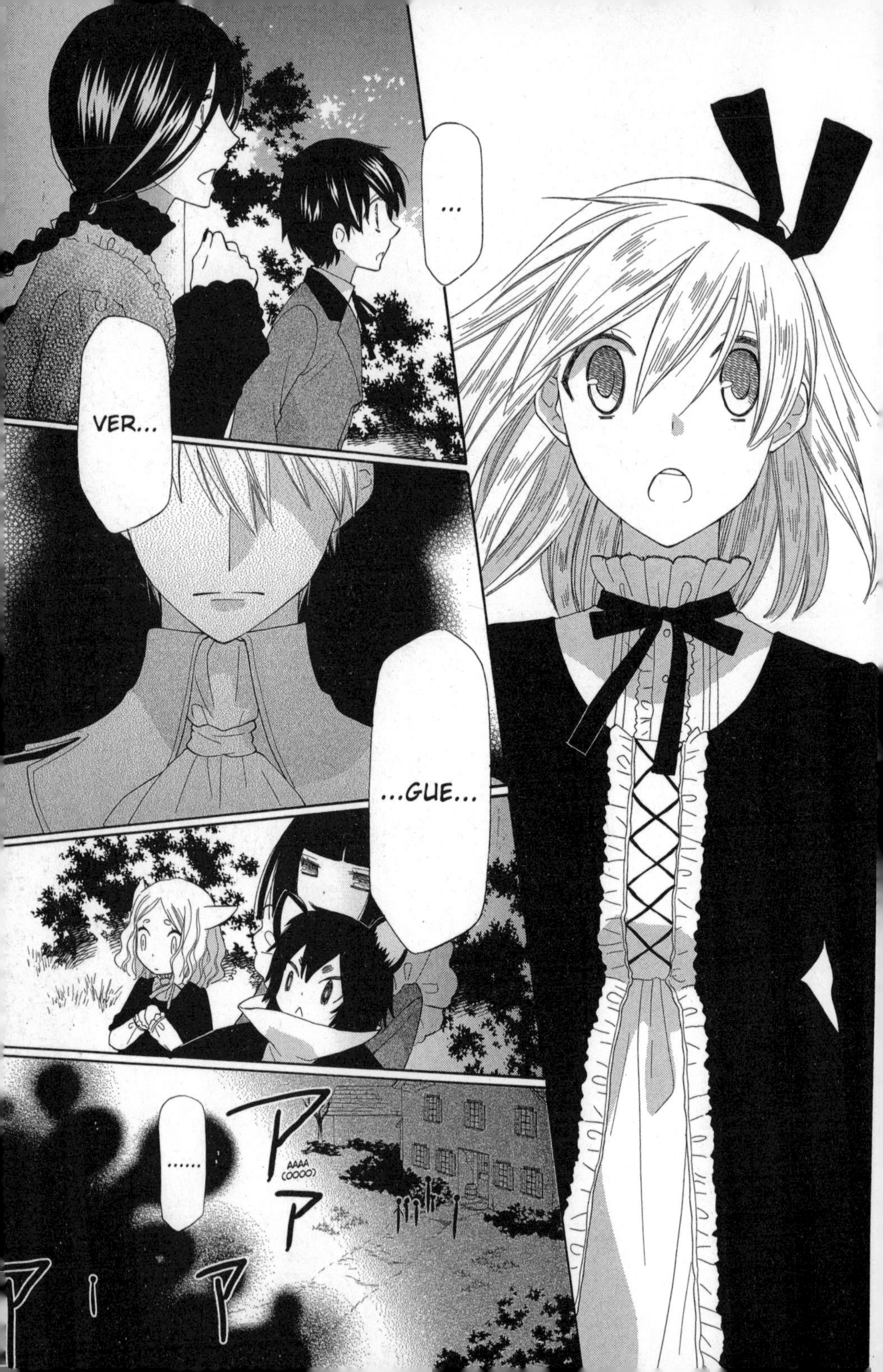
...
VER...
...GUE...
......
AAAA (OOOO)

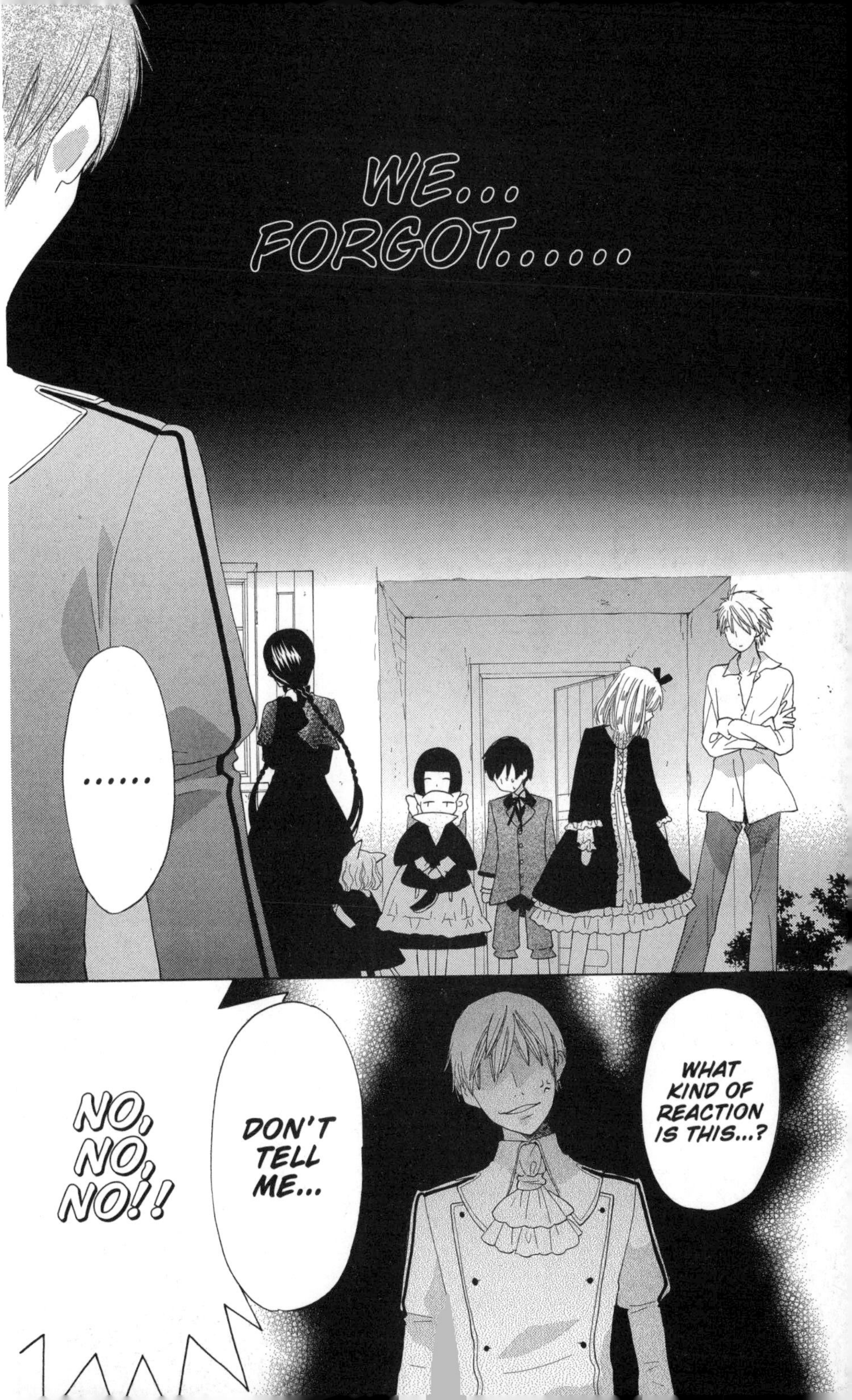
WE... FORGOT......
......
WHAT KIND OF REACTION IS THIS...?
DON'T TELL ME...
NO, NO, NO!!

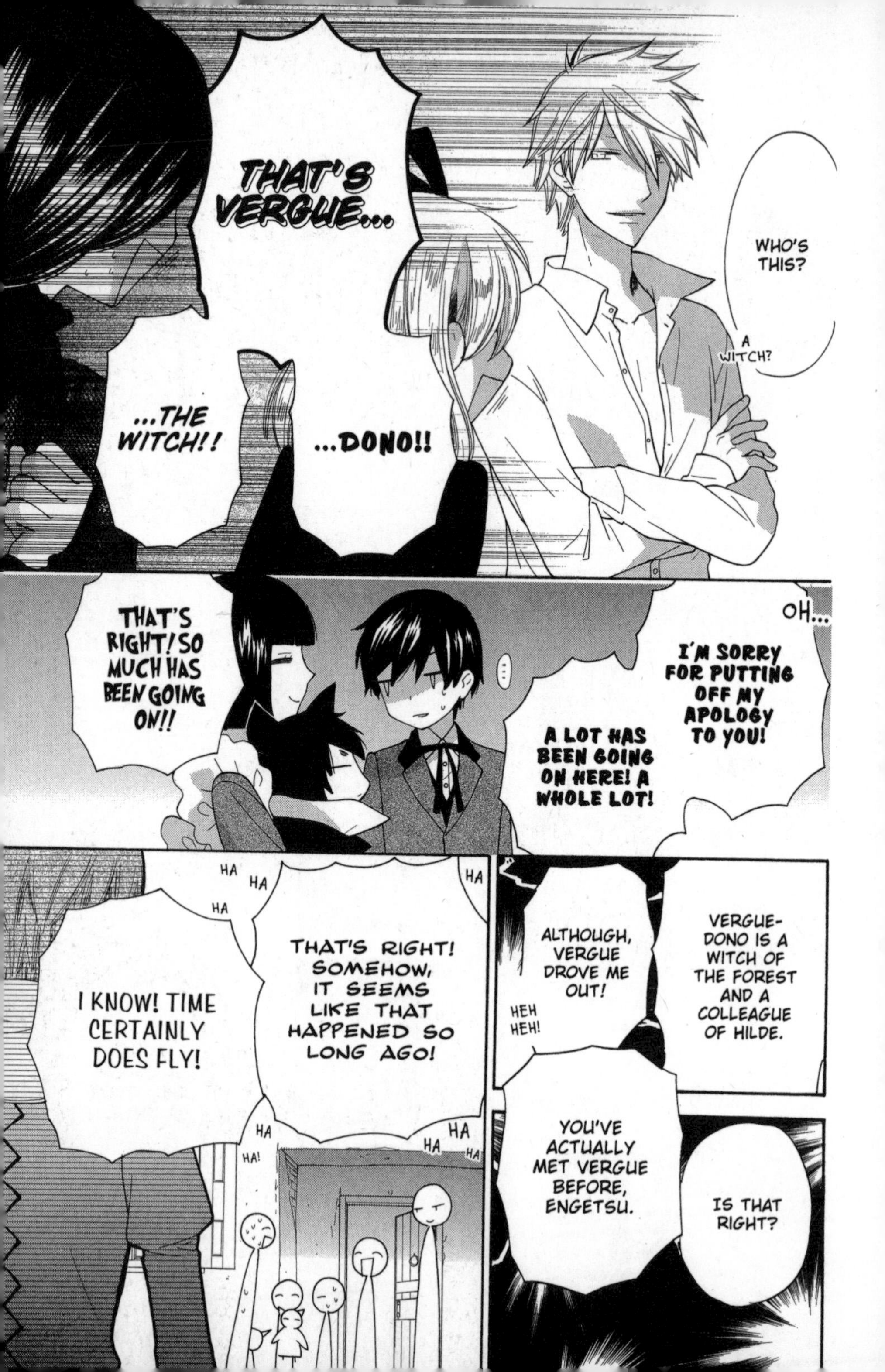
WHO'S THIS?
A WITCH?
THAT'S VERGUE...
...DONO!!
...THE WITCH!!
OH...
I'M SORRY FOR PUTTING OFF MY APOLOGY TO YOU!
A LOT HAS BEEN GOING ON HERE! A WHOLE LOT!
...
THAT'S RIGHT! SO MUCH HAS BEEN GOING ON!!
VERGUE-DONO IS A WITCH OF THE FOREST AND A COLLEAGUE OF HILDE.
ALTHOUGH, VERGUE DROVE ME OUT!
HEH HEH!
YOU'VE ACTUALLY MET VERGUE BEFORE, ENGETSU.
IS THAT RIGHT?
HA
HA
HA
HA
THAT'S RIGHT! SOMEHOW, IT SEEMS LIKE THAT HAPPENED SO LONG AGO!
I KNOW! TIME CERTAINLY DOES FLY!
HA
HA
HA
HA!
HA

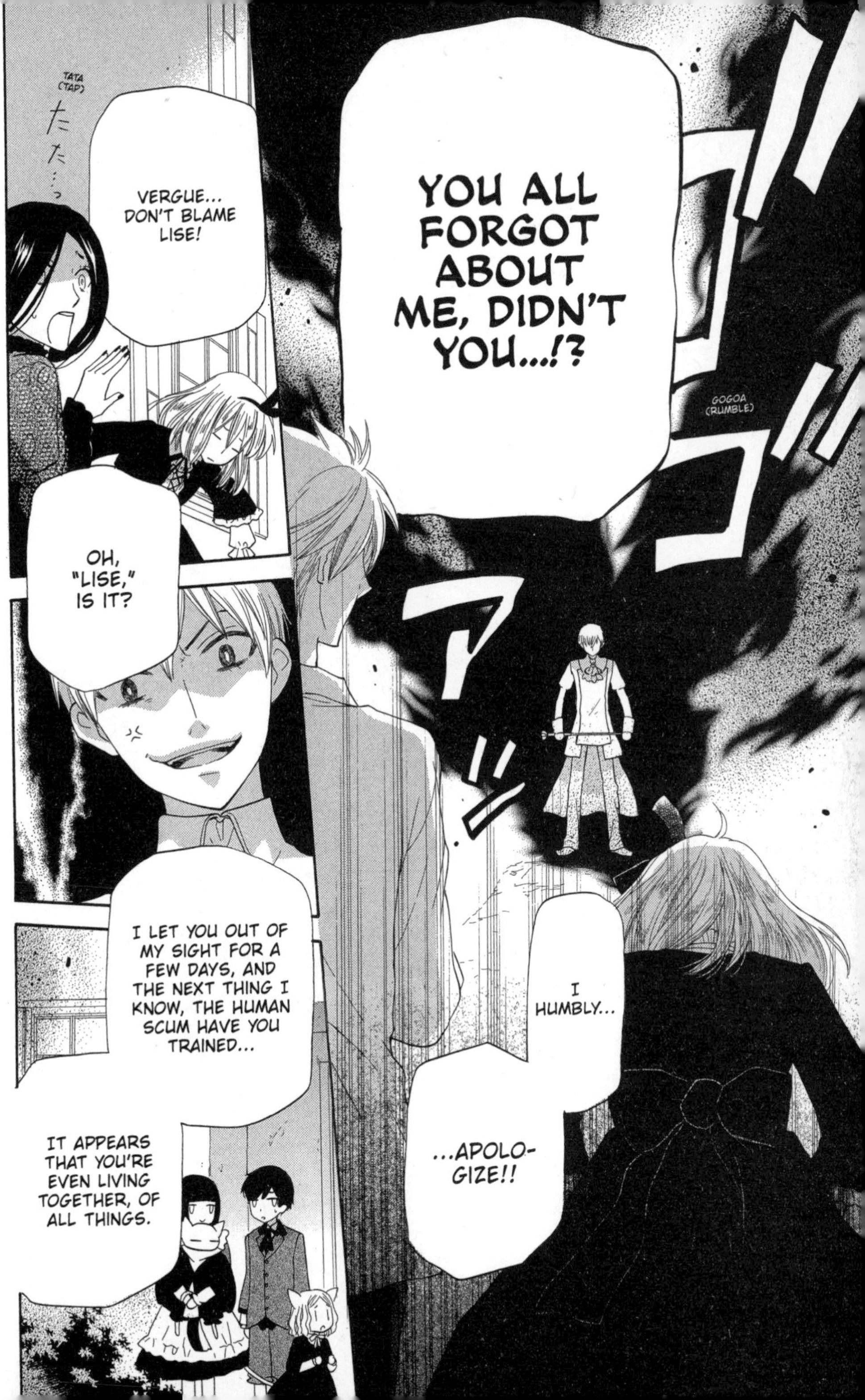
YOU ALL FORGOT ABOUT ME, DIDN'T YOU...!?
GOGOA (RUMBLE)
I HUMBLY...
...APOLO-GIZE!!
TATA (TAP)
VERGUE... DON'T BLAME LISE!
OH, "LISE," IS IT?
I LET YOU OUT OF MY SIGHT FOR A FEW DAYS, AND THE NEXT THING I KNOW, THE HUMAN SCUM HAVE YOU TRAINED...
IT APPEARS THAT YOU'RE EVEN LIVING TOGETHER, OF ALL THINGS.

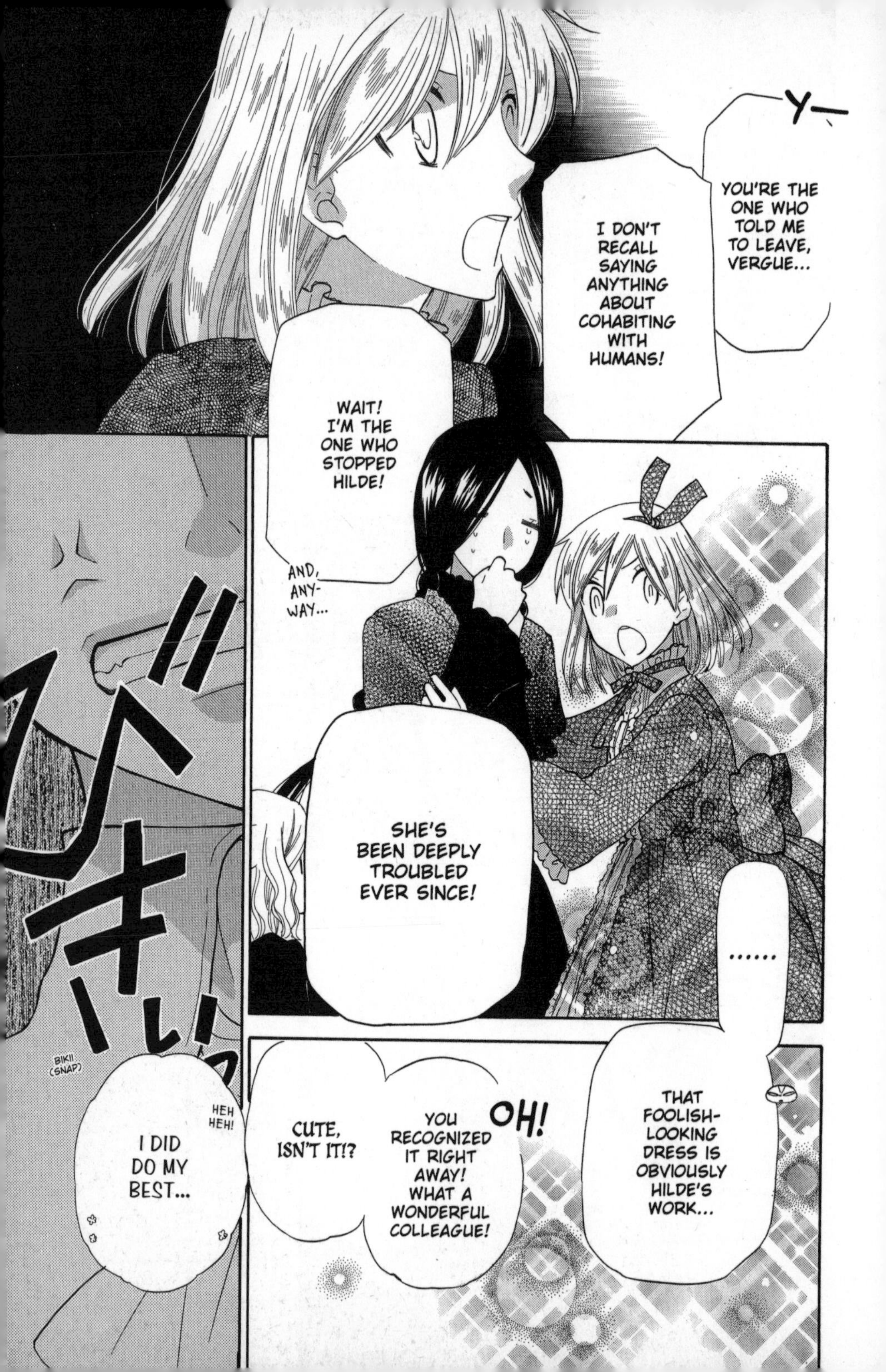
Y—
YOU'RE THE ONE WHO TOLD ME TO LEAVE, VERGUE...
I DON'T RECALL SAYING ANYTHING ABOUT COHABITING WITH HUMANS!
WAIT! I'M THE ONE WHO STOPPED HILDE!
AND, ANY-WAY...
SHE'S BEEN DEEPLY TROUBLED EVER SINCE!
......
THAT FOOLISH-LOOKING DRESS IS OBVIOUSLY HILDE'S WORK...
OH!
YOU RECOGNIZED IT RIGHT AWAY! WHAT A WONDERFUL COLLEAGUE!
CUTE, ISN'T IT!?
I DID DO MY BEST...
HEH HEH!
BIKII (SNAP)

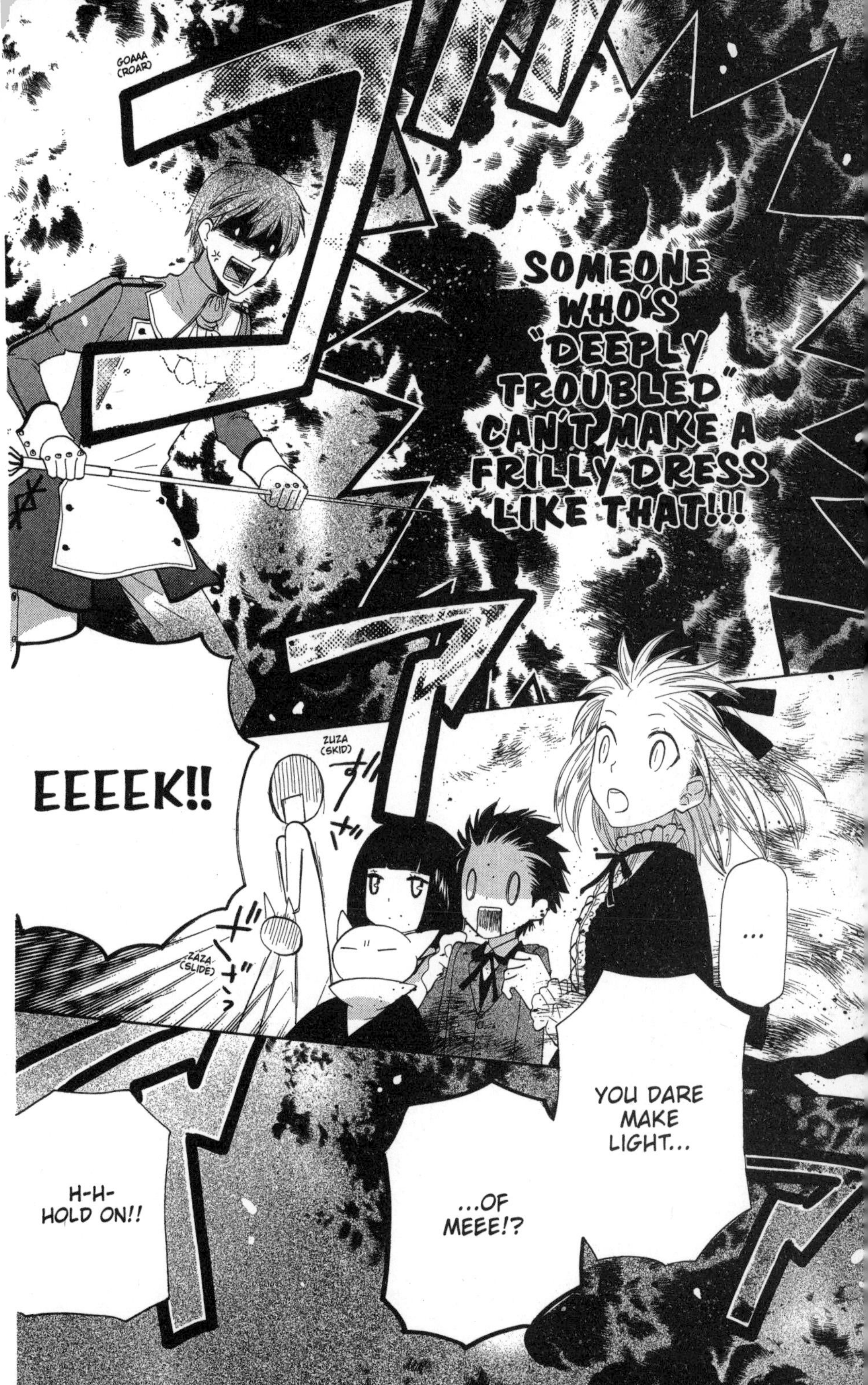
SOMEONE WHO'S "DEEPLY TROUBLED" CAN'T MAKE A FRILLY DRESS LIKE THAT!!!
GOAAA (ROAR)
...
ZUZA (SKID)
EEEEK!!
ZAZA (SLIDE)
YOU DARE MAKE LIGHT...
...OF MEEE!?
H-H-HOLD ON!!

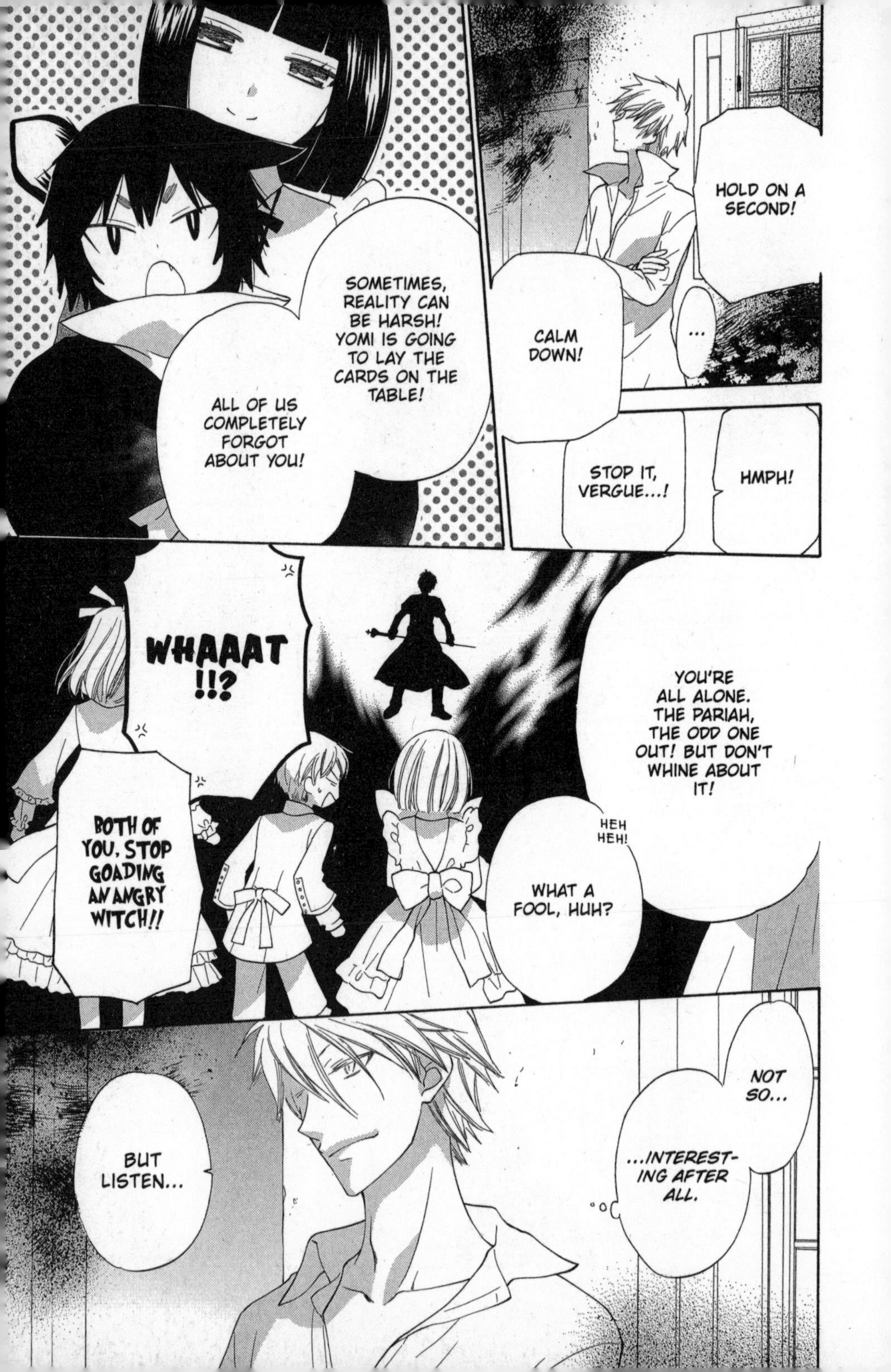
HOLD ON A SECOND!
...
CALM DOWN!
HMPH!
STOP IT, VERGUE...!
SOMETIMES, REALITY CAN BE HARSH! YOMI IS GOING TO LAY THE CARDS ON THE TABLE!
ALL OF US COMPLETELY FORGOT ABOUT YOU!
YOU'RE ALL ALONE. THE PARIAH, THE ODD ONE OUT! BUT DON'T WHINE ABOUT IT!
HEH HEH!
WHAT A FOOL, HUH?
WHAAAT!!?
BOTH OF YOU. STOP GOADING AN ANGRY WITCH!!
NOT SO...
...INTERESTING AFTER ALL.
BUT LISTEN...

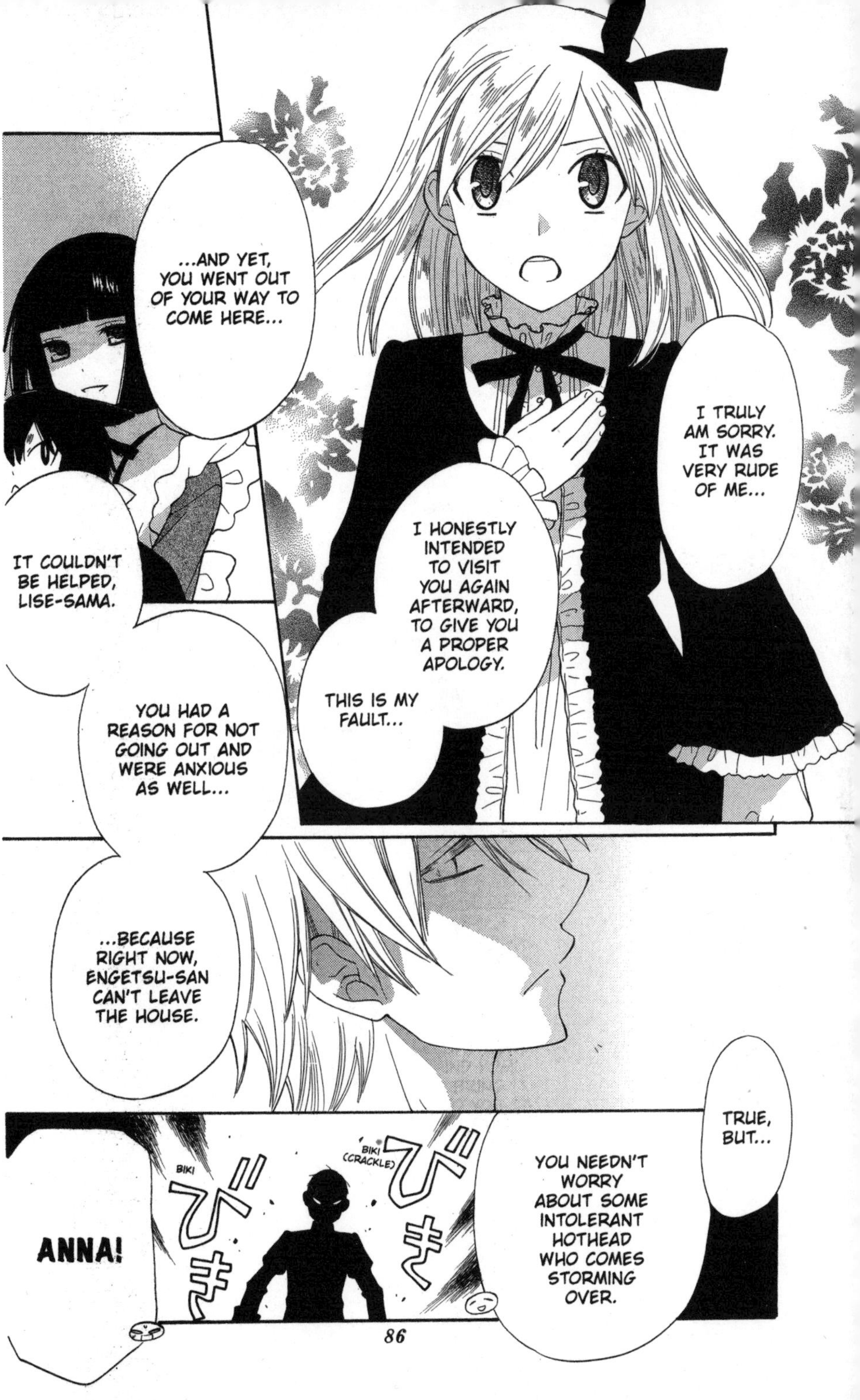
I TRULY AM SORRY. IT WAS VERY RUDE OF ME...
I HONESTLY INTENDED TO VISIT YOU AGAIN AFTERWARD, TO GIVE YOU A PROPER APOLOGY.
THIS IS MY FAULT...
...AND YET, YOU WENT OUT OF YOUR WAY TO COME HERE...
IT COULDN'T BE HELPED, LISE-SAMA.
YOU HAD A REASON FOR NOT GOING OUT AND WERE ANXIOUS AS WELL...
...BECAUSE RIGHT NOW, ENGETSU-SAN CAN'T LEAVE THE HOUSE.
TRUE, BUT...
YOU NEEDN'T WORRY ABOUT SOME INTOLERANT HOTHEAD WHO COMES STORMING OVER.
BIKI (CRACKLE)
BIKI
ANNA!

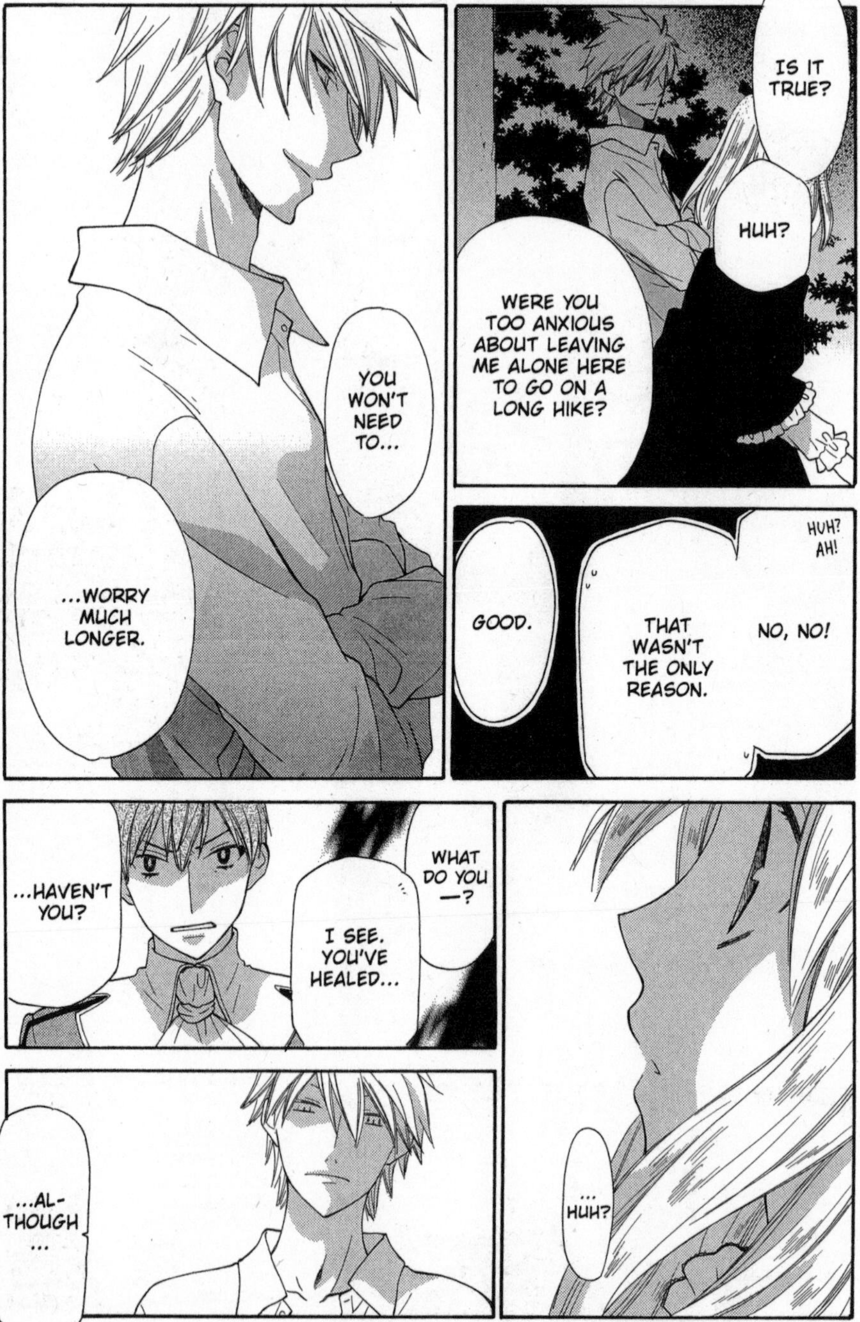
IS IT TRUE?
HUH?
WERE YOU TOO ANXIOUS ABOUT LEAVING ME ALONE HERE TO GO ON A LONG HIKE?
HUH? AH!
NO, NO!
THAT WASN'T THE ONLY REASON.
GOOD.
YOU WON'T NEED TO...
...WORRY MUCH LONGER.
... HUH?
WHAT DO YOU —?
I SEE. YOU'VE HEALED...
...HAVEN'T YOU?
...AL-THOUGH ...

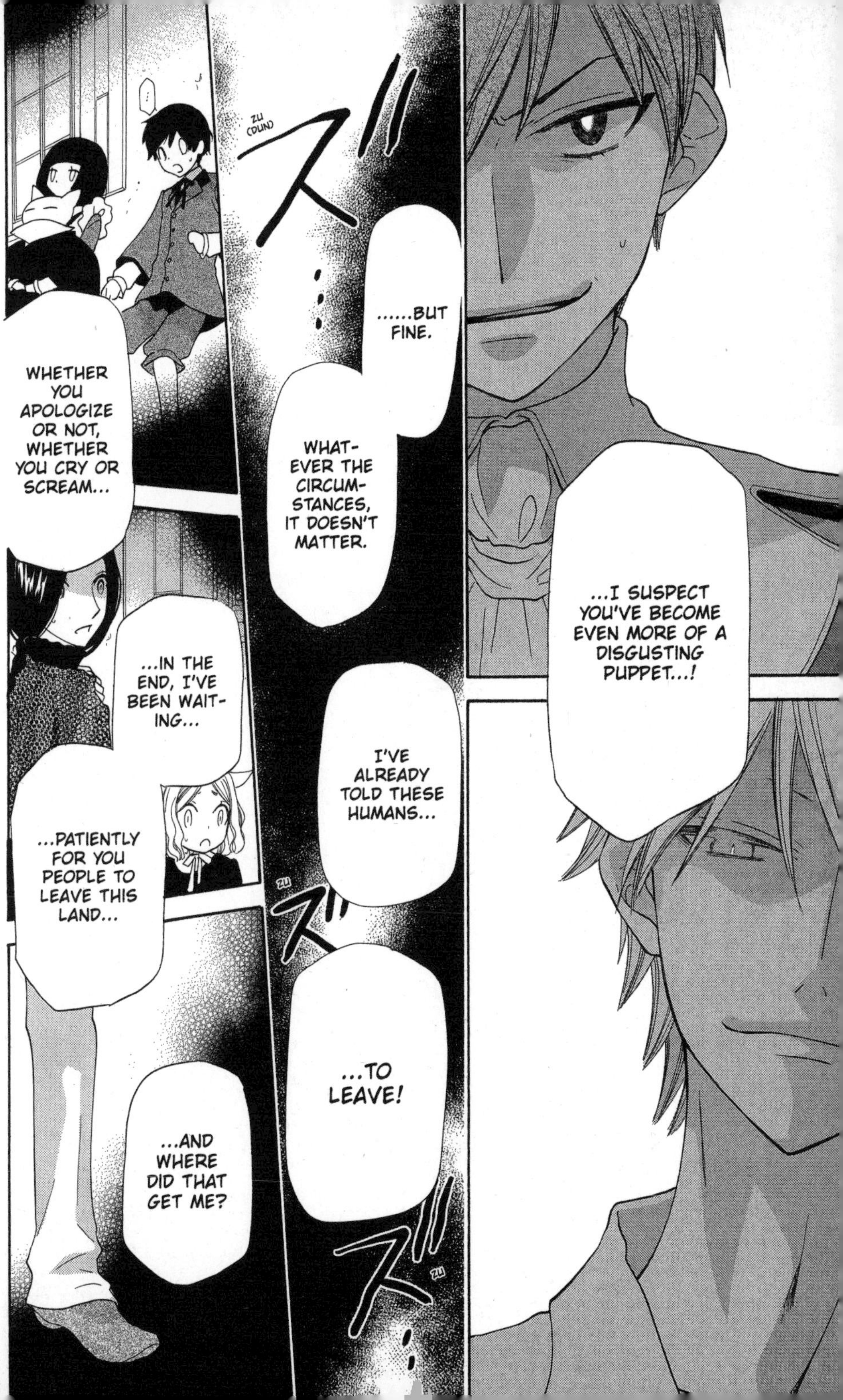
...I SUSPECT YOU'VE BECOME EVEN MORE OF A DISGUSTING PUPPET...!
ZU (DUN)
......BUT FINE.
WHAT-EVER THE CIRCUM-STANCES, IT DOESN'T MATTER.
I'VE ALREADY TOLD THESE HUMANS...
ZU
...TO LEAVE!
ZU
WHETHER YOU APOLOGIZE OR NOT, WHETHER YOU CRY OR SCREAM...
...IN THE END, I'VE BEEN WAIT-ING...
...PATIENTLY FOR YOU PEOPLE TO LEAVE THIS LAND...
...AND WHERE DID THAT GET ME?

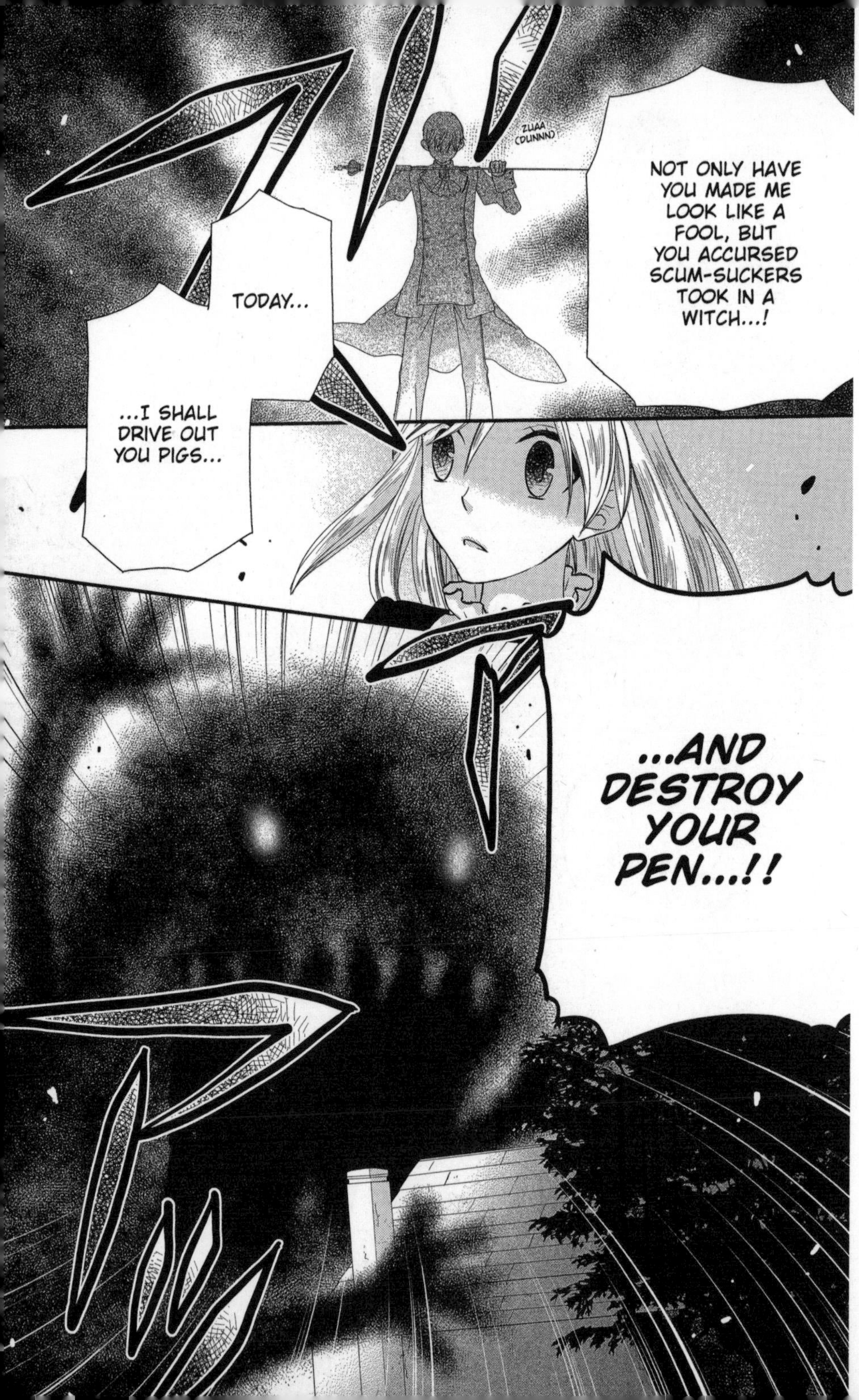
NOT ONLY HAVE YOU MADE ME LOOK LIKE A FOOL, BUT YOU ACCURSED SCUM-SUCKERS TOOK IN A WITCH...!
ZUAA (DUNNNN)
TODAY...
...I SHALL DRIVE OUT YOU PIGS...
...AND DESTROY YOUR PEN...!!

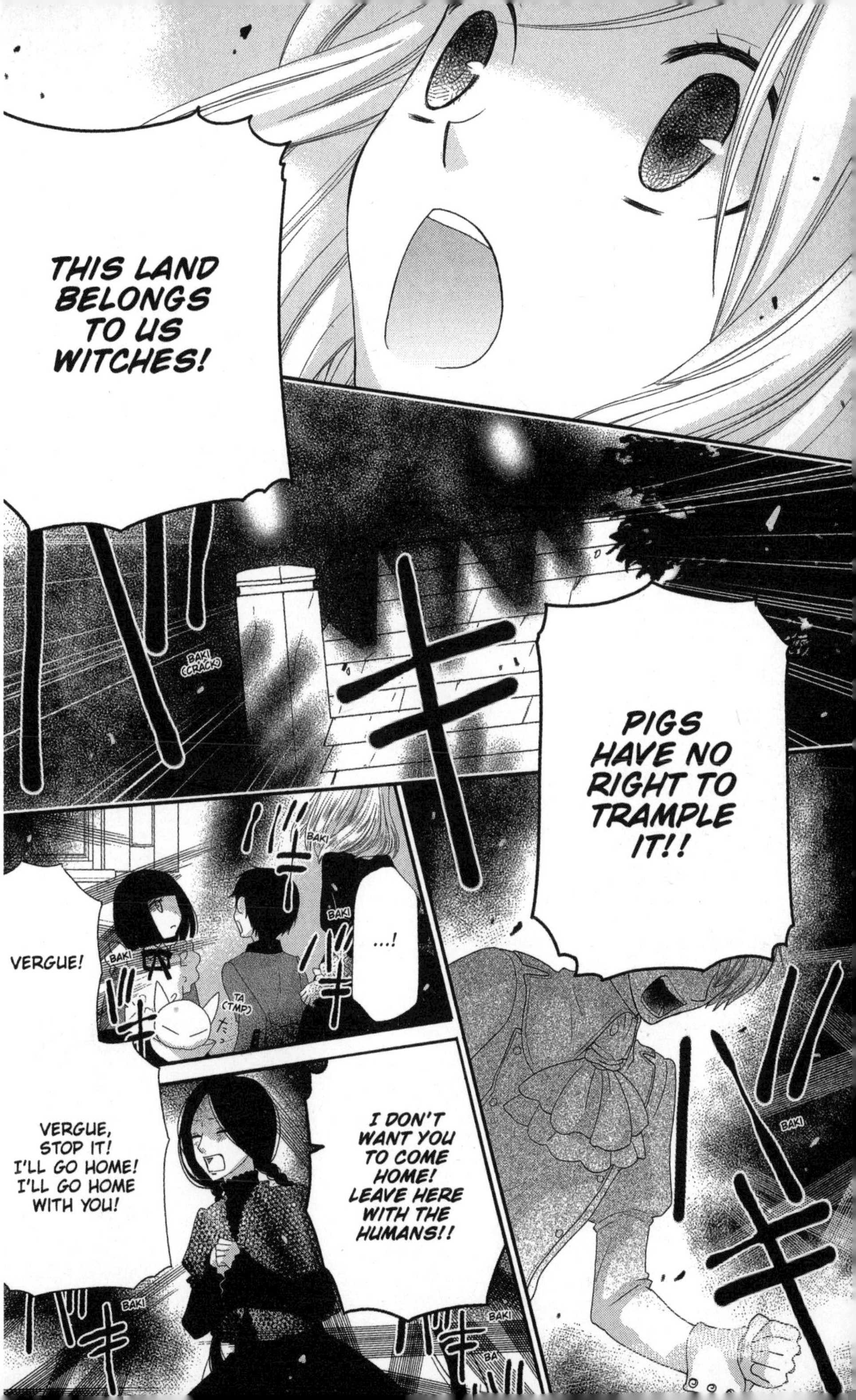
THIS LAND BELONGS TO US WITCHES!
PIGS HAVE NO RIGHT TO TRAMPLE IT!!
BAKI (CRACK)
BAKI
I DON'T WANT YOU TO COME HOME! LEAVE HERE WITH THE HUMANS!!
BAKI
BAKI
...!
BAKI
VERGUE!
BAKI
TA (TMP)
VERGUE, STOP IT! I'LL GO HOME! I'LL GO HOME WITH YOU!
BAKI
BAKI
BA

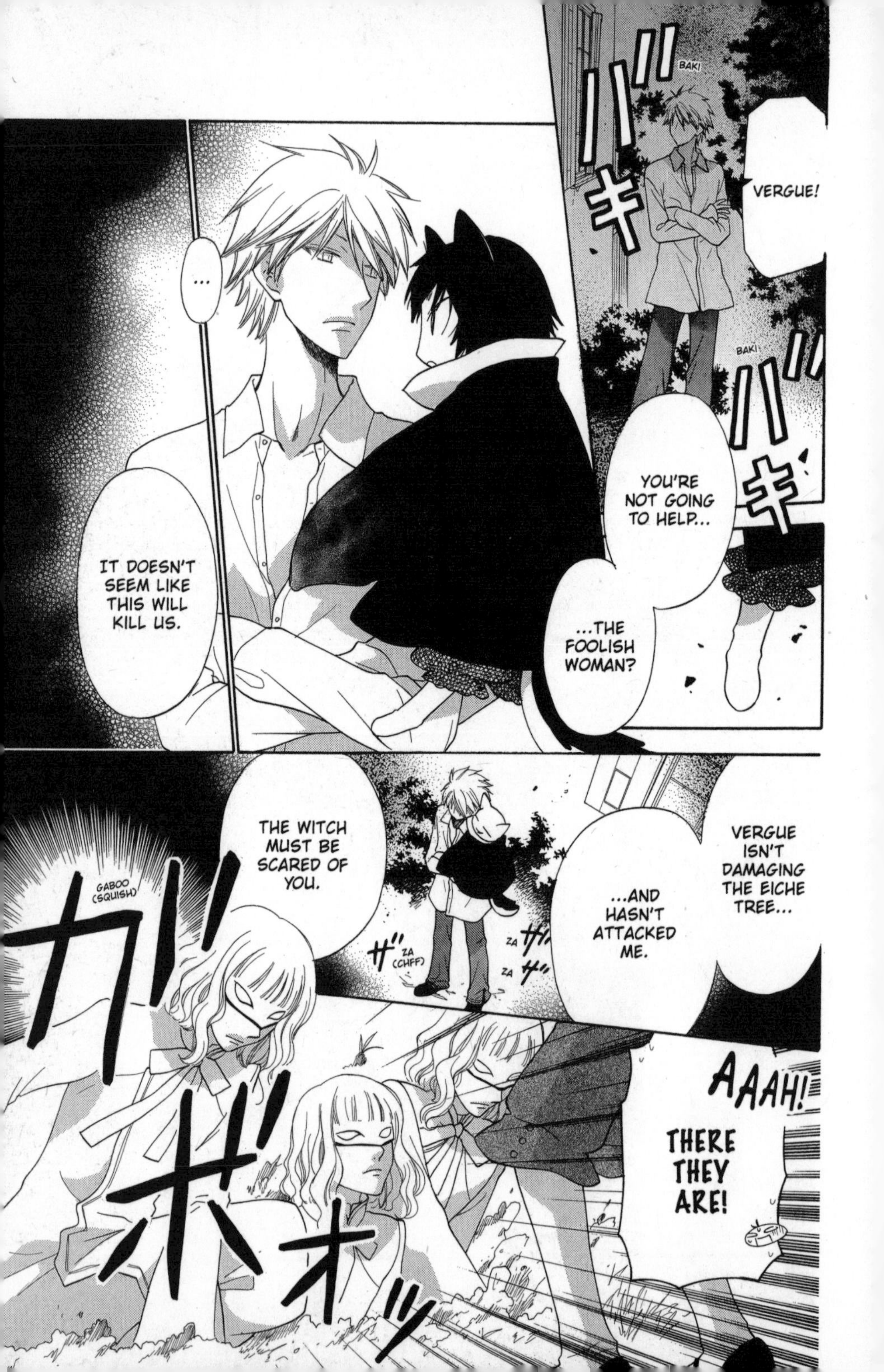
BAKI
VERGUE!
BAKI
YOU'RE NOT GOING TO HELP...
...THE FOOLISH WOMAN?
...
IT DOESN'T SEEM LIKE THIS WILL KILL US.
VERGUE ISN'T DAMAGING THE EICHE TREE...
...AND HASN'T ATTACKED ME.
ZA
ZA
THE WITCH MUST BE SCARED OF YOU.
ZA (CHFF)
AAAH!
THERE THEY ARE!
GABOO (SQUISH)

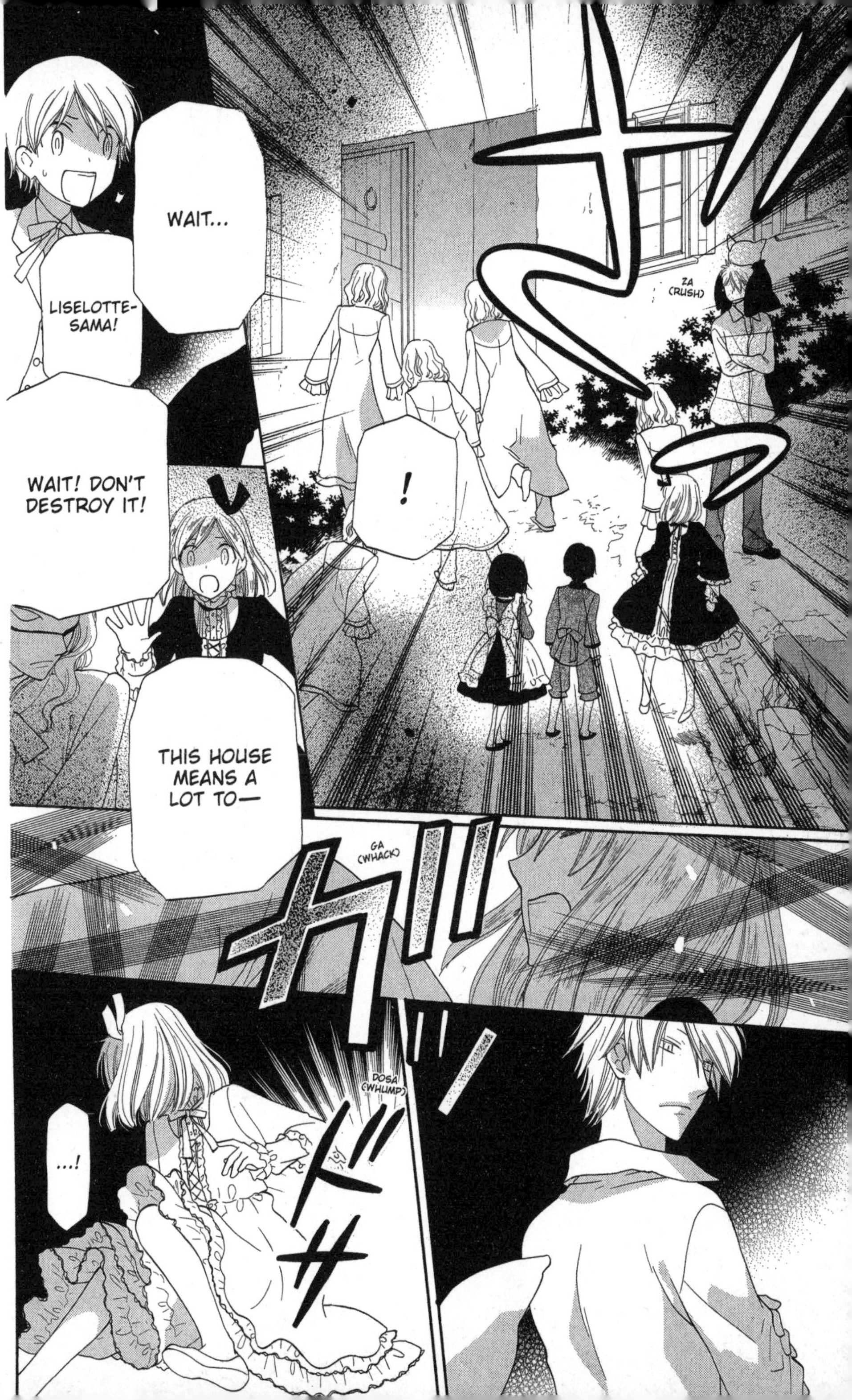
ZA
(RUSH)
!
WAIT...
LISELOTTE-SAMA!
WAIT! DON'T DESTROY IT!
THIS HOUSE MEANS A LOT TO—
GA
(WHACK)
DOSA
(WHUMP)
...!

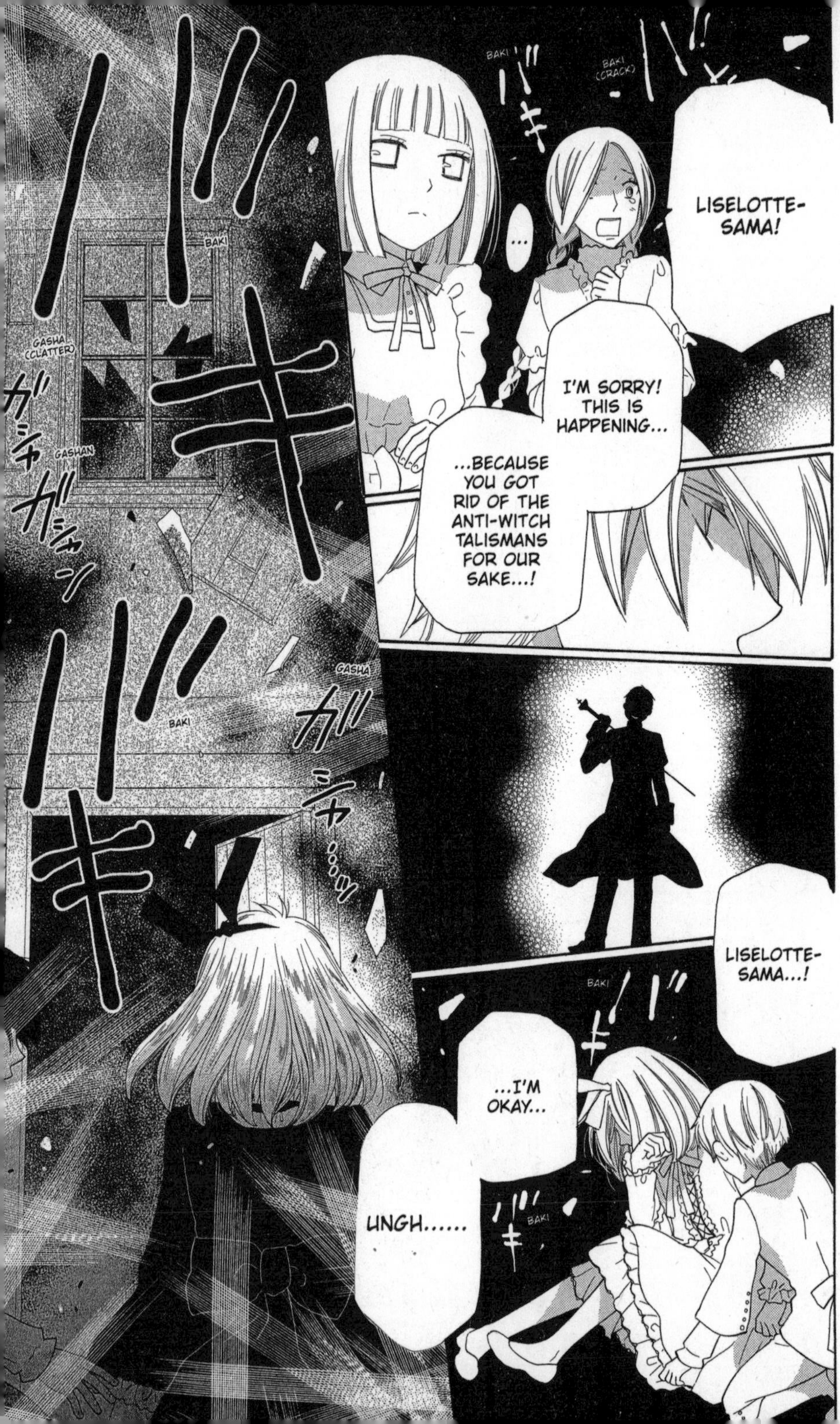
BAKI
BAKI (CRACK)
LISELOTTE-SAMA!
...
I'M SORRY! THIS IS HAPPENING...
...BECAUSE YOU GOT RID OF THE ANTI-WITCH TALISMANS FOR OUR SAKE...!
LISELOTTE-SAMA...!
BAKI
...I'M OKAY...
UNGH......
BAKI
BAKI
GASHA (CLATTER)
GASHAN
BAKI
GASHA

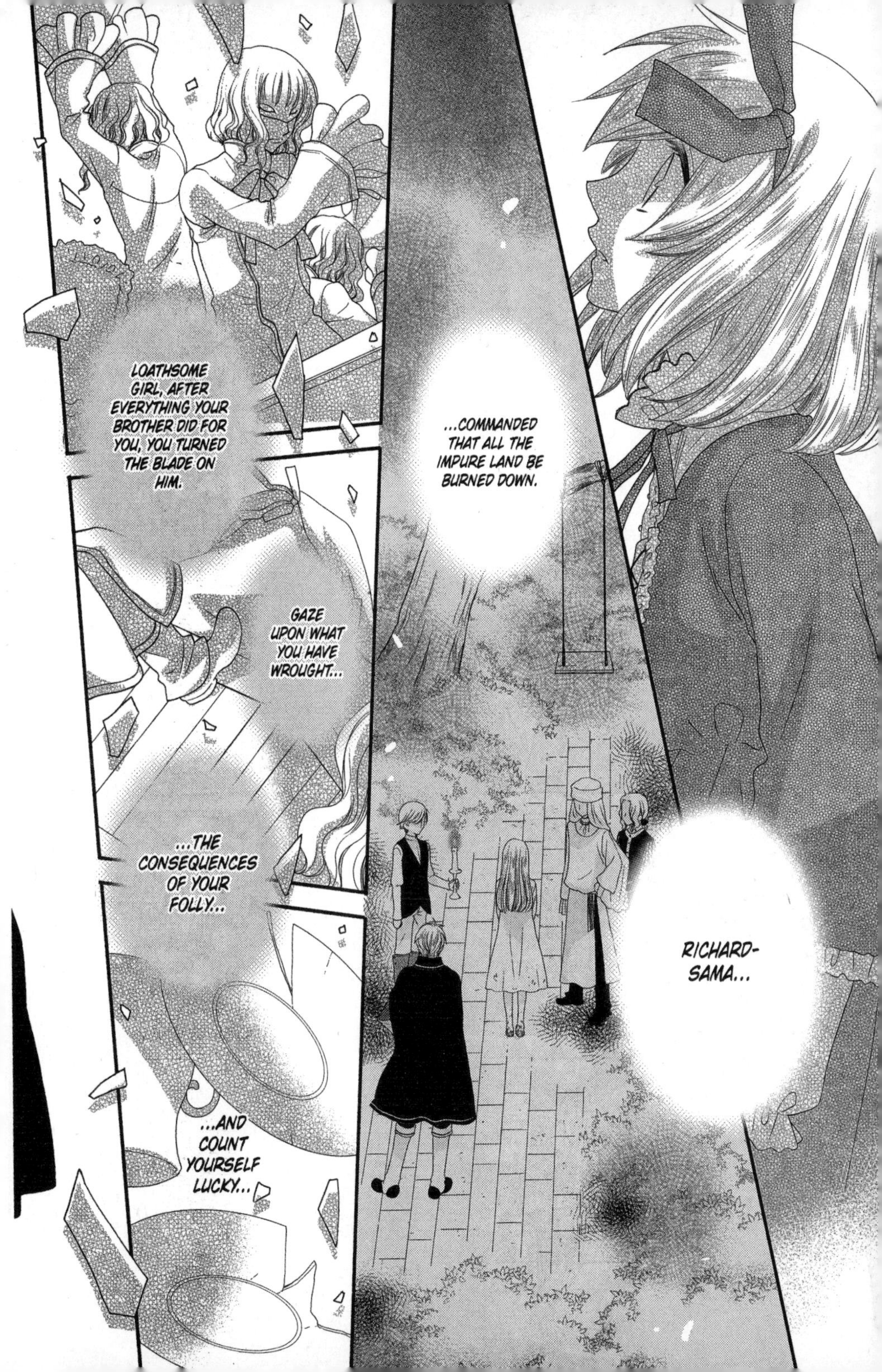
RICHARD-SAMA...
...COMMANDED THAT ALL THE IMPURE LAND BE BURNED DOWN.
LOATHSOME GIRL, AFTER EVERYTHING YOUR BROTHER DID FOR YOU, YOU TURNED THE BLADE ON HIM.
GAZE UPON WHAT YOU HAVE WROUGHT...
...THE CONSEQUENCES OF YOUR FOLLY...
...AND COUNT YOURSELF LUCKY...

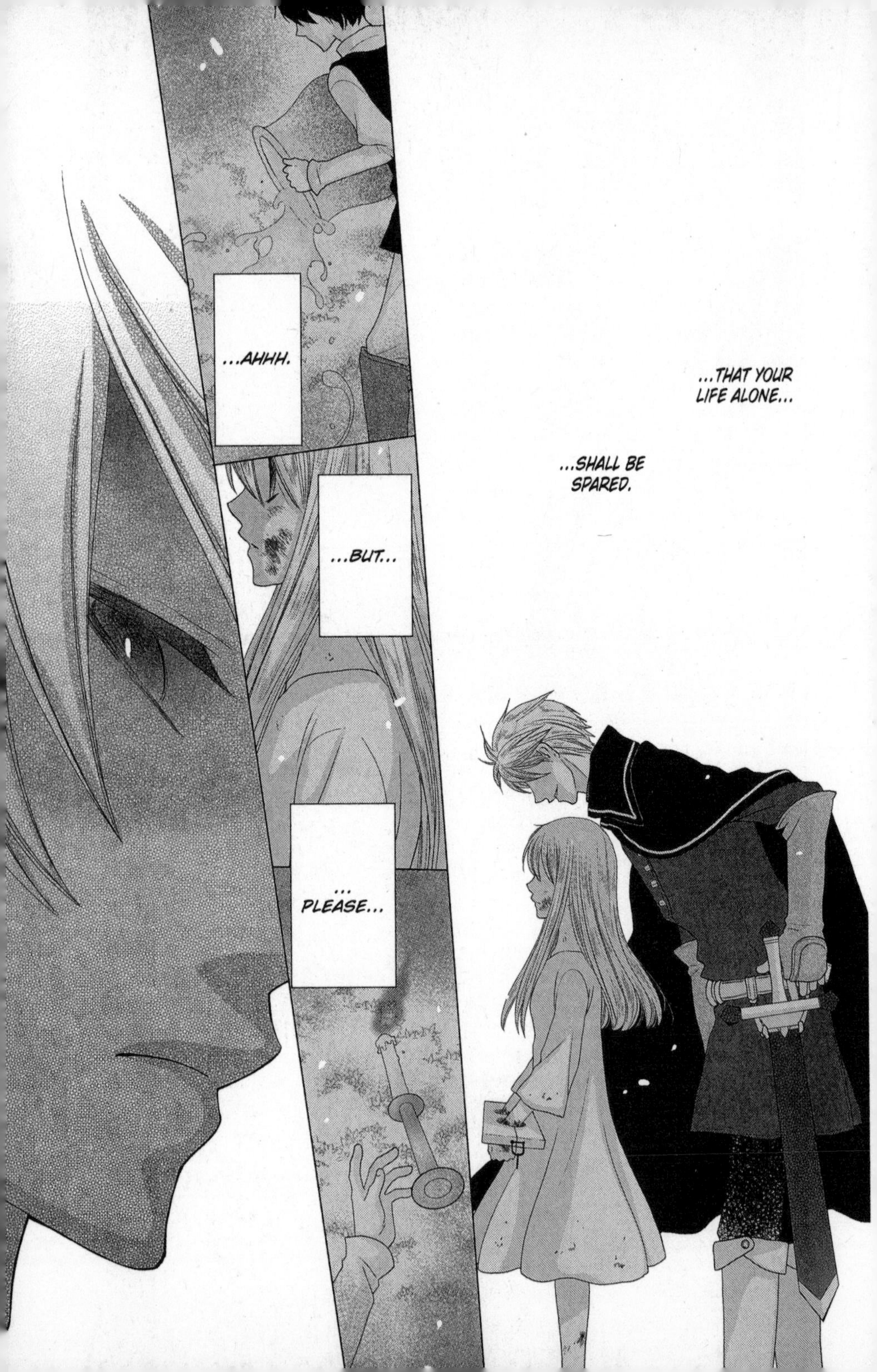
...THAT YOUR LIFE ALONE...
...SHALL BE SPARED.
...AHHH.
...BUT...
...PLEASE...

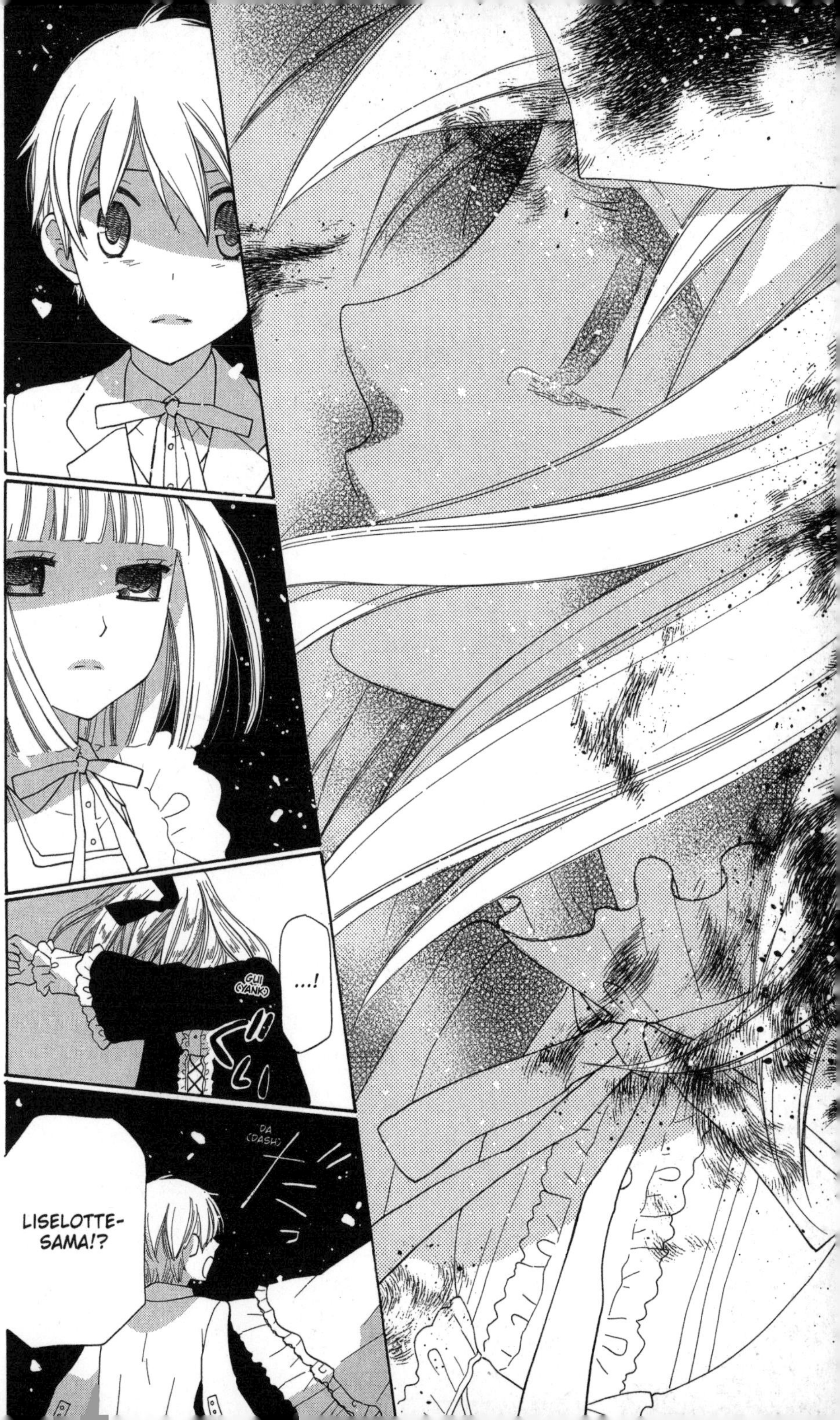
...!
GUI (YANK)
DA (DASH)
LISELOTTE-SAMA!?

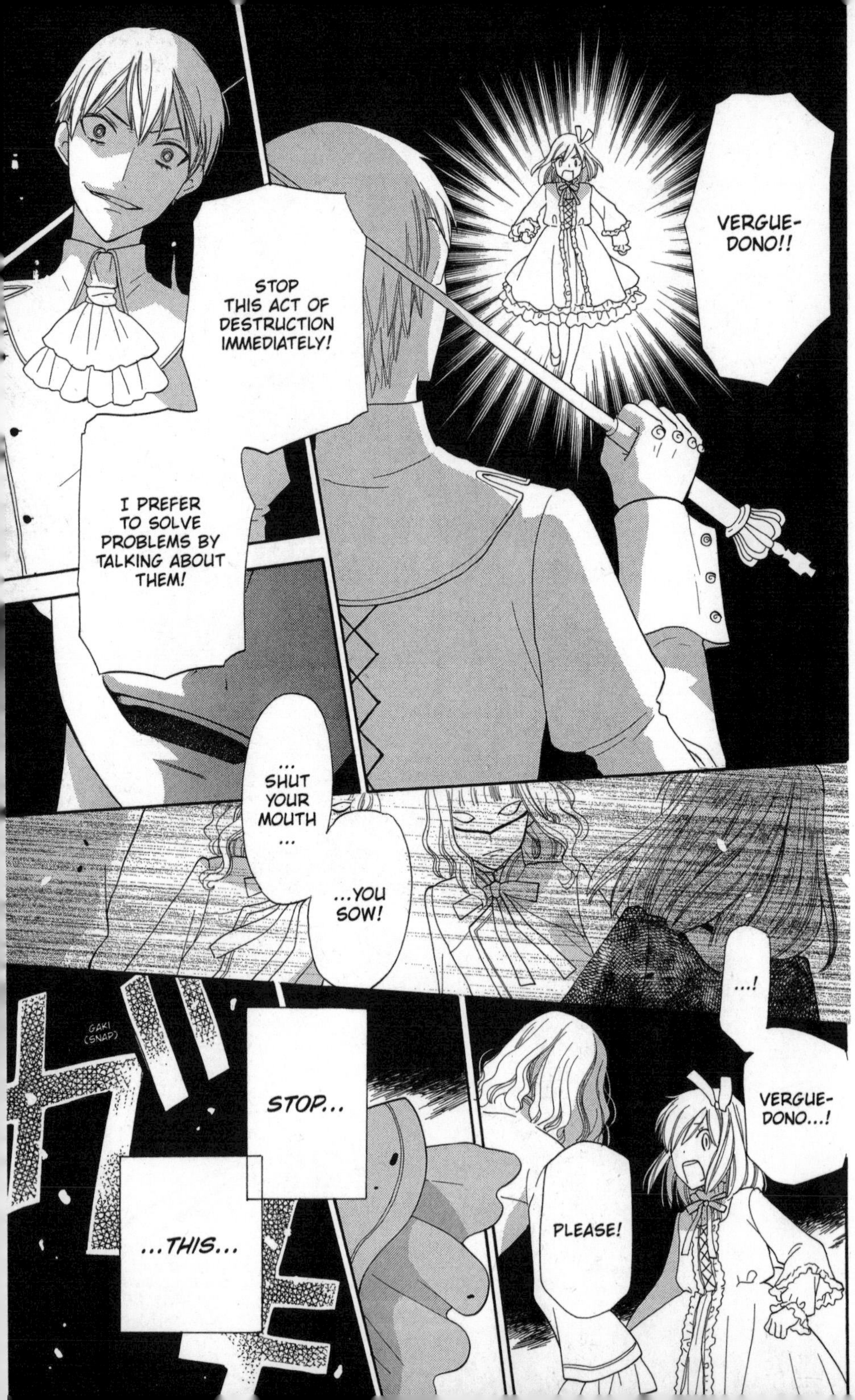
VERGUE-DONO!!
STOP THIS ACT OF DESTRUCTION IMMEDIATELY!
I PREFER TO SOLVE PROBLEMS BY TALKING ABOUT THEM!
...SHUT YOUR MOUTH...
...YOU SOW!
...!
VERGUE-DONO...!
PLEASE!
STOP...
...THIS...
GAKI (SNAP)

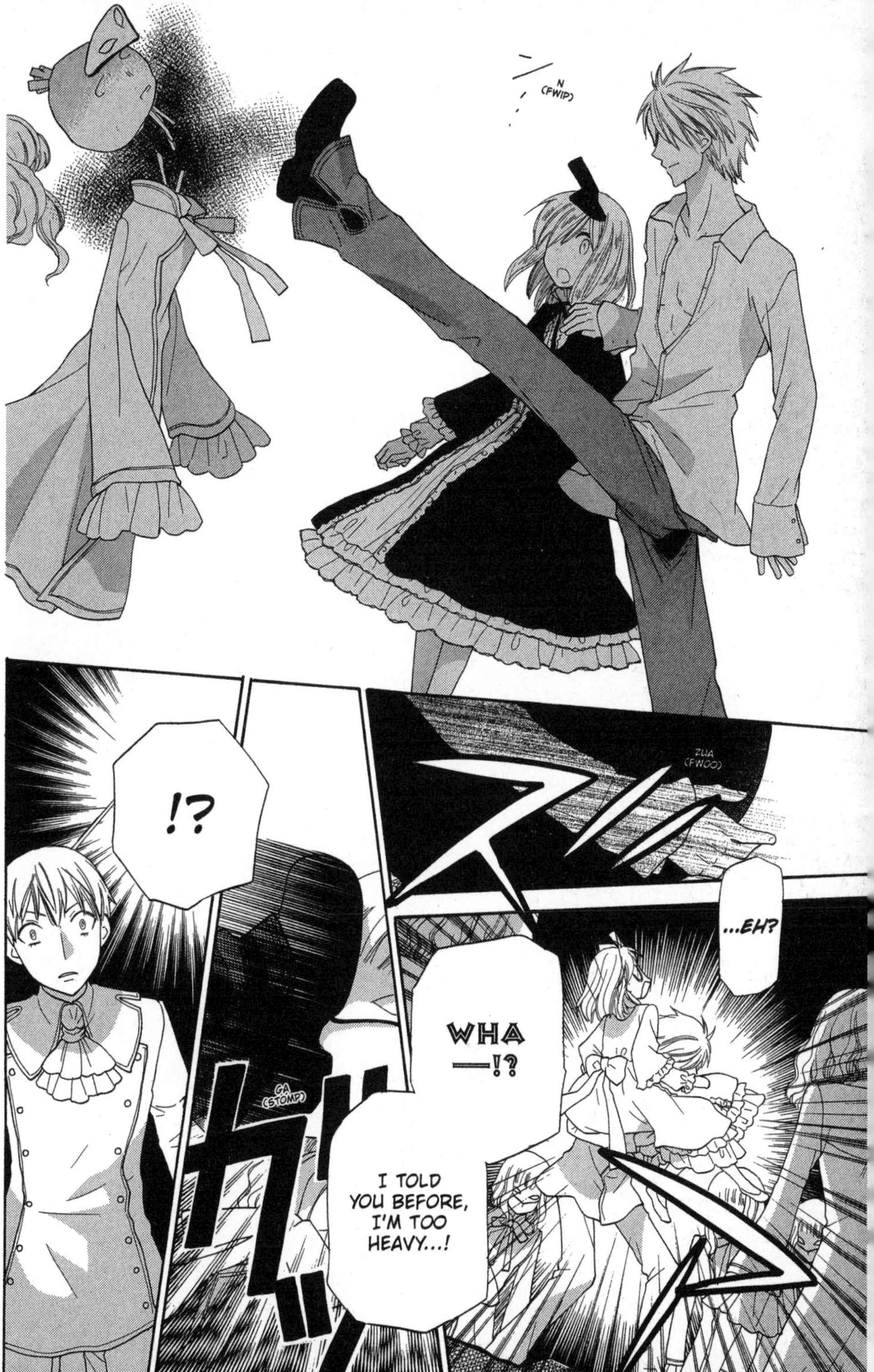
N
(FWIP)
ZUA
(FWOO)
...EH?
WHA—!?
I TOLD YOU BEFORE, I'M TOO HEAVY...!
GA
(STOMP)
!?

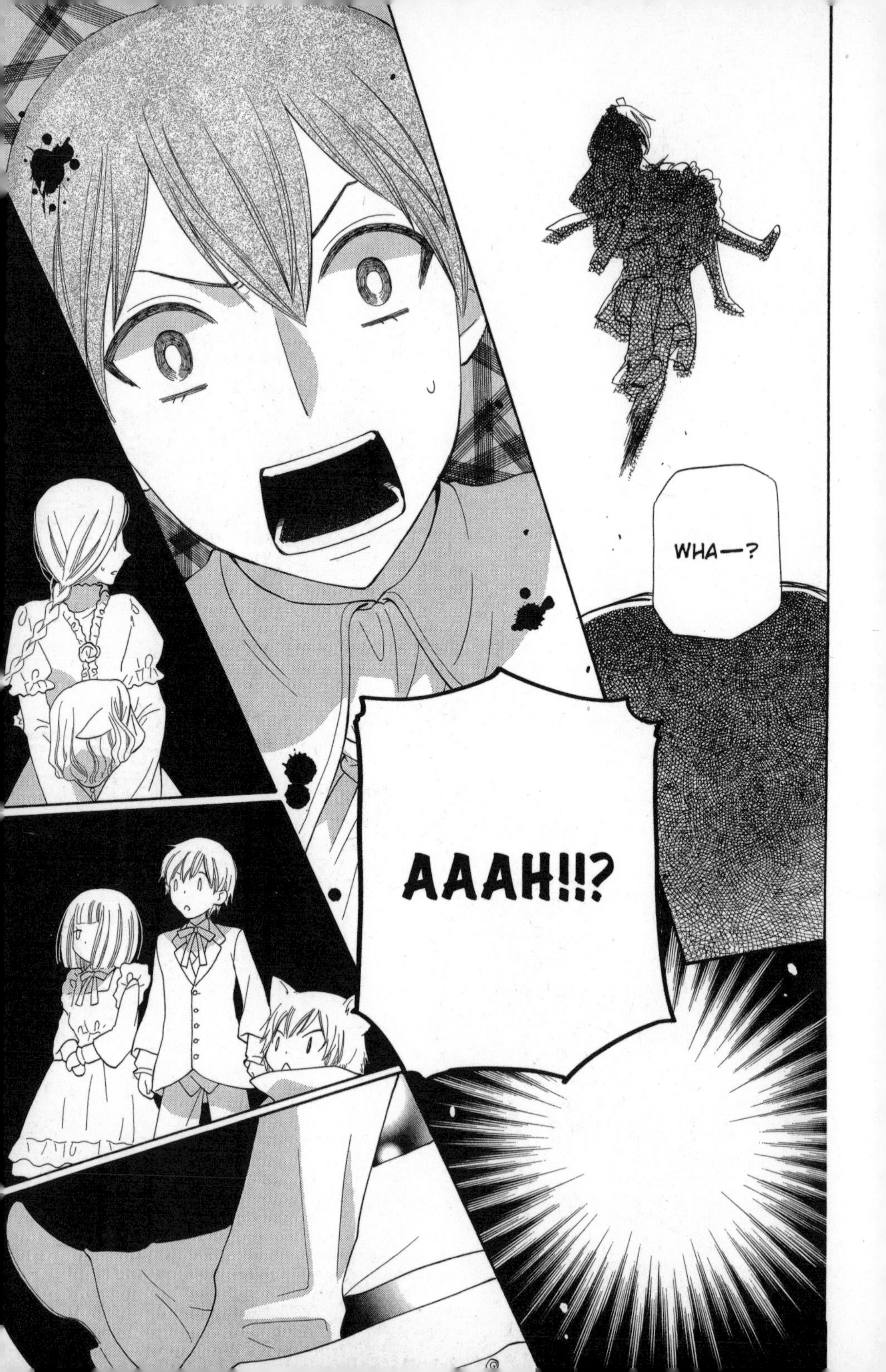
WHA—?
AAAH!!?

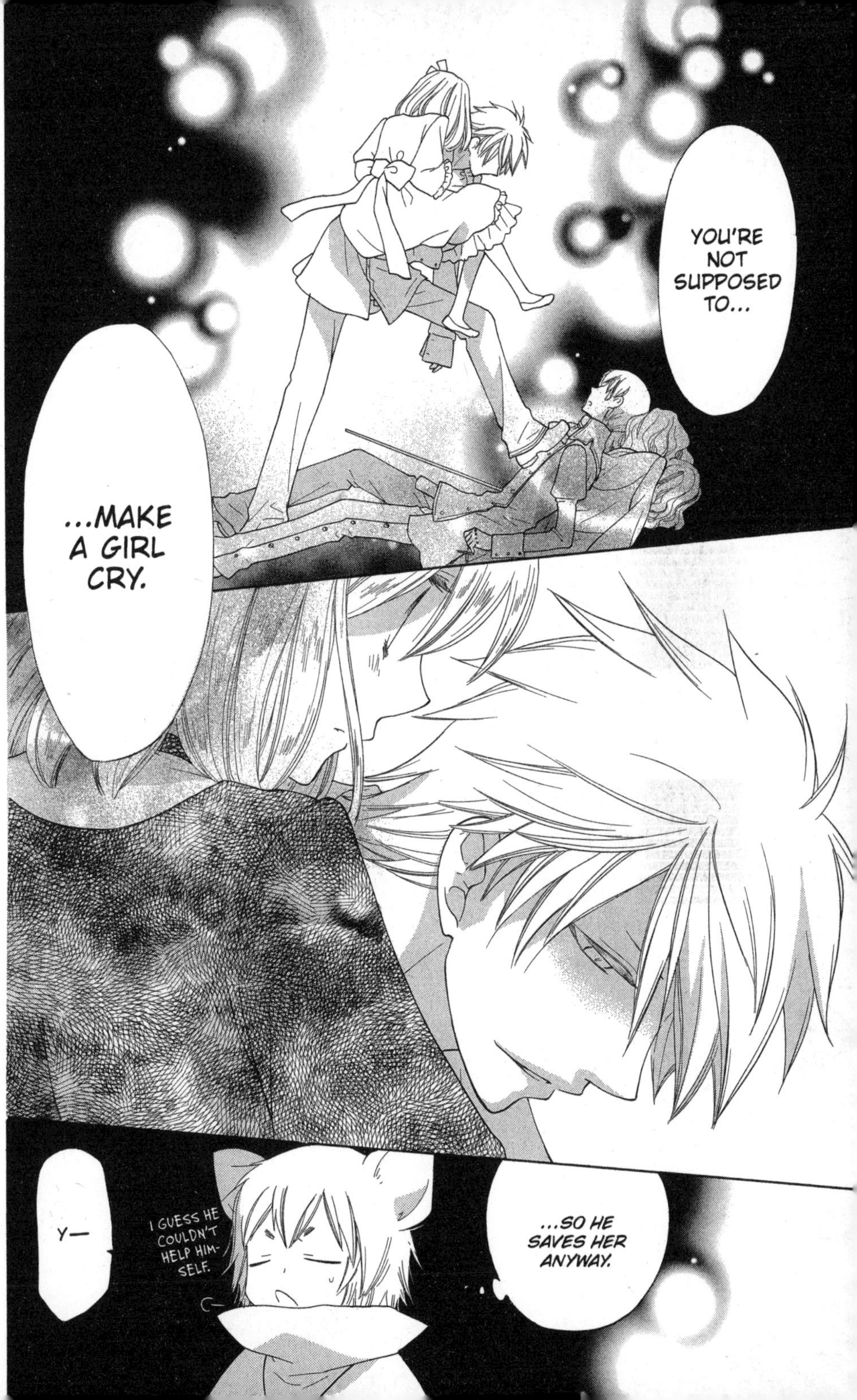
YOU'RE NOT SUPPOSED TO...
...MAKE A GIRL CRY.
...SO HE SAVES HER ANYWAY.
I GUESS HE COULDN'T HELP HIM-SELF.
Y—

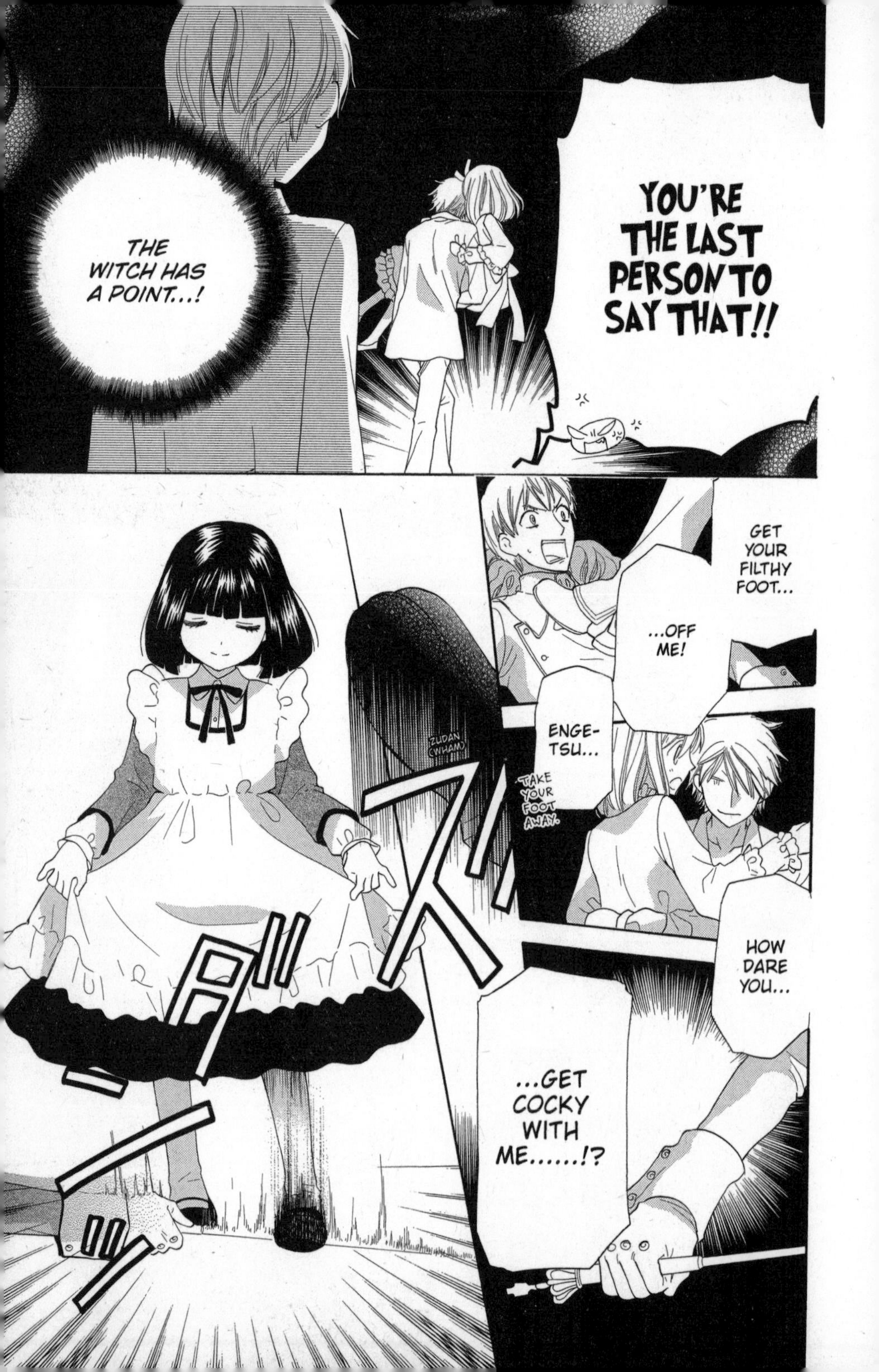
YOU'RE THE LAST PERSON TO SAY THAT!!
THE WITCH HAS A POINT...!
GET YOUR FILTHY FOOT...
...OFF ME!
ENGE-TSU...
TAKE YOUR FOOT AWAY.
HOW DARE YOU...
...GET COCKY WITH ME......!?
ZUDAN (WHAM)

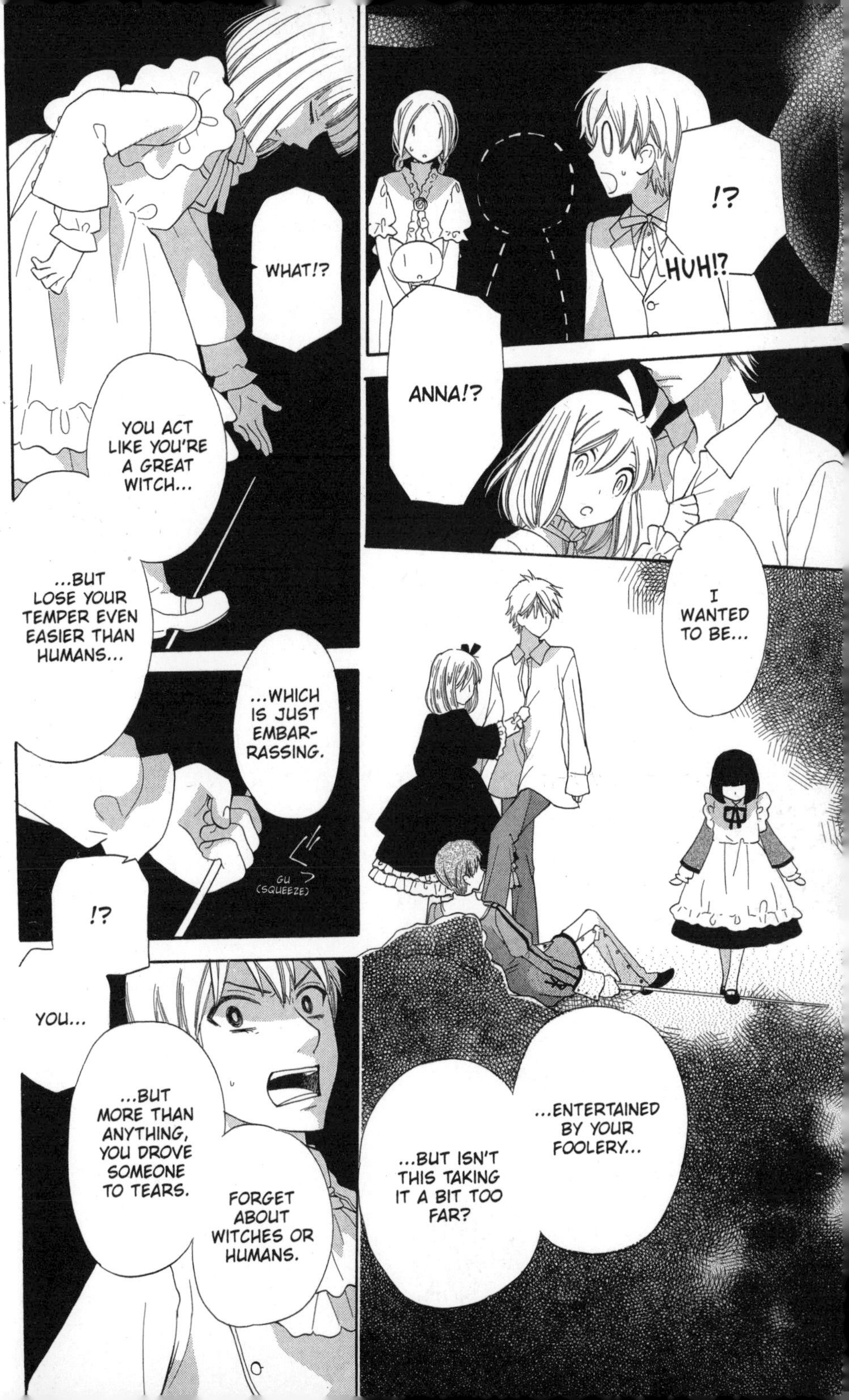
!?
HUH!?
ANNA!?
WHAT!?
YOU ACT LIKE YOU'RE A GREAT WITCH...
...BUT LOSE YOUR TEMPER EVEN EASIER THAN HUMANS...
...WHICH IS JUST EMBARRASSING.
GU (SQUEEZE)
!?
I WANTED TO BE...
...ENTERTAINED BY YOUR FOOLERY...
...BUT ISN'T THIS TAKING IT A BIT TOO FAR?
YOU...
FORGET ABOUT WITCHES OR HUMANS.
...BUT MORE THAN ANYTHING, YOU DROVE SOMEONE TO TEARS.

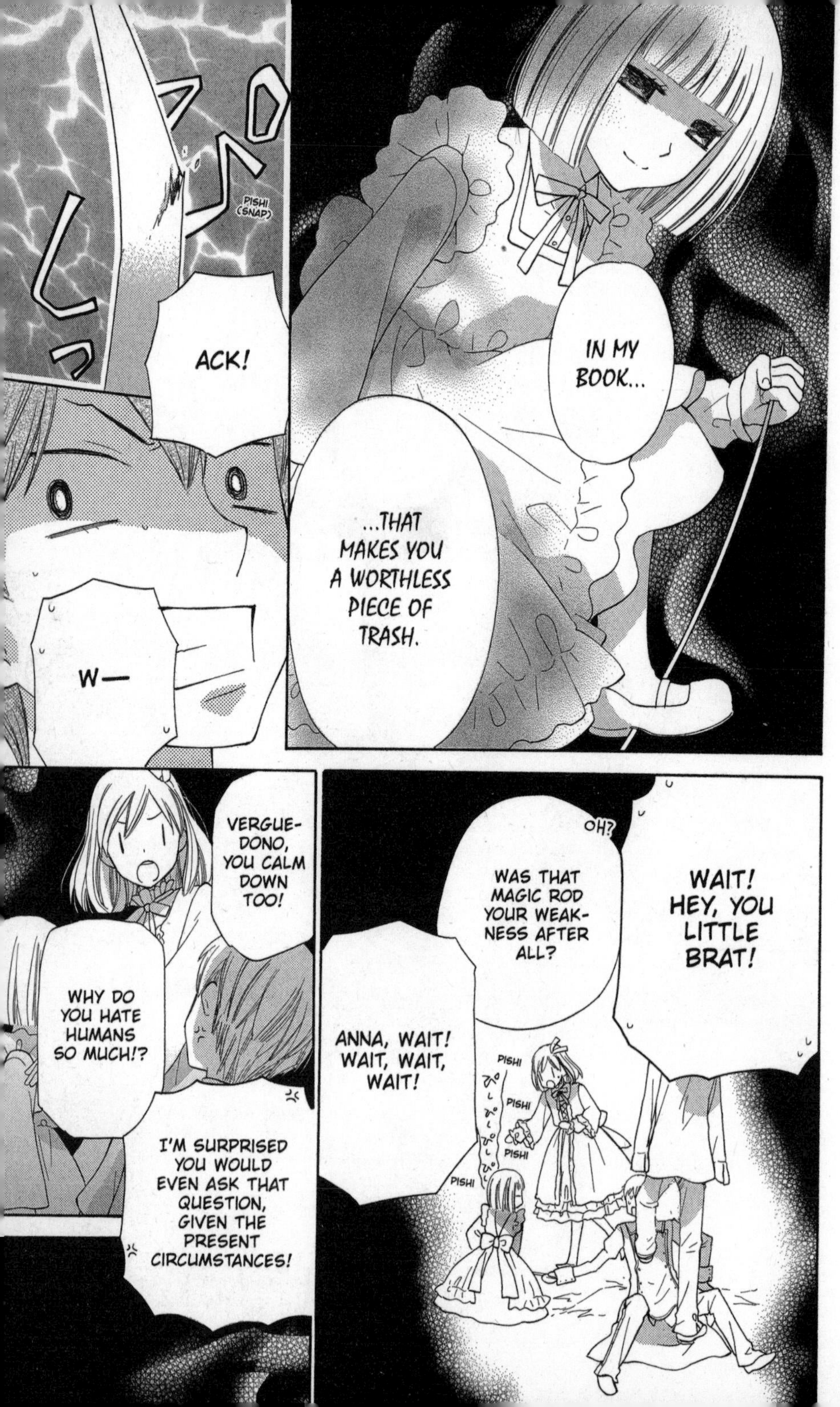
IN MY BOOK...
...THAT MAKES YOU A WORTHLESS PIECE OF TRASH.
PISHI (SNAP)
ACK!
W—
WAIT! HEY, YOU LITTLE BRAT!
OH?
WAS THAT MAGIC ROD YOUR WEAKNESS AFTER ALL?
ANNA, WAIT! WAIT, WAIT, WAIT!
PISHI
PISHI
PISHI
PISHI
VERGUE-DONO, YOU CALM DOWN TOO!
WHY DO YOU HATE HUMANS SO MUCH!?
I'M SURPRISED YOU WOULD EVEN ASK THAT QUESTION, GIVEN THE PRESENT CIRCUMSTANCES!

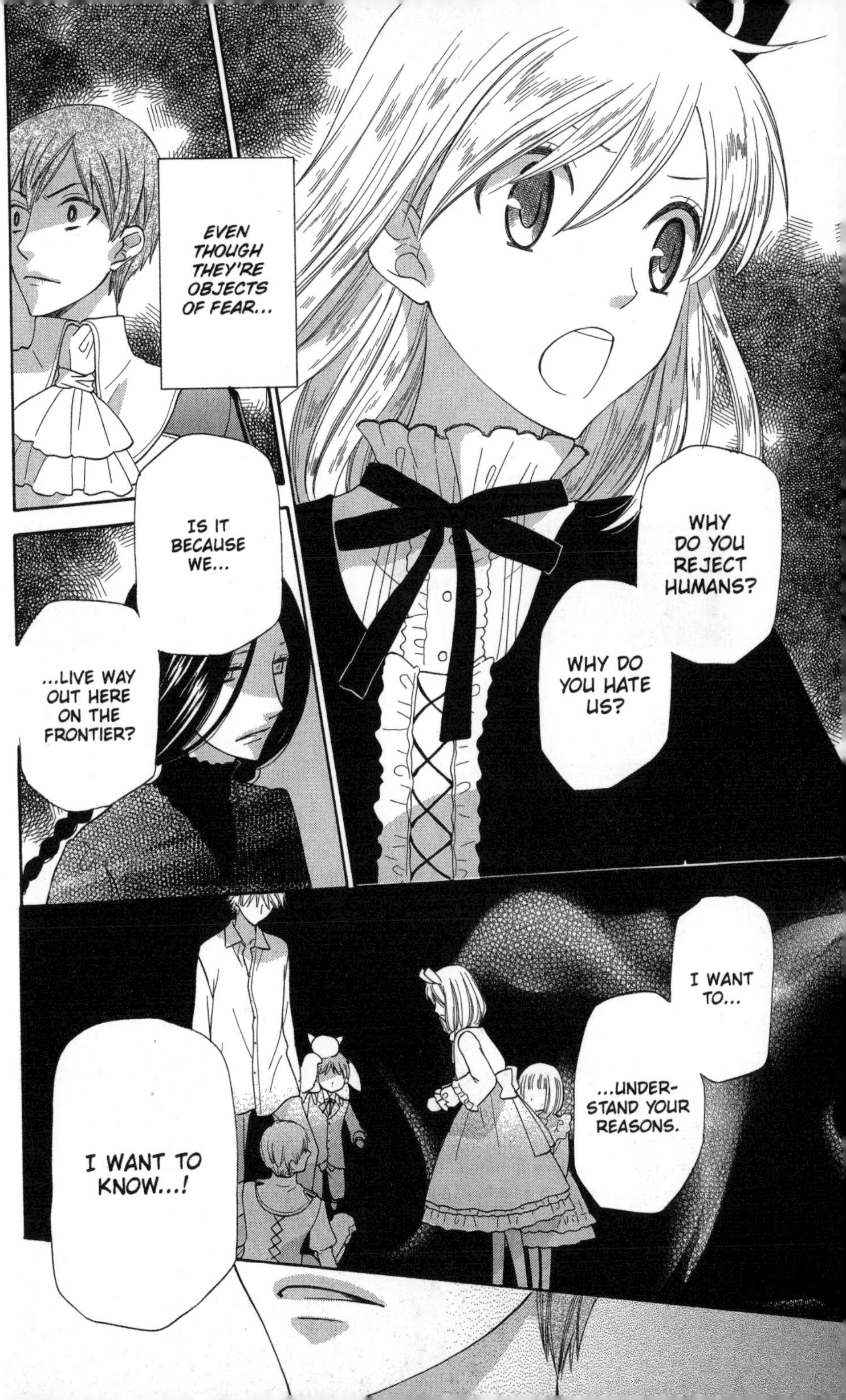
WHY DO YOU REJECT HUMANS?
WHY DO YOU HATE US?
EVEN THOUGH THEY'RE OBJECTS OF FEAR...
IS IT BECAUSE WE...
...LIVE WAY OUT HERE ON THE FRONTIER?
I WANT TO...
...UNDER-STAND YOUR REASONS.
I WANT TO KNOW...!

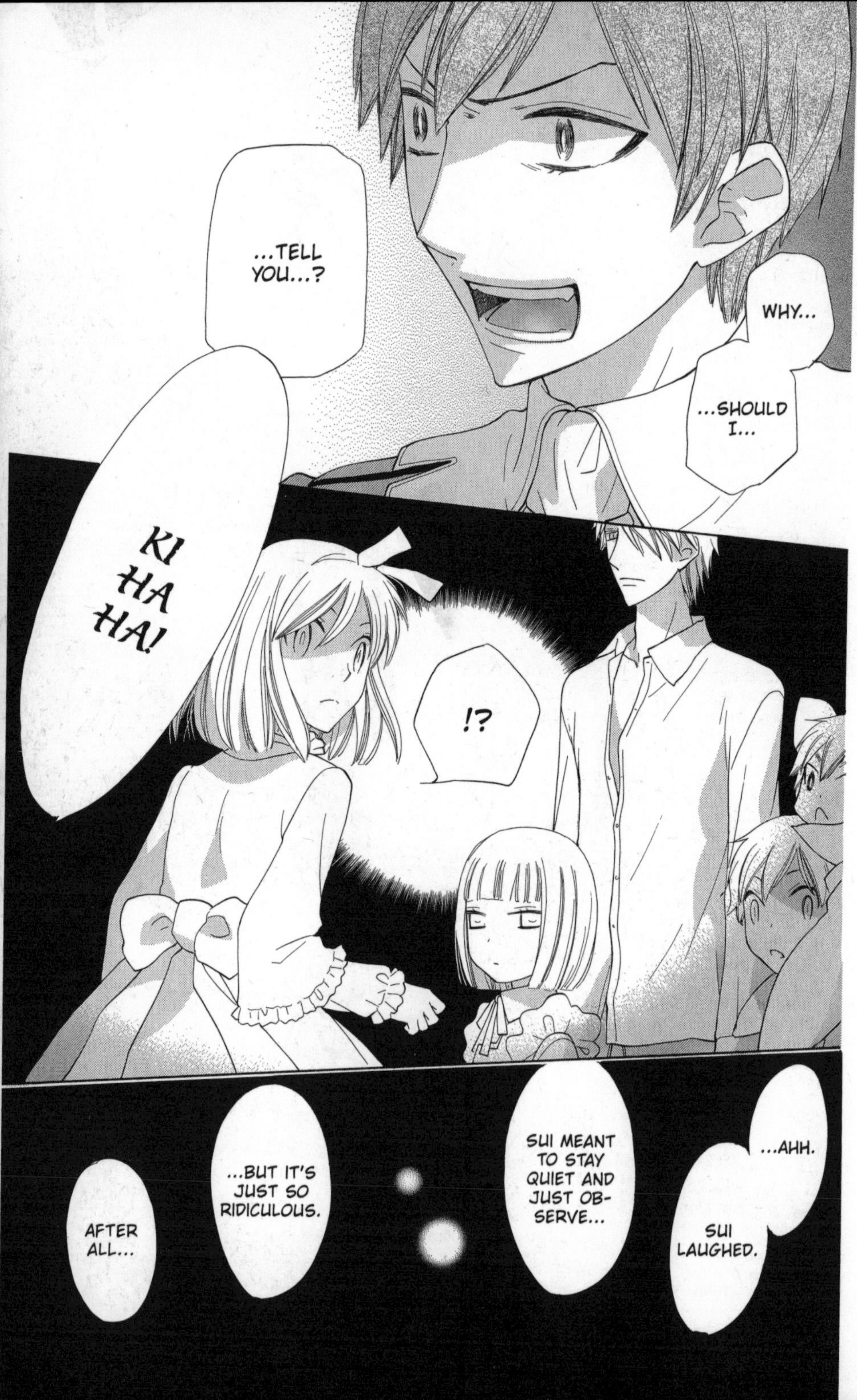
WHY...
...SHOULD I...
...TELL YOU...?
KI HA HA!
!?
...AHH.
SUI LAUGHED.
SUI MEANT TO STAY QUIET AND JUST OB- SERVE...
...BUT IT'S JUST SO RIDICULOUS.
AFTER ALL...

KAKON (CLACK)
...SUI KNOWS HOW VERGUE...
...WAS ORIGINALLY...
...A WORTH-LESS PIECE OF TRASH...
...HUMAN TOO.

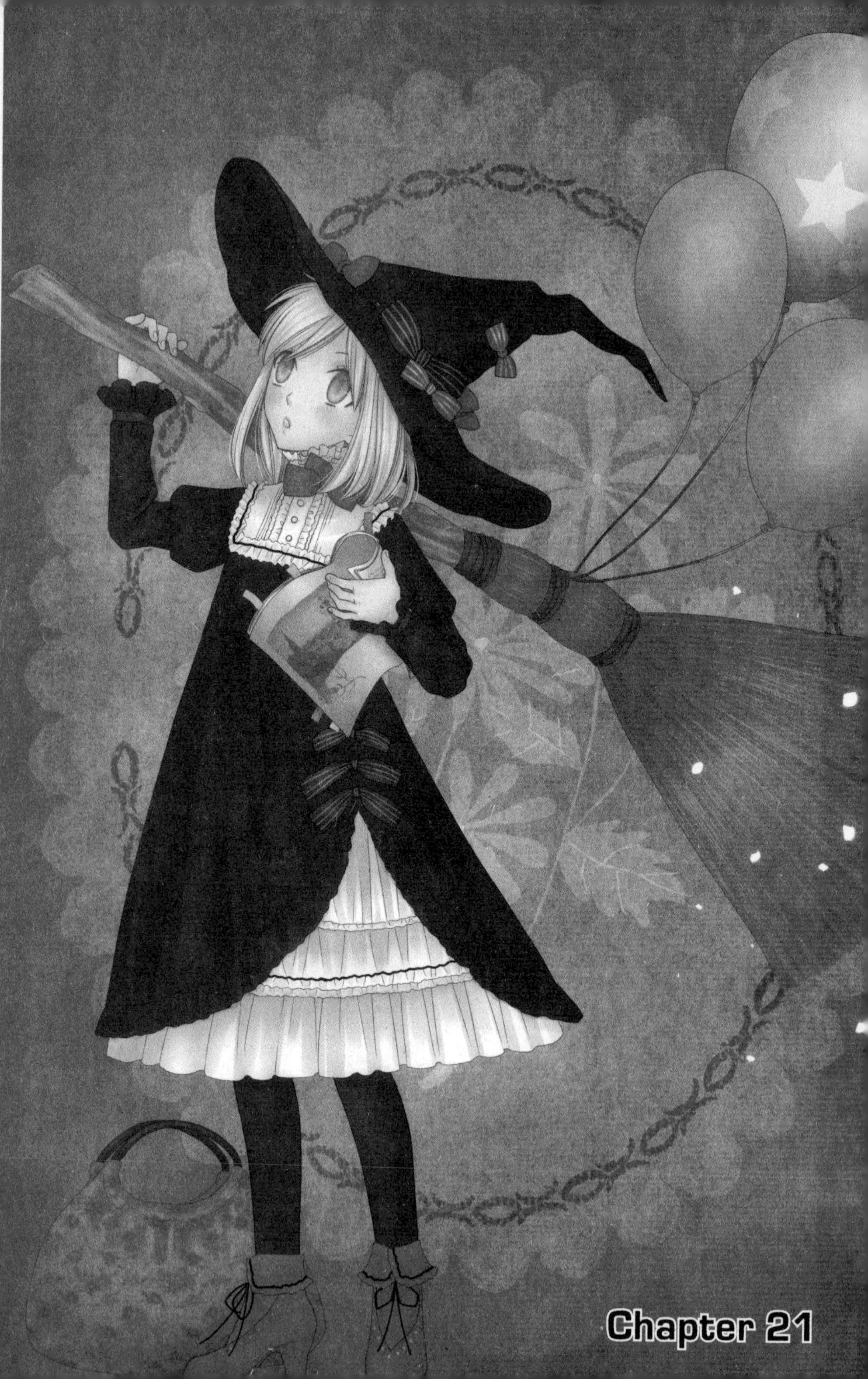

Chapter 21

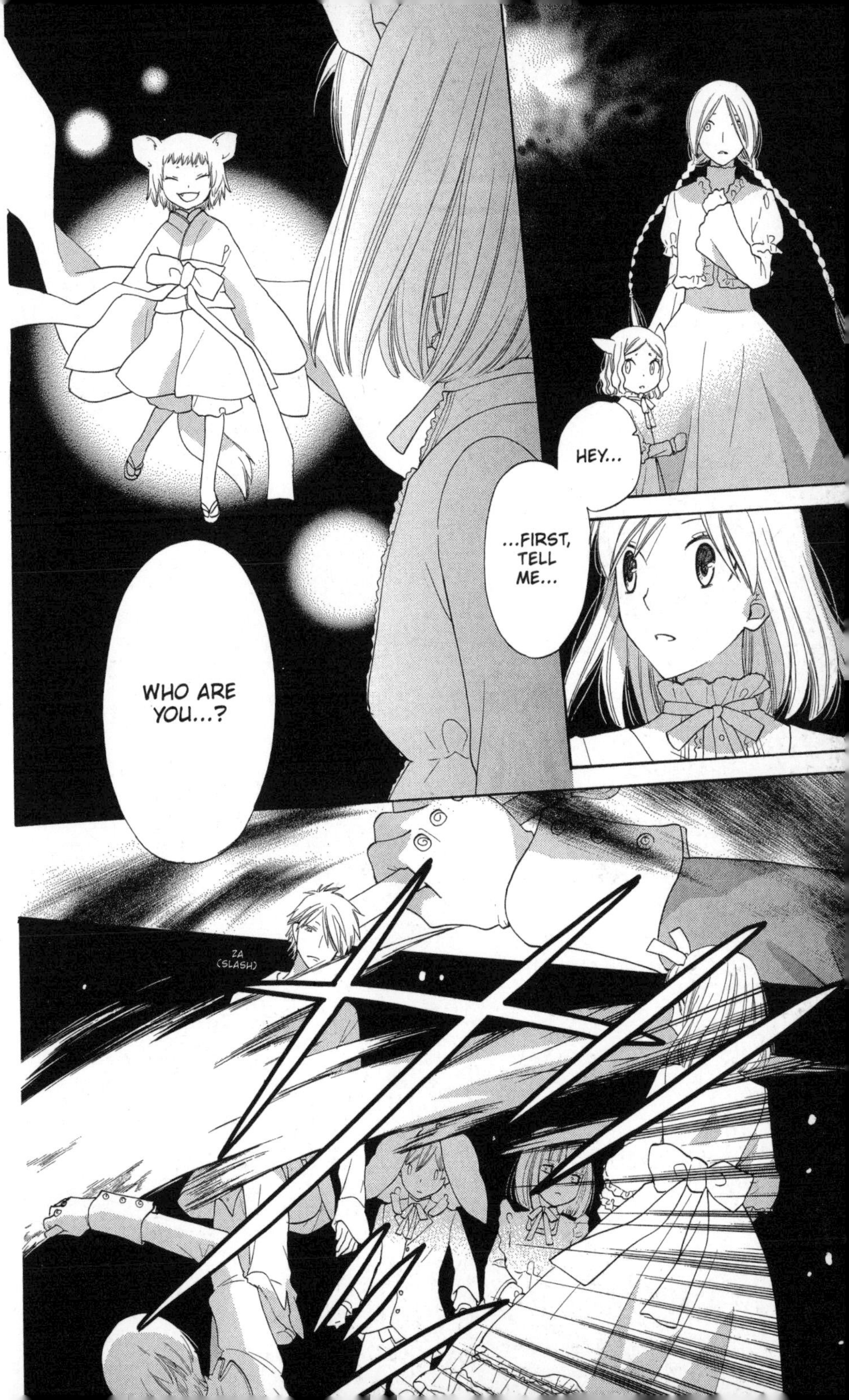
HEY...
...FIRST, TELL ME...
WHO ARE YOU...?
ZA (SLASH)

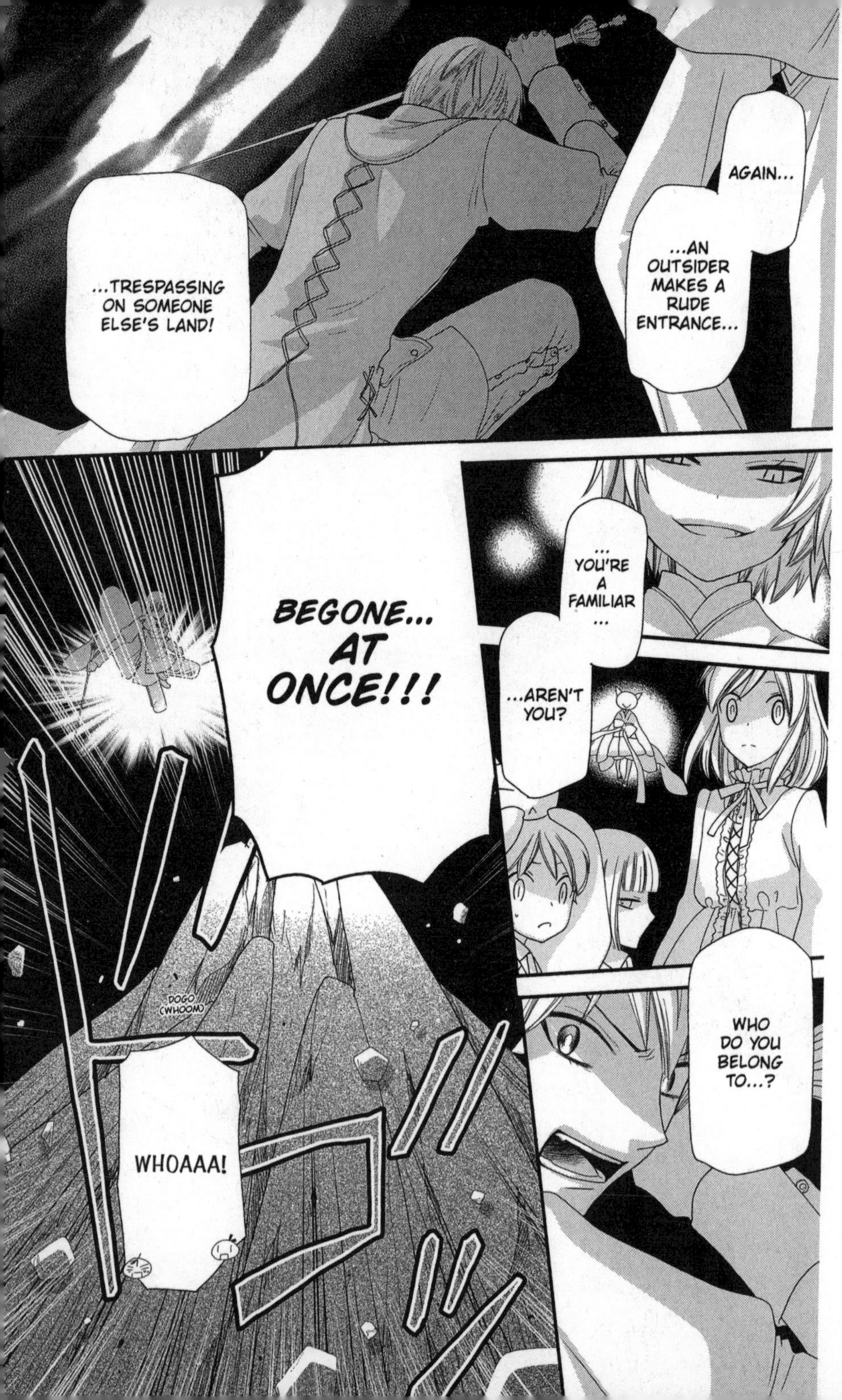
AGAIN...
...AN OUTSIDER MAKES A RUDE ENTRANCE...
...TRESPASSING ON SOMEONE ELSE'S LAND!
... YOU'RE A FAMILIAR ...
...AREN'T YOU?
WHO DO YOU BELONG TO...?
BEGONE... AT ONCE!!!
DOGO (WHOOM)
WHOAAA!

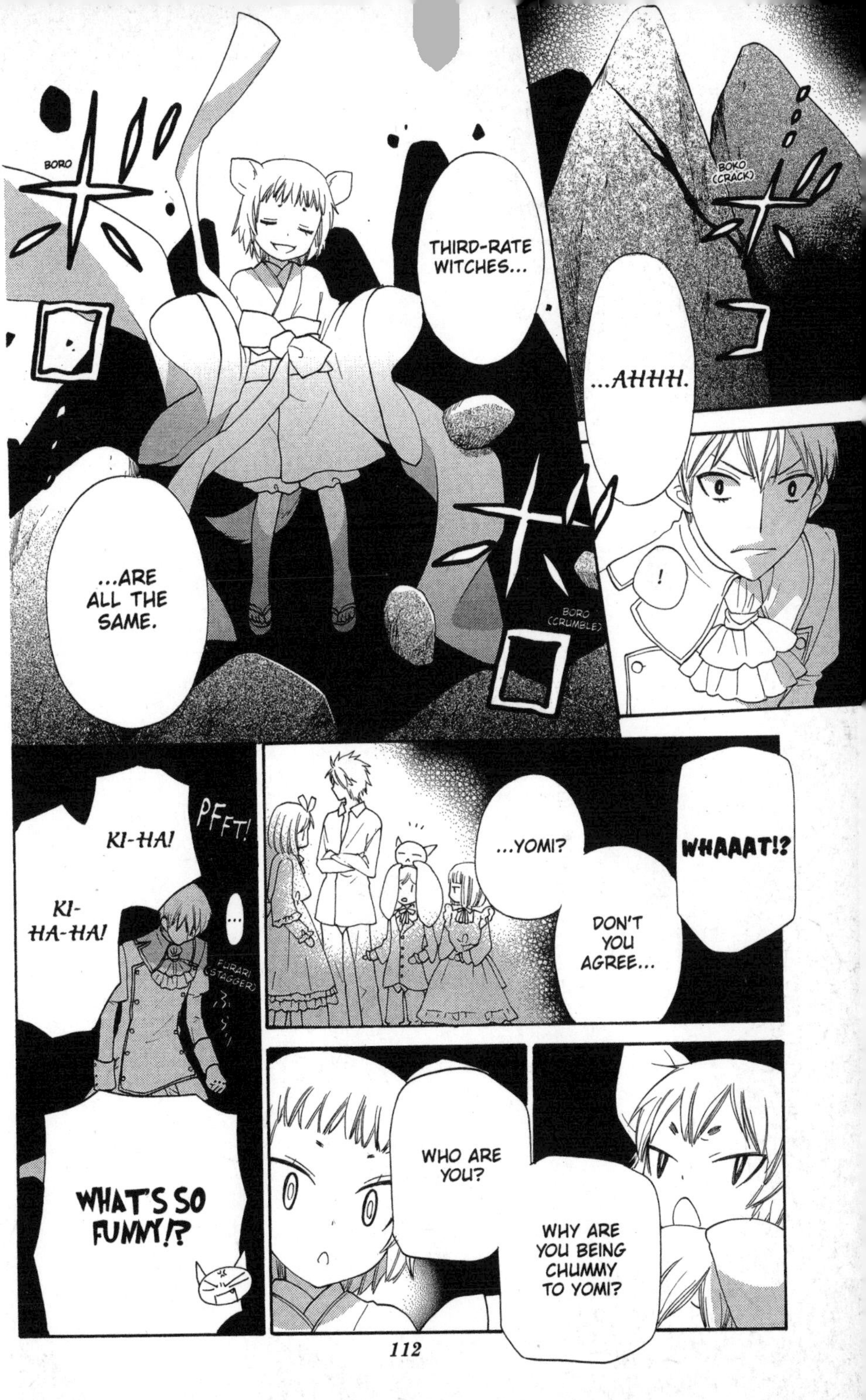
BOKO (CRACK)
...AHHH.
!
THIRD-RATE WITCHES...
BORO
...ARE ALL THE SAME.
BORO (CRUMBLE)
WHAAAT!?
...YOMI?
DON'T YOU AGREE...
WHO ARE YOU?
WHY ARE YOU BEING CHUMMY TO YOMI?
PFFT!
KI-HA!
KI-HA-HA!
...
FURARI (STAGGER)
WHAT'S SO FUNNY!?

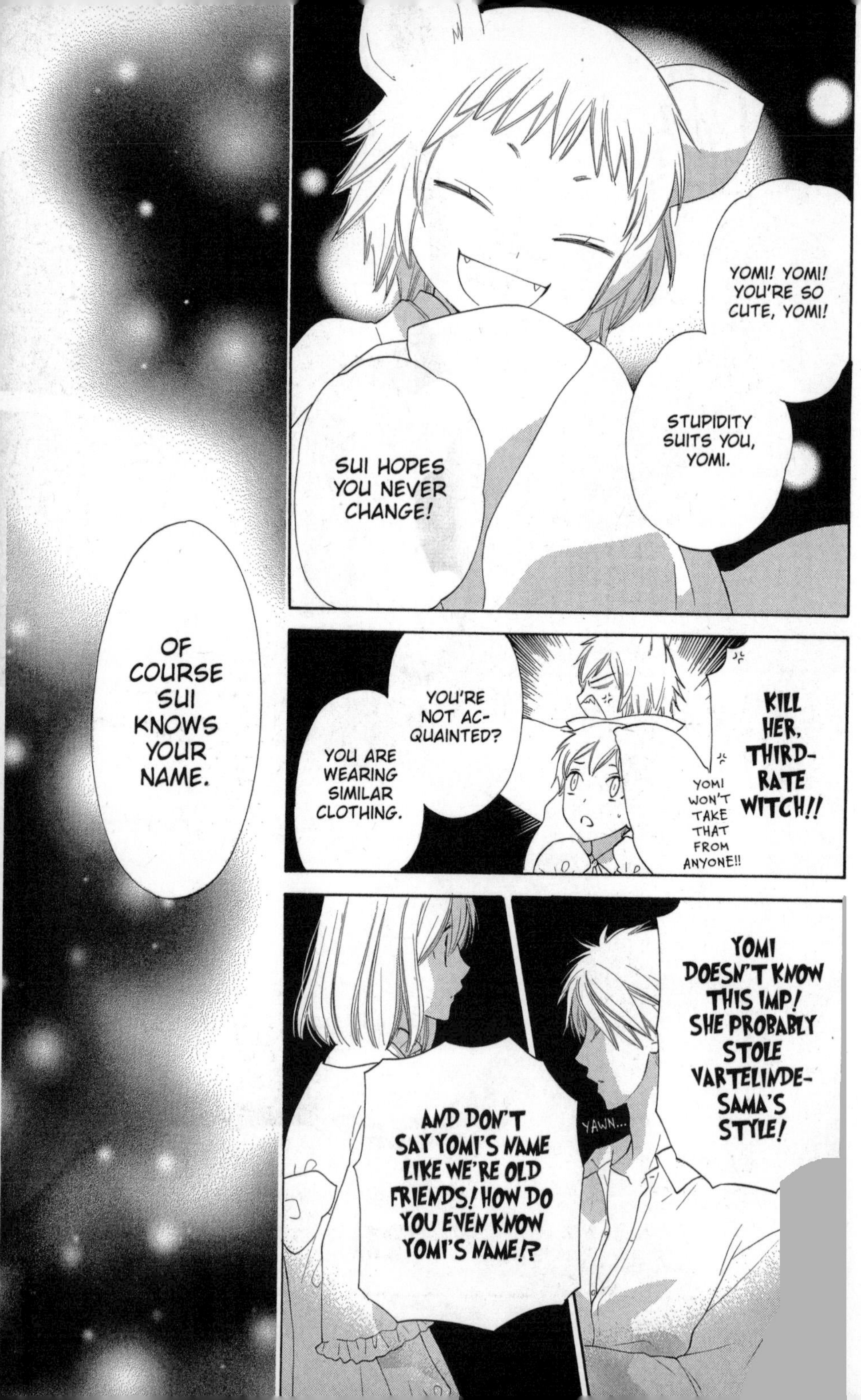
YOMI! YOMI! YOU'RE SO CUTE, YOMI!
STUPIDITY SUITS YOU, YOMI.
SUI HOPES YOU NEVER CHANGE!
KILL HER, THIRD-RATE WITCH!!
YOMI WON'T TAKE THAT FROM ANYONE!!
YOU'RE NOT AC-QUAINTED?
YOU ARE WEARING SIMILAR CLOTHING.
YOMI DOESN'T KNOW THIS IMP! SHE PROBABLY STOLE VARTELINDE-SAMA'S STYLE!
YAWN...
AND DON'T SAY YOMI'S NAME LIKE WE'RE OLD FRIENDS! HOW DO YOU EVEN KNOW YOMI'S NAME!?
OF COURSE SUI KNOWS YOUR NAME.

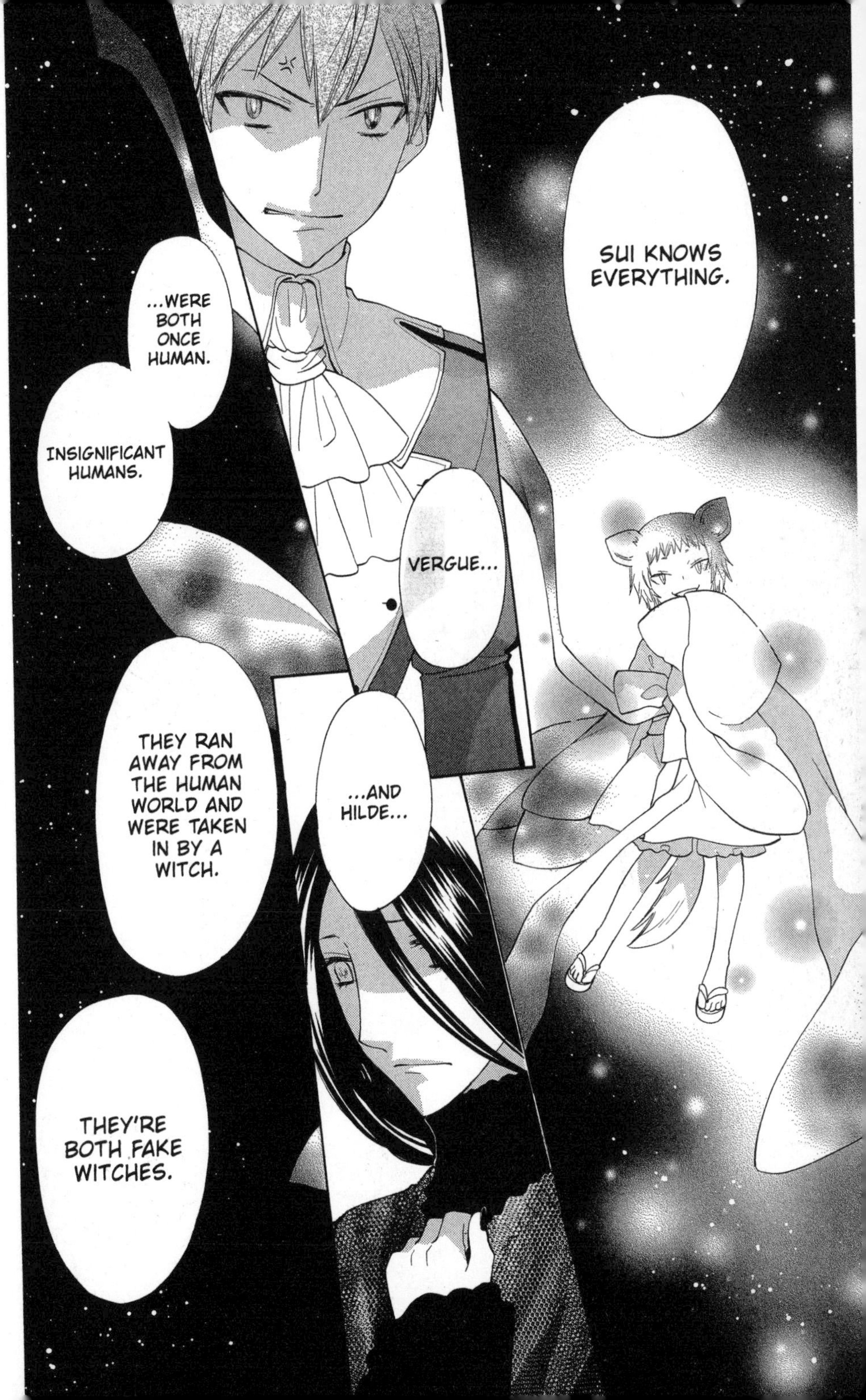
SUI KNOWS EVERYTHING.
VERGUE...
...WERE BOTH ONCE HUMAN.
INSIGNIFICANT HUMANS.
...AND HILDE...
THEY RAN AWAY FROM THE HUMAN WORLD AND WERE TAKEN IN BY A WITCH.
THEY'RE BOTH FAKE WITCHES.

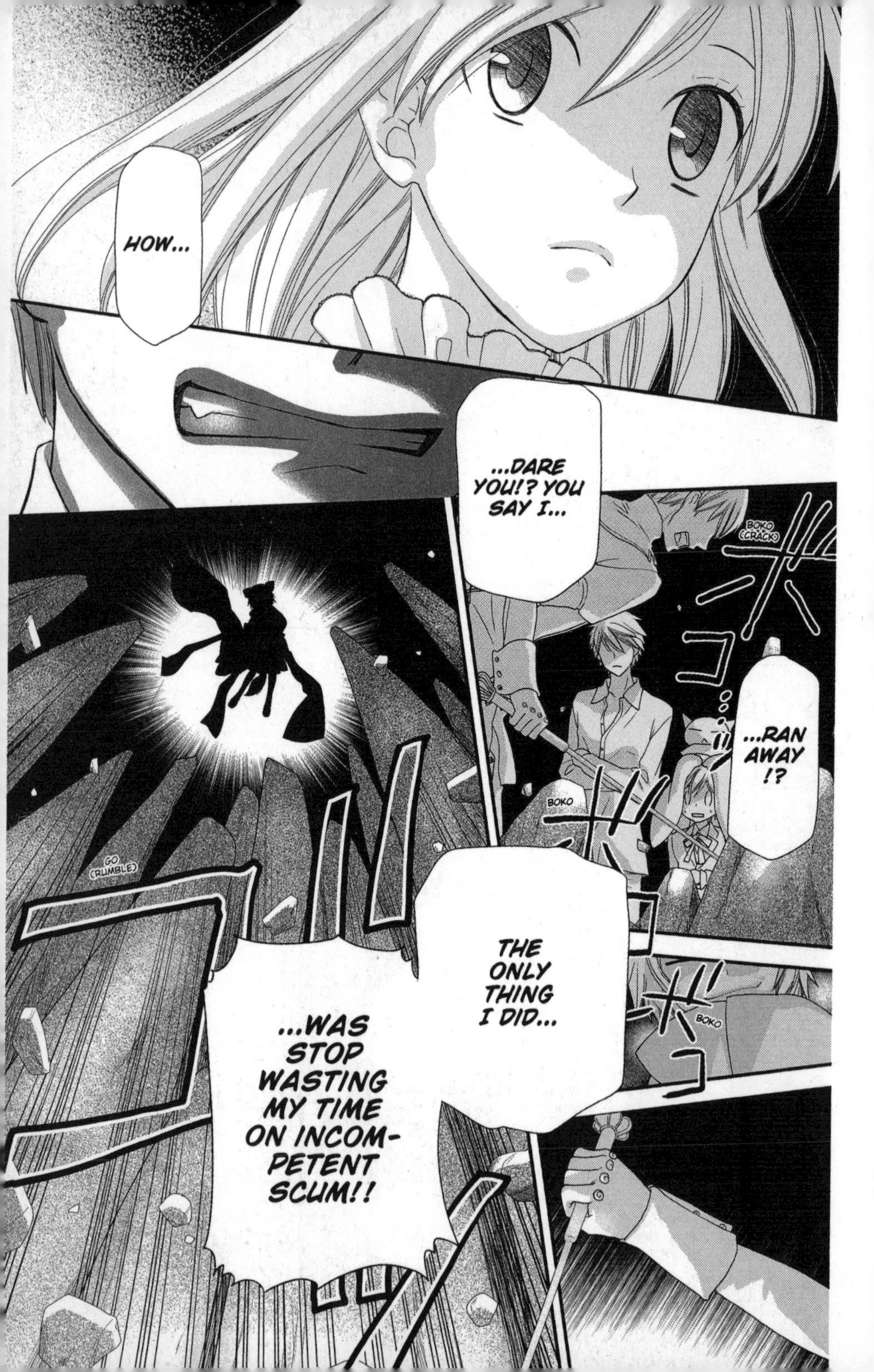
HOW...
...DARE YOU!? YOU SAY I...
BOKO (CRACK)
...RAN AWAY !?
BOKO
THE ONLY THING I DID...
BOKO
GO (RUMBLE)
...WAS STOP WASTING MY TIME ON INCOM-PETENT SCUM!!

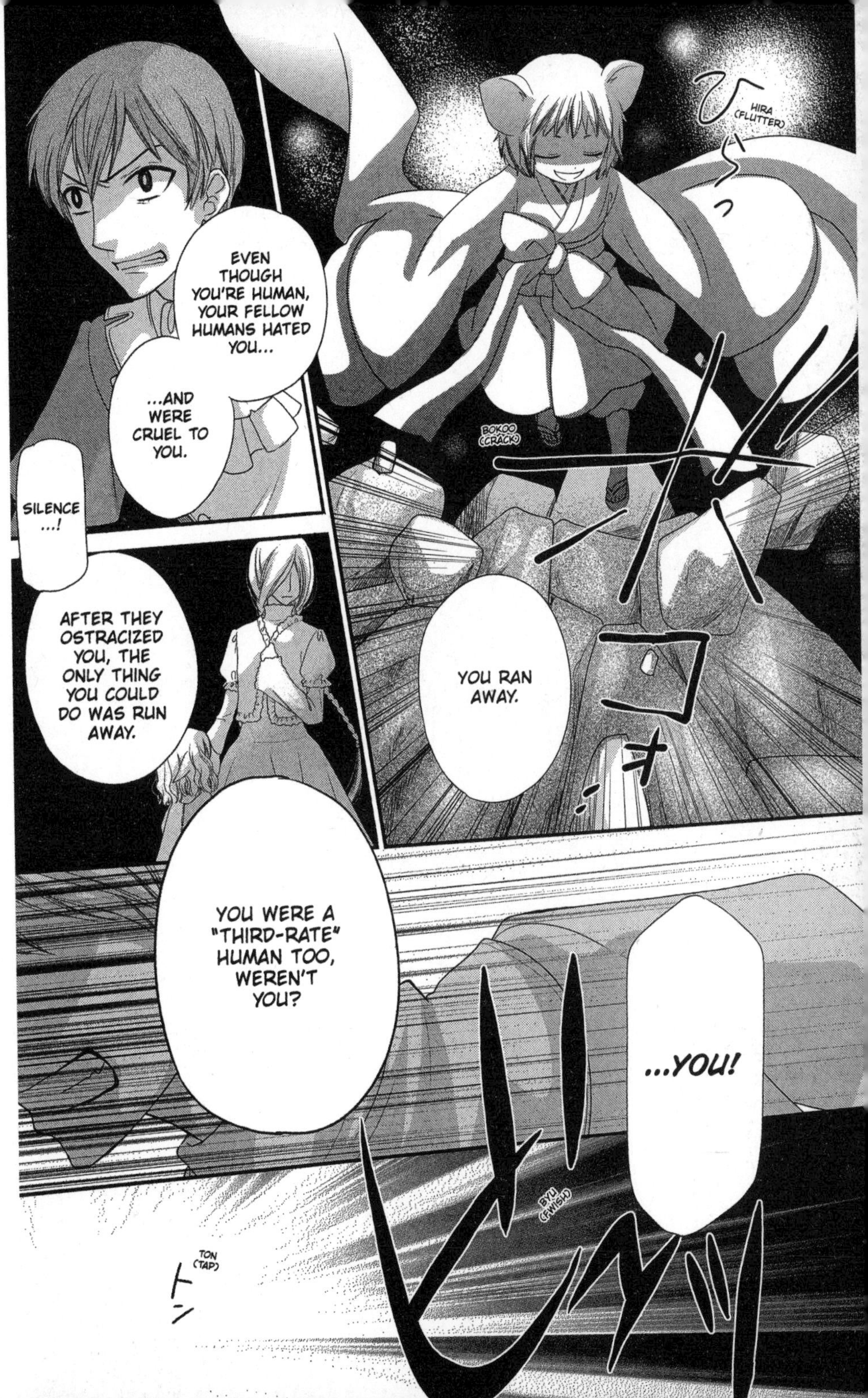
HIRA (FLUTTER)
BOKOO (CRACK)
EVEN THOUGH YOU'RE HUMAN, YOUR FELLOW HUMANS HATED YOU...
...AND WERE CRUEL TO YOU.
SILENCE ...!
AFTER THEY OSTRACIZED YOU, THE ONLY THING YOU COULD DO WAS RUN AWAY.
YOU RAN AWAY.
YOU WERE A "THIRD-RATE" HUMAN TOO, WEREN'T YOU?
...YOU!
BYU (FWISH)
TON (TAP)

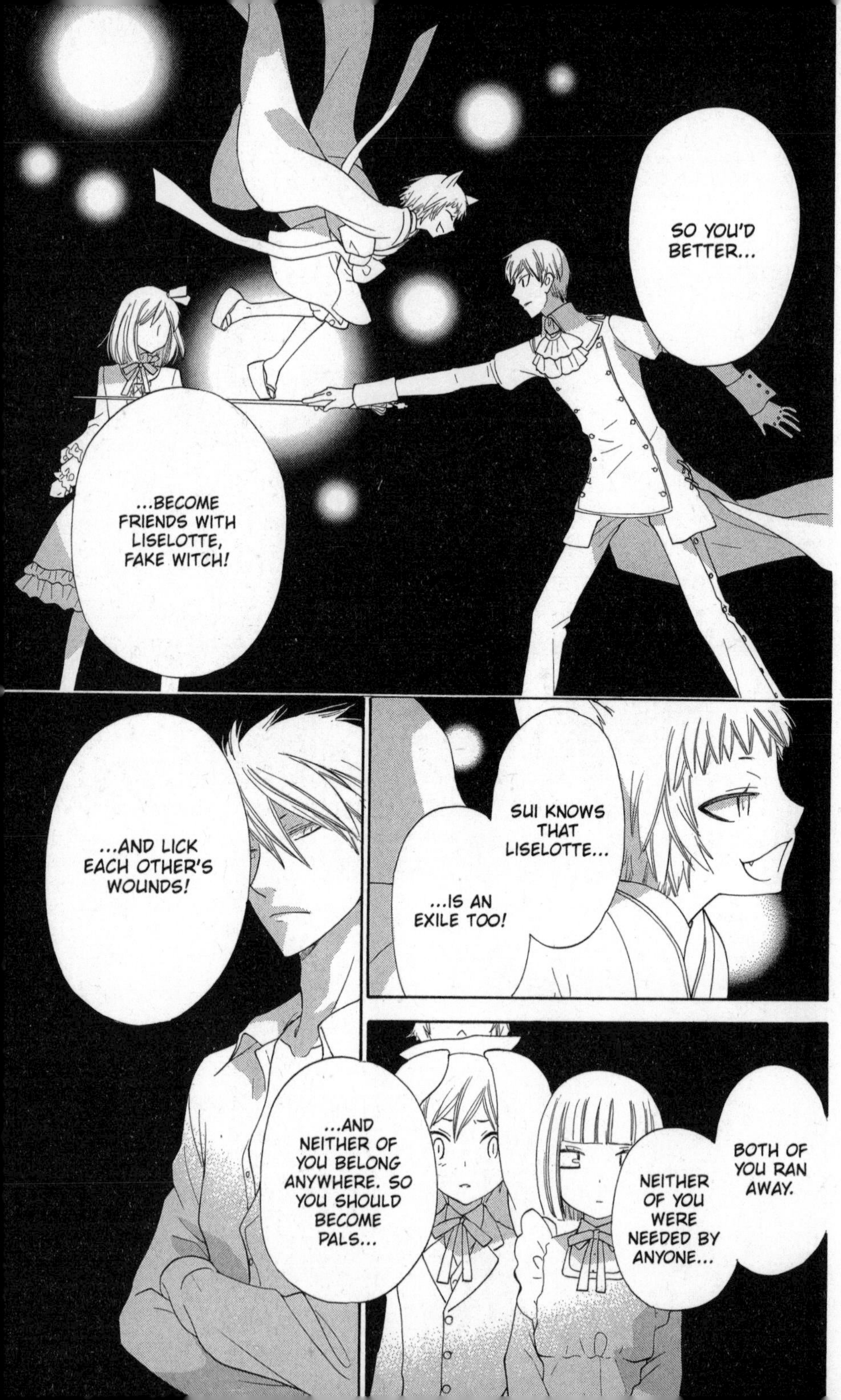
SO YOU'D BETTER...
...BECOME FRIENDS WITH LISELOTTE, FAKE WITCH!
SUI KNOWS THAT LISELOTTE...
...IS AN EXILE TOO!
BOTH OF YOU RAN AWAY.
NEITHER OF YOU WERE NEEDED BY ANYONE...
...AND NEITHER OF YOU BELONG ANYWHERE. SO YOU SHOULD BECOME PALS...
...AND LICK EACH OTHER'S WOUNDS!

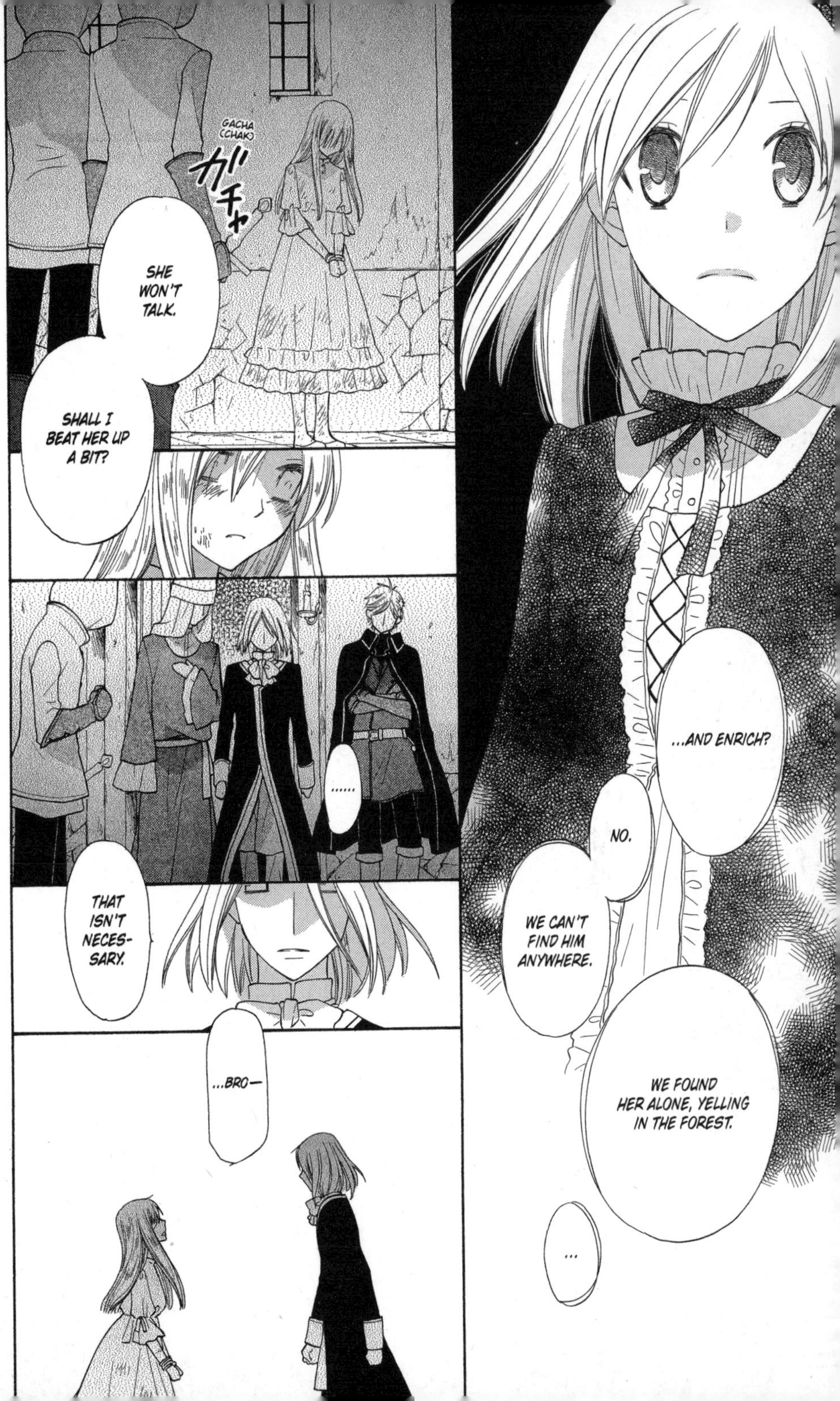
...AND ENRICH?
NO.
WE CAN'T FIND HIM ANYWHERE.
WE FOUND HER ALONE, YELLING IN THE FOREST.
...
GACHA (CHAK)
ガチャ
SHE WON'T TALK.
SHALL I BEAT HER UP A BIT?
......
THAT ISN'T NECES-SARY.
...BRO—

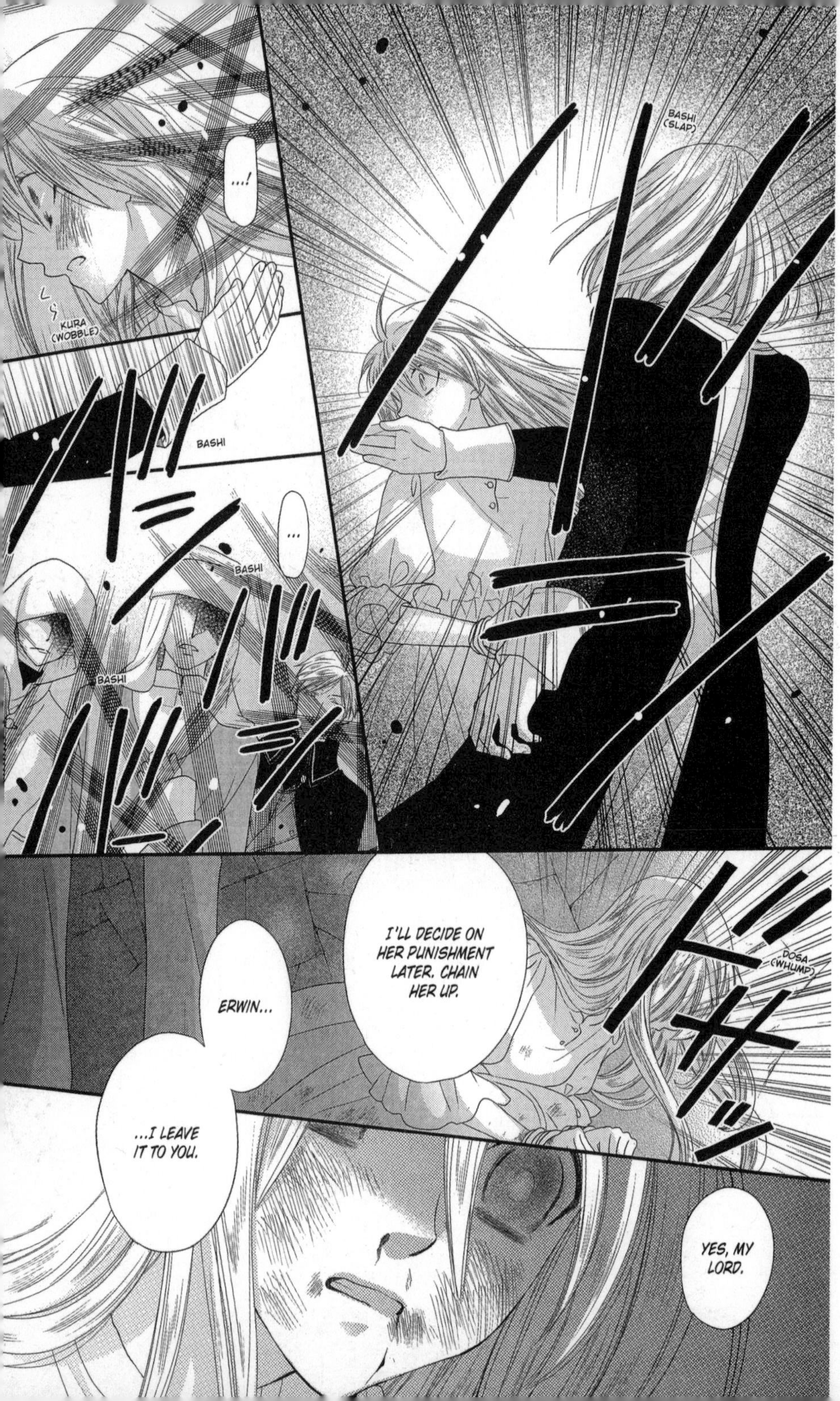
BASHI (SLAP)
...!
KURA (WOBBLE)
BASHI
...
BASHI
BASHI
DOSA (WHUMP)
I'LL DECIDE ON HER PUNISHMENT LATER. CHAIN HER UP.
ERWIN...
...I LEAVE IT TO YOU.
YES, MY LORD.

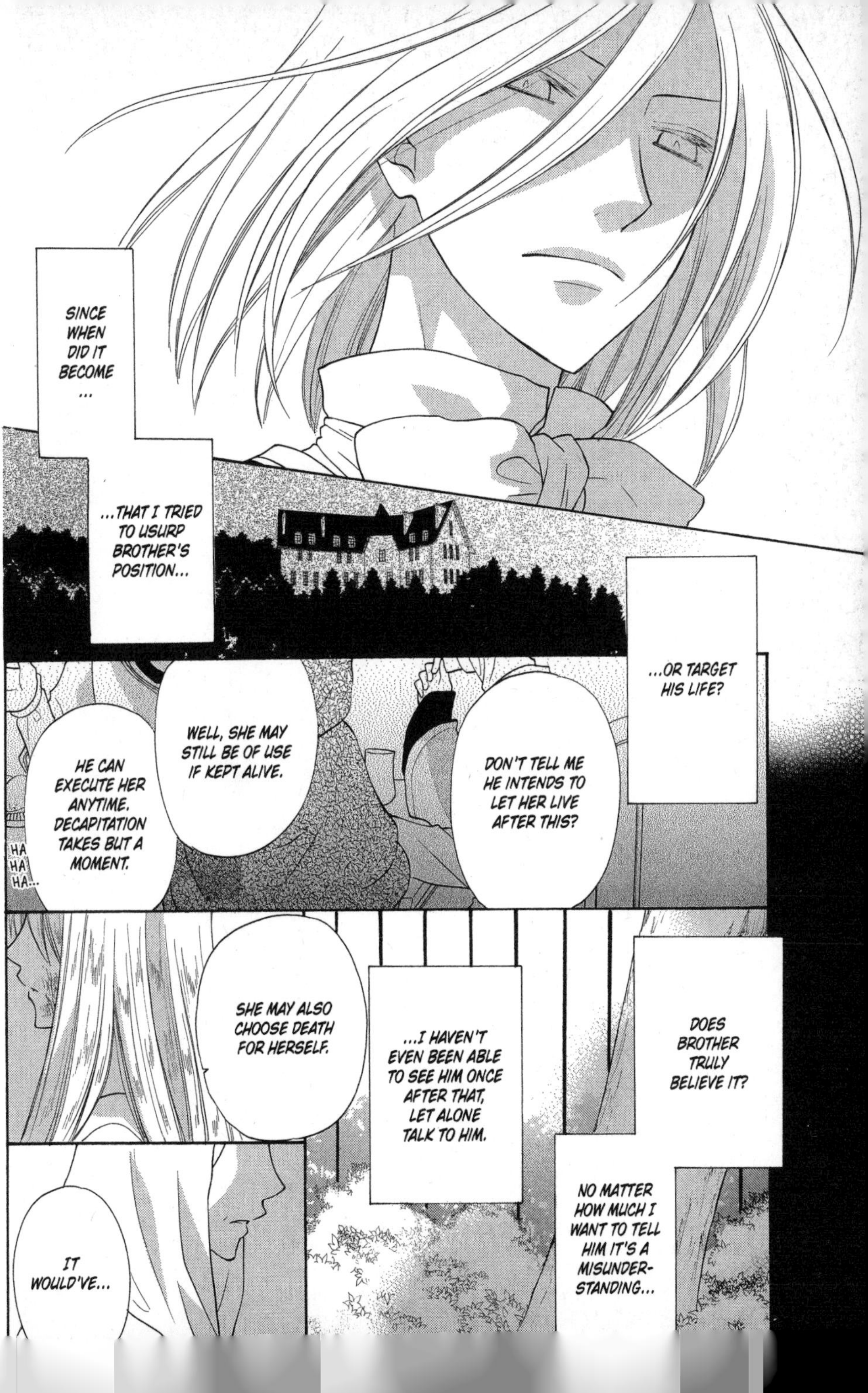
SINCE WHEN DID IT BECOME ...
...THAT I TRIED TO USURP BROTHER'S POSITION...
...OR TARGET HIS LIFE?
DON'T TELL ME HE INTENDS TO LET HER LIVE AFTER THIS?
WELL, SHE MAY STILL BE OF USE IF KEPT ALIVE.
HE CAN EXECUTE HER ANYTIME. DECAPITATION TAKES BUT A MOMENT.
HA HA HA...
DOES BROTHER TRULY BELIEVE IT?
NO MATTER HOW MUCH I WANT TO TELL HIM IT'S A MISUNDERSTANDING...
...I HAVEN'T EVEN BEEN ABLE TO SEE HIM ONCE AFTER THAT, LET ALONE TALK TO HIM.
SHE MAY ALSO CHOOSE DEATH FOR HERSELF.
IT WOULD'VE...

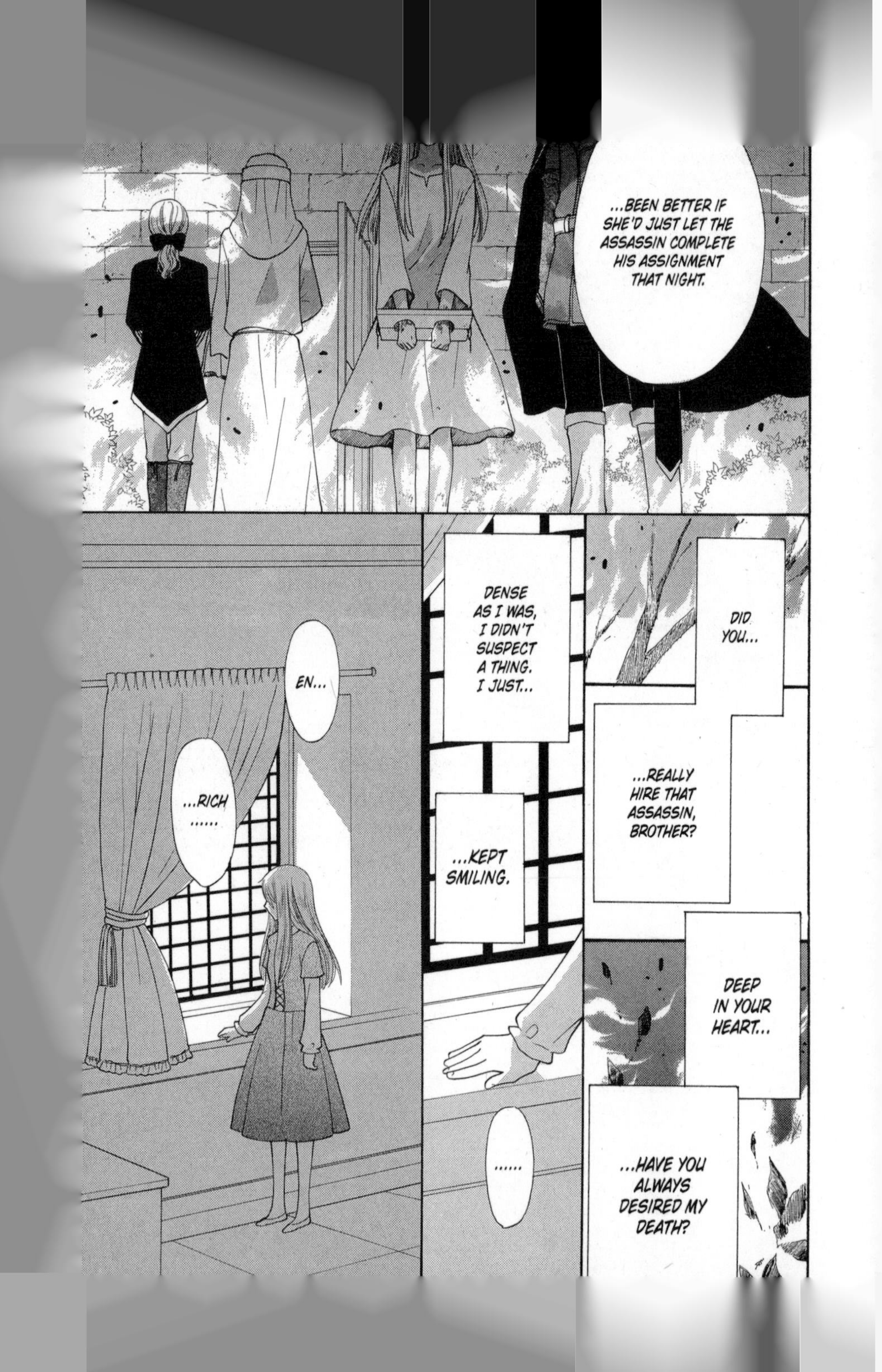
...BEEN BETTER IF SHE'D JUST LET THE ASSASSIN COMPLETE HIS ASSIGNMENT THAT NIGHT.
DID YOU...
...REALLY HIRE THAT ASSASSIN, BROTHER?
DEEP IN YOUR HEART...
...HAVE YOU ALWAYS DESIRED MY DEATH?
DENSE AS I WAS, I DIDN'T SUSPECT A THING. I JUST...
...KEPT SMILING.
......
EN...
...RICH ......

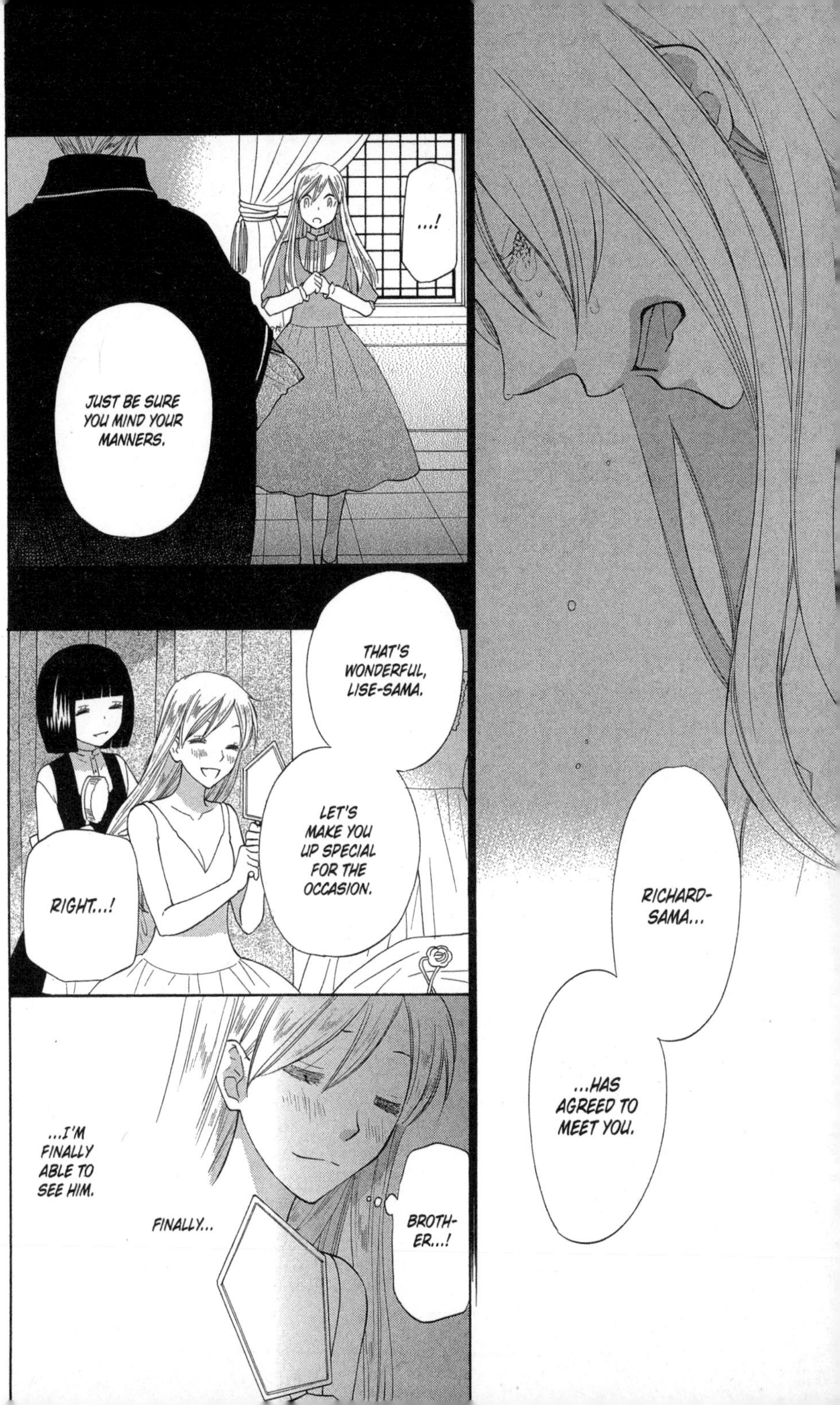
RICHARD-SAMA...
...HAS AGREED TO MEET YOU.
...!
JUST BE SURE YOU MIND YOUR MANNERS.
THAT'S WONDERFUL, LISE-SAMA.
LET'S MAKE YOU UP SPECIAL FOR THE OCCASION.
RIGHT...!
BROTH-ER...!
FINALLY...
...I'M FINALLY ABLE TO SEE HIM.

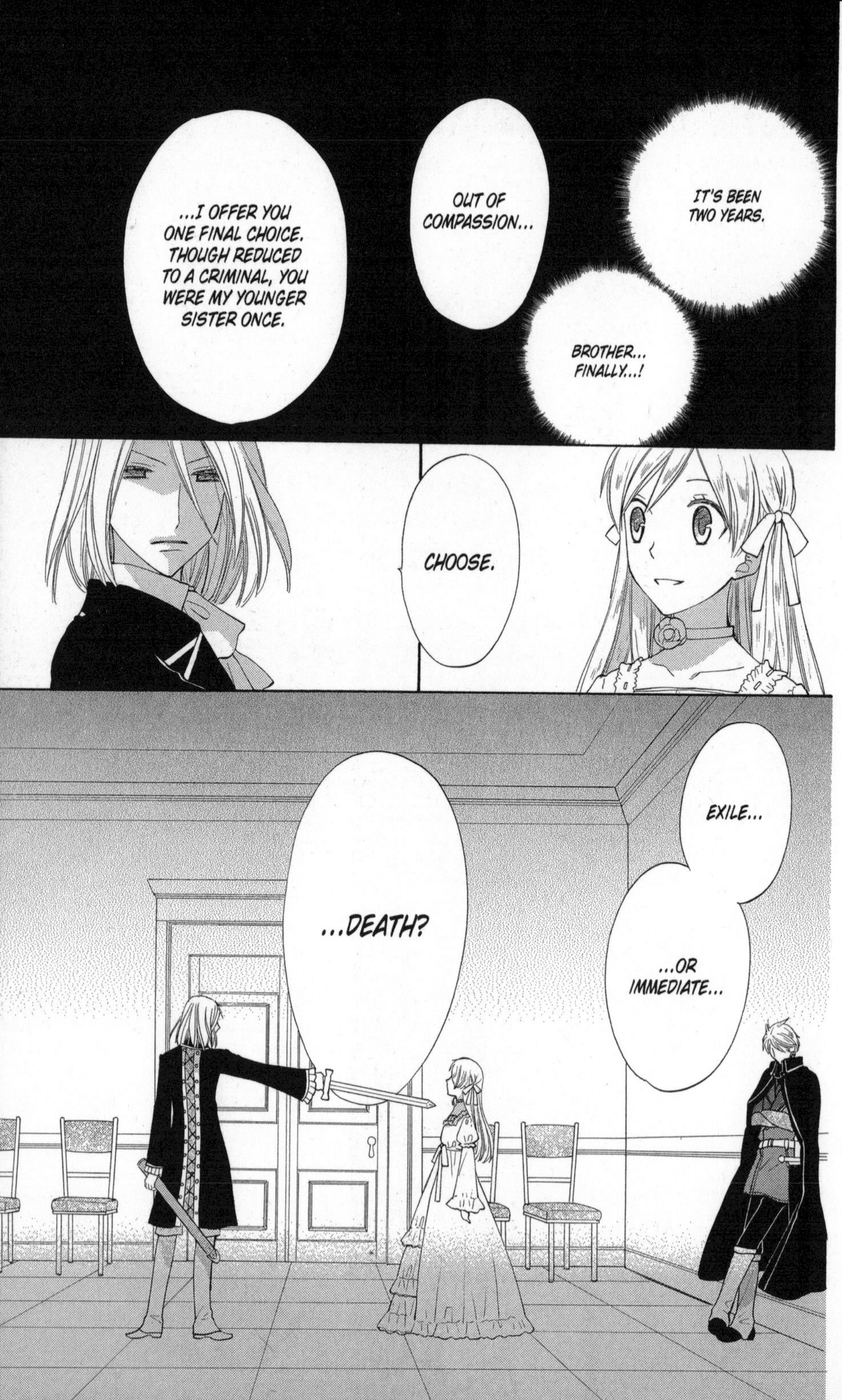
IT'S BEEN TWO YEARS.
BROTHER... FINALLY...!
OUT OF COMPASSION...
...I OFFER YOU ONE FINAL CHOICE. THOUGH REDUCED TO A CRIMINAL, YOU WERE MY YOUNGER SISTER ONCE.
CHOOSE.
EXILE...
...OR IMMEDIATE...
...DEATH?

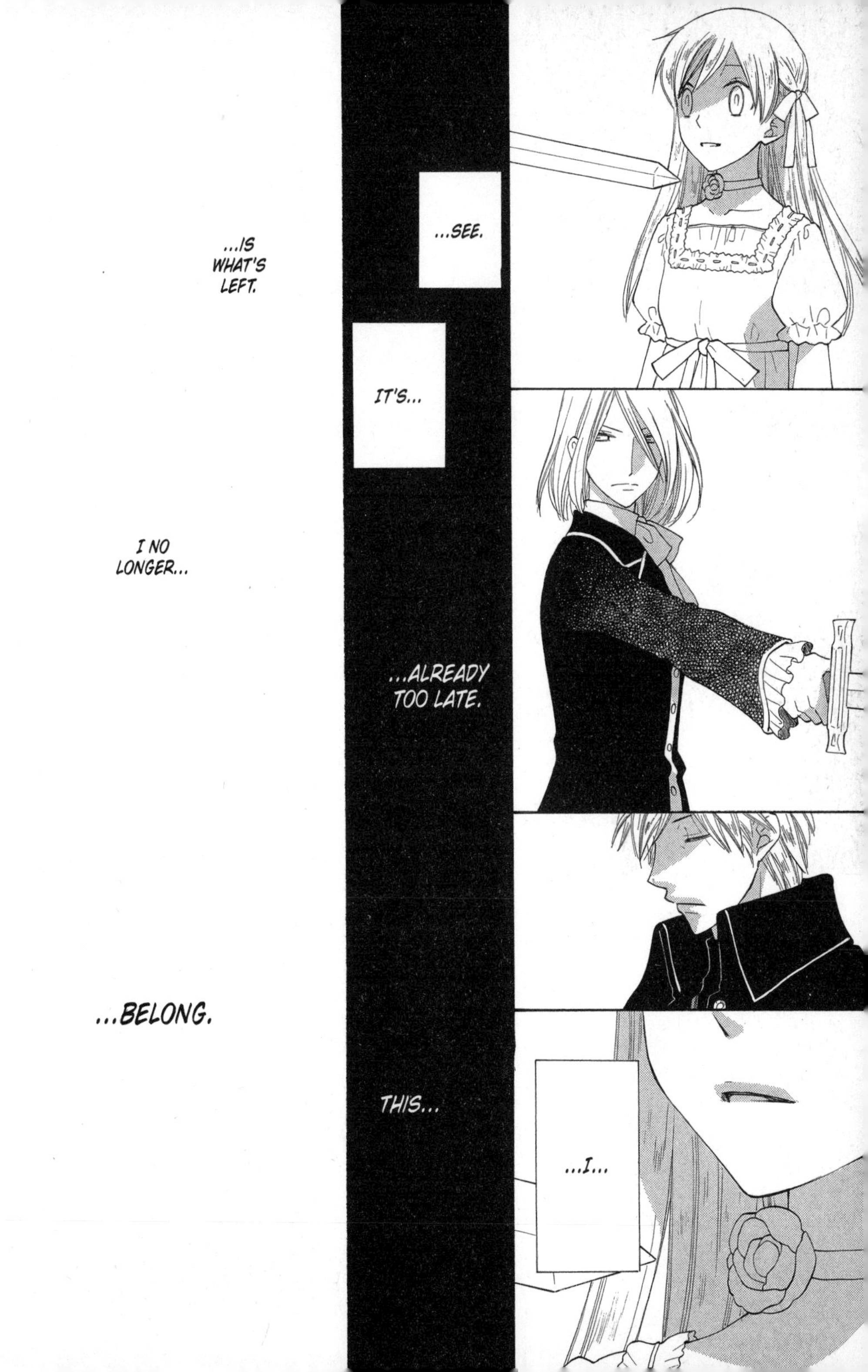
...SEE.
IT'S...
...ALREADY TOO LATE.
THIS...
...I...
...IS WHAT'S LEFT.
I NO LONGER...
...BELONG.

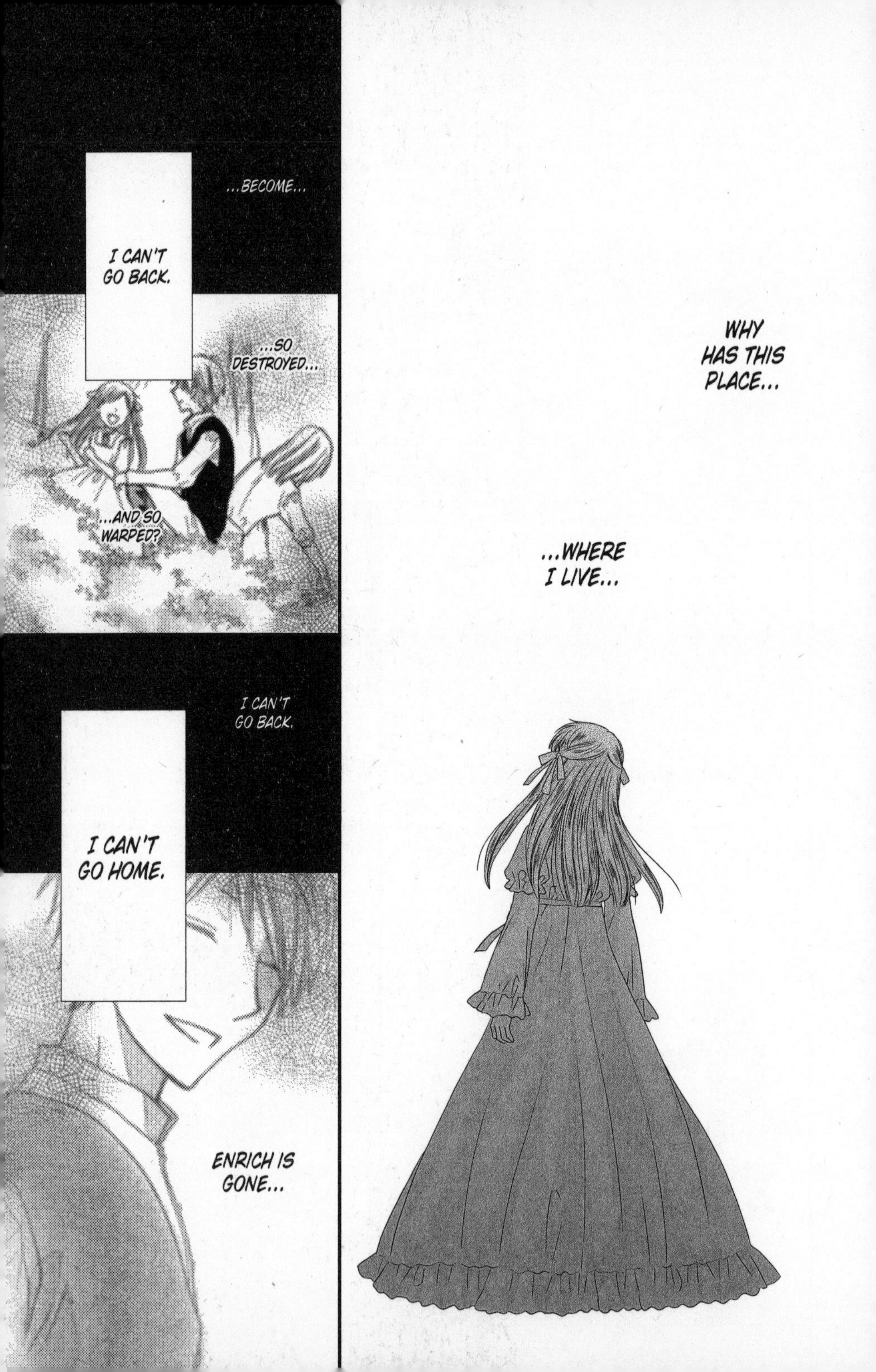
WHY HAS THIS PLACE...
...WHERE I LIVE...
...BECOME...
I CAN'T GO BACK.
...SO DESTROYED...
...AND SO WARPED?
I CAN'T GO BACK.
I CAN'T GO HOME.
ENRICH IS GONE...

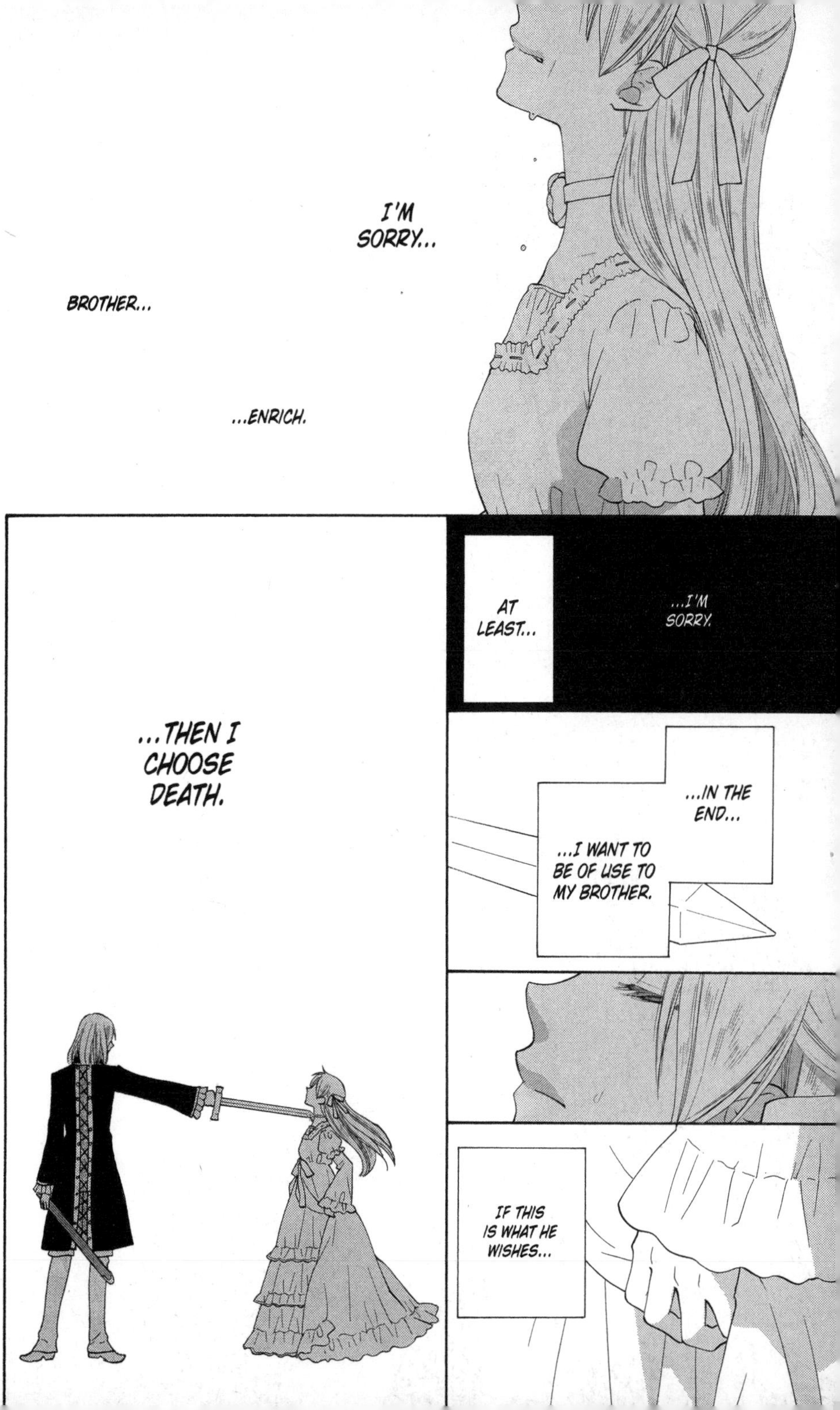
I'M SORRY...
BROTHER...
...ENRICH.
...I'M SORRY.
AT LEAST...
...IN THE END...
...I WANT TO BE OF USE TO MY BROTHER.
IF THIS IS WHAT HE WISHES...
...THEN I CHOOSE DEATH.

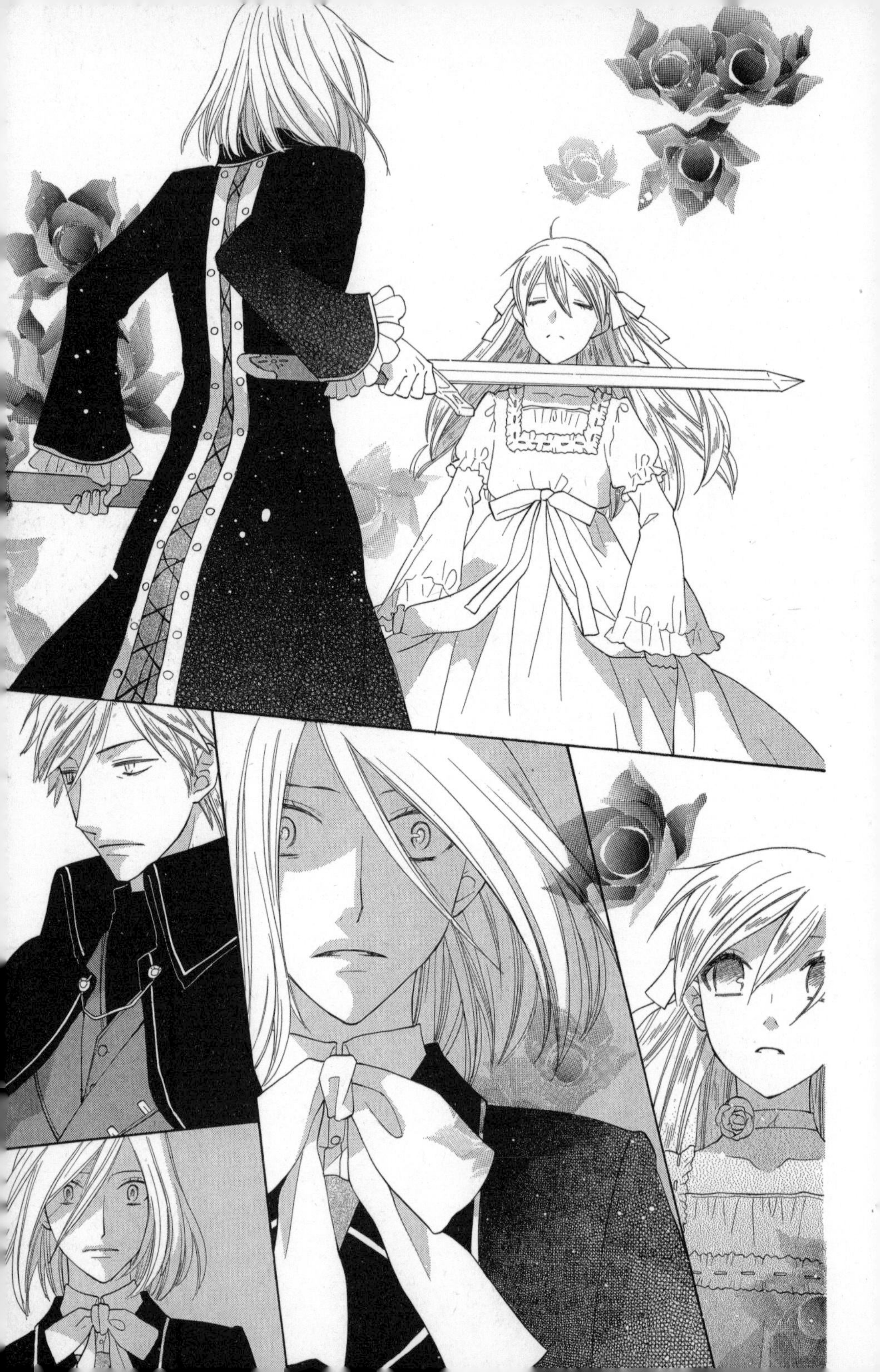

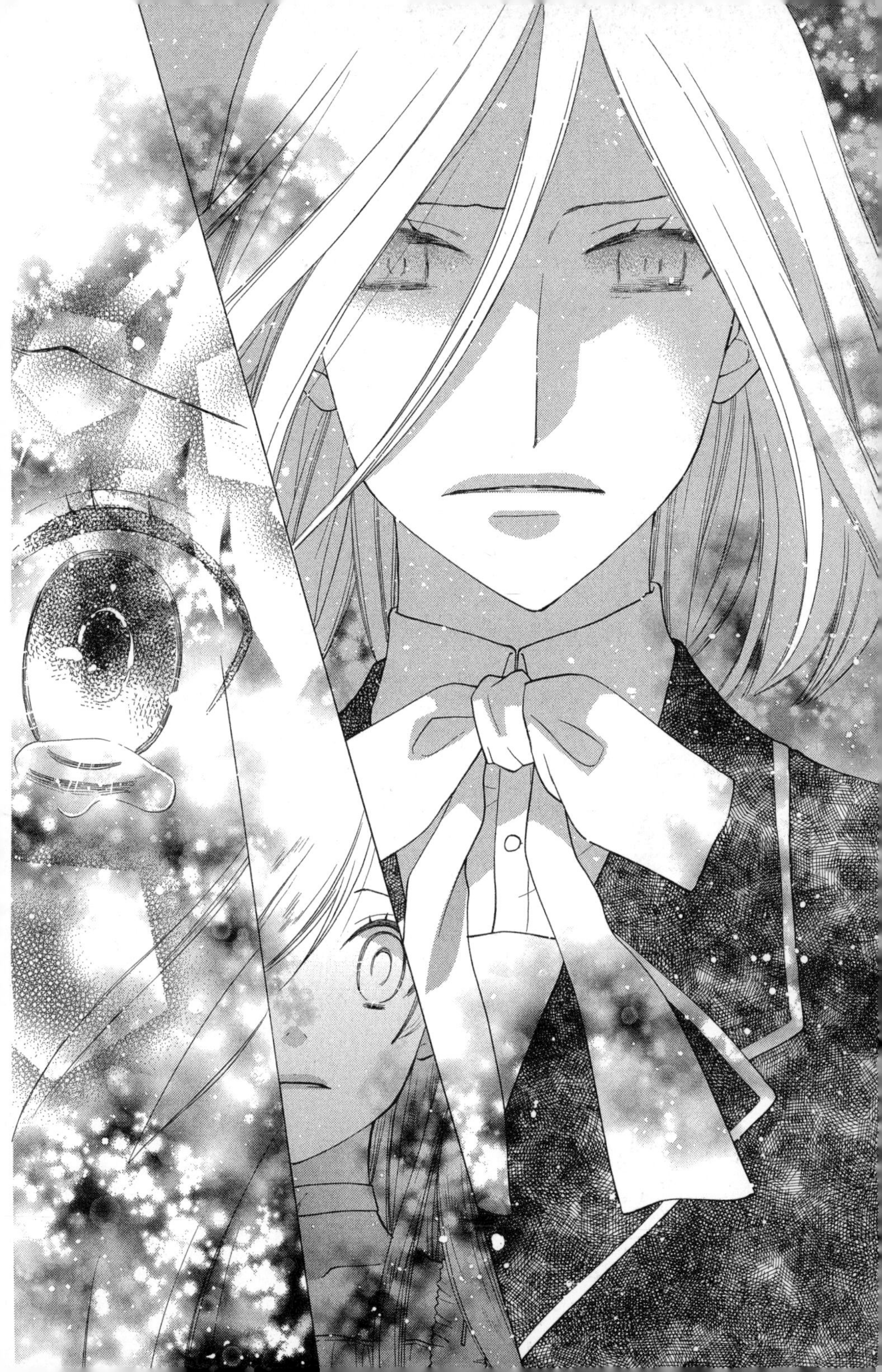

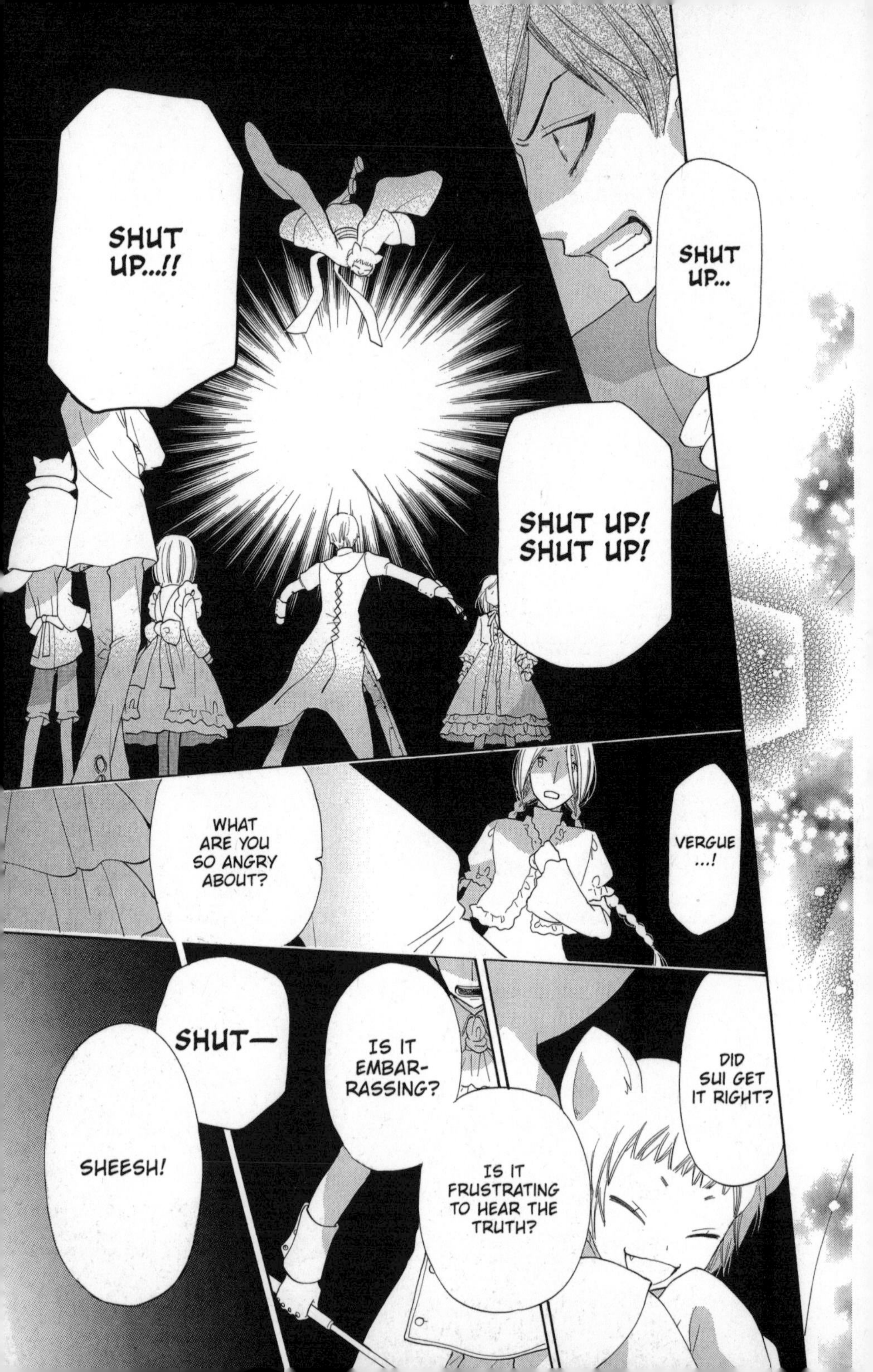
SHUT UP...
SHUT UP! SHUT UP!
SHUT UP...!!
VERGUE ...!
WHAT ARE YOU SO ANGRY ABOUT?
DID SUI GET IT RIGHT?
IS IT FRUSTRATING TO HEAR THE TRUTH?
IS IT EMBARRASSING?
SHUT—
SHEESH!

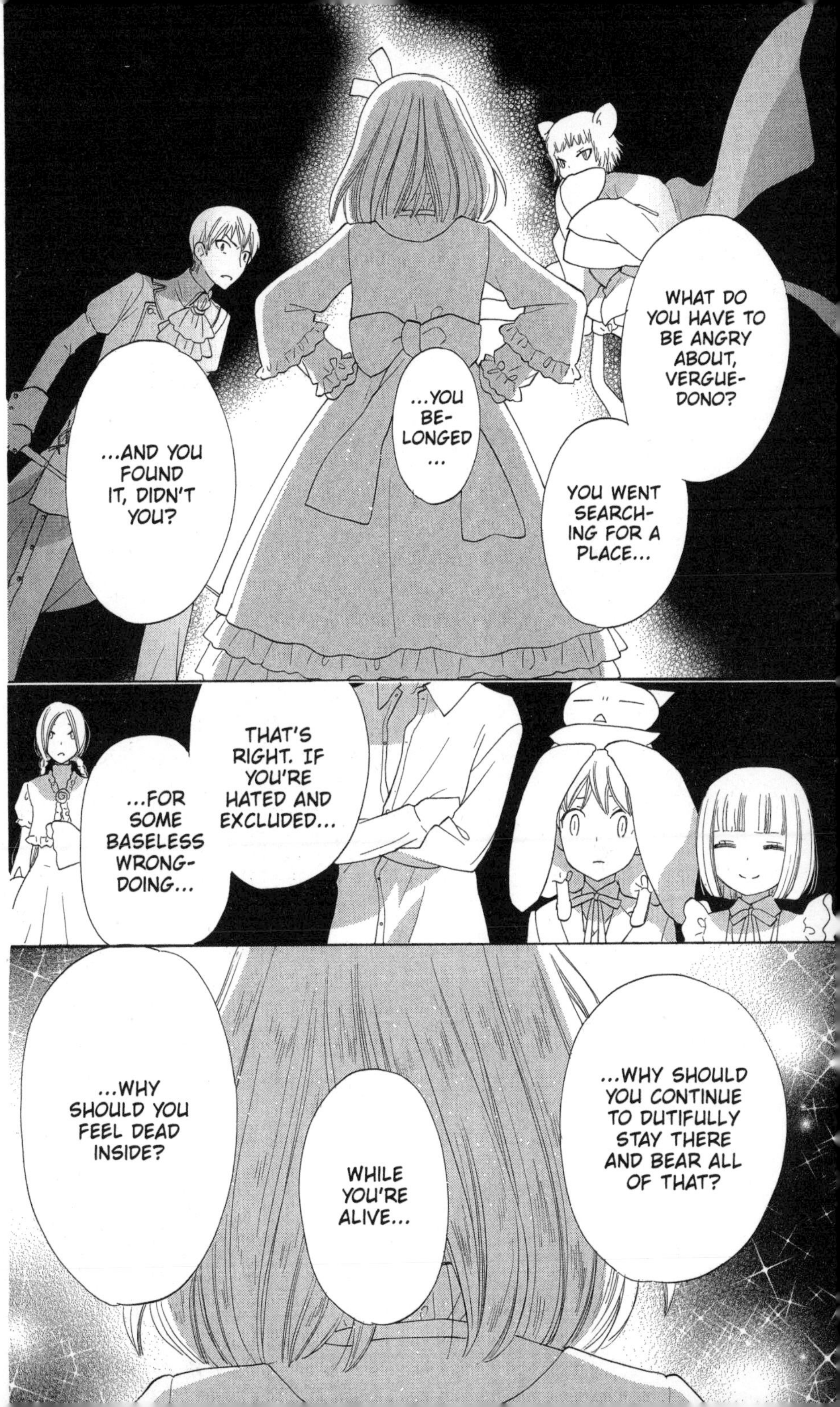
WHAT DO YOU HAVE TO BE ANGRY ABOUT, VERGUE-DONO?
YOU WENT SEARCHING FOR A PLACE...
...YOU BELONGED...
...AND YOU FOUND IT, DIDN'T YOU?
THAT'S RIGHT. IF YOU'RE HATED AND EXCLUDED...
...FOR SOME BASELESS WRONGDOING...
...WHY SHOULD YOU CONTINUE TO DUTIFULLY STAY THERE AND BEAR ALL OF THAT?
WHILE YOU'RE ALIVE...
...WHY SHOULD YOU FEEL DEAD INSIDE?

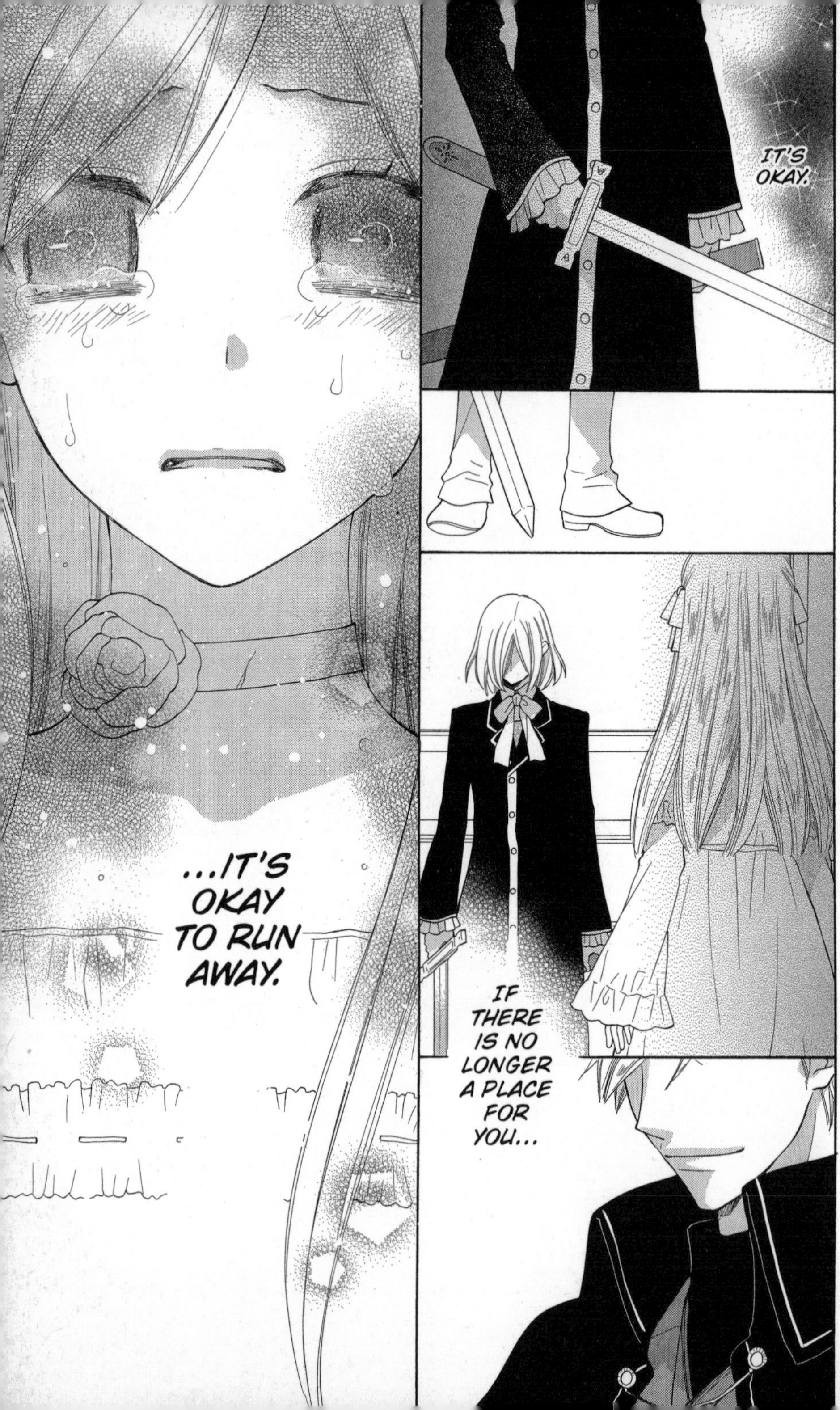
IT'S OKAY.
IF THERE IS NO LONGER A PLACE FOR YOU...
...IT'S OKAY TO RUN AWAY.

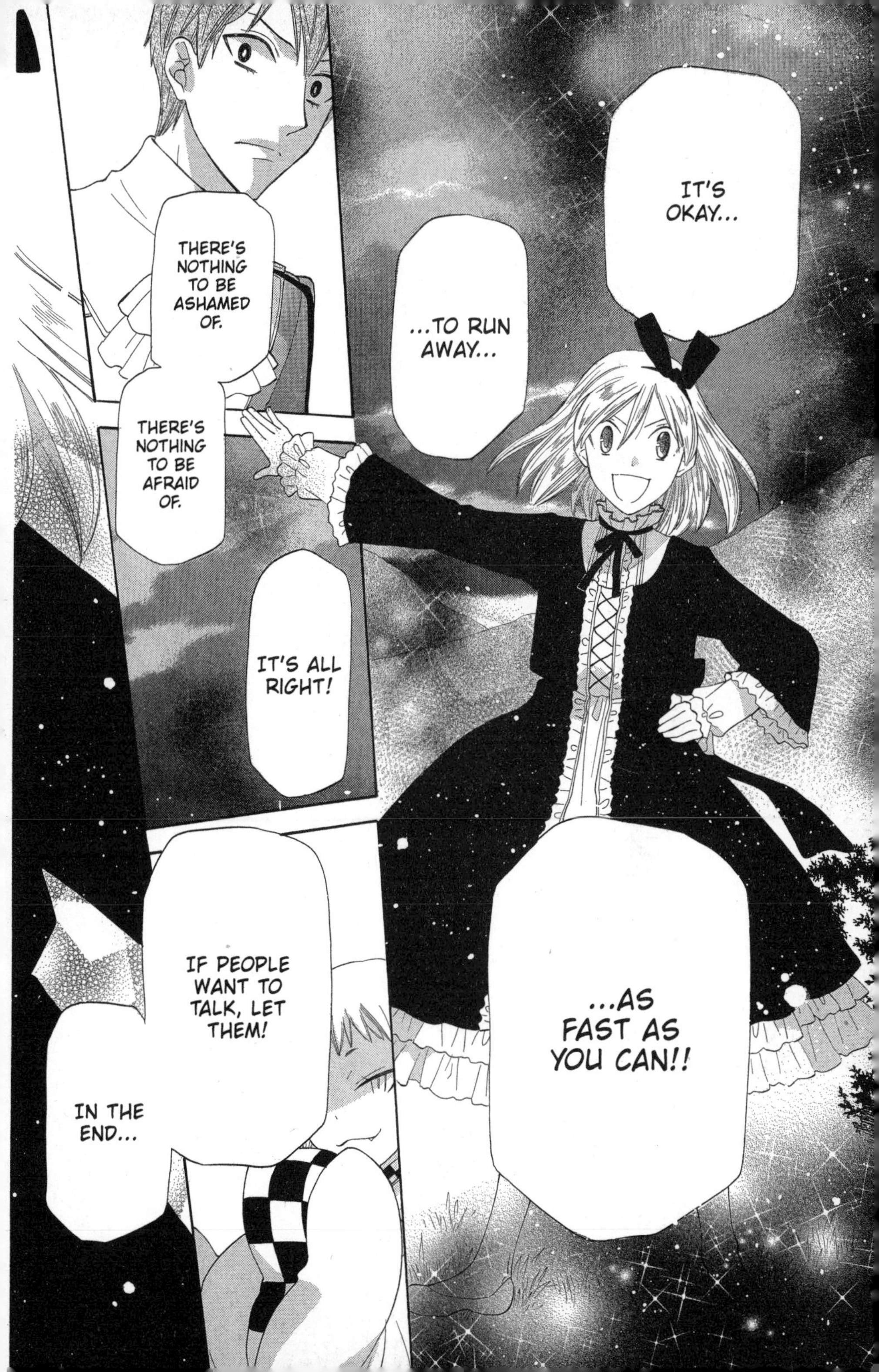
IT'S OKAY...
...TO RUN AWAY...
...AS FAST AS YOU CAN!!
THERE'S NOTHING TO BE ASHAMED OF.
THERE'S NOTHING TO BE AFRAID OF.
IT'S ALL RIGHT!
IF PEOPLE WANT TO TALK, LET THEM!
IN THE END...

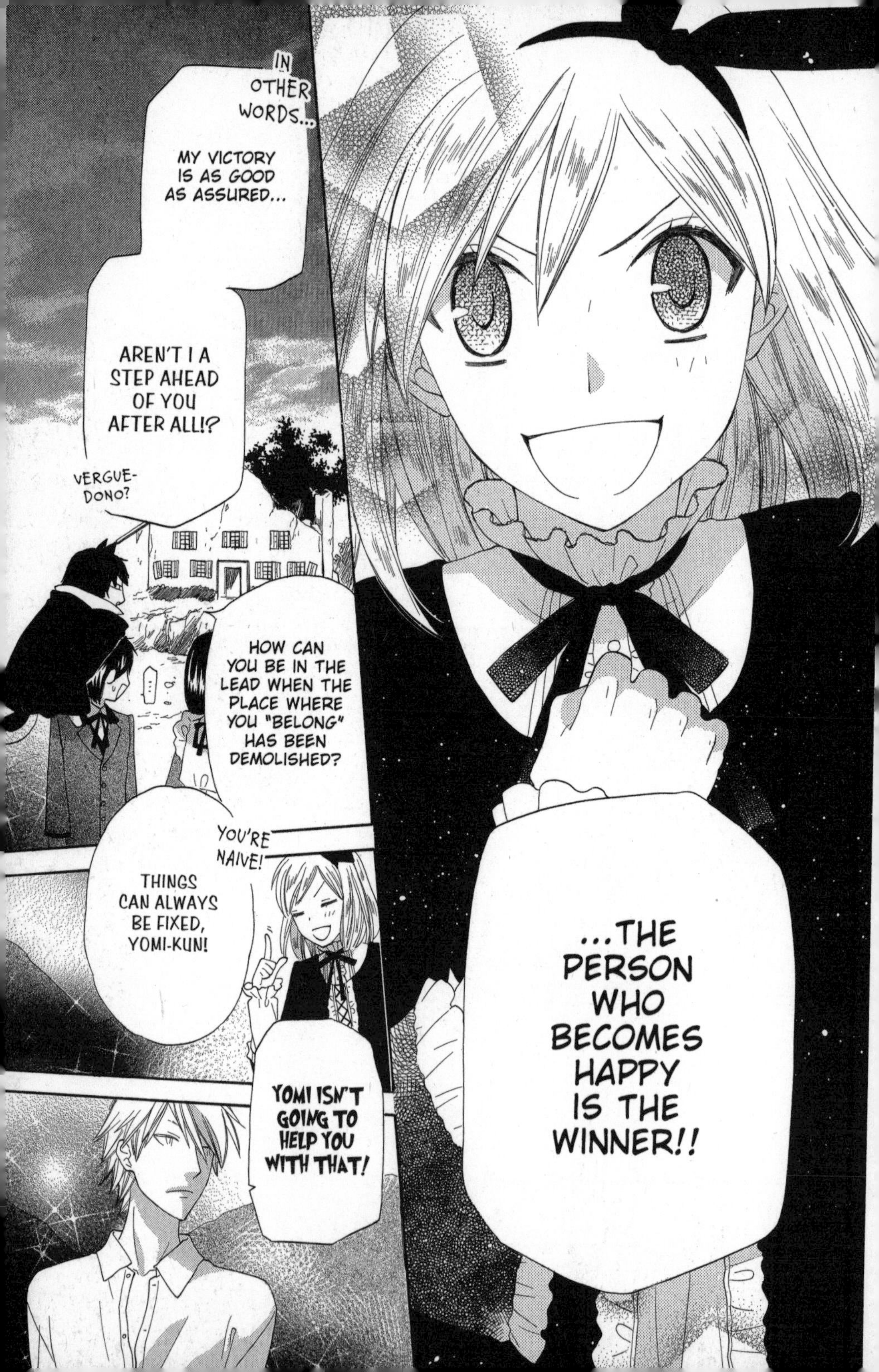

IN OTHER WORDS...
MY VICTORY IS AS GOOD AS ASSURED...
AREN'T I A STEP AHEAD OF YOU AFTER ALL!?
VERGUE-DONO?
HOW CAN YOU BE IN THE LEAD WHEN THE PLACE WHERE YOU "BELONG" HAS BEEN DEMOLISHED?
YOU'RE NAIVE!
THINGS CAN ALWAYS BE FIXED, YOMI-KUN!
YOMI ISN'T GOING TO HELP YOU WITH THAT!
...THE PERSON WHO BECOMES HAPPY IS THE WINNER!!

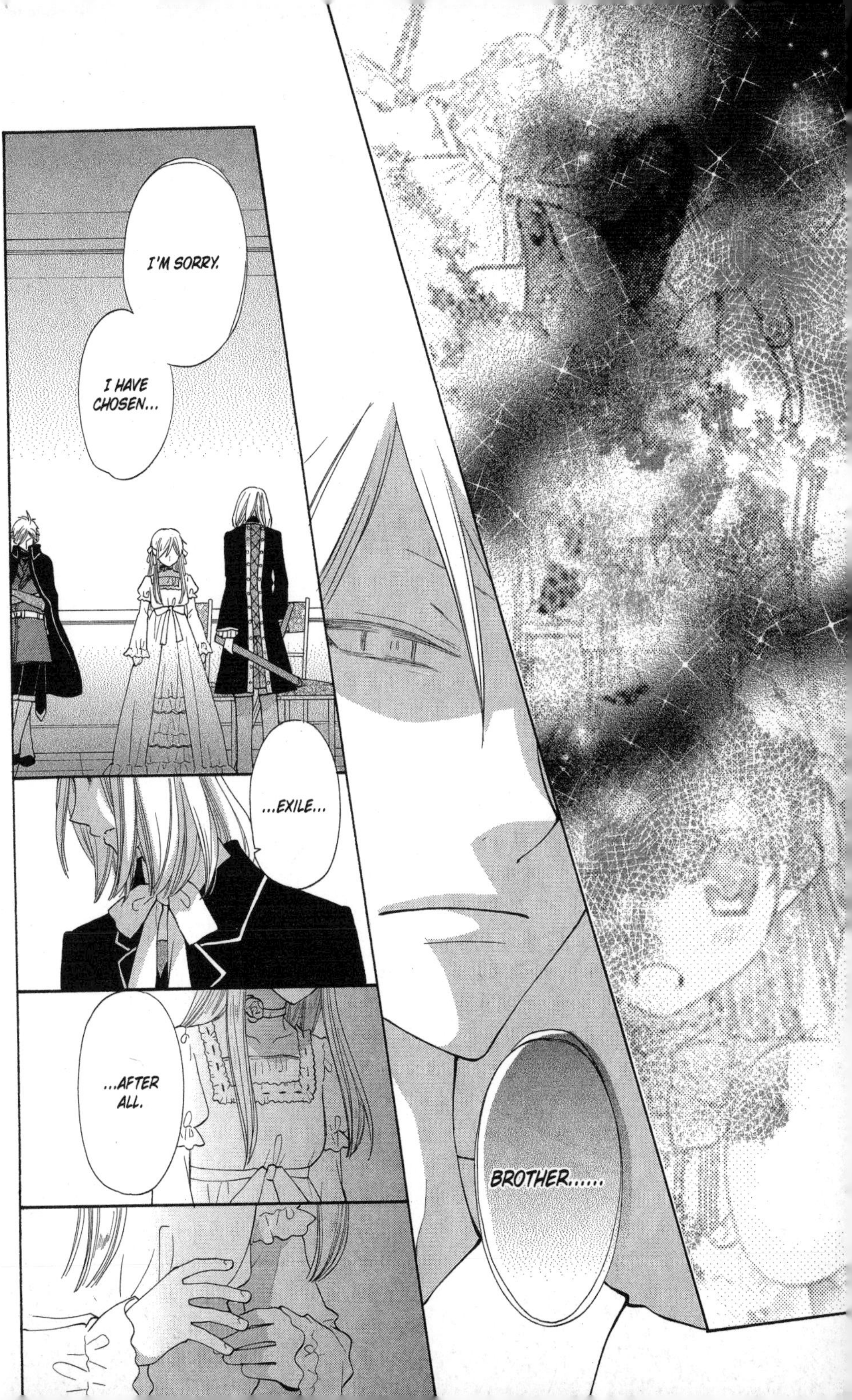
BROTHER......
I'M SORRY.
I HAVE CHOSEN...
...EXILE...
...AFTER ALL.

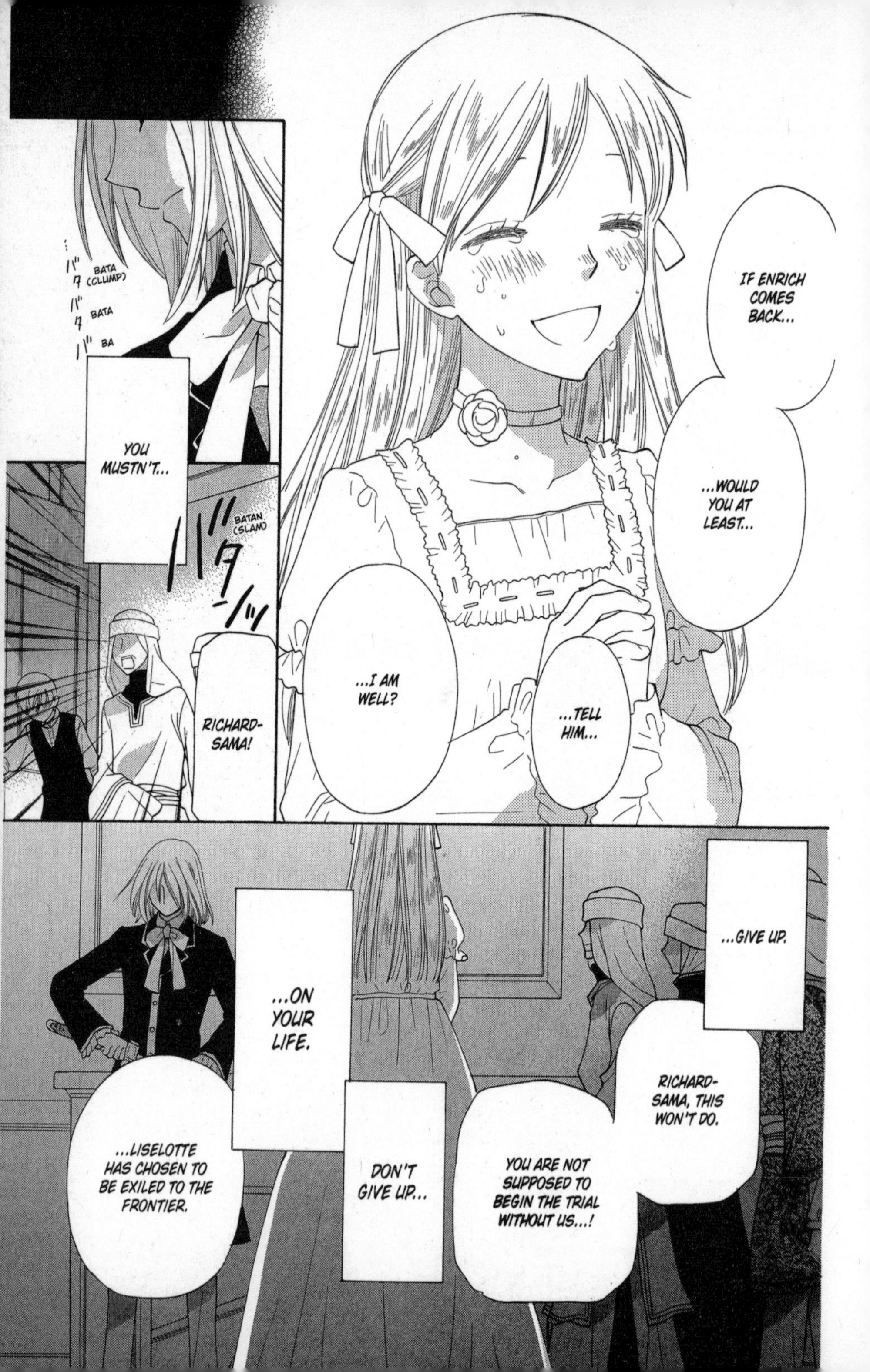
IF ENRICH COMES BACK...
...WOULD YOU AT LEAST...
...TELL HIM...
...I AM WELL?
BATA (CLUMP)
BATA
BA
YOU MUSTN'T...
BATAN (SLAM)
RICHARD-SAMA!
...GIVE UP.
RICHARD-SAMA, THIS WON'T DO.
YOU ARE NOT SUPPOSED TO BEGIN THE TRIAL WITHOUT US...!
DON'T GIVE UP...
...ON YOUR LIFE.
...LISELOTTE HAS CHOSEN TO BE EXILED TO THE FRONTIER.

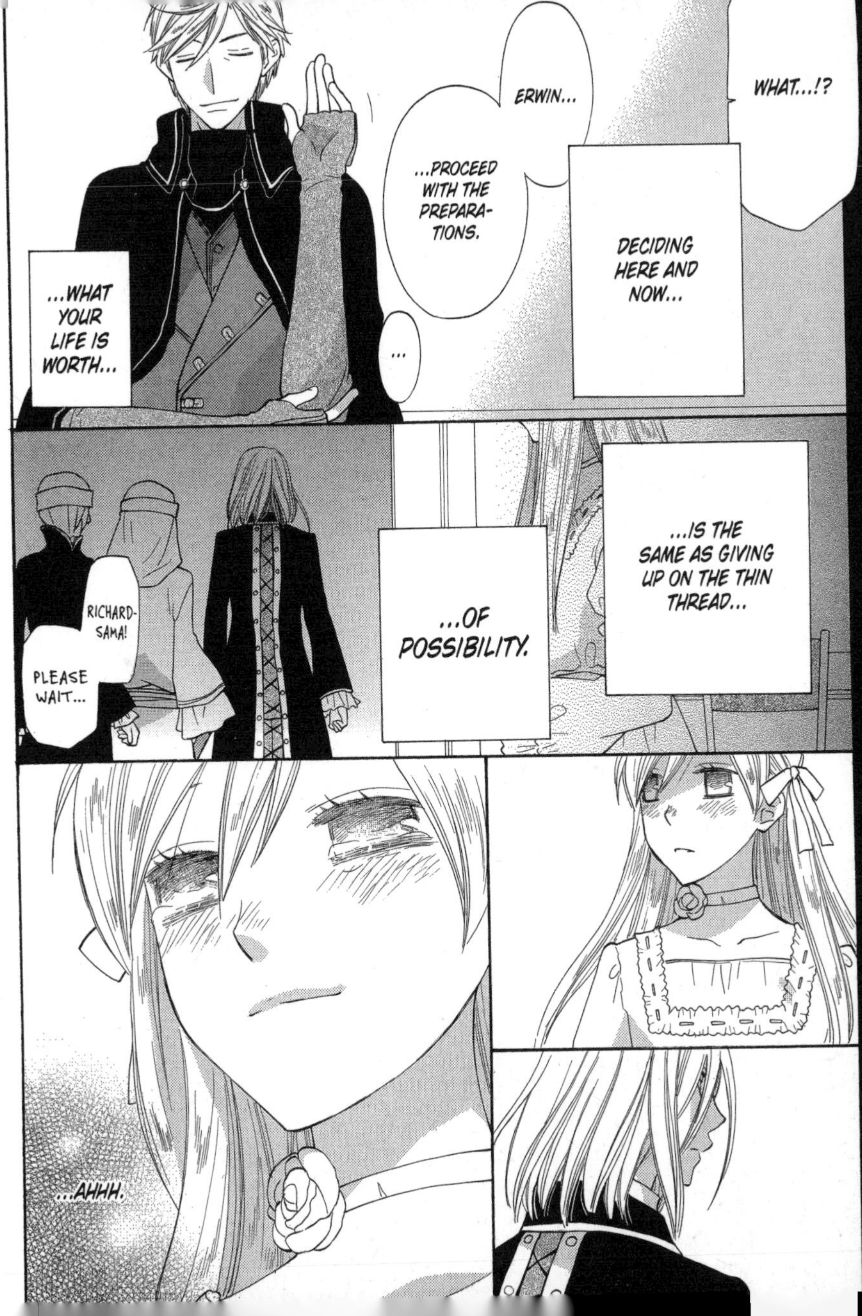
WHAT...!?
ERWIN...
...PROCEED WITH THE PREPARATIONS.
DECIDING HERE AND NOW...
...
...WHAT YOUR LIFE IS WORTH...
...IS THE SAME AS GIVING UP ON THE THIN THREAD...
...OF POSSIBILITY.
RICHARD-SAMA!
PLEASE WAIT...
...AHHH.

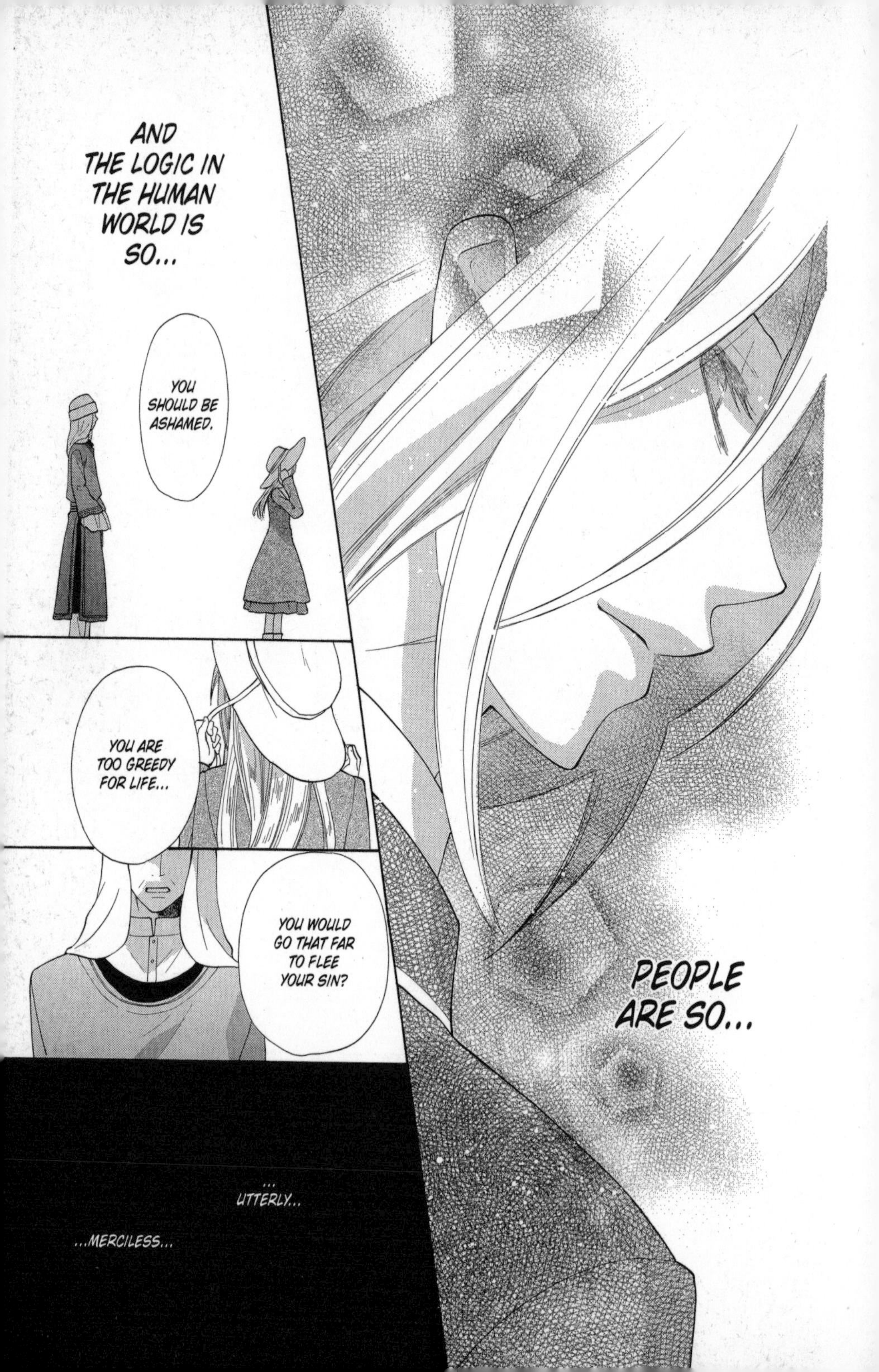
PEOPLE ARE SO...
AND THE LOGIC IN THE HUMAN WORLD IS SO...
YOU SHOULD BE ASHAMED.
YOU ARE TOO GREEDY FOR LIFE...
YOU WOULD GO THAT FAR TO FLEE YOUR SIN?
... UTTERLY...
...MERCILESS...

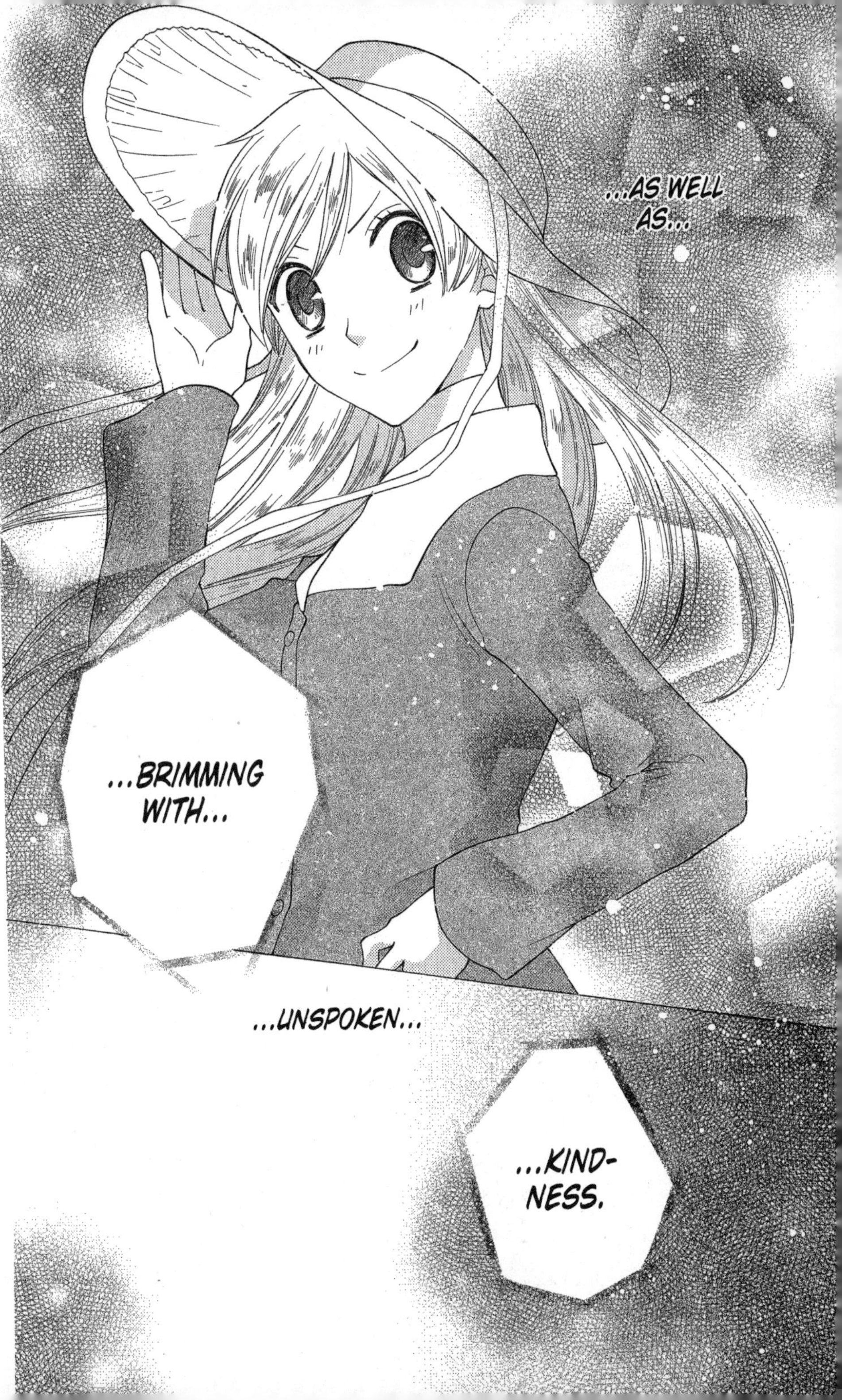
...AS WELL AS...
...BRIMMING WITH...
...UNSPOKEN...
...KIND-NESS.

Chapter 22

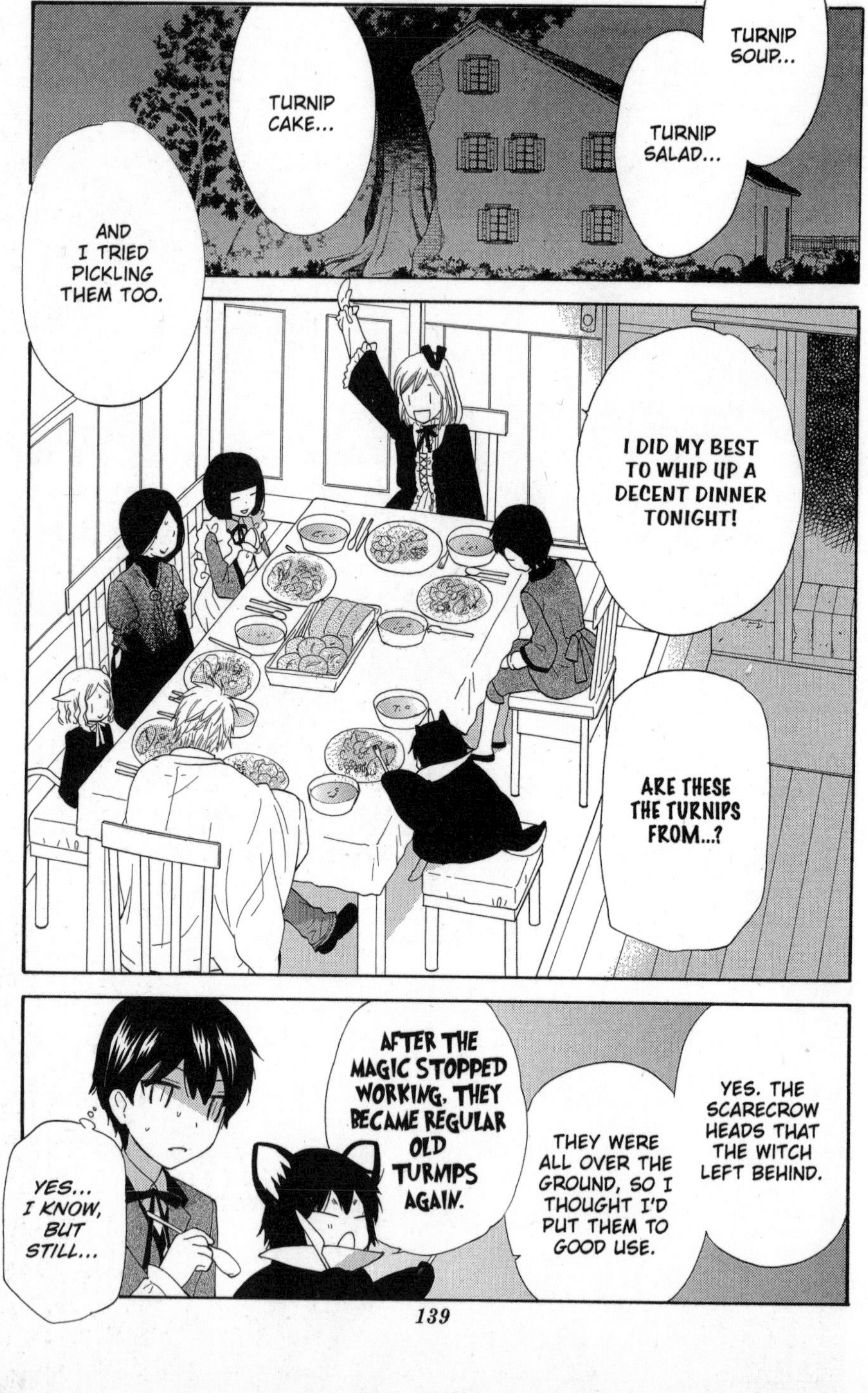
TURNIP SOUP...
TURNIP SALAD...
TURNIP CAKE...
AND I TRIED PICKLING THEM TOO.
I DID MY BEST TO WHIP UP A DECENT DINNER TONIGHT!
ARE THESE THE TURNIPS FROM...?
YES. THE SCARECROW HEADS THAT THE WITCH LEFT BEHIND.
THEY WERE ALL OVER THE GROUND, SO I THOUGHT I'D PUT THEM TO GOOD USE.
AFTER THE MAGIC STOPPED WORKING, THEY BECAME REGULAR OLD TURMPS AGAIN.
YES... I KNOW, BUT STILL...

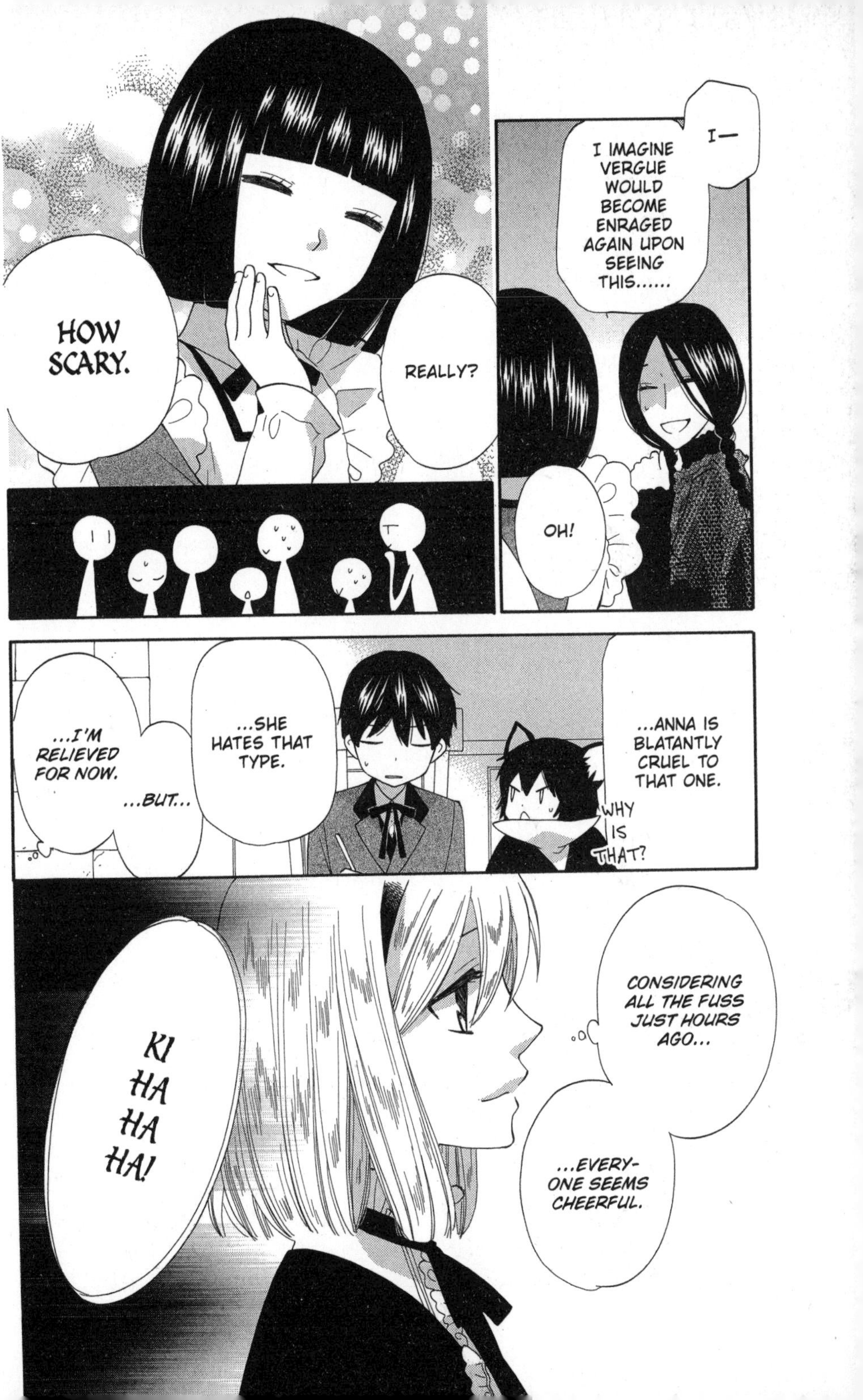
I—
I IMAGINE VERGUE WOULD BECOME ENRAGED AGAIN UPON SEEING THIS......
OH!
REALLY?
HOW SCARY.
...ANNA IS BLATANTLY CRUEL TO THAT ONE.
WHY IS THAT?
...SHE HATES THAT TYPE.
...BUT...
...I'M RELIEVED FOR NOW.
CONSIDERING ALL THE FUSS JUST HOURS AGO...
...EVERY-ONE SEEMS CHEERFUL.
KI HA HA HA!

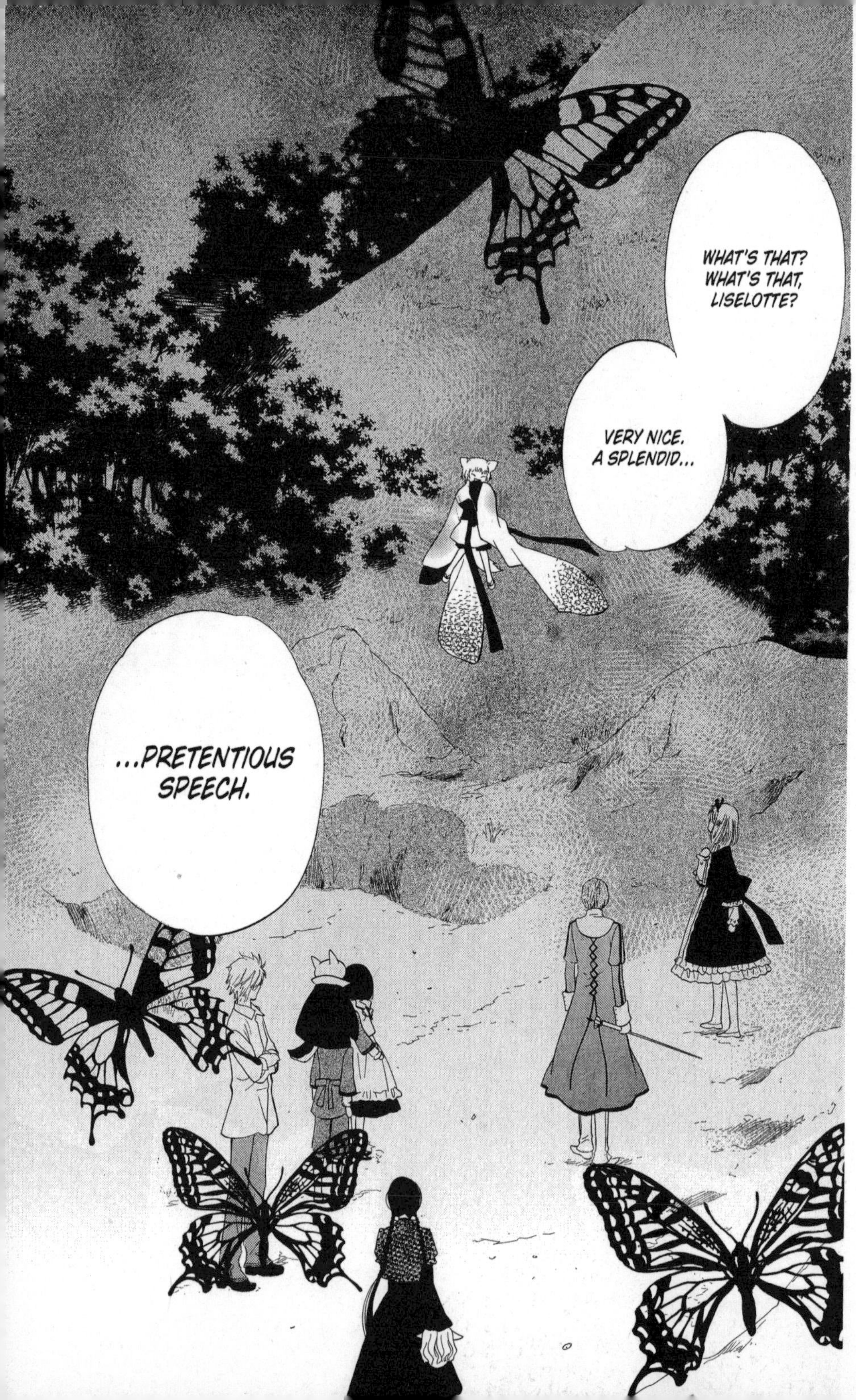
WHAT'S THAT? WHAT'S THAT, LISELOTTE?
VERY NICE. A SPLENDID...
...PRETENTIOUS SPEECH.

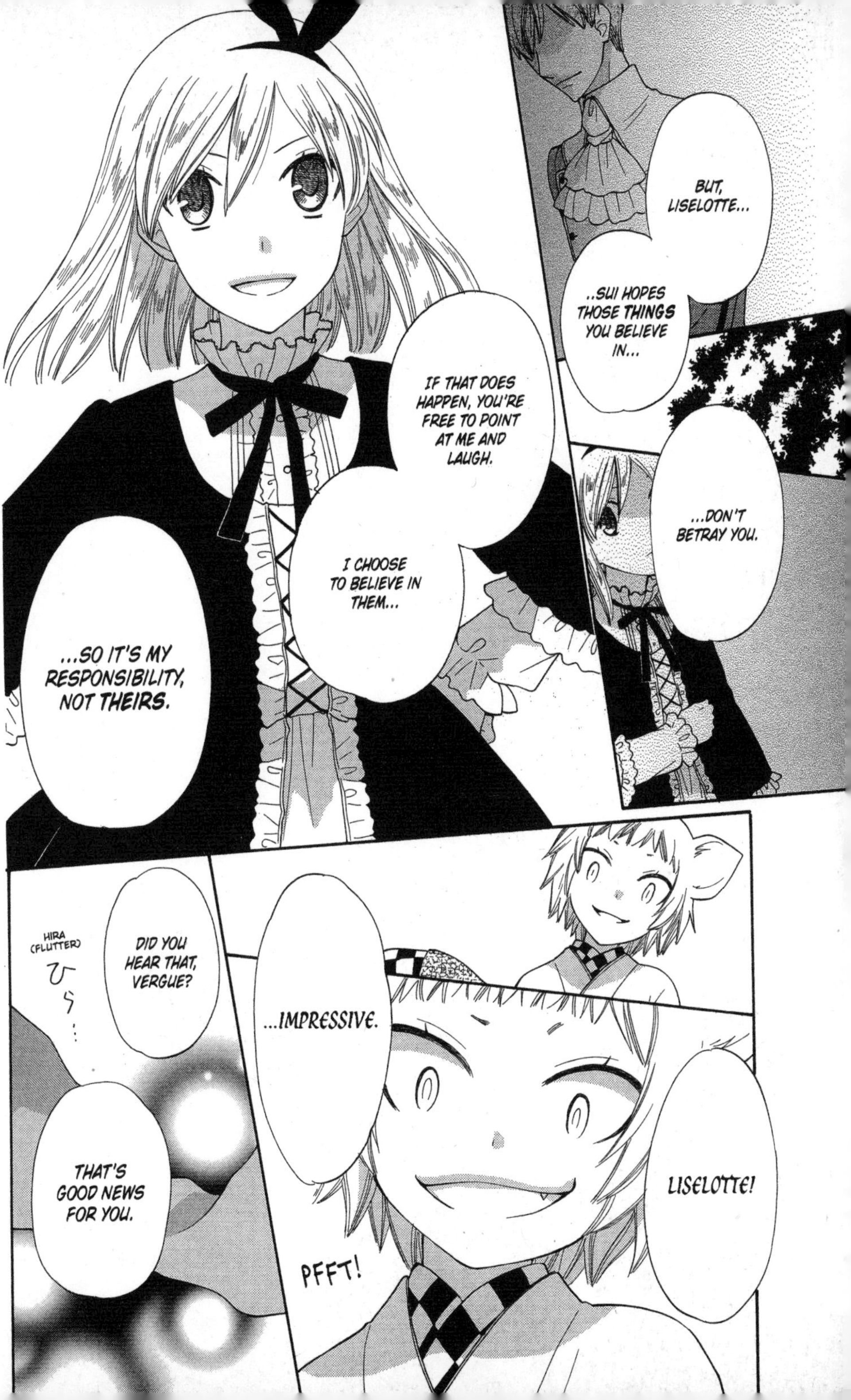
BUT, LISELOTTE...
...SUI HOPES THOSE THINGS YOU BELIEVE IN...
...DON'T BETRAY YOU.
IF THAT DOES HAPPEN, YOU'RE FREE TO POINT AT ME AND LAUGH.
I CHOOSE TO BELIEVE IN THEM...
...SO IT'S MY RESPONSIBILITY, NOT THEIRS.
...IMPRESSIVE.
LISELOTTE!
PFFT!
DID YOU HEAR THAT, VERGUE?
HIRA (FLUTTER)
ひら…
THAT'S GOOD NEWS FOR YOU.

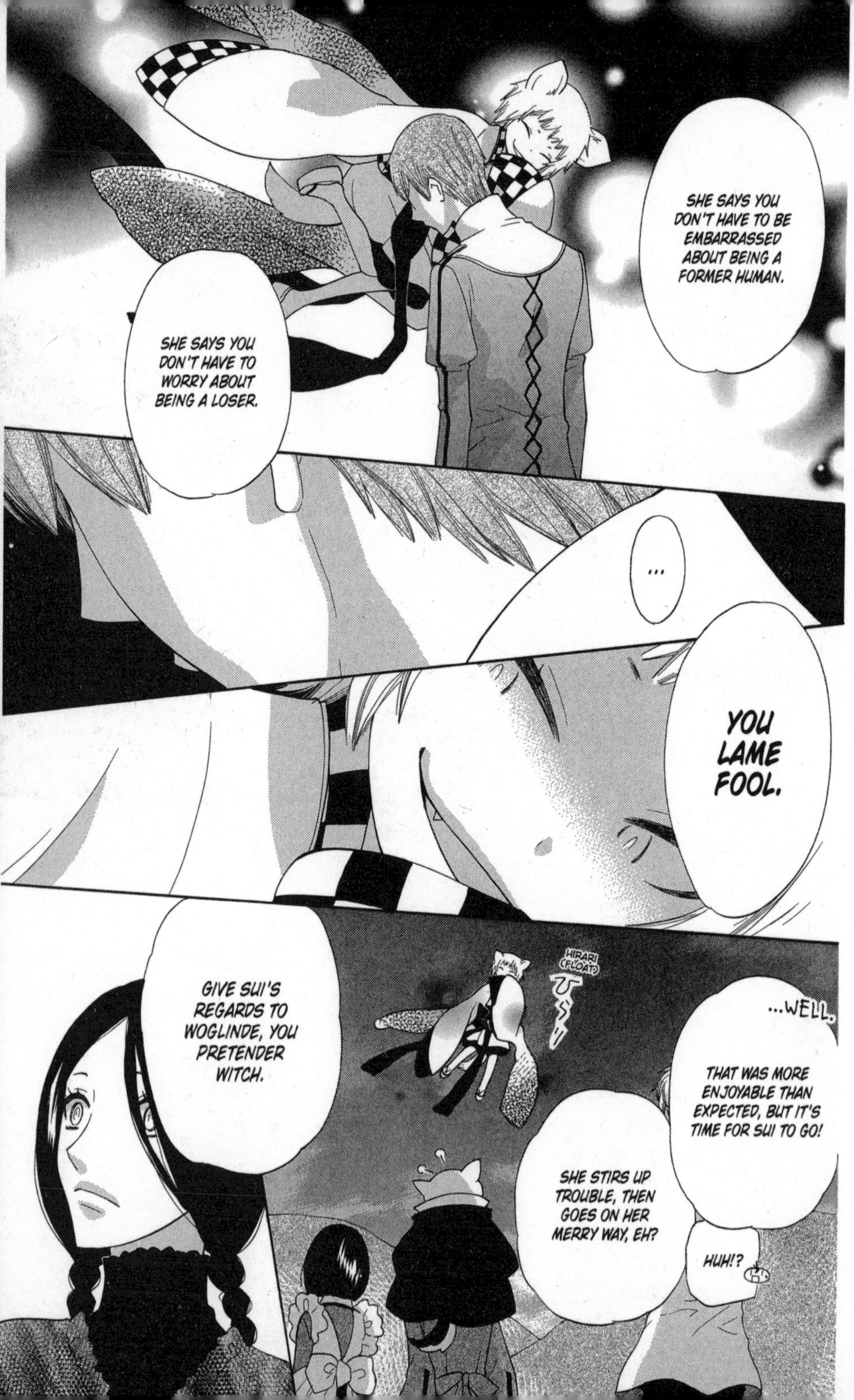
SHE SAYS YOU DON'T HAVE TO BE EMBARRASSED ABOUT BEING A FORMER HUMAN.
SHE SAYS YOU DON'T HAVE TO WORRY ABOUT BEING A LOSER.
...
YOU LAME FOOL.
...WELL.
THAT WAS MORE ENJOYABLE THAN EXPECTED, BUT IT'S TIME FOR SUI TO GO!
HIRARI (FLOAT)
SHE STIRS UP TROUBLE, THEN GOES ON HER MERRY WAY, EH?
HUH!?
GIVE SUI'S REGARDS TO WOGLINDE, YOU PRETENDER WITCH.

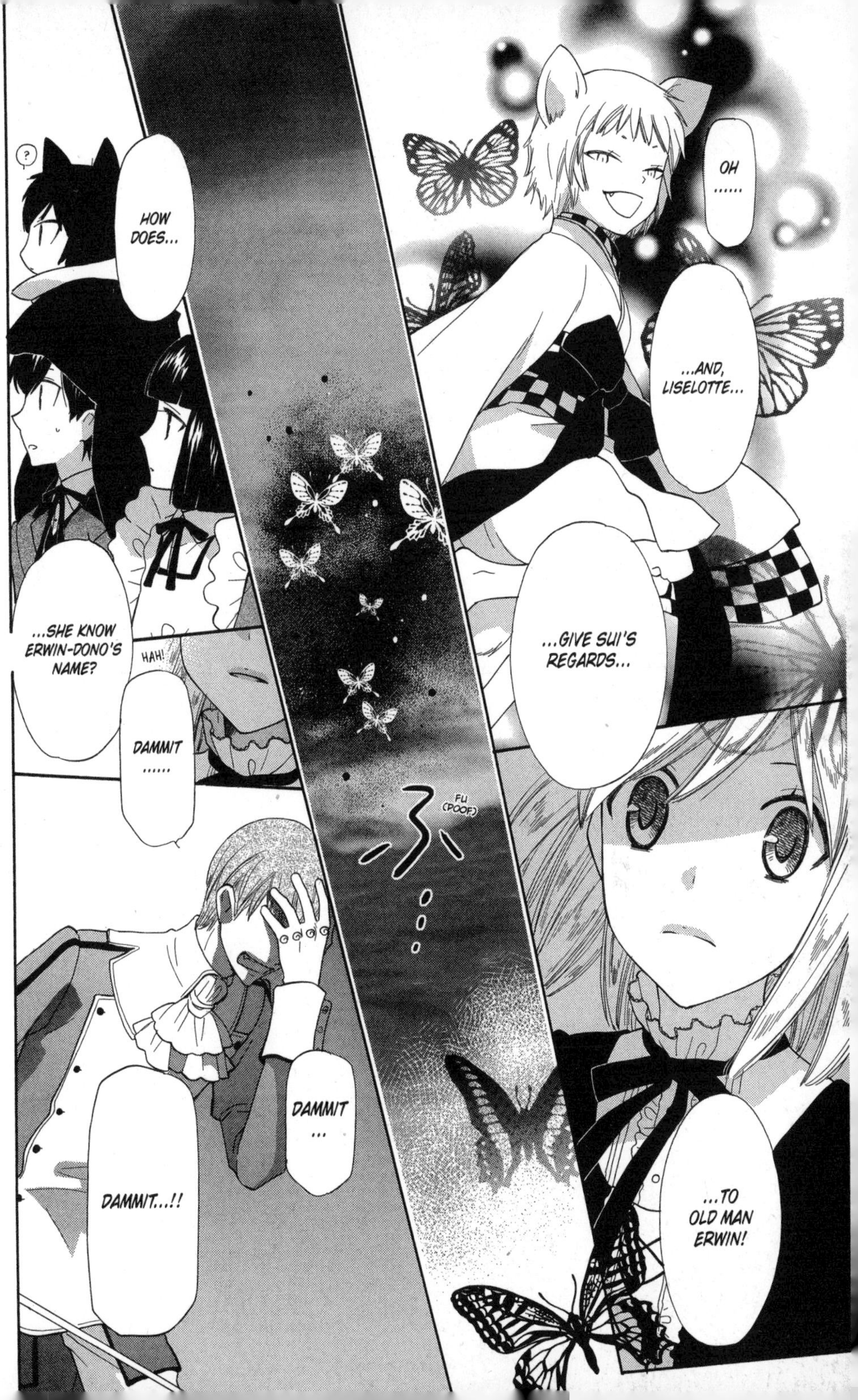

OH ......
...AND, LISELOTTE...
...GIVE SUI'S REGARDS...
...TO OLD MAN ERWIN!
ふ
FU (POOF)
?
HOW DOES...
...SHE KNOW ERWIN-DONO'S NAME?
HAH!
DAMMIT ......
DAMMIT ...
DAMMIT...!!

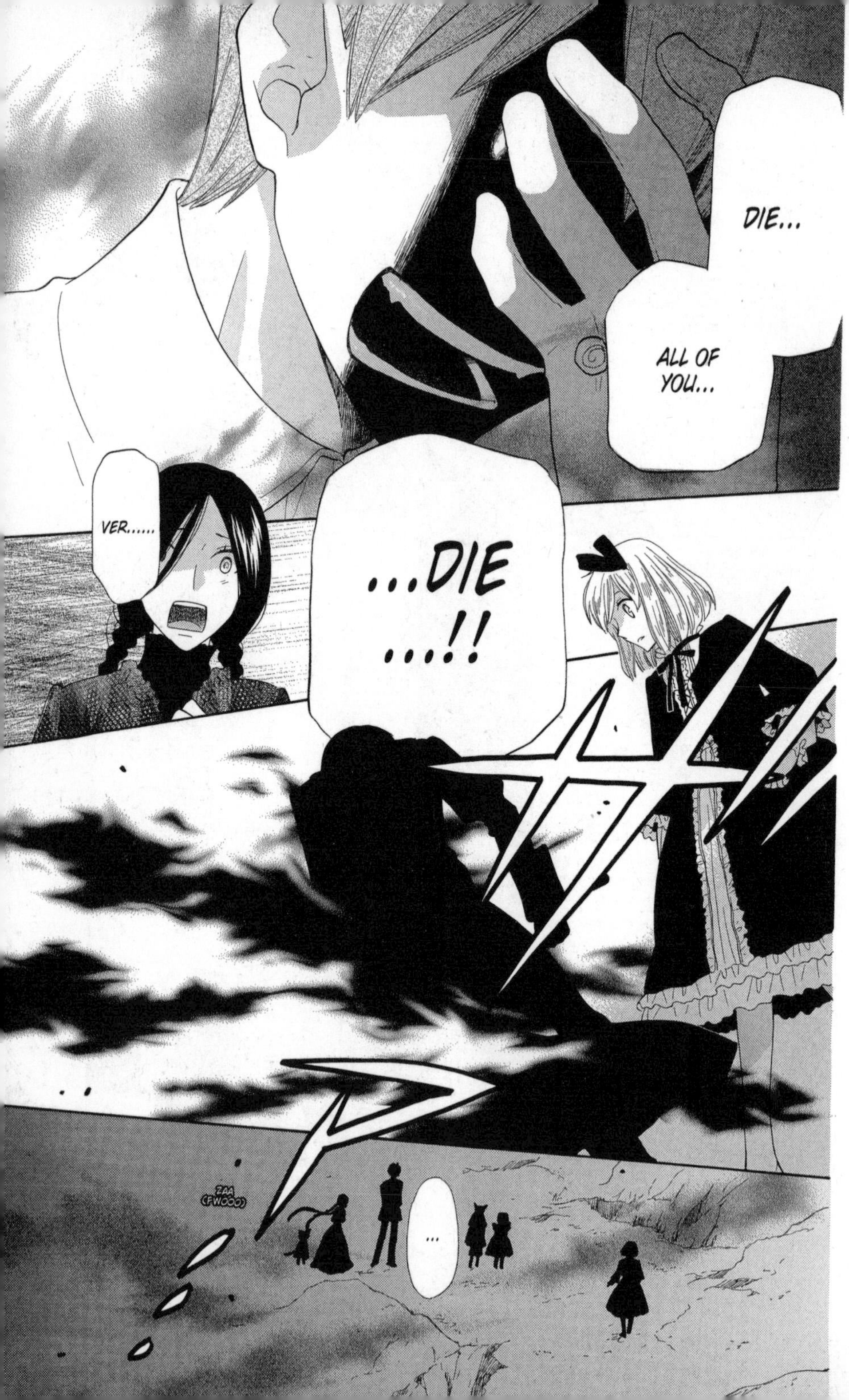
DIE...
ALL OF YOU...
...DIE ...!!
VER......
...
ZAA (FWOOO)

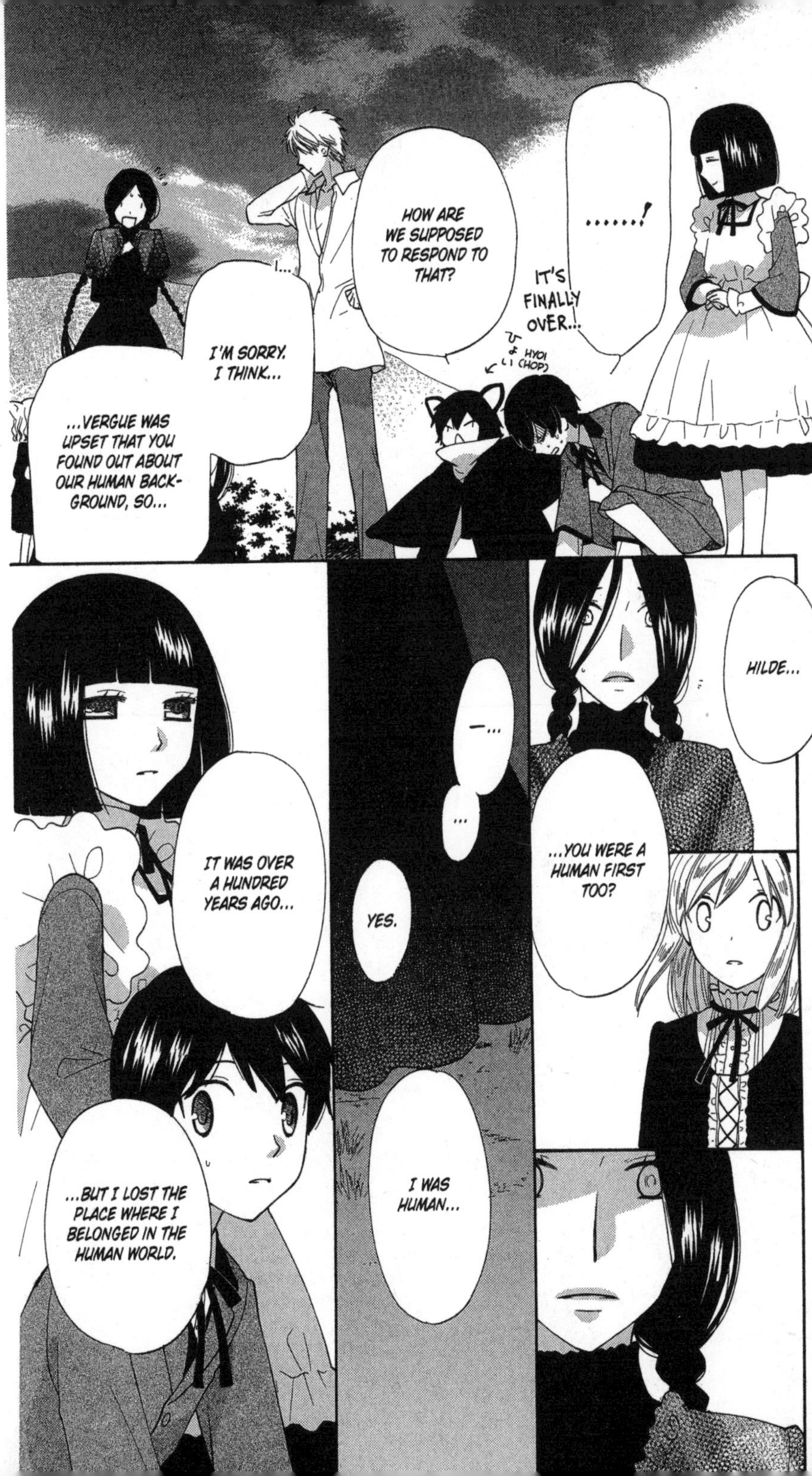

......!
IT'S FINALLY OVER...!
HYOI (HOP)
HOW ARE WE SUPPOSED TO RESPOND TO THAT?
I...
I'M SORRY. I THINK...
...VERGUE WAS UPSET THAT YOU FOUND OUT ABOUT OUR HUMAN BACKGROUND, SO...
HILDE...
...YOU WERE A HUMAN FIRST TOO?
—...
...
YES.
I WAS HUMAN...
IT WAS OVER A HUNDRED YEARS AGO...
...BUT I LOST THE PLACE WHERE I BELONGED IN THE HUMAN WORLD.

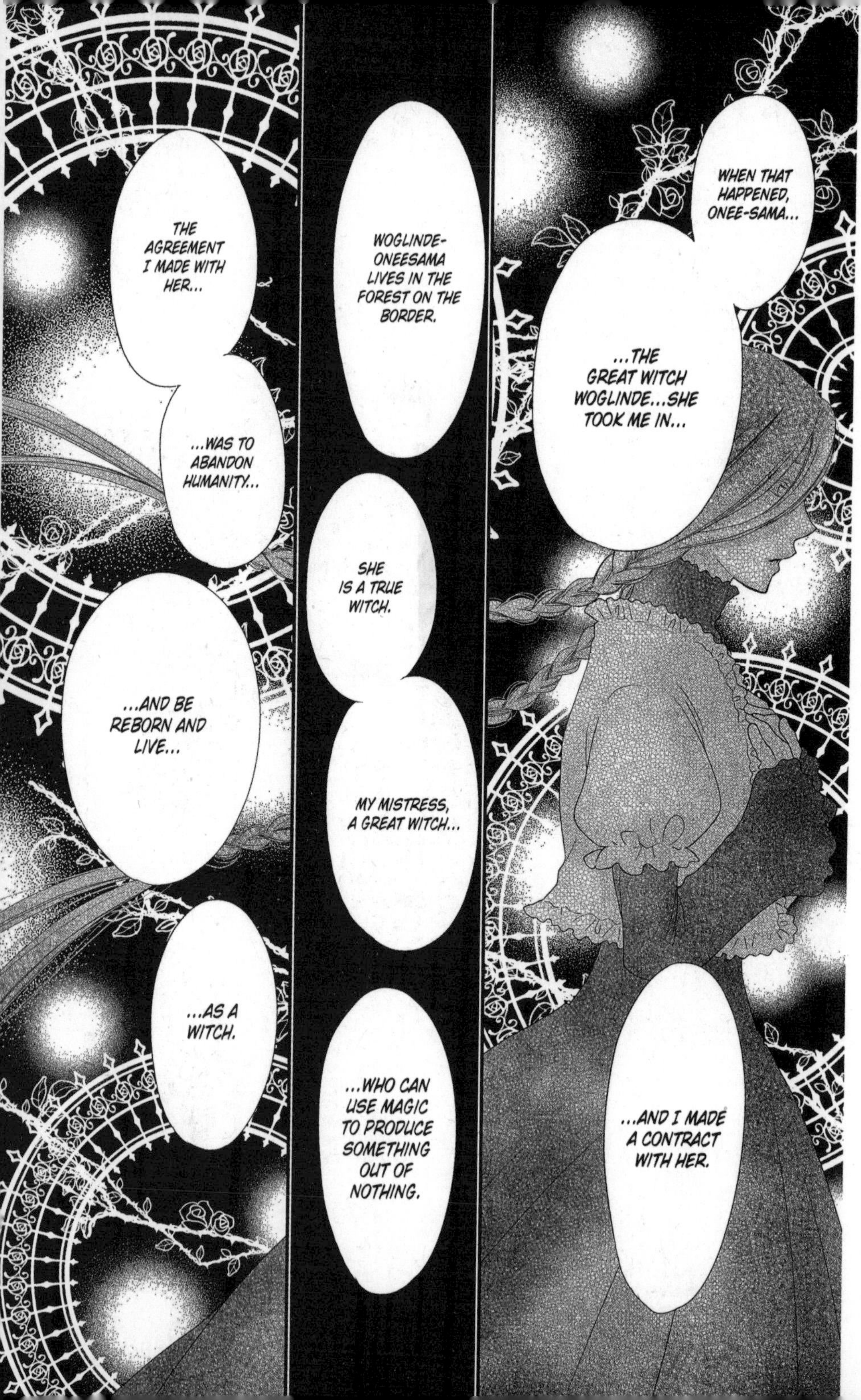
WHEN THAT HAPPENED, ONEE-SAMA...
...THE GREAT WITCH WOGLINDE...SHE TOOK ME IN...
...AND I MADE A CONTRACT WITH HER.
WOGLINDE-ONEESAMA LIVES IN THE FOREST ON THE BORDER.
SHE IS A TRUE WITCH.
MY MISTRESS, A GREAT WITCH...
...WHO CAN USE MAGIC TO PRODUCE SOMETHING OUT OF NOTHING.
THE AGREEMENT I MADE WITH HER...
...WAS TO ABANDON HUMANITY...
...AND BE REBORN AND LIVE...
...AS A WITCH.

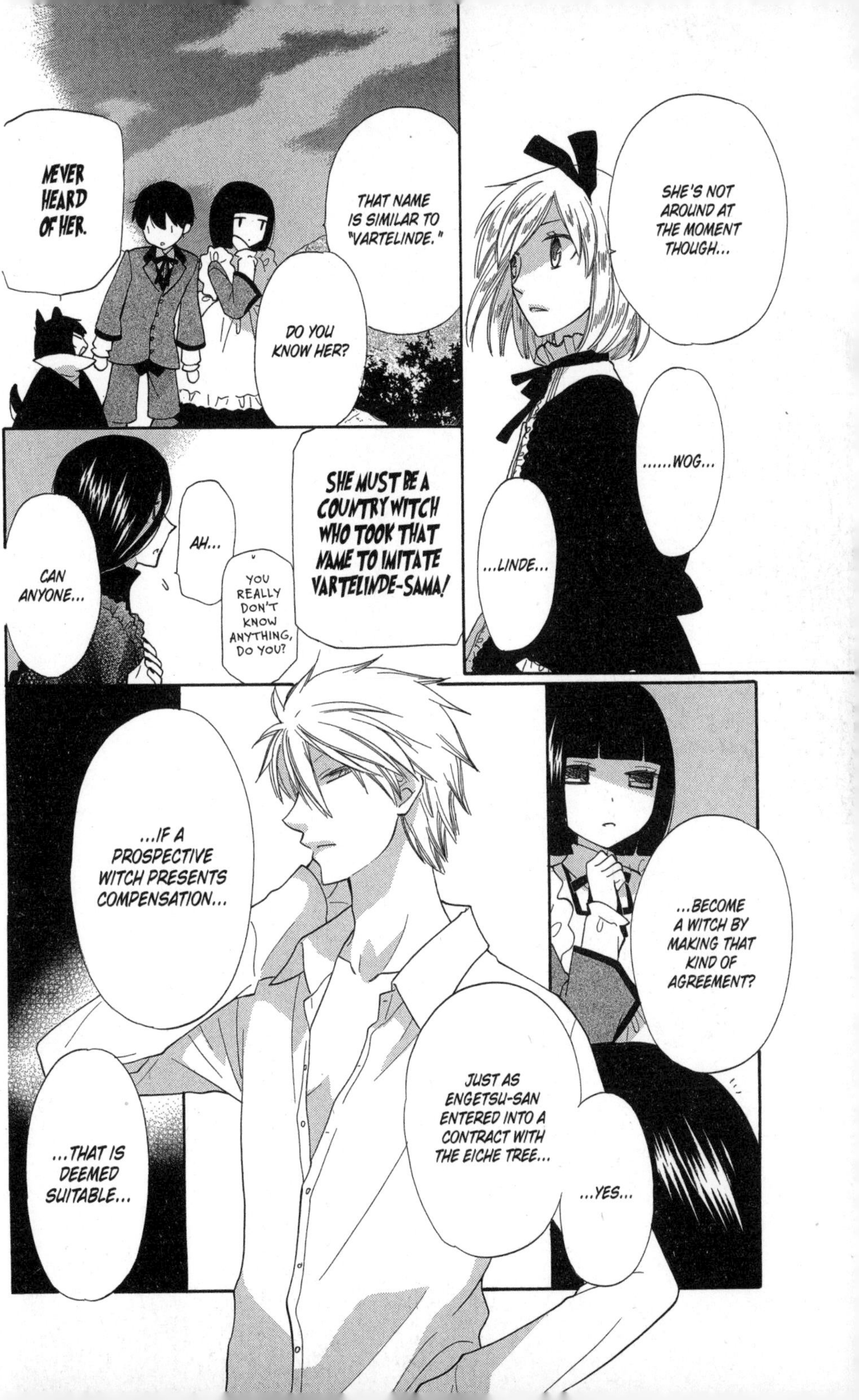
SHE'S NOT AROUND AT THE MOMENT THOUGH...
......WOG...
...LINDE...
THAT NAME IS SIMILAR TO "VARTELINDE."
DO YOU KNOW HER?
NEVER HEARD OF HER.
SHE MUST BE A COUNTRY WITCH WHO TOOK THAT NAME TO IMITATE VARTELINDE-SAMA!
AH...
YOU REALLY DON'T KNOW ANYTHING, DO YOU?
CAN ANYONE...
...BECOME A WITCH BY MAKING THAT KIND OF AGREEMENT?
...YES...
...IF A PROSPECTIVE WITCH PRESENTS COMPENSATION...
...THAT IS DEEMED SUITABLE...
JUST AS ENGETSU-SAN ENTERED INTO A CONTRACT WITH THE EICHE TREE...

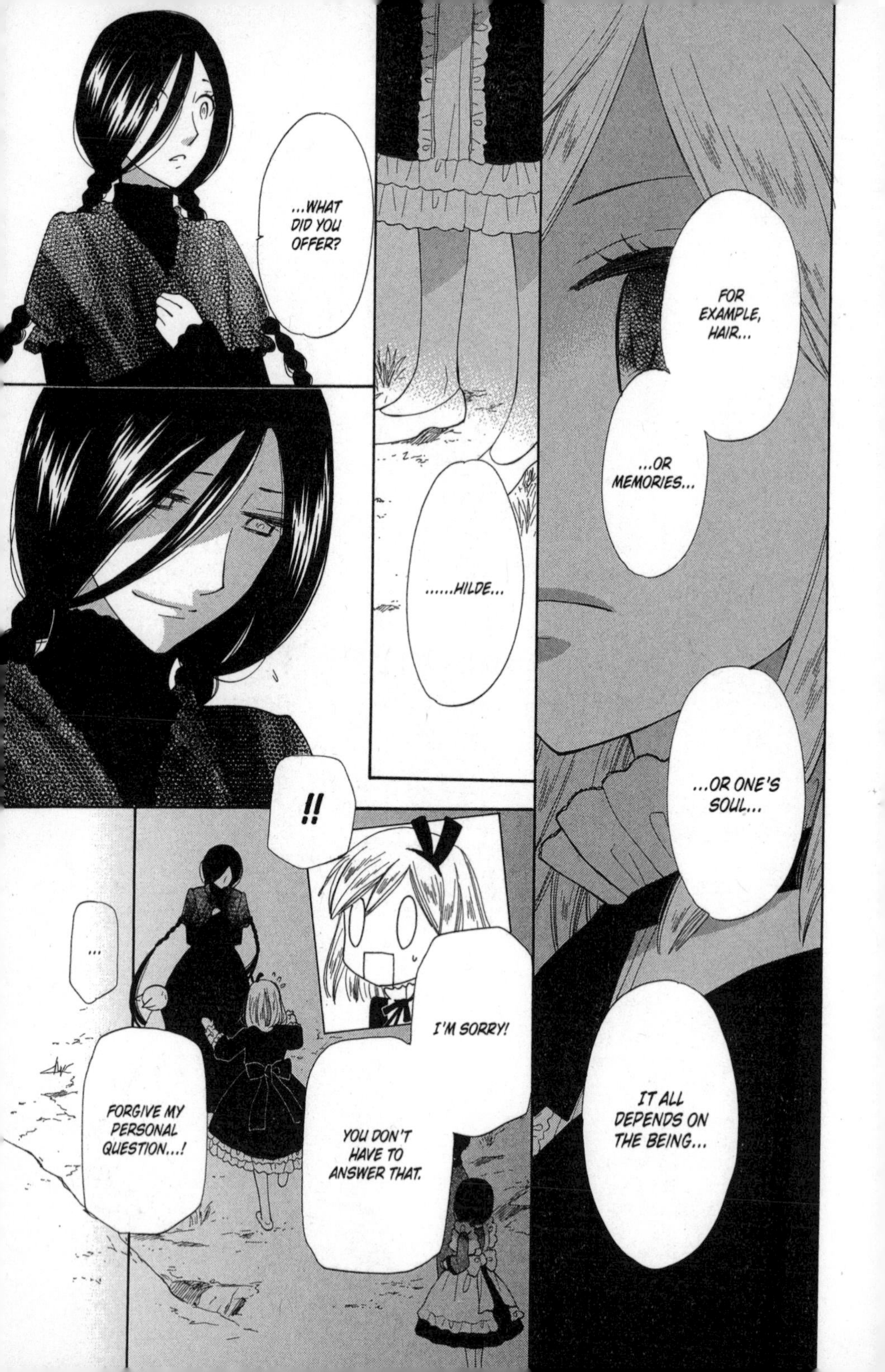
FOR EXAMPLE, HAIR...
...OR MEMORIES...
...OR ONE'S SOUL...
IT ALL DEPENDS ON THE BEING...
......HILDE...
...WHAT DID YOU OFFER?
!!
I'M SORRY!
YOU DON'T HAVE TO ANSWER THAT.
...
FORGIVE MY PERSONAL QUESTION...!

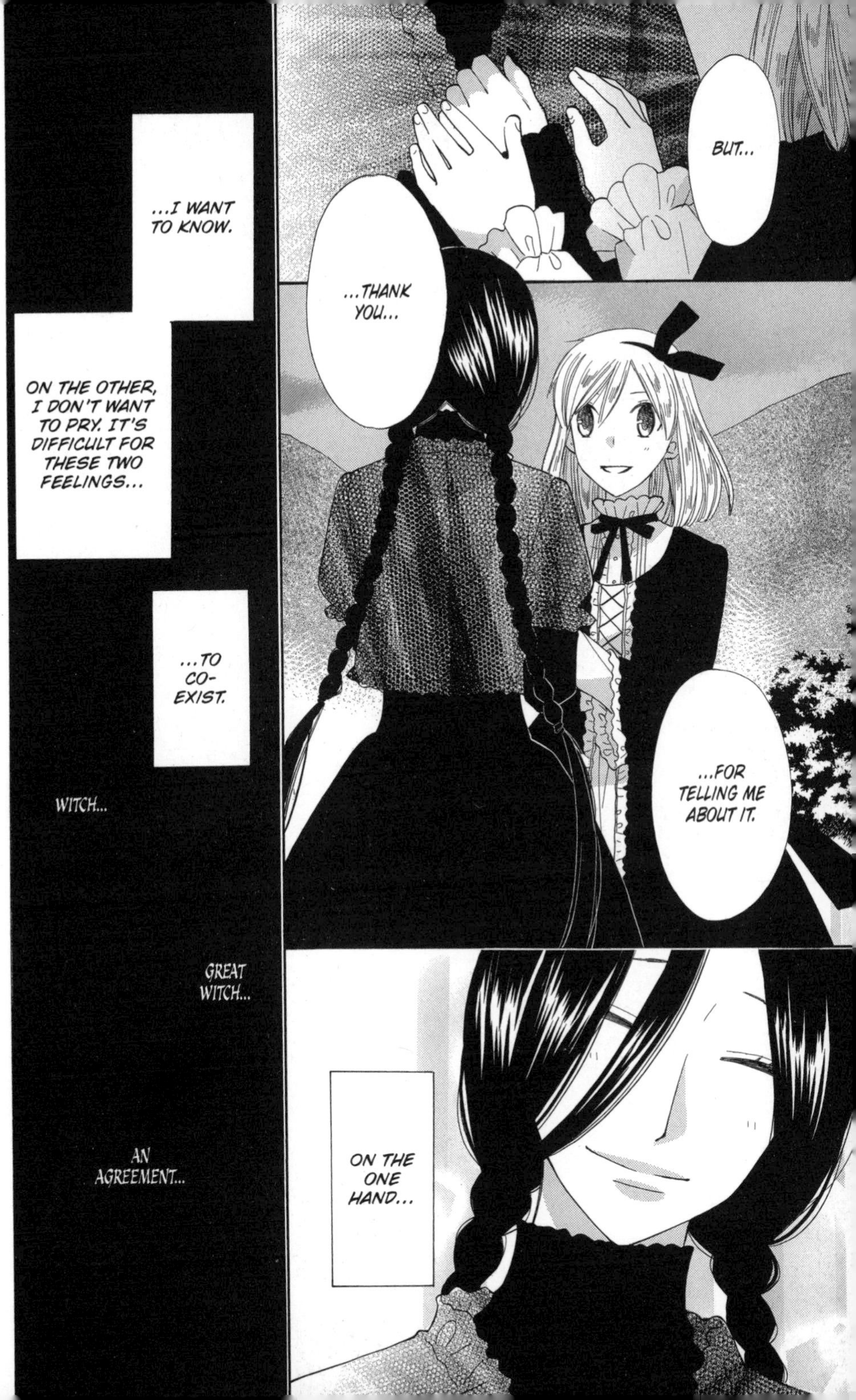
BUT...
...THANK YOU...
...FOR TELLING ME ABOUT IT.
ON THE ONE HAND...
...I WANT TO KNOW.
ON THE OTHER, I DON'T WANT TO PRY. IT'S DIFFICULT FOR THESE TWO FEELINGS...
...TO CO-EXIST.
WITCH...
GREAT WITCH...
AN AGREEMENT...

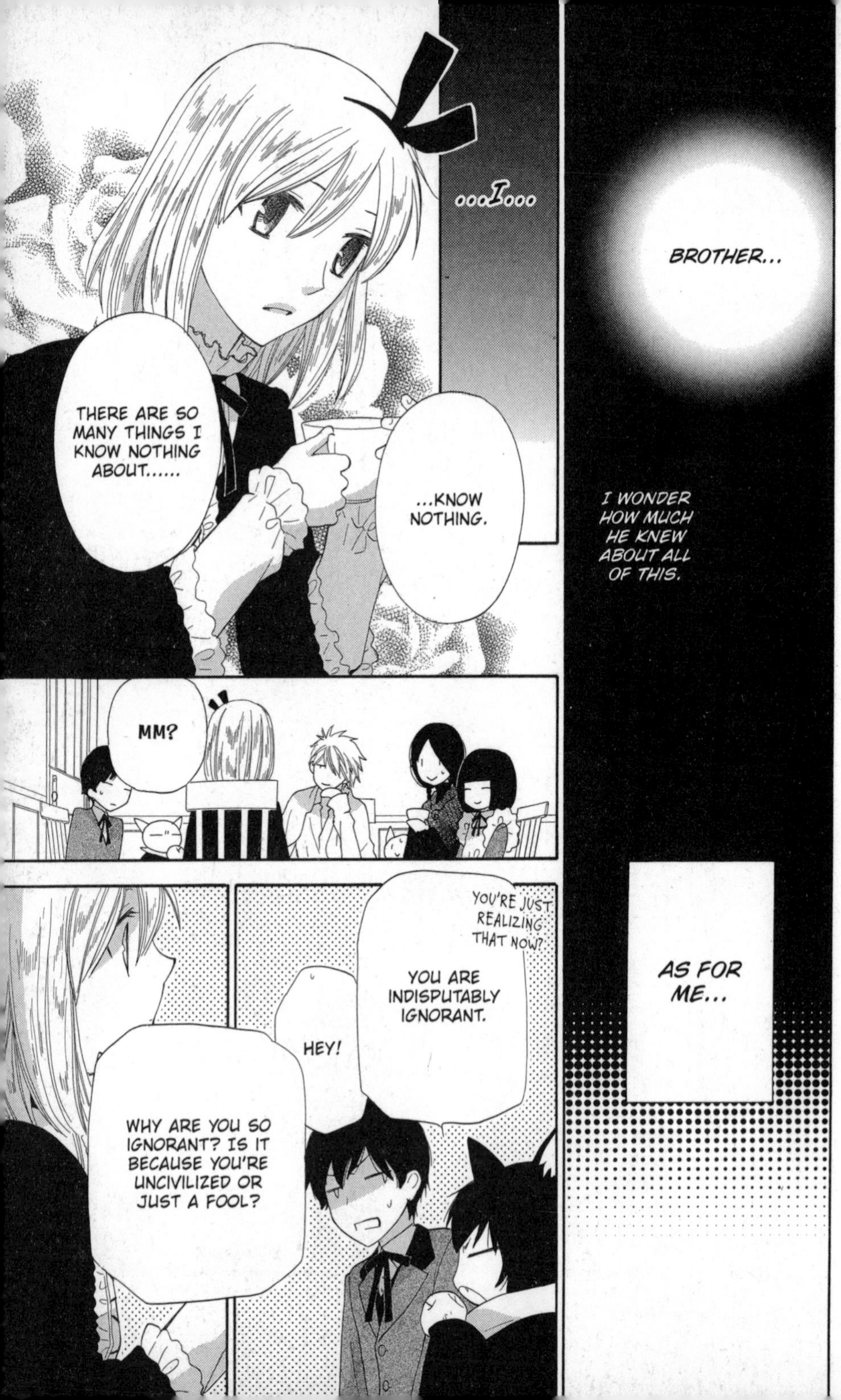
BROTHER...
I WONDER HOW MUCH HE KNEW ABOUT ALL OF THIS.
AS FOR ME...
...I...
THERE ARE SO MANY THINGS I KNOW NOTHING ABOUT......
...KNOW NOTHING.
MM?
YOU'RE JUST REALIZING THAT NOW?
YOU ARE INDISPUTABLY IGNORANT.
HEY!
WHY ARE YOU SO IGNORANT? IS IT BECAUSE YOU'RE UNCIVILIZED OR JUST A FOOL?

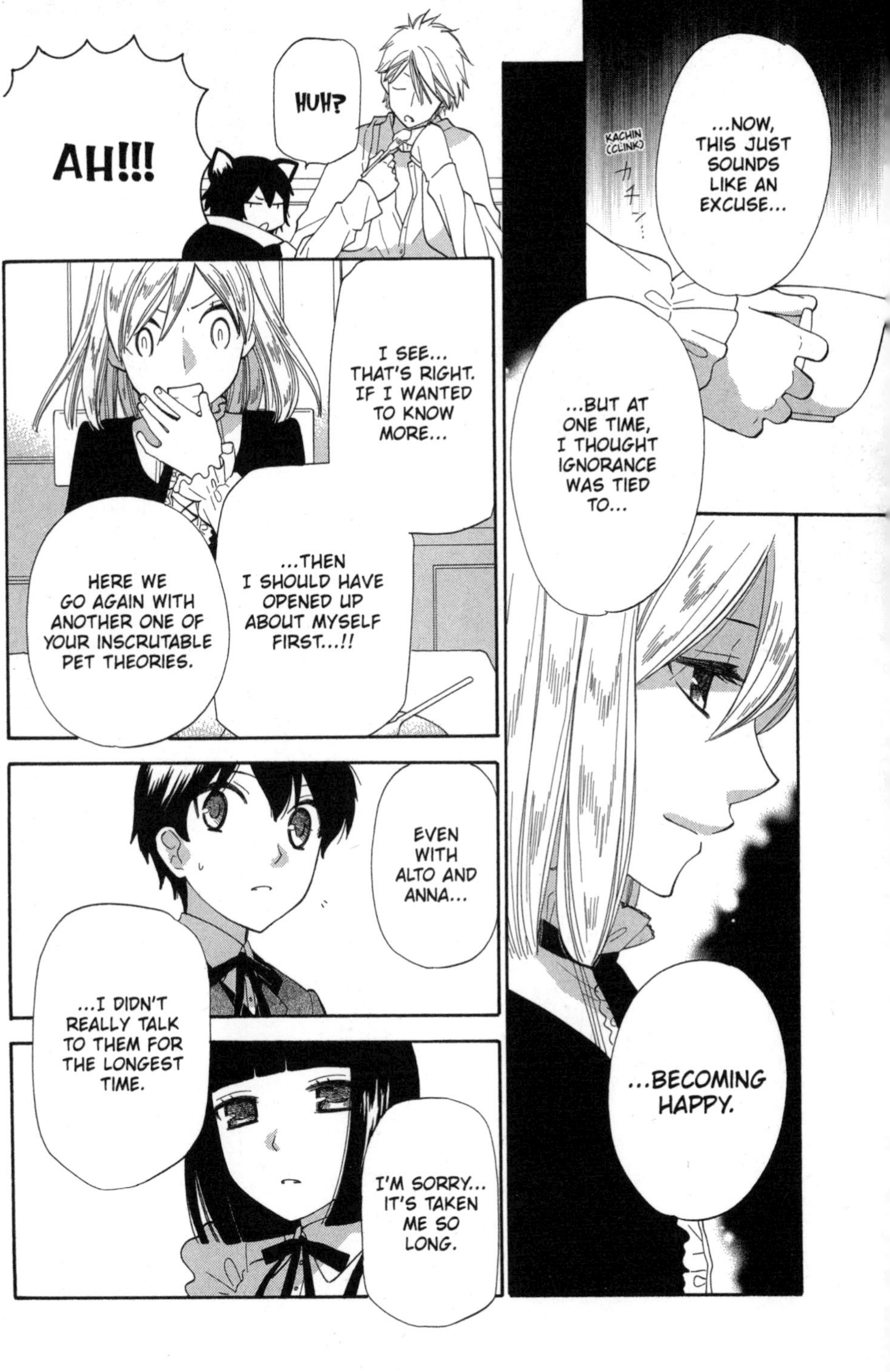
KACHIN (CLINK)
...NOW, THIS JUST SOUNDS LIKE AN EXCUSE...
...BUT AT ONE TIME, I THOUGHT IGNORANCE WAS TIED TO...
...BECOMING HAPPY.
AH!!!
HUH?
I SEE... THAT'S RIGHT. IF I WANTED TO KNOW MORE...
...THEN I SHOULD HAVE OPENED UP ABOUT MYSELF FIRST...!!
HERE WE GO AGAIN WITH ANOTHER ONE OF YOUR INSCRUTABLE PET THEORIES.
EVEN WITH ALTO AND ANNA...
...I DIDN'T REALLY TALK TO THEM FOR THE LONGEST TIME.
I'M SORRY... IT'S TAKEN ME SO LONG.

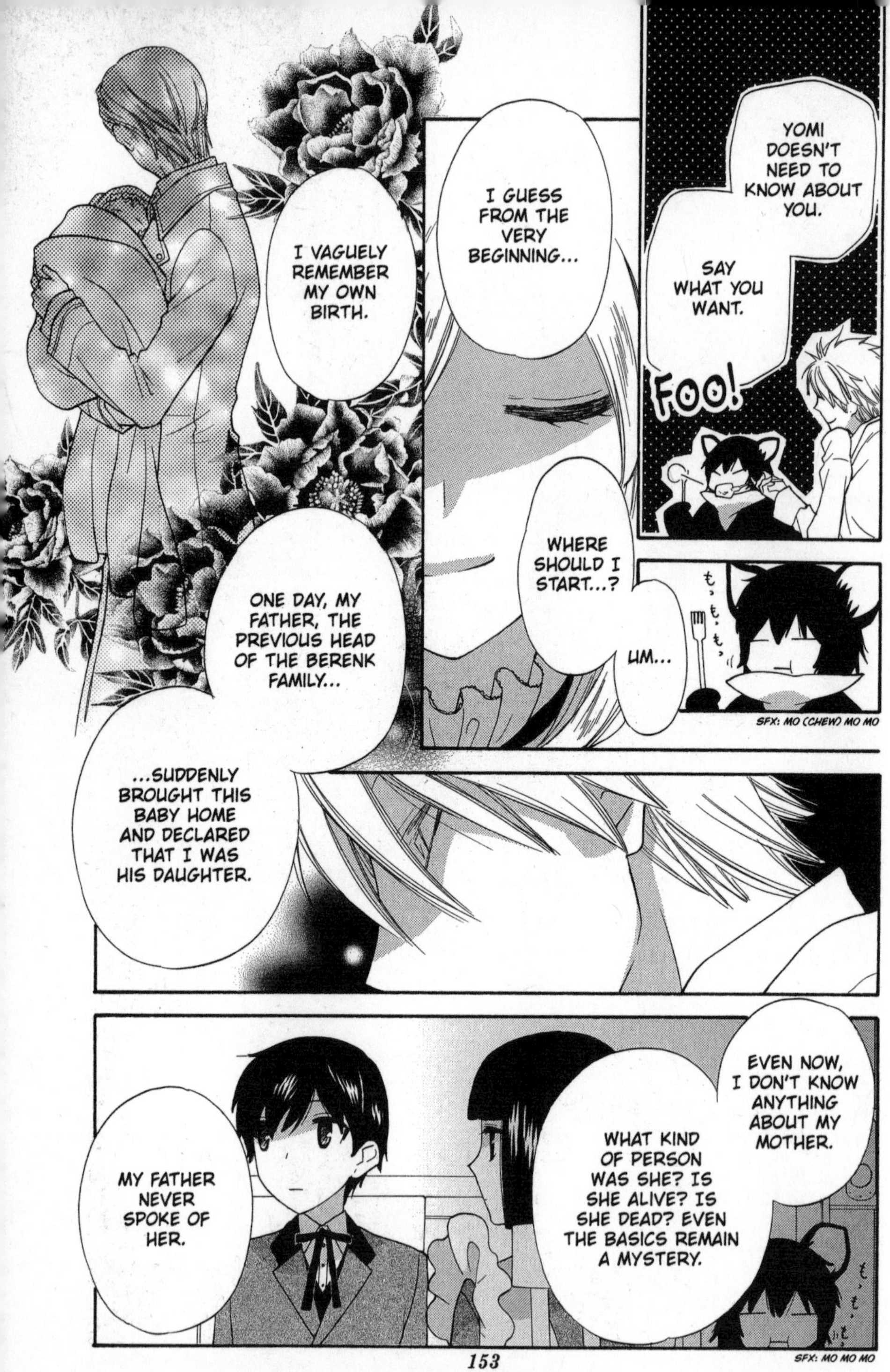
YOMI DOESN'T NEED TO KNOW ABOUT YOU.
SAY WHAT YOU WANT.
FOO!
UM...
もっもっもっ
SFX: MO (CHEW) MO MO
I GUESS FROM THE VERY BEGINNING...
WHERE SHOULD I START...?
I VAGUELY REMEMBER MY OWN BIRTH.
ONE DAY, MY FATHER, THE PREVIOUS HEAD OF THE BERENK FAMILY...
...SUDDENLY BROUGHT THIS BABY HOME AND DECLARED THAT I WAS HIS DAUGHTER.
EVEN NOW, I DON'T KNOW ANYTHING ABOUT MY MOTHER.
WHAT KIND OF PERSON WAS SHE? IS SHE ALIVE? IS SHE DEAD? EVEN THE BASICS REMAIN A MYSTERY.
MY FATHER NEVER SPOKE OF HER.
SFX: MO MO MO

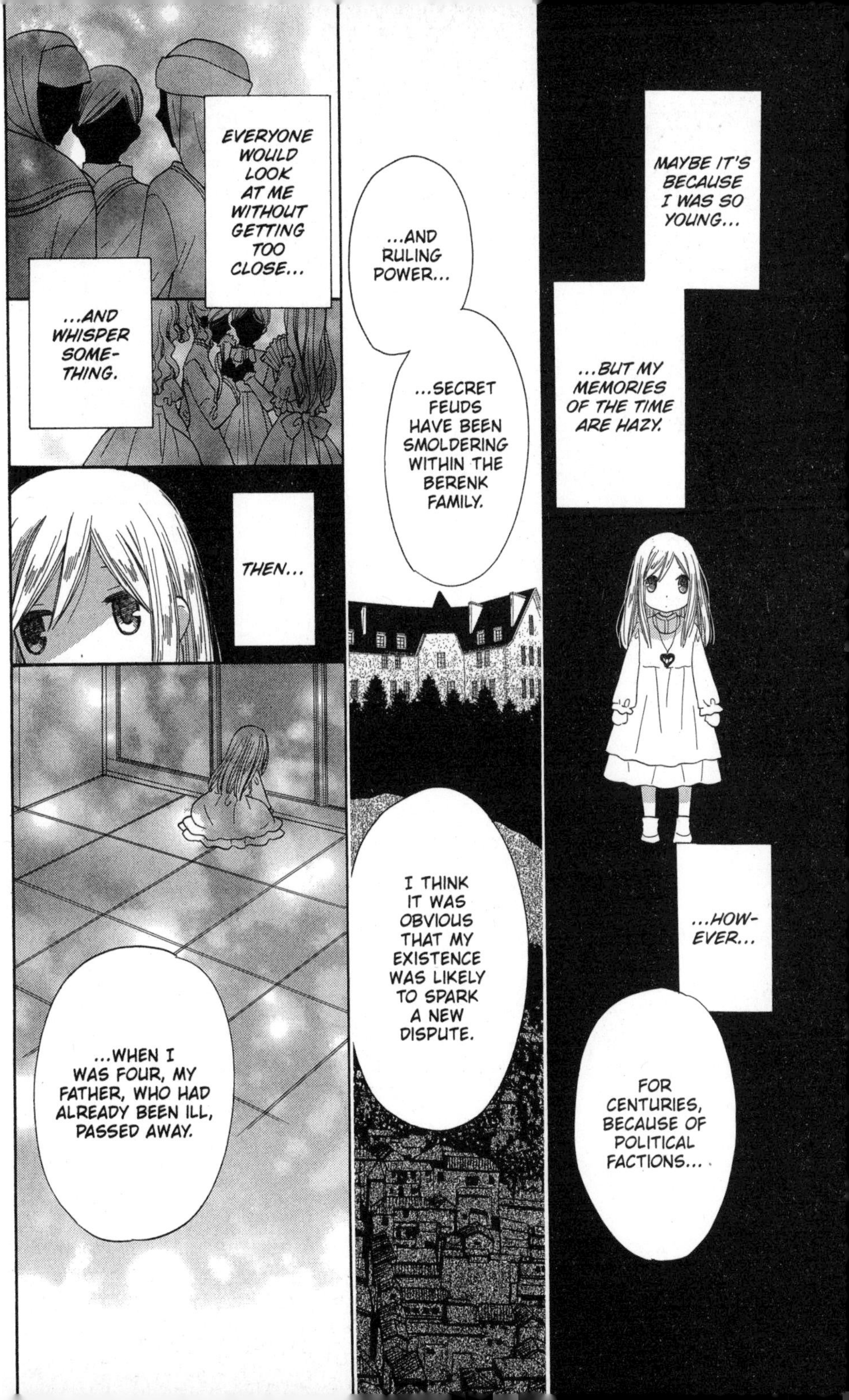
MAYBE IT'S BECAUSE I WAS SO YOUNG...
...BUT MY MEMORIES OF THE TIME ARE HAZY.
...HOW-EVER...
FOR CENTURIES, BECAUSE OF POLITICAL FACTIONS...
...AND RULING POWER...
...SECRET FEUDS HAVE BEEN SMOLDERING WITHIN THE BERENK FAMILY.
I THINK IT WAS OBVIOUS THAT MY EXISTENCE WAS LIKELY TO SPARK A NEW DISPUTE.
EVERYONE WOULD LOOK AT ME WITHOUT GETTING TOO CLOSE...
...AND WHISPER SOME-THING.
THEN...
...WHEN I WAS FOUR, MY FATHER, WHO HAD ALREADY BEEN ILL, PASSED AWAY.

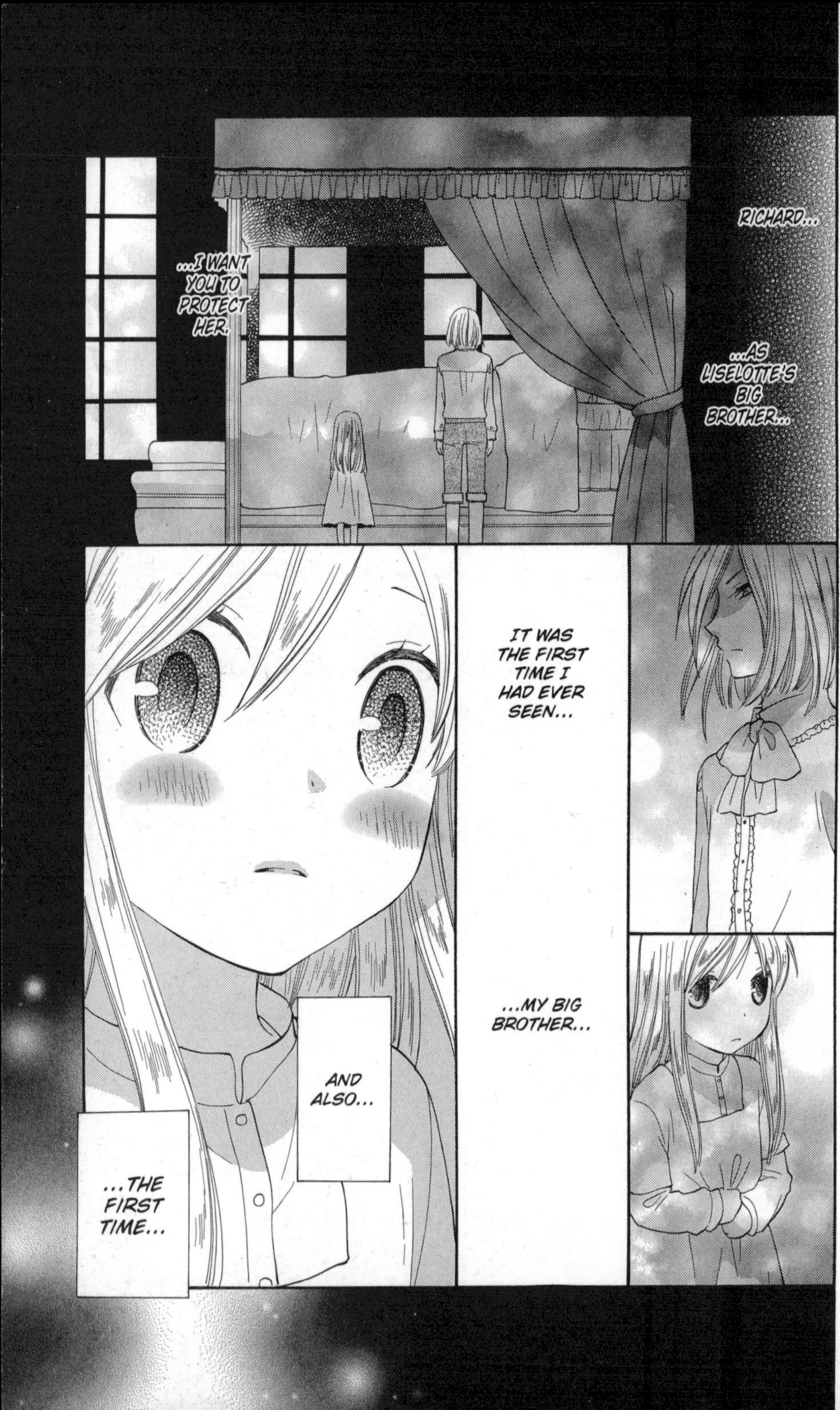
RICHARD...
...AS LISELOTTE'S BIG BROTHER...
...I WANT YOU TO PROTECT HER.
IT WAS THE FIRST TIME I HAD EVER SEEN...
...MY BIG BROTHER...
AND ALSO...
...THE FIRST TIME...

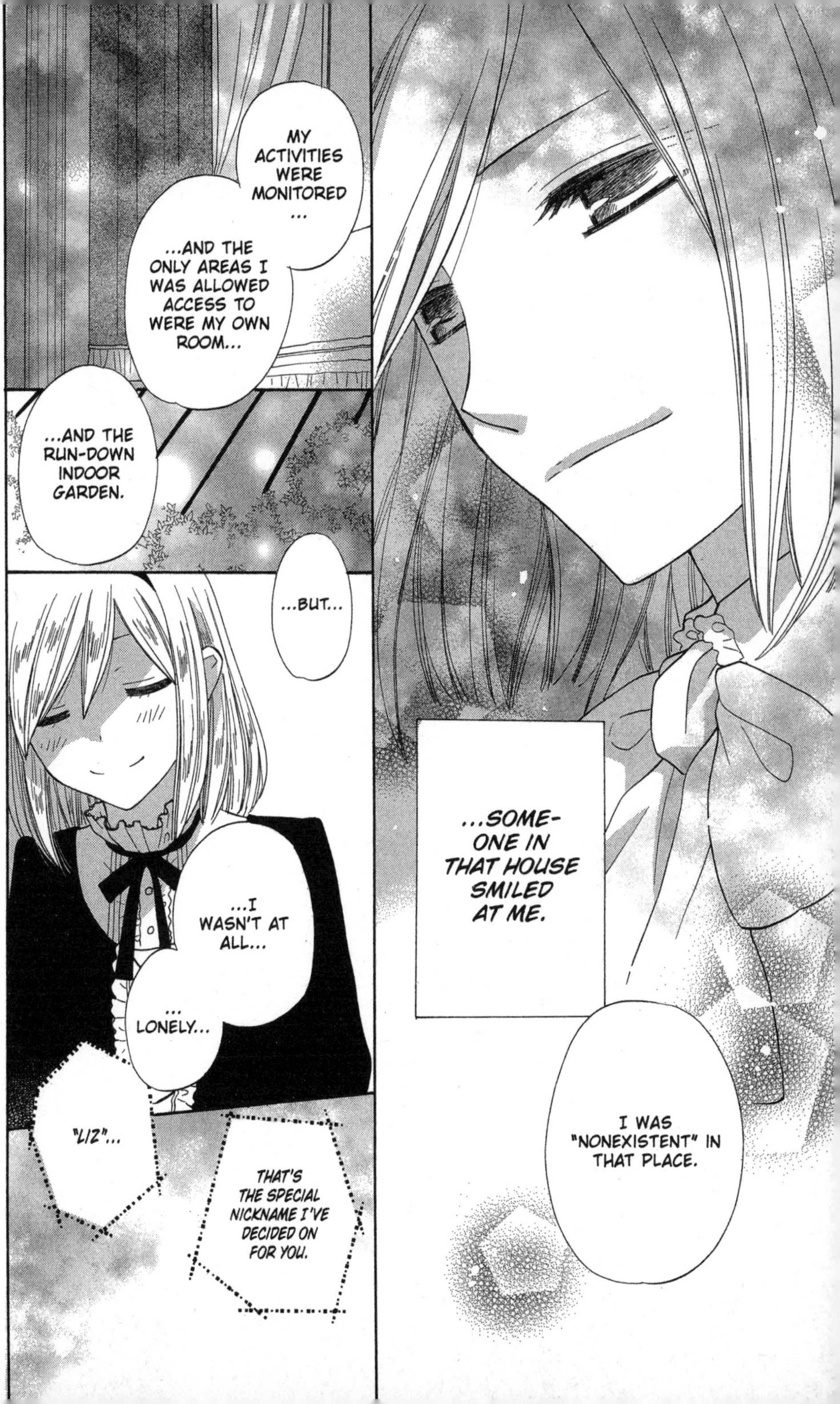
...SOME-ONE IN THAT HOUSE SMILED AT ME.
I WAS "NONEXISTENT" IN THAT PLACE.
MY ACTIVITIES WERE MONITORED ...
...AND THE ONLY AREAS I WAS ALLOWED ACCESS TO WERE MY OWN ROOM...
...AND THE RUN-DOWN INDOOR GARDEN.
...BUT...
...I WASN'T AT ALL...
... LONELY...
"LIZ"...
THAT'S THE SPECIAL NICKNAME I'VE DECIDED ON FOR YOU.

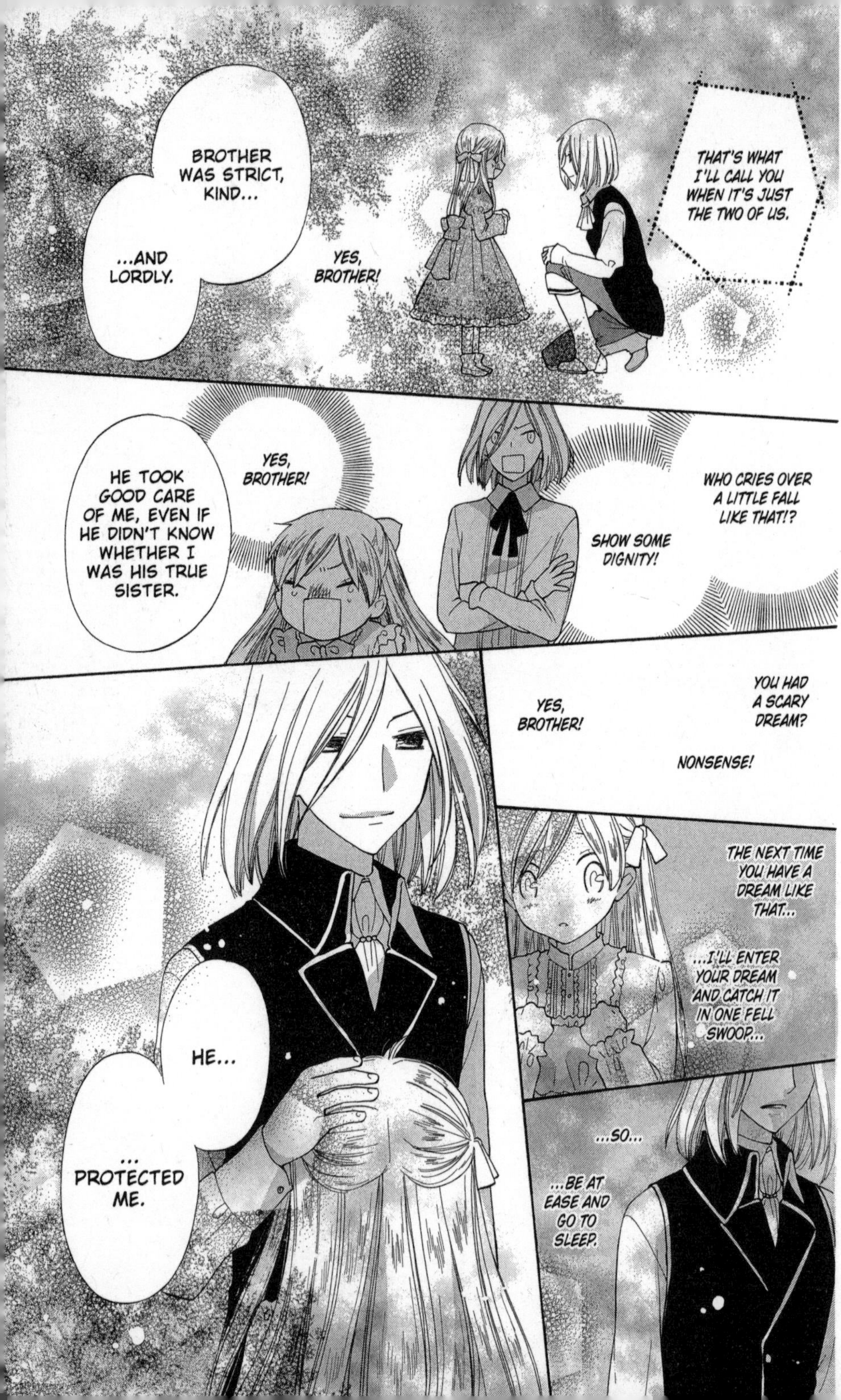
THAT'S WHAT I'LL CALL YOU WHEN IT'S JUST THE TWO OF US.
YES, BROTHER!
BROTHER WAS STRICT, KIND...
...AND LORDLY.
WHO CRIES OVER A LITTLE FALL LIKE THAT!?
SHOW SOME DIGNITY!
YES, BROTHER!
HE TOOK GOOD CARE OF ME, EVEN IF HE DIDN'T KNOW WHETHER I WAS HIS TRUE SISTER.
YOU HAD A SCARY DREAM?
NONSENSE!
YES, BROTHER!
THE NEXT TIME YOU HAVE A DREAM LIKE THAT...
...I'LL ENTER YOUR DREAM AND CATCH IT IN ONE FELL SWOOP...
...SO...
...BE AT EASE AND GO TO SLEEP.
HE...
...PROTECTED ME.

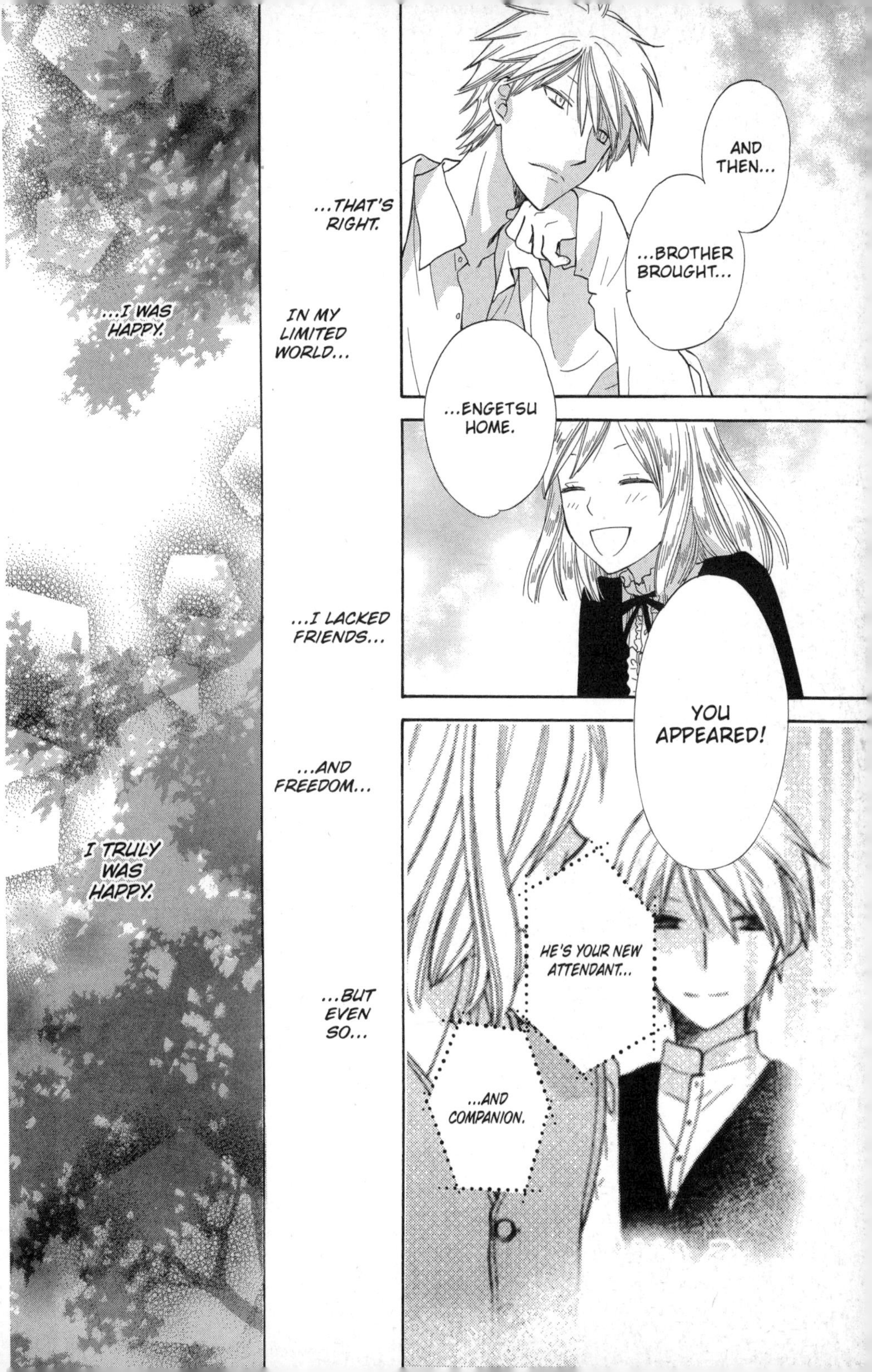
AND THEN...
...BROTHER BROUGHT...
...ENGETSU HOME.
YOU APPEARED!
HE'S YOUR NEW ATTENDANT...
...AND COMPANION.
...THAT'S RIGHT.
IN MY LIMITED WORLD...
...I LACKED FRIENDS...
...AND FREEDOM...
...BUT EVEN SO...
...I WAS HAPPY.
I TRULY WAS HAPPY.

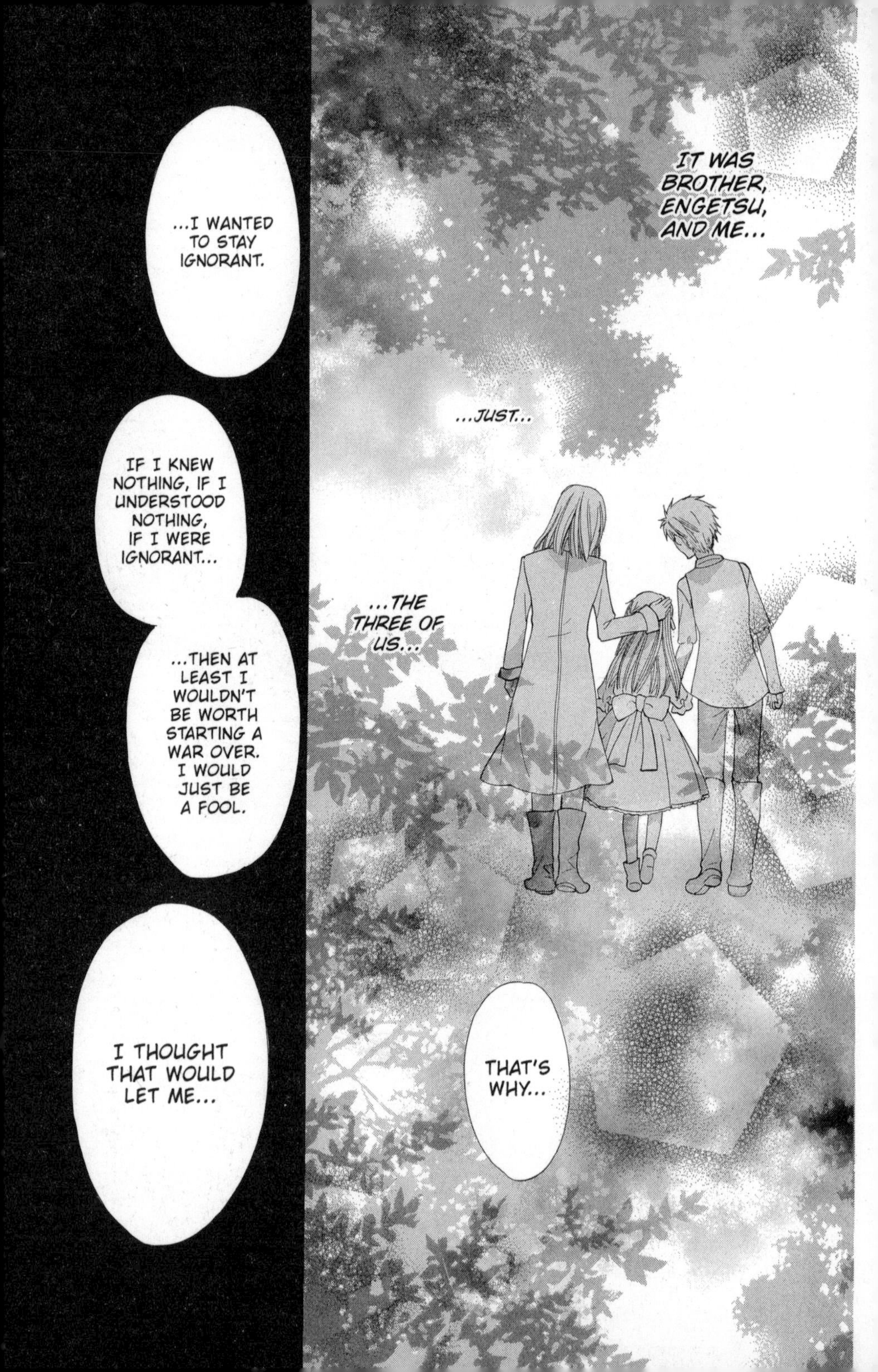
IT WAS BROTHER, ENGETSU, AND ME...
...JUST...
...THE THREE OF US...
THAT'S WHY...
...I WANTED TO STAY IGNORANT.
IF I KNEW NOTHING, IF I UNDERSTOOD NOTHING, IF I WERE IGNORANT...
...THEN AT LEAST I WOULDN'T BE WORTH STARTING A WAR OVER. I WOULD JUST BE A FOOL.
I THOUGHT THAT WOULD LET ME...

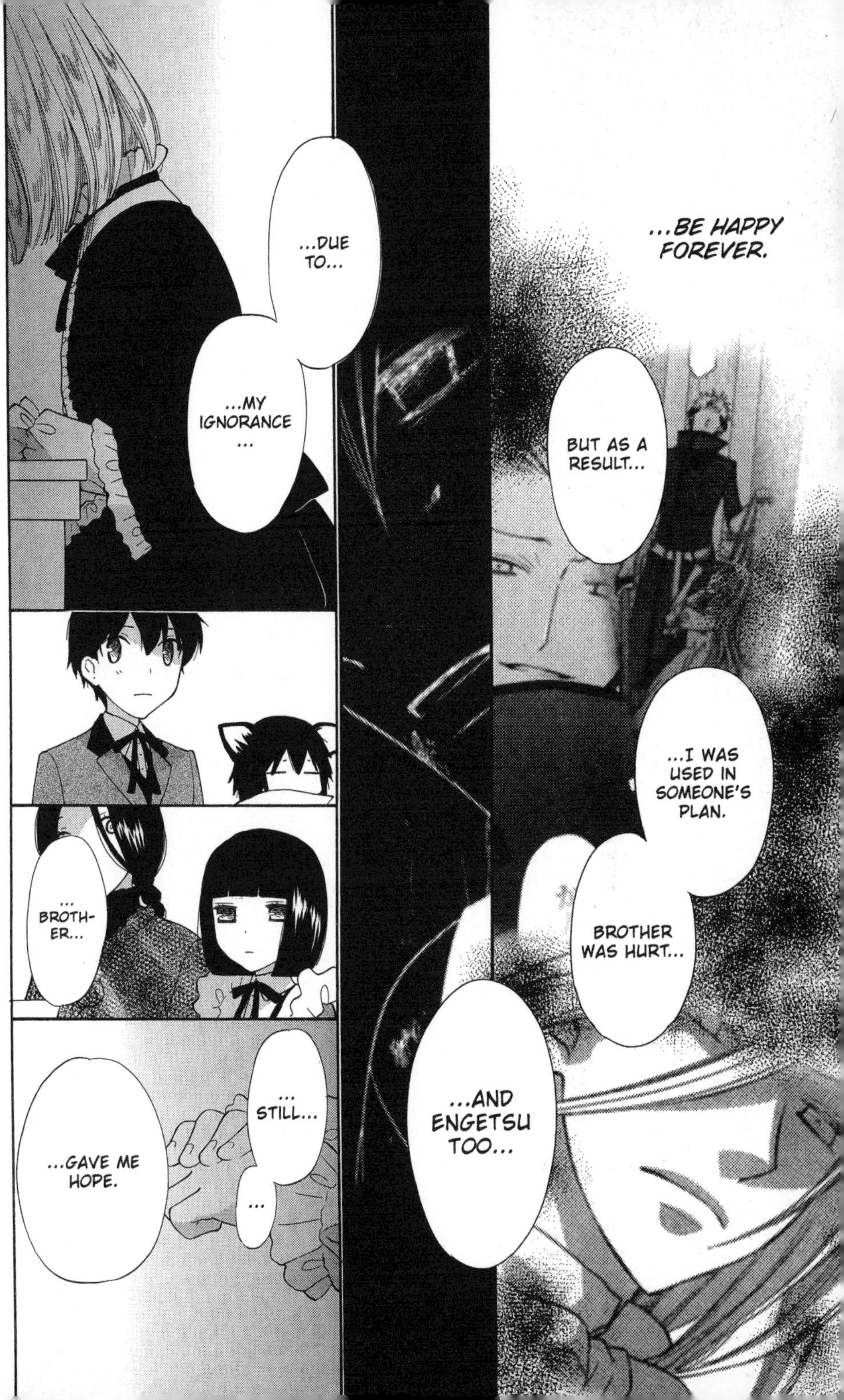
...BE HAPPY FOREVER.
BUT AS A RESULT...
...I WAS USED IN SOMEONE'S PLAN.
BROTHER WAS HURT...
...AND ENGETSU TOO...
...DUE TO...
...MY IGNORANCE ...
... BROTH-ER...
... STILL...
...
...GAVE ME HOPE.

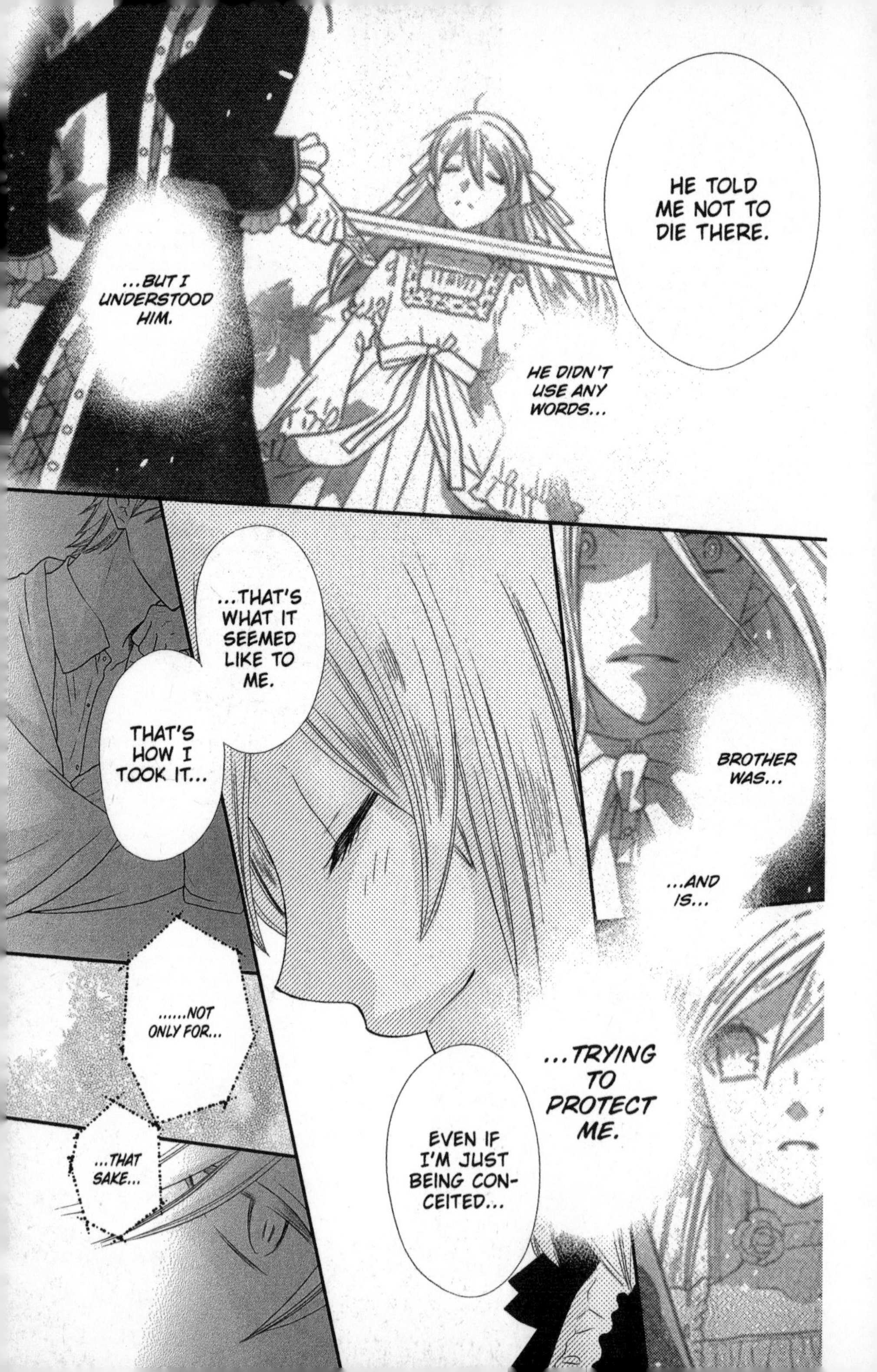
HE TOLD ME NOT TO DIE THERE.
HE DIDN'T USE ANY WORDS...
...BUT I UNDERSTOOD HIM.
BROTHER WAS...
...AND IS...
...TRYING TO PROTECT ME.
...THAT'S WHAT IT SEEMED LIKE TO ME.
THAT'S HOW I TOOK IT...
EVEN IF I'M JUST BEING CON-CEITED...
......NOT ONLY FOR...
...THAT SAKE...

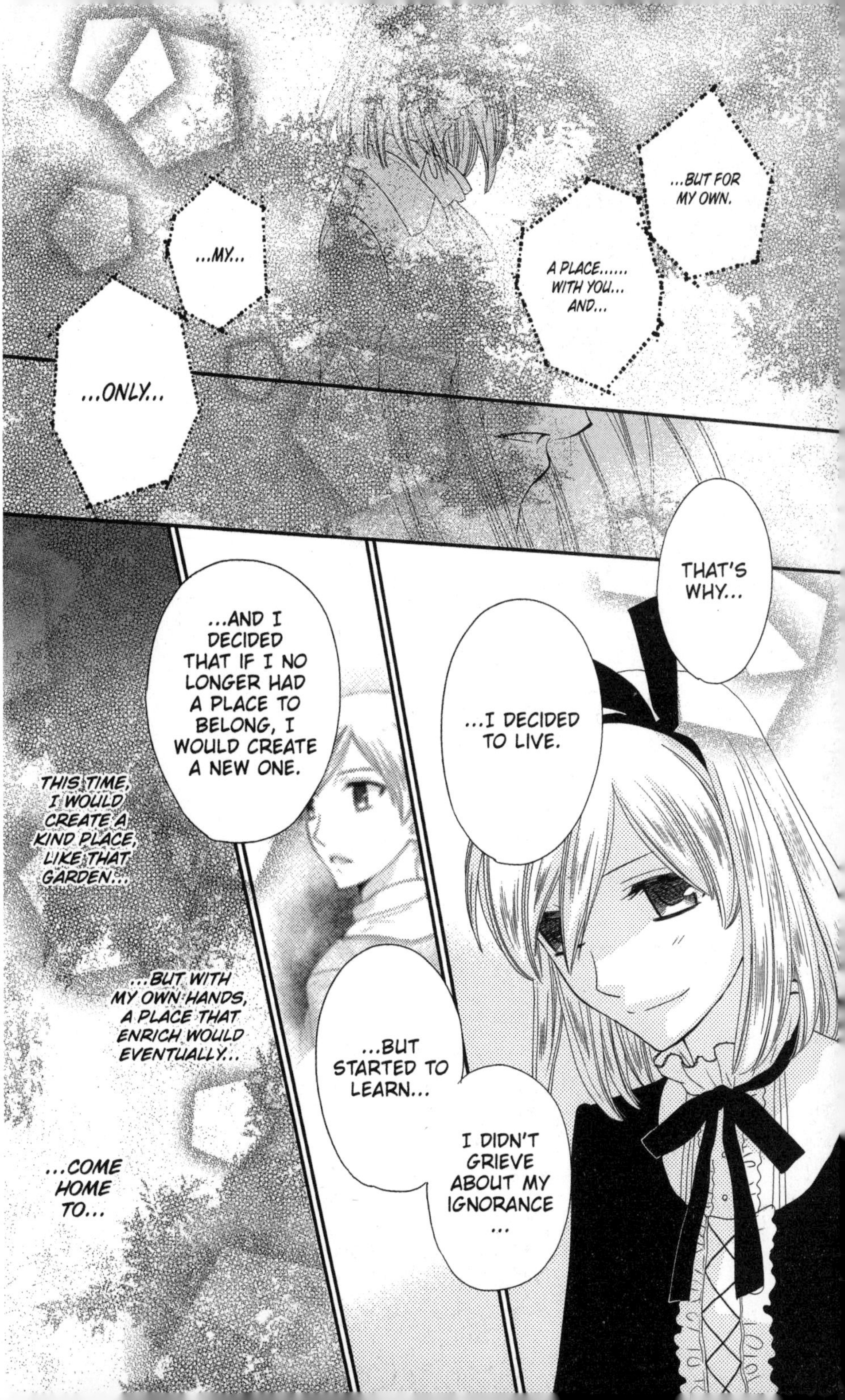

...BUT FOR MY OWN.
A PLACE...... WITH YOU... AND...
...MY...
...ONLY...
THAT'S WHY...
...I DECIDED TO LIVE.
I DIDN'T GRIEVE ABOUT MY IGNORANCE ...
...BUT STARTED TO LEARN...
...AND I DECIDED THAT IF I NO LONGER HAD A PLACE TO BELONG, I WOULD CREATE A NEW ONE.
THIS TIME, I WOULD CREATE A KIND PLACE, LIKE THAT GARDEN...
...BUT WITH MY OWN HANDS, A PLACE THAT ENRICH WOULD EVENTUALLY...
...COME HOME TO...

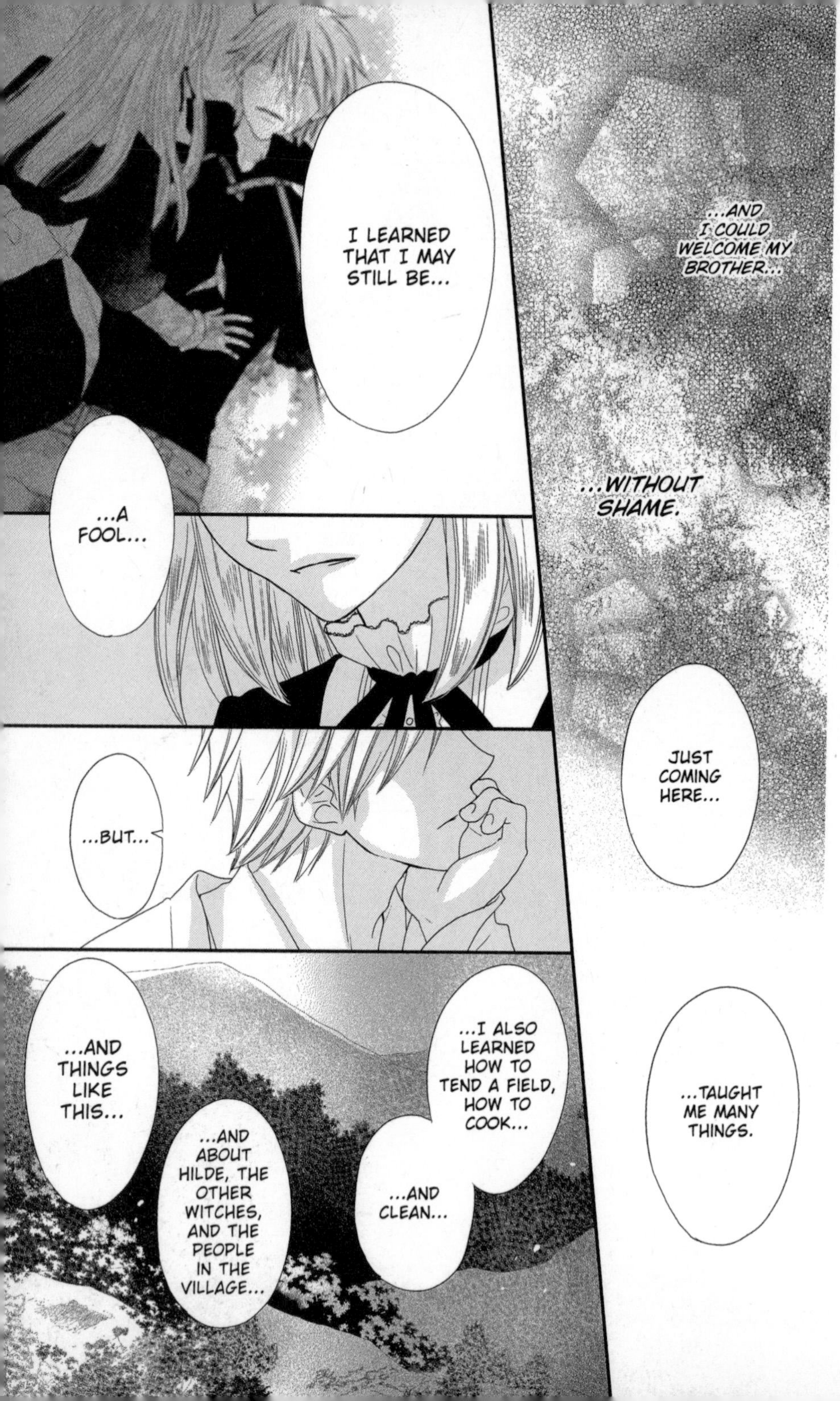

...AND I COULD WELCOME MY BROTHER...
...WITHOUT SHAME.
JUST COMING HERE...
...TAUGHT ME MANY THINGS.
I LEARNED THAT I MAY STILL BE...
...A FOOL...
...BUT...
...I ALSO LEARNED HOW TO TEND A FIELD, HOW TO COOK...
...AND CLEAN...
...AND ABOUT HILDE, THE OTHER WITCHES, AND THE PEOPLE IN THE VILLAGE...
...AND THINGS LIKE THIS...

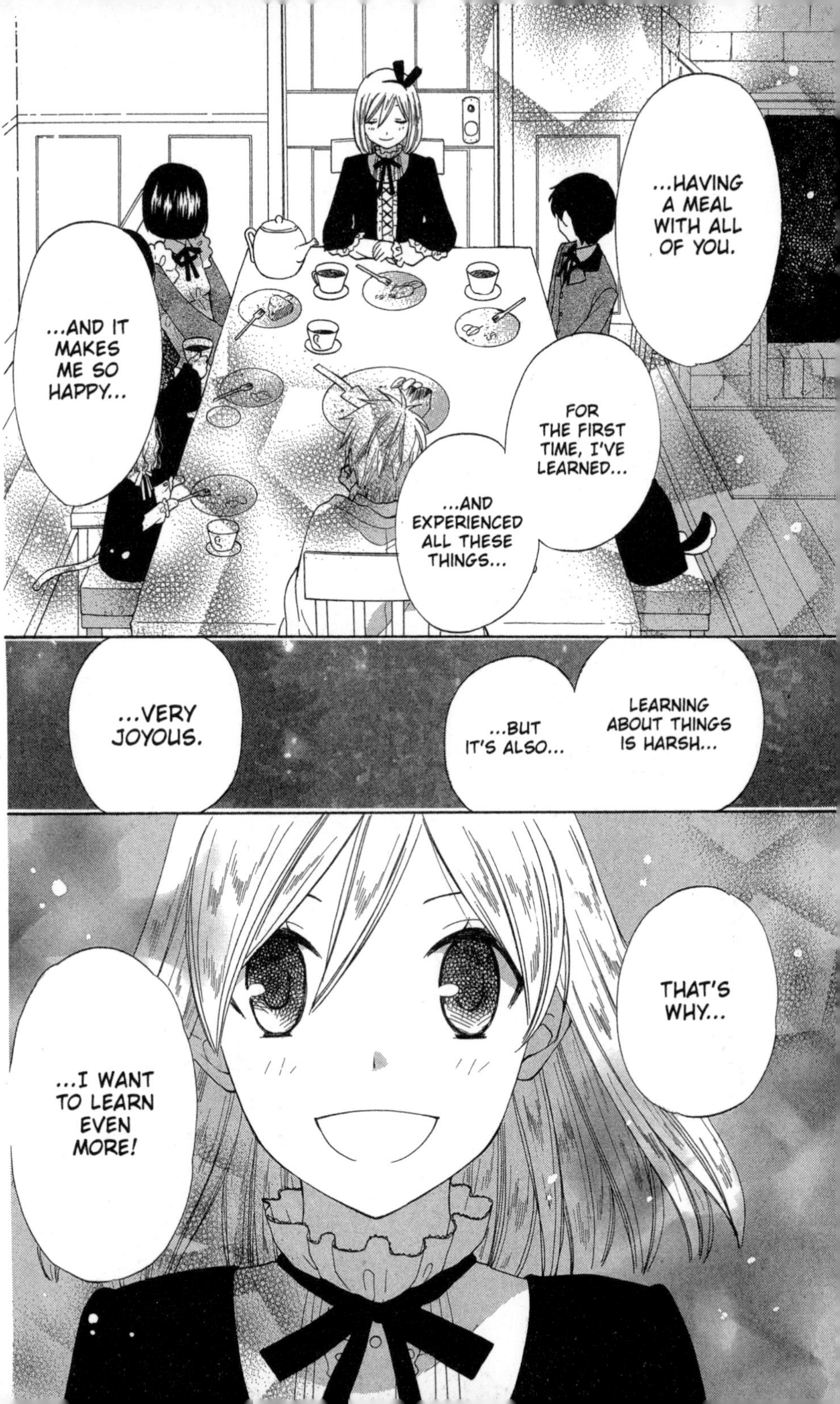
...HAVING A MEAL WITH ALL OF YOU.
FOR THE FIRST TIME, I'VE LEARNED...
...AND EXPERIENCED ALL THESE THINGS...
...AND IT MAKES ME SO HAPPY...
LEARNING ABOUT THINGS IS HARSH...
...BUT IT'S ALSO...
...VERY JOYOUS.
THAT'S WHY...
...I WANT TO LEARN EVEN MORE!

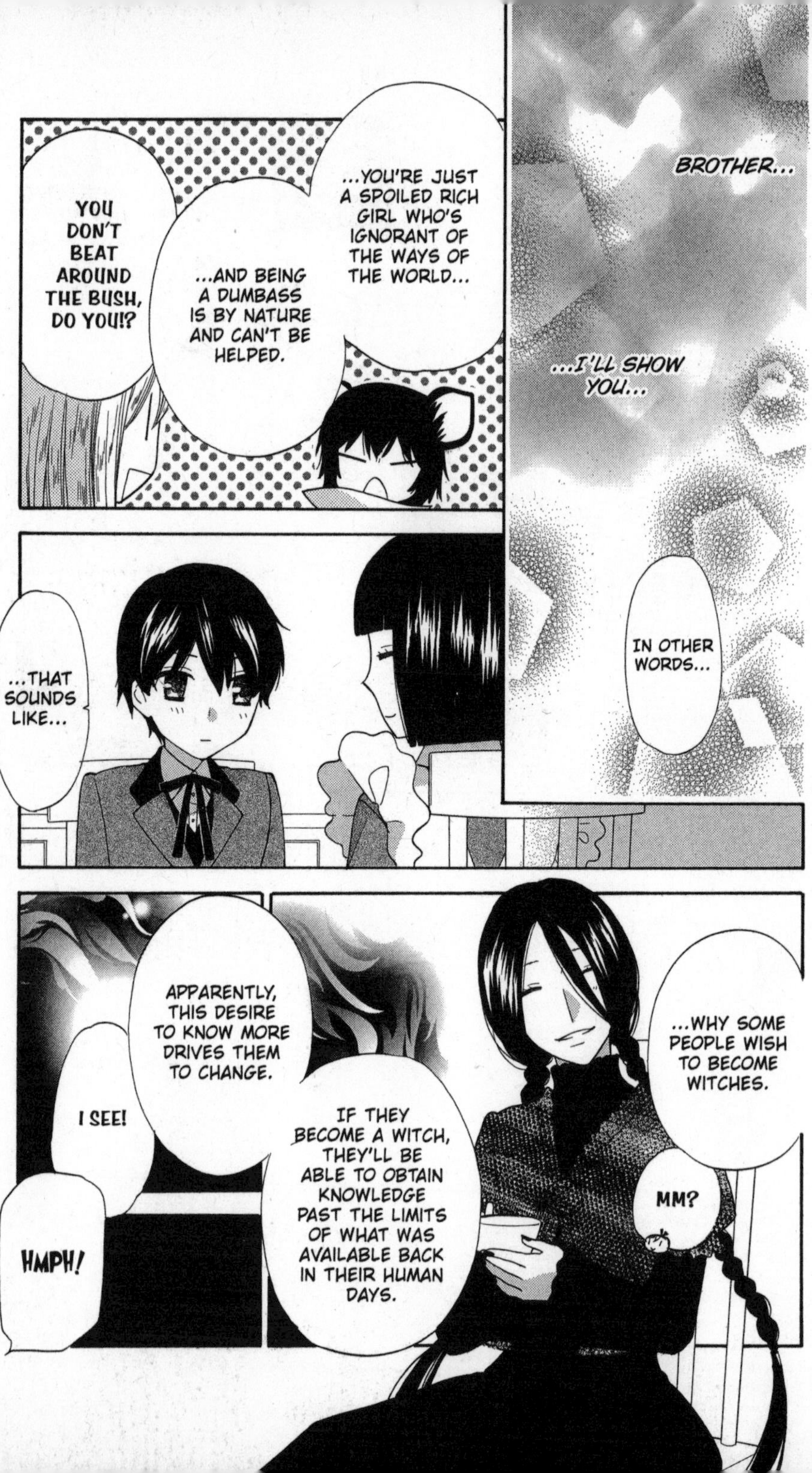
BROTHER...
...I'LL SHOW YOU...
IN OTHER WORDS...
...YOU'RE JUST A SPOILED RICH GIRL WHO'S IGNORANT OF THE WAYS OF THE WORLD...
...AND BEING A DUMBASS IS BY NATURE AND CAN'T BE HELPED.
YOU DON'T BEAT AROUND THE BUSH, DO YOU!?
...THAT SOUNDS LIKE...
...WHY SOME PEOPLE WISH TO BECOME WITCHES.
MM?
APPARENTLY, THIS DESIRE TO KNOW MORE DRIVES THEM TO CHANGE.
IF THEY BECOME A WITCH, THEY'LL BE ABLE TO OBTAIN KNOWLEDGE PAST THE LIMITS OF WHAT WAS AVAILABLE BACK IN THEIR HUMAN DAYS.
I SEE!
HMPH!

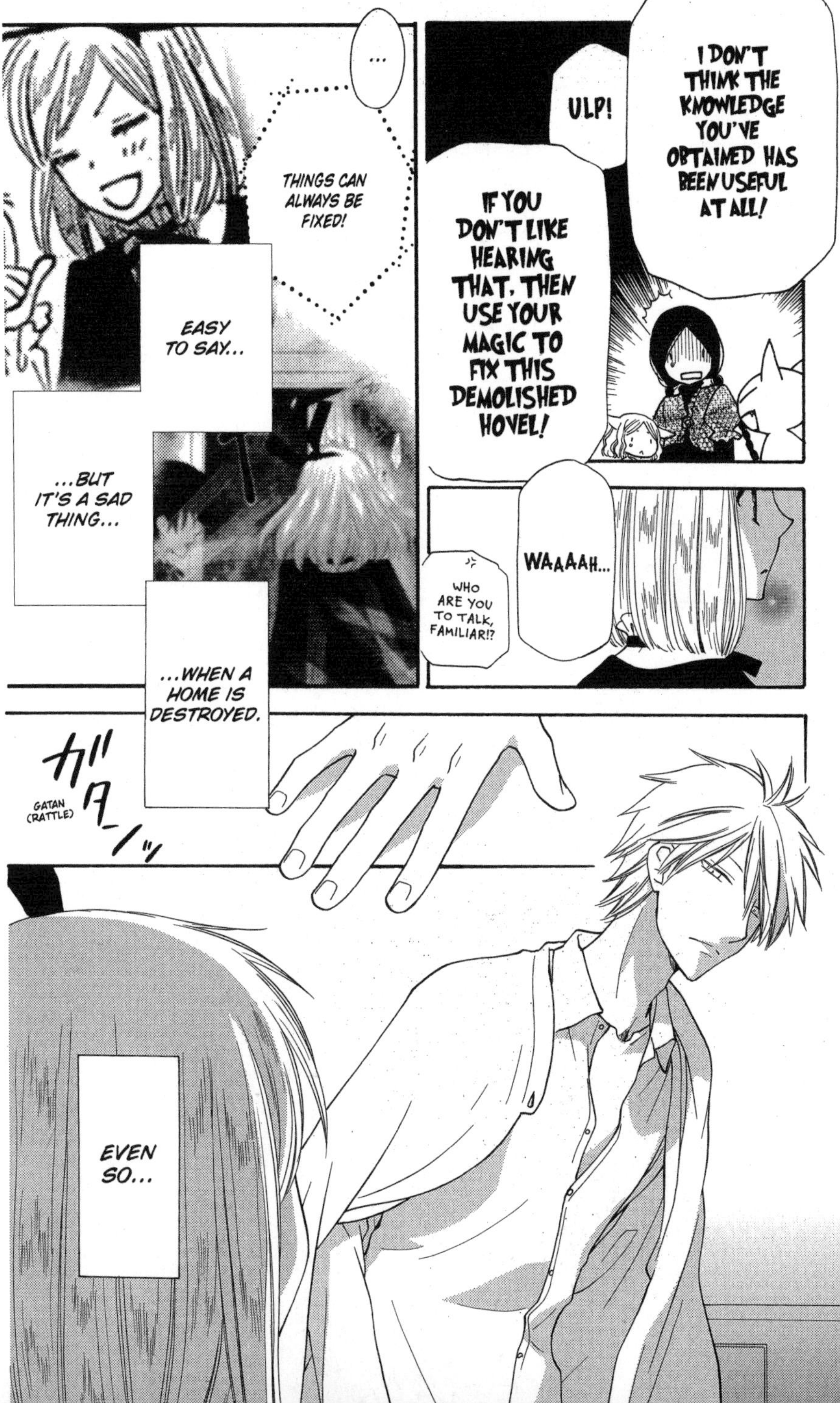
I DON'T THINK THE KNOWLEDGE YOU'VE OBTAINED HAS BEEN USEFUL AT ALL!
ULP!
IF YOU DON'T LIKE HEARING THAT, THEN USE YOUR MAGIC TO FIX THIS DEMOLISHED HOVEL!
WAAAAH...
WHO ARE YOU TO TALK, FAMILIAR!?
...
THINGS CAN ALWAYS BE FIXED!
EASY TO SAY...
...BUT IT'S A SAD THING...
...WHEN A HOME IS DESTROYED.
ガタンッ
GATAN (RATTLE)
EVEN SO...

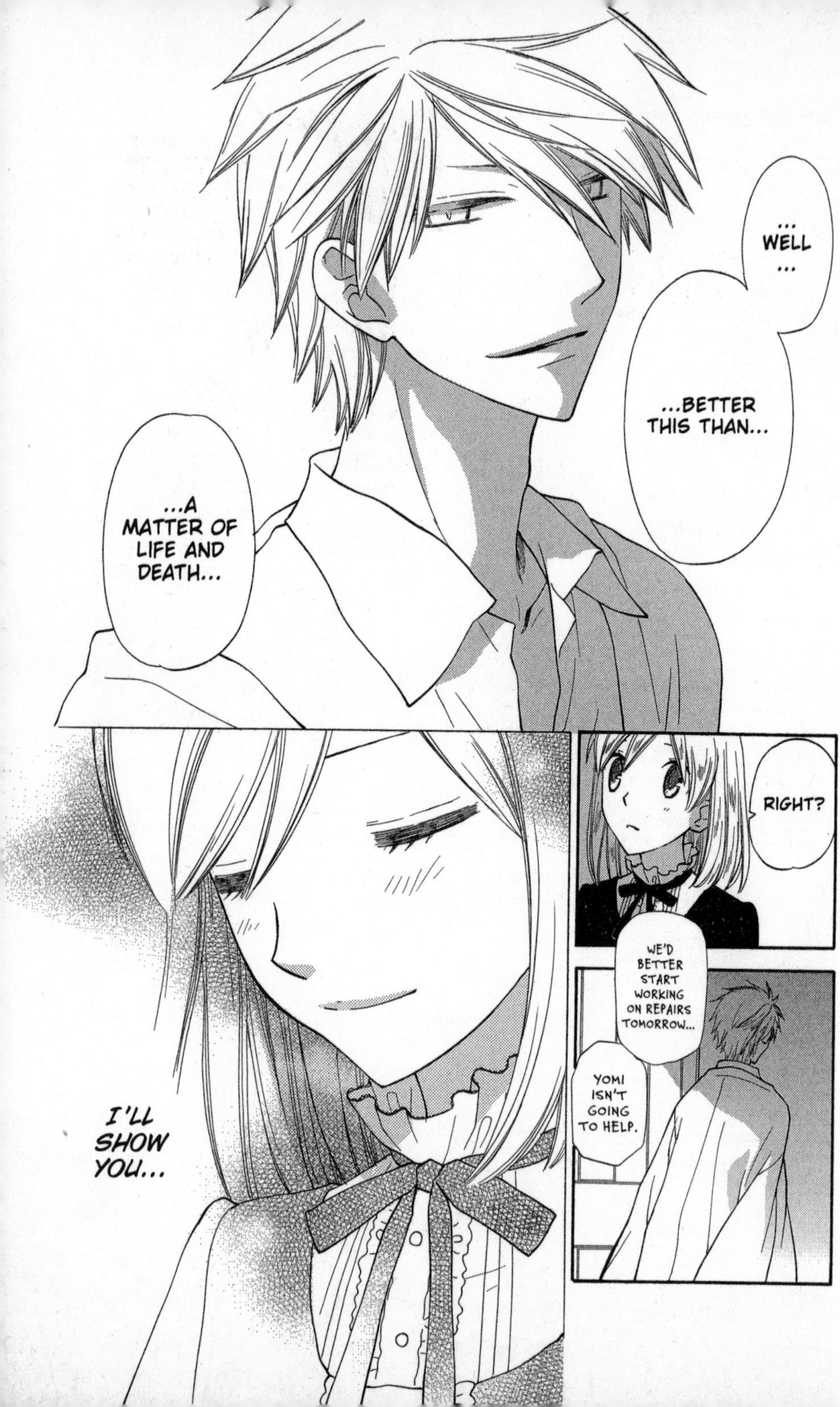
...WELL...
...BETTER THIS THAN...
...A MATTER OF LIFE AND DEATH...
RIGHT?
WE'D BETTER START WORKING ON REPAIRS TOMORROW...
YOMI ISN'T GOING TO HELP.
I'LL SHOW YOU...

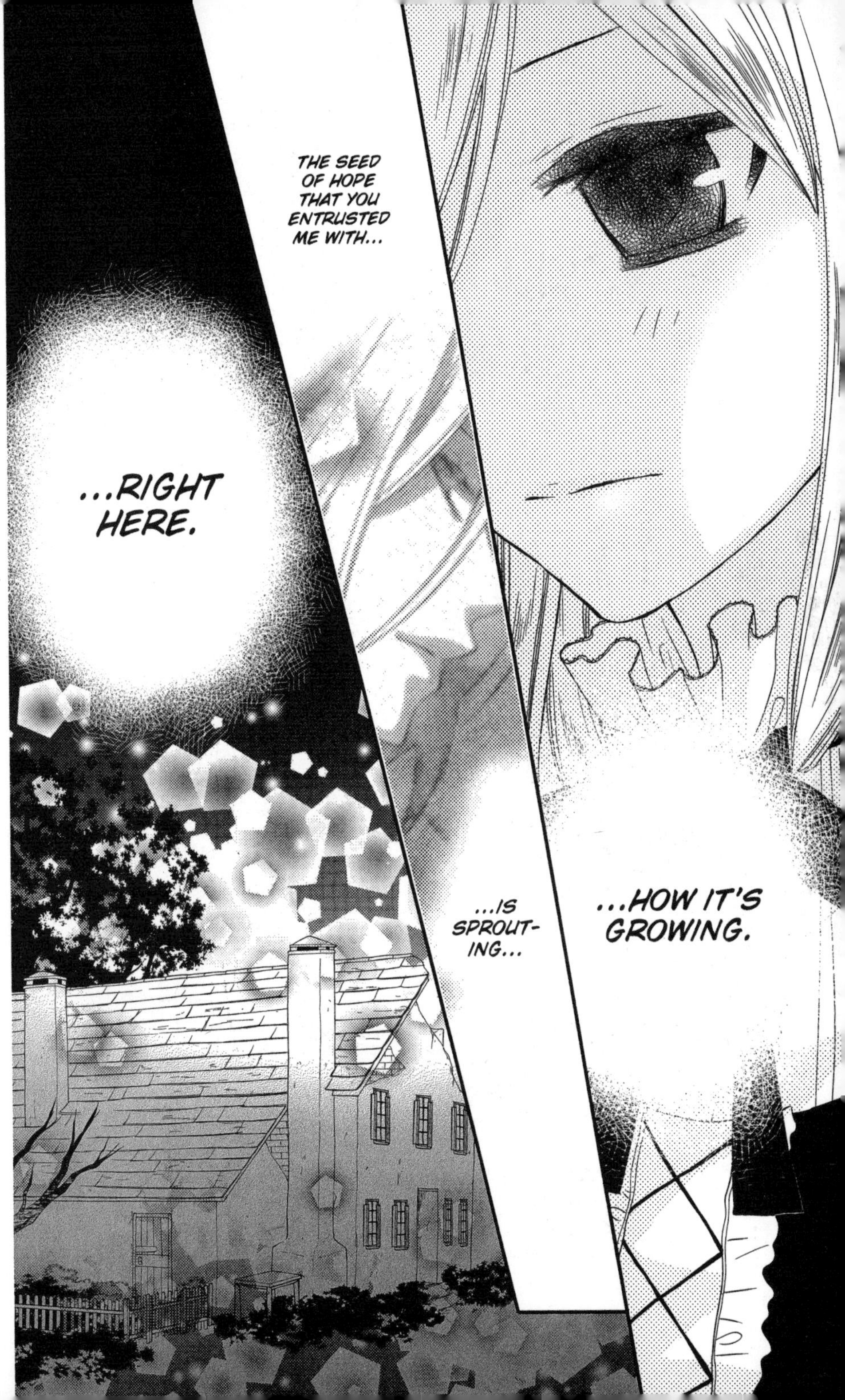
THE SEED OF HOPE THAT YOU ENTRUSTED ME WITH...
...RIGHT HERE.
...IS SPROUT-ING...
...HOW IT'S GROWING.

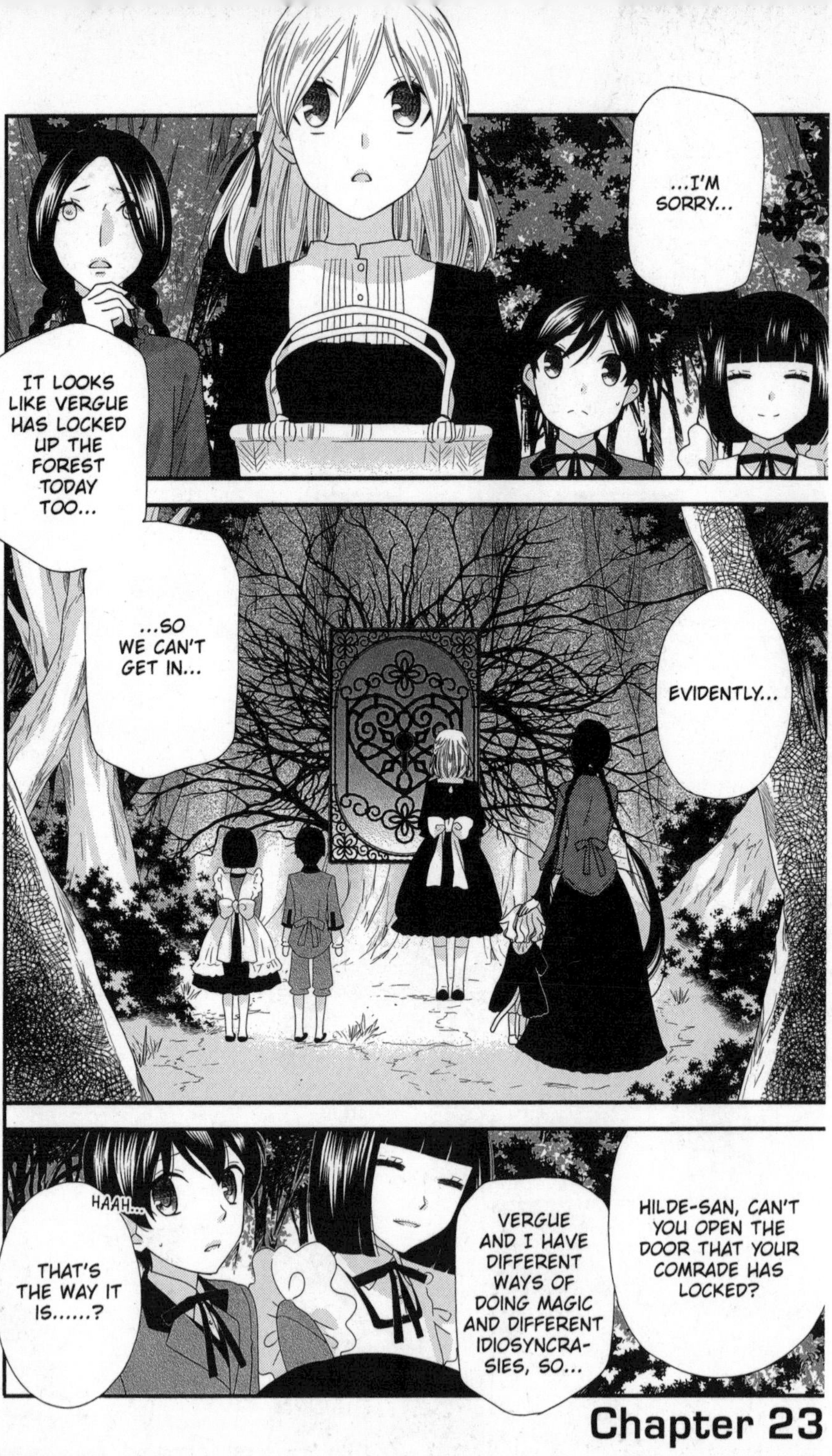
...I'M SORRY...
IT LOOKS LIKE VERGUE HAS LOCKED UP THE FOREST TODAY TOO...
...SO WE CAN'T GET IN...
EVIDENTLY...
HILDE-SAN, CAN'T YOU OPEN THE DOOR THAT YOUR COMRADE HAS LOCKED?
VERGUE AND I HAVE DIFFERENT WAYS OF DOING MAGIC AND DIFFERENT IDIOSYNCRA-SIES, SO...
HAAH...
THAT'S THE WAY IT IS......?

Chapter 23

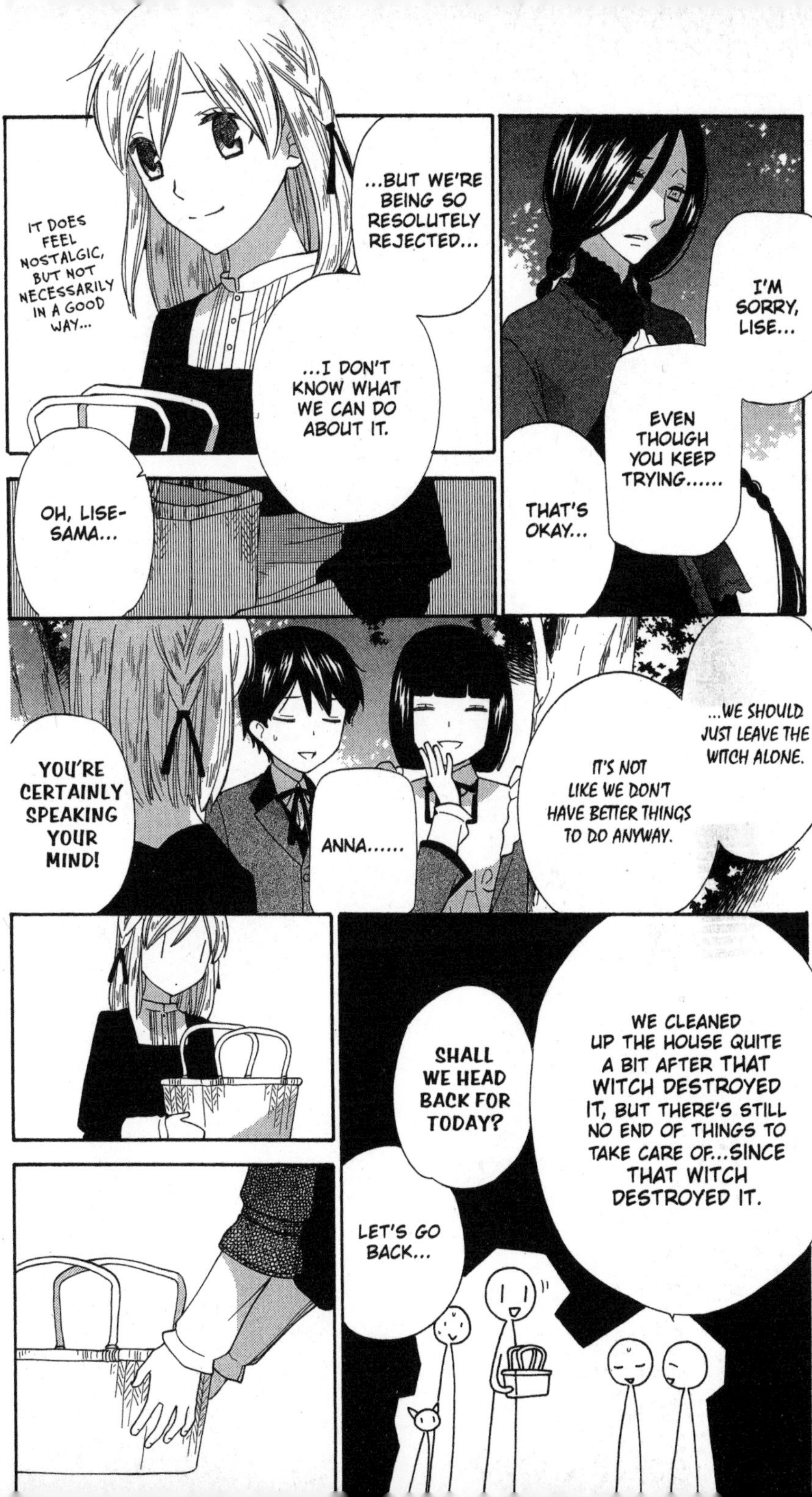
I'M SORRY, LISE...
EVEN THOUGH YOU KEEP TRYING......
THAT'S OKAY...
...BUT WE'RE BEING SO RESOLUTELY REJECTED...
IT DOES FEEL NOSTALGIC, BUT NOT NECESSARILY IN A GOOD WAY...
...I DON'T KNOW WHAT WE CAN DO ABOUT IT.
OH, LISE-SAMA...
...WE SHOULD JUST LEAVE THE WITCH ALONE.
IT'S NOT LIKE WE DON'T HAVE BETTER THINGS TO DO ANYWAY.
ANNA......
YOU'RE CERTAINLY SPEAKING YOUR MIND!
WE CLEANED UP THE HOUSE QUITE A BIT AFTER THAT WITCH DESTROYED IT, BUT THERE'S STILL NO END OF THINGS TO TAKE CARE OF...SINCE THAT WITCH DESTROYED IT.
SHALL WE HEAD BACK FOR TODAY?
LET'S GO BACK...

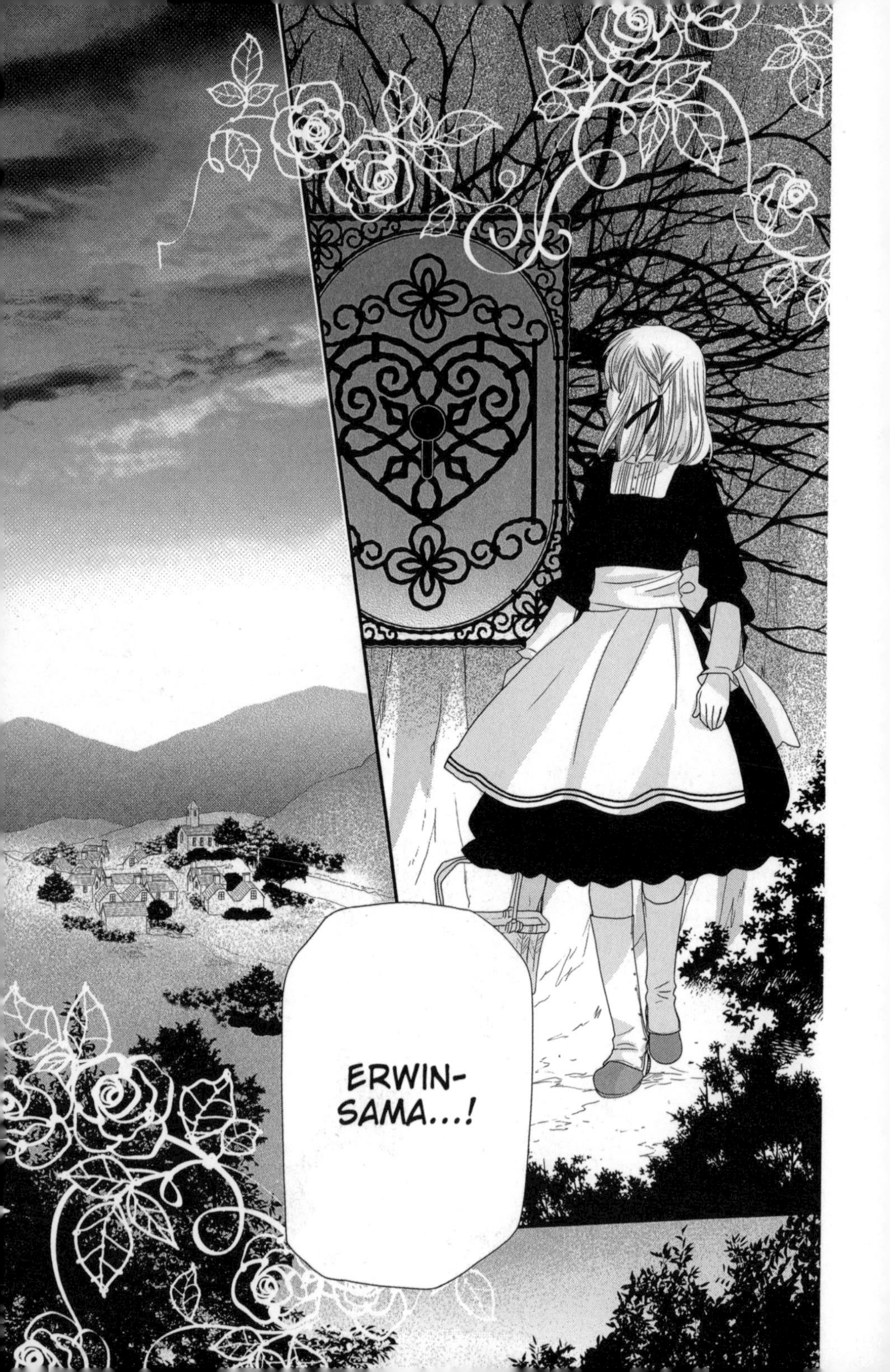
ERWIN-
SAMA...!

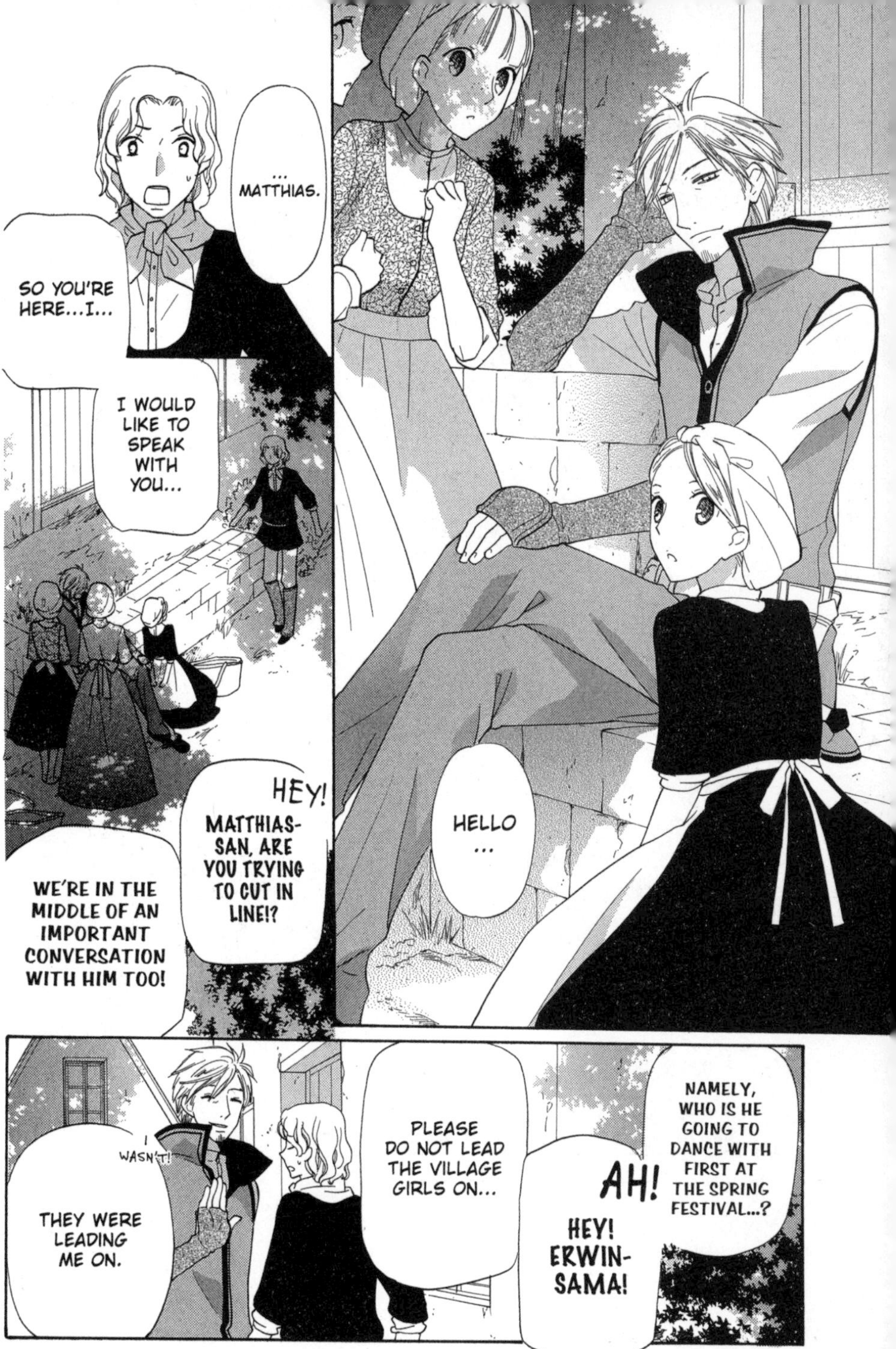
HELLO ...
... MATTHIAS.
SO YOU'RE HERE...I...
I WOULD LIKE TO SPEAK WITH YOU...
HEY!
MATTHIAS-SAN, ARE YOU TRYING TO CUT IN LINE!?
WE'RE IN THE MIDDLE OF AN IMPORTANT CONVERSATION WITH HIM TOO!
NAMELY, WHO IS HE GOING TO DANCE WITH FIRST AT THE SPRING FESTIVAL...?
AH!
HEY! ERWIN-SAMA!
PLEASE DO NOT LEAD THE VILLAGE GIRLS ON...
I WASN'T!
THEY WERE LEADING ME ON.

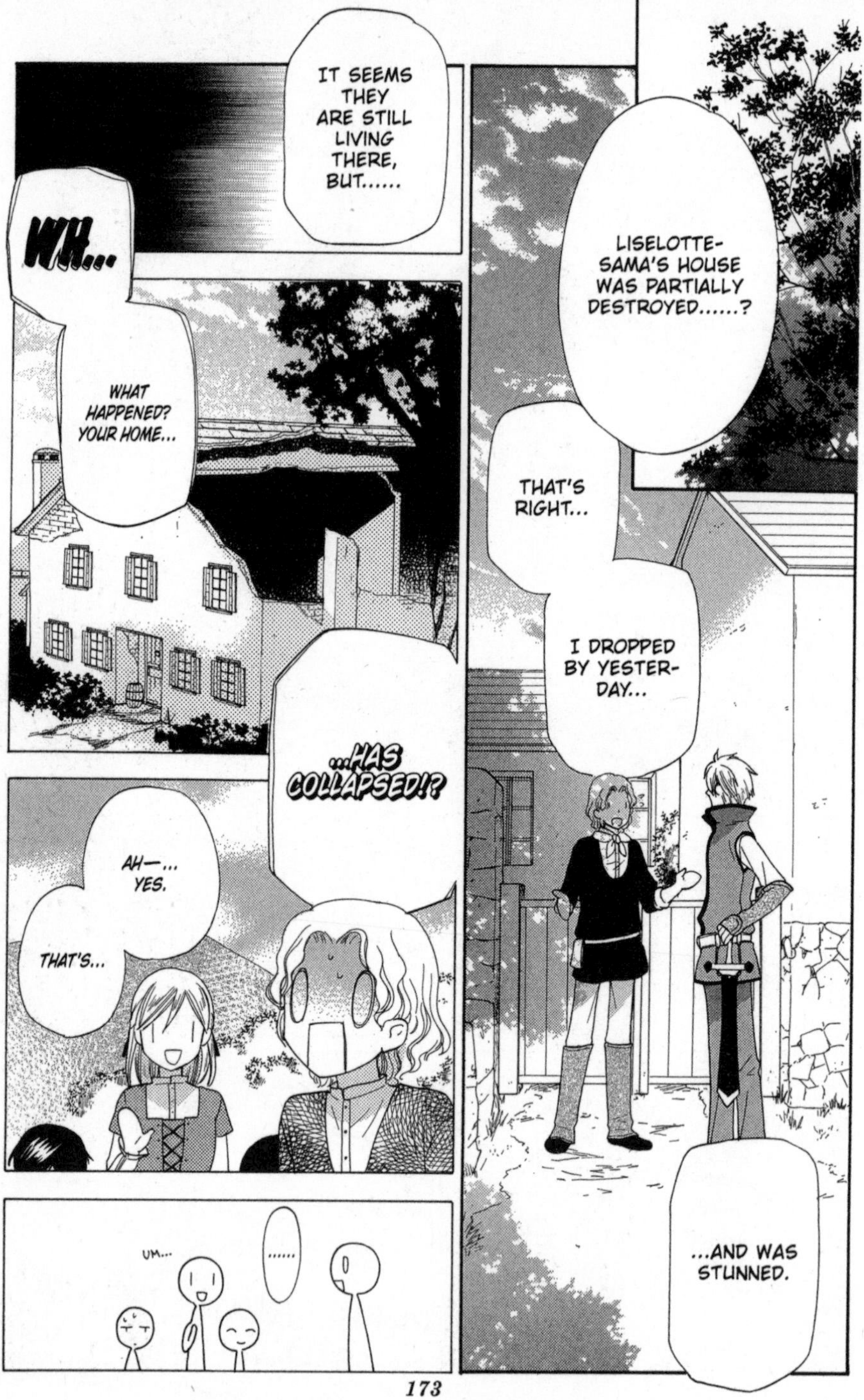
LISELOTTE-SAMA'S HOUSE WAS PARTIALLY DESTROYED......?
THAT'S RIGHT...
I DROPPED BY YESTER-DAY...
...AND WAS STUNNED.
IT SEEMS THEY ARE STILL LIVING THERE, BUT......
WH...
WHAT HAPPENED? YOUR HOME...
...HAS COLLAPSED!?
AH—... YES.
THAT'S...
......
UM...

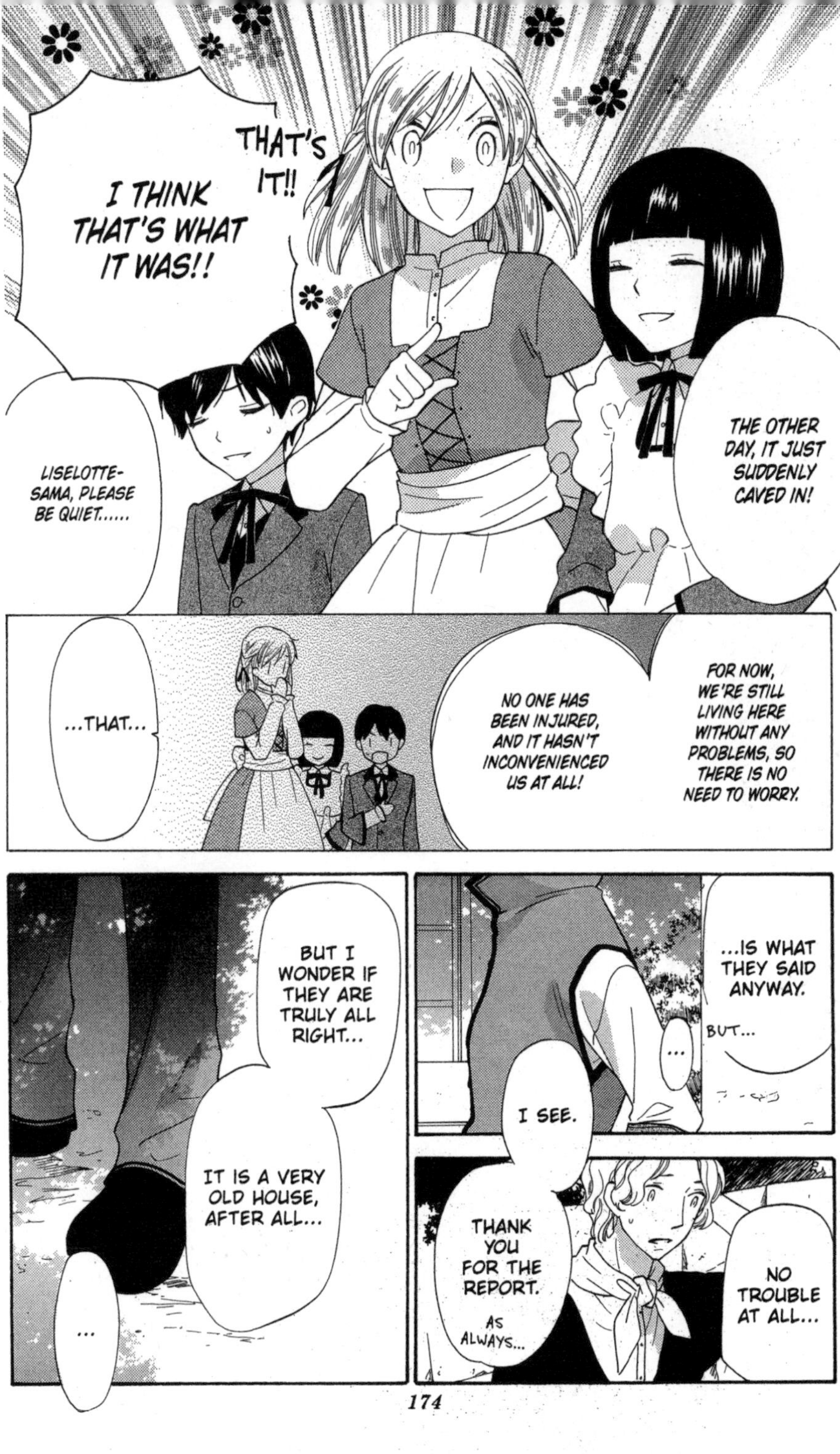
THE OTHER DAY, IT JUST SUDDENLY CAVED IN!
THAT'S IT!!
I THINK THAT'S WHAT IT WAS!!
LISELOTTE-SAMA, PLEASE BE QUIET......
FOR NOW, WE'RE STILL LIVING HERE WITHOUT ANY PROBLEMS, SO THERE IS NO NEED TO WORRY.
NO ONE HAS BEEN INJURED, AND IT HASN'T INCONVENIENCED US AT ALL!
...THAT...
...IS WHAT THEY SAID ANYWAY.
BUT...
...
I SEE.
NO TROUBLE AT ALL...
THANK YOU FOR THE REPORT.
AS ALWAYS...
BUT I WONDER IF THEY ARE TRULY ALL RIGHT...
IT IS A VERY OLD HOUSE, AFTER ALL...
...

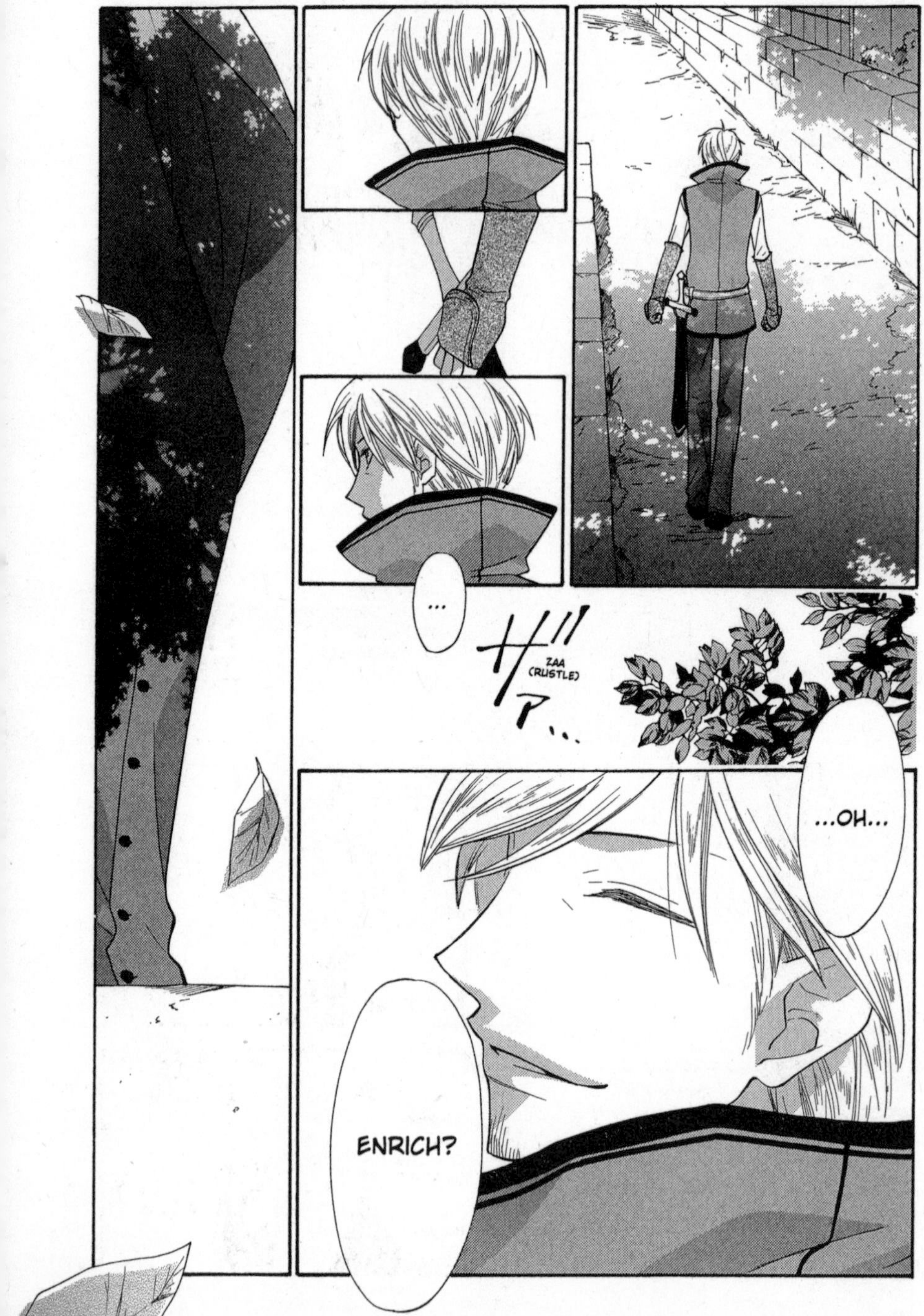
...
ザァ...
ZAA (RUSTLE)
...OH...
ENRICH?

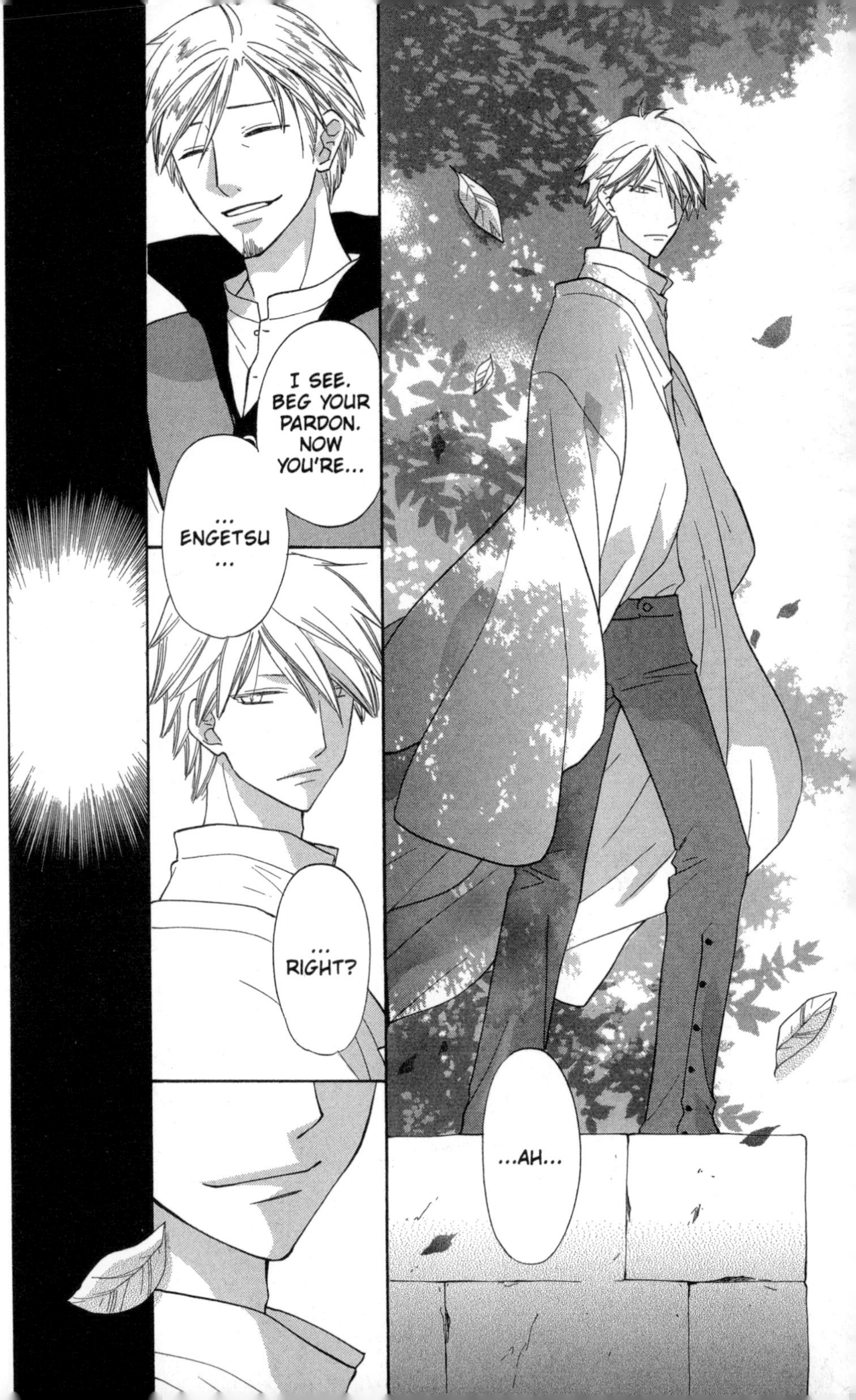
...AH...
I SEE. BEG YOUR PARDON. NOW YOU'RE...
...ENGETSU...
...RIGHT?

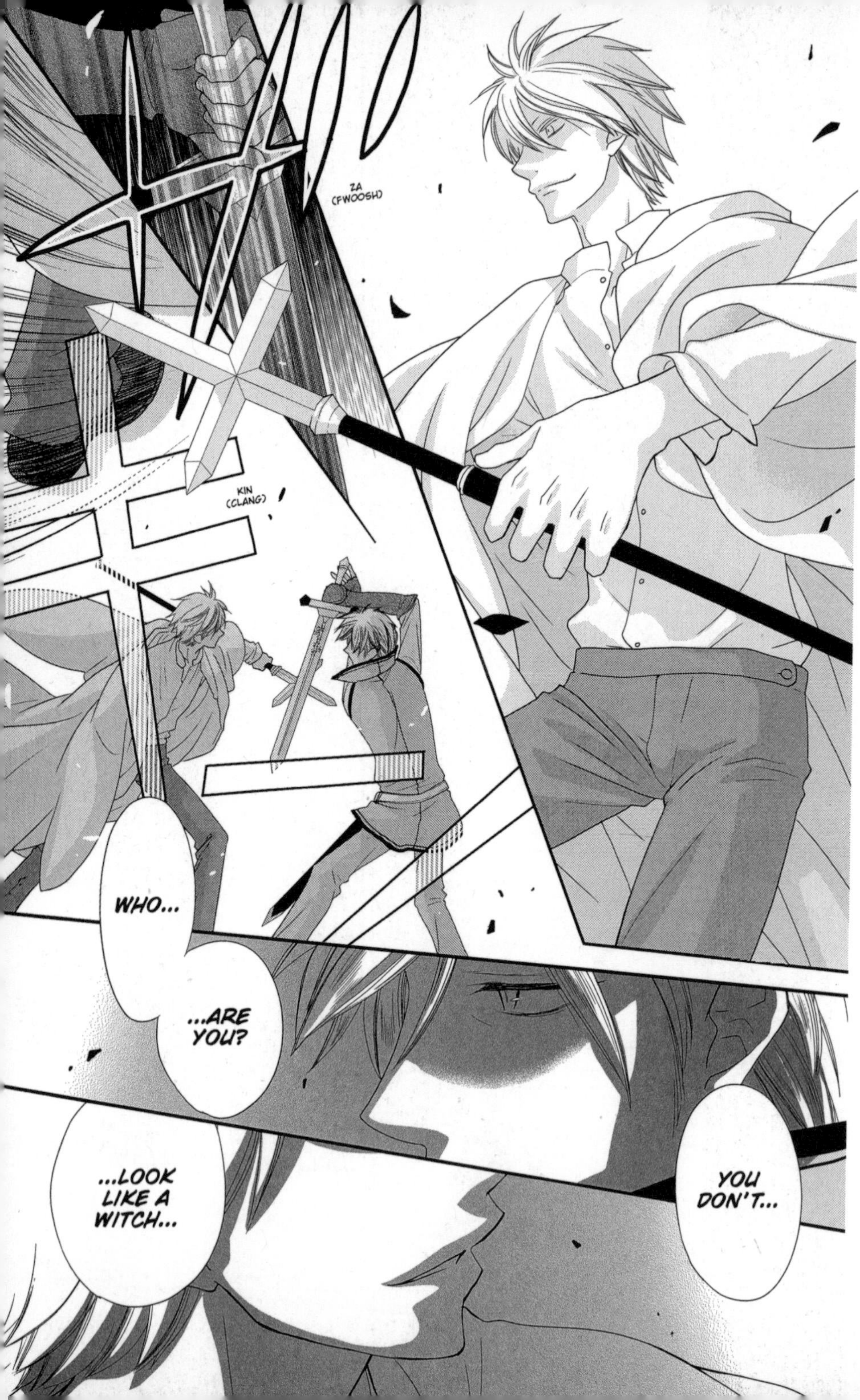
ZA (FWOOSH)
KIN (CLANG)
WHO...
...ARE YOU?
YOU DON'T...
...LOOK LIKE A WITCH...

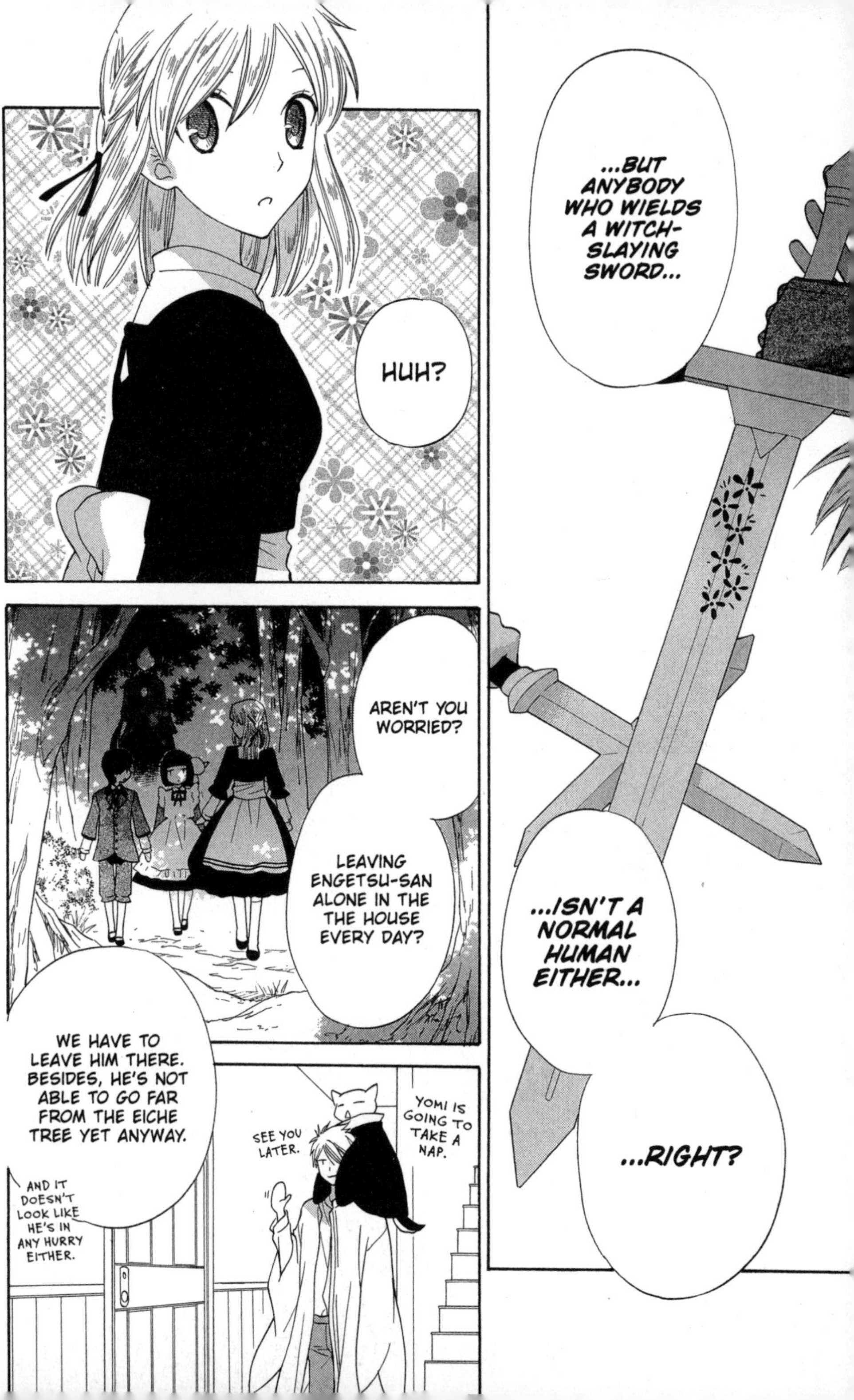
...BUT ANYBODY WHO WIELDS A WITCH-SLAYING SWORD...
...ISN'T A NORMAL HUMAN EITHER...
...RIGHT?
HUH?
AREN'T YOU WORRIED?
LEAVING ENGETSU-SAN ALONE IN THE THE HOUSE EVERY DAY?
WE HAVE TO LEAVE HIM THERE. BESIDES, HE'S NOT ABLE TO GO FAR FROM THE EICHE TREE YET ANYWAY.
AND IT DOESN'T LOOK LIKE HE'S IN ANY HURRY EITHER.
YOMI IS GOING TO TAKE A NAP.
SEE YOU LATER.

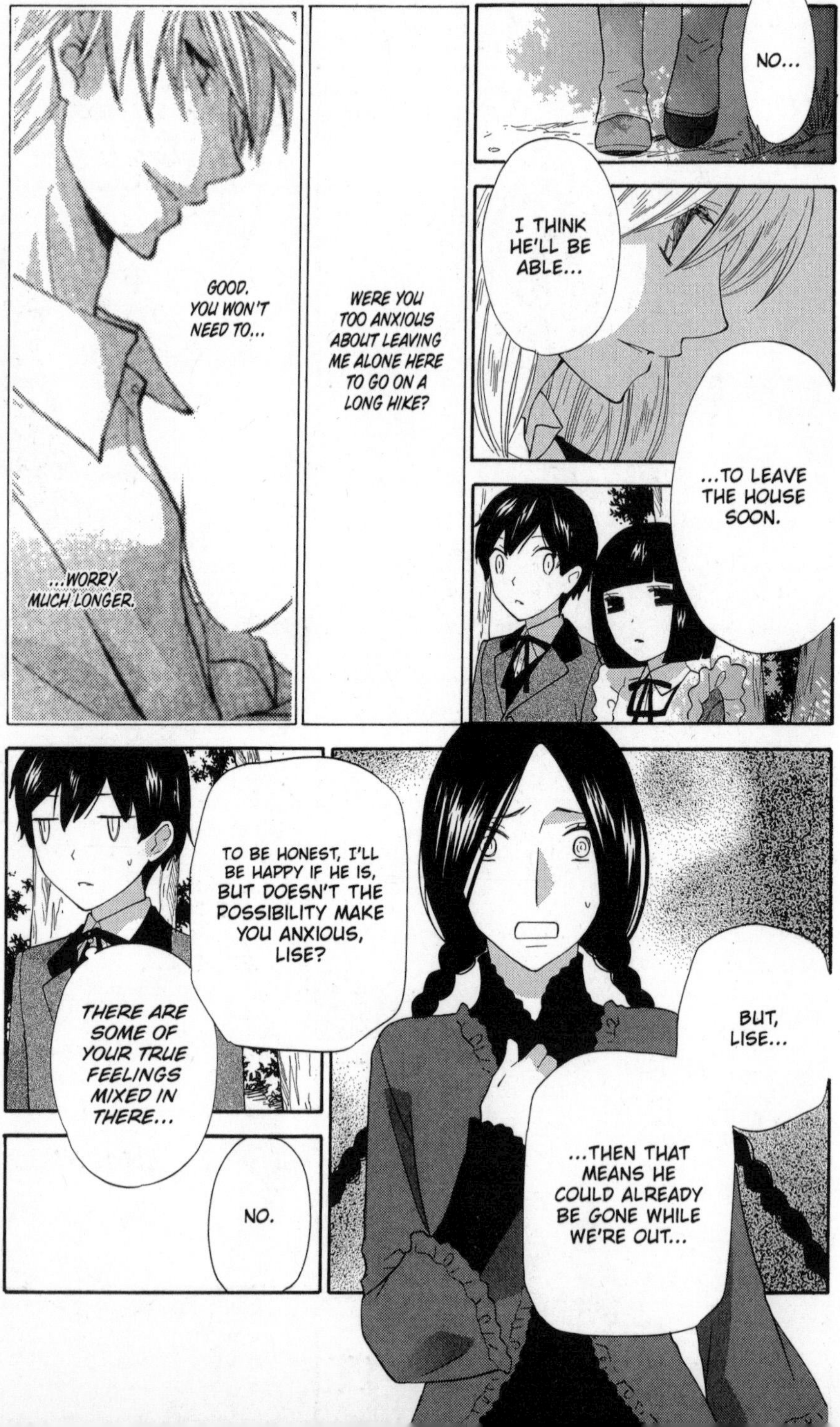
NO...
I THINK HE'LL BE ABLE...
...TO LEAVE THE HOUSE SOON.
WERE YOU TOO ANXIOUS ABOUT LEAVING ME ALONE HERE TO GO ON A LONG HIKE?
GOOD. YOU WON'T NEED TO...
...WORRY MUCH LONGER.
BUT, LISE...
...THEN THAT MEANS HE COULD ALREADY BE GONE WHILE WE'RE OUT...
TO BE HONEST, I'LL BE HAPPY IF HE IS, BUT DOESN'T THE POSSIBILITY MAKE YOU ANXIOUS, LISE?
THERE ARE SOME OF YOUR TRUE FEELINGS MIXED IN THERE...
NO.

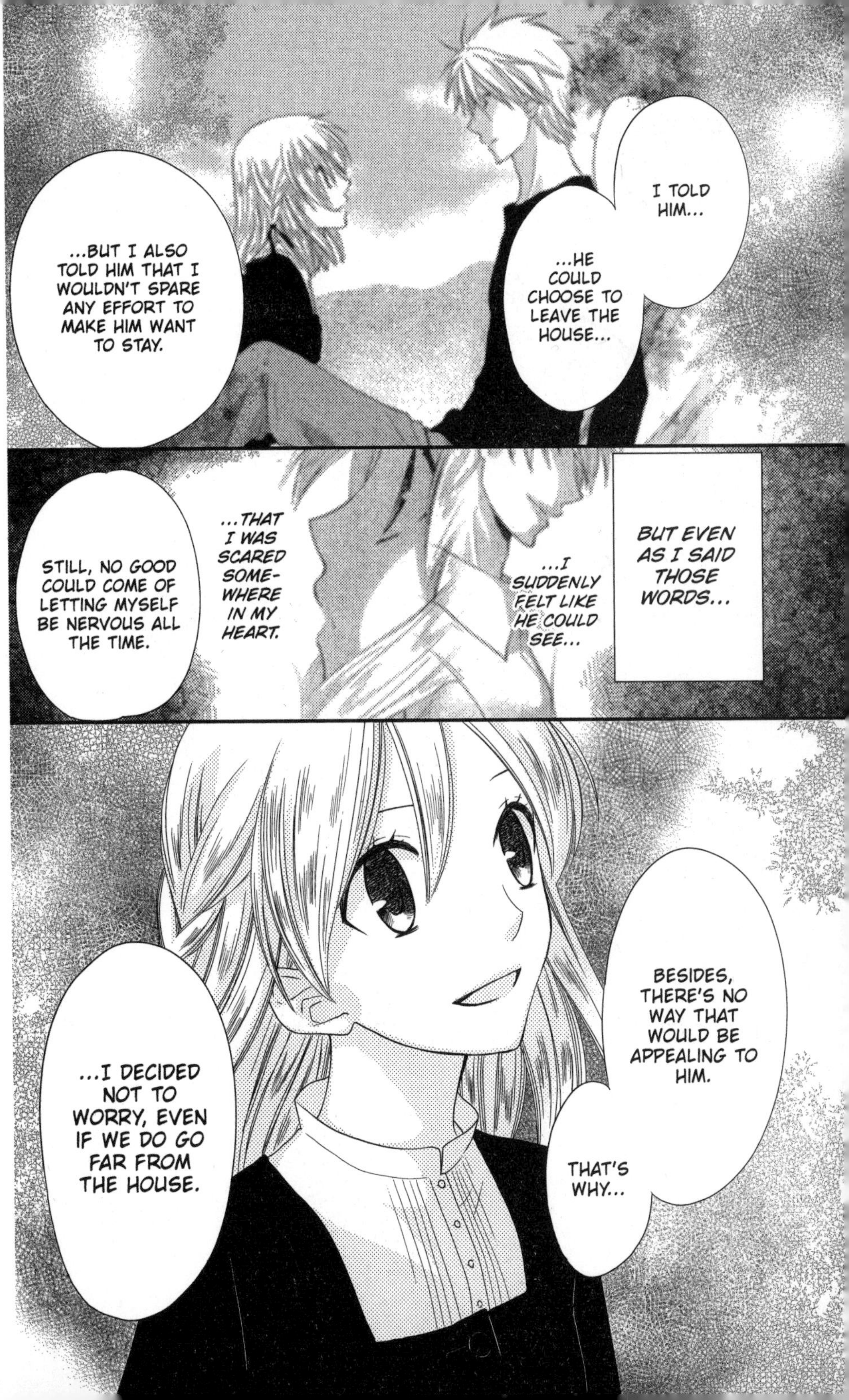
I TOLD HIM...
...HE COULD CHOOSE TO LEAVE THE HOUSE...
...BUT I ALSO TOLD HIM THAT I WOULDN'T SPARE ANY EFFORT TO MAKE HIM WANT TO STAY.
BUT EVEN AS I SAID THOSE WORDS...
...I SUDDENLY FELT LIKE HE COULD SEE...
...THAT I WAS SCARED SOME-WHERE IN MY HEART.
STILL, NO GOOD COULD COME OF LETTING MYSELF BE NERVOUS ALL THE TIME.
BESIDES, THERE'S NO WAY THAT WOULD BE APPEALING TO HIM.
THAT'S WHY...
...I DECIDED NOT TO WORRY, EVEN IF WE DO GO FAR FROM THE HOUSE.

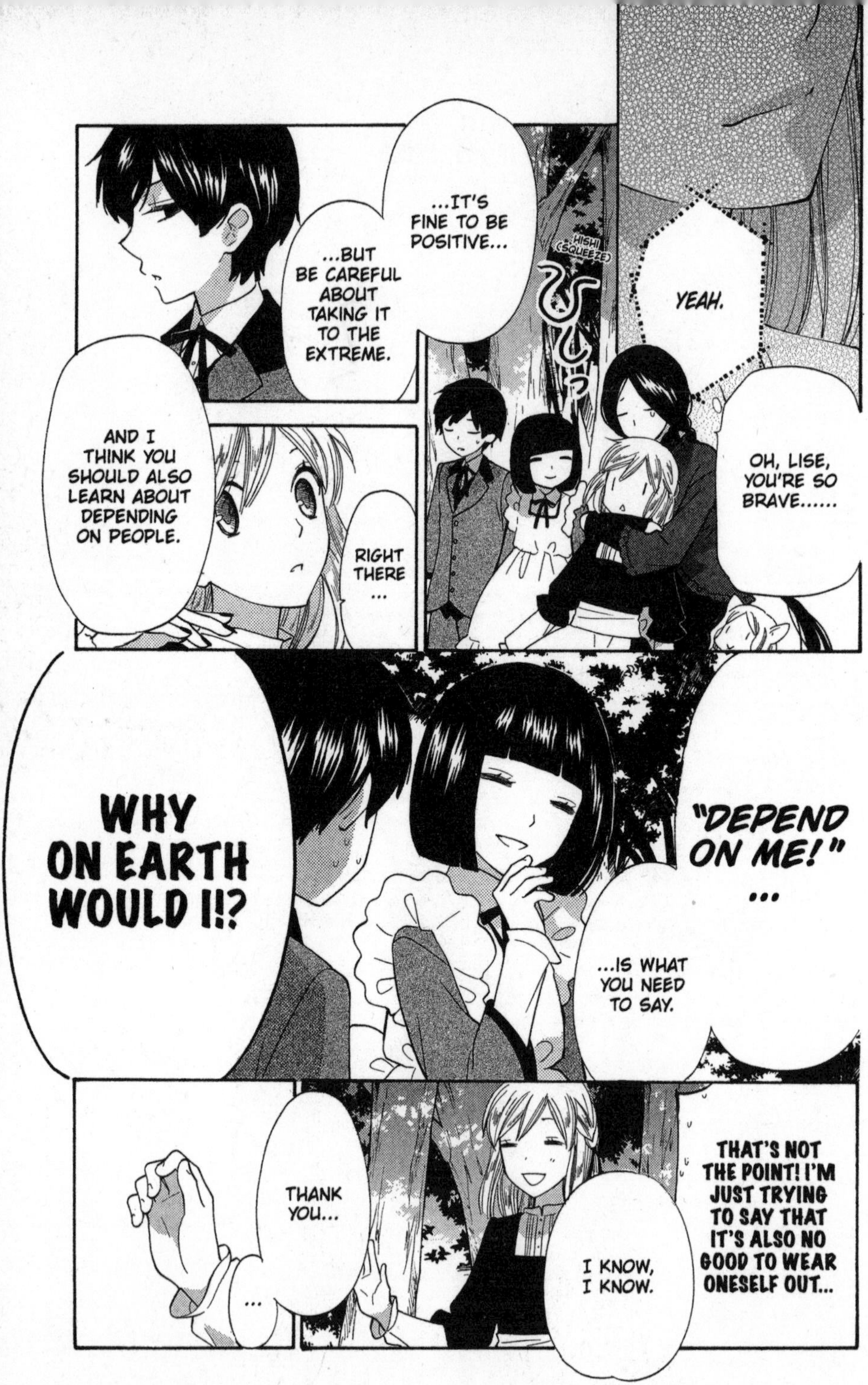
YEAH.
...IT'S FINE TO BE POSITIVE...
...BUT BE CAREFUL ABOUT TAKING IT TO THE EXTREME.
HISHI (SQUEEZE)
OH, LISE, YOU'RE SO BRAVE......
AND I THINK YOU SHOULD ALSO LEARN ABOUT DEPENDING ON PEOPLE.
RIGHT THERE ...
"DEPEND ON ME!" ...
...IS WHAT YOU NEED TO SAY.
WHY ON EARTH WOULD I!?
THAT'S NOT THE POINT! I'M JUST TRYING TO SAY THAT IT'S ALSO NO GOOD TO WEAR ONESELF OUT...
I KNOW, I KNOW.
THANK YOU...
...

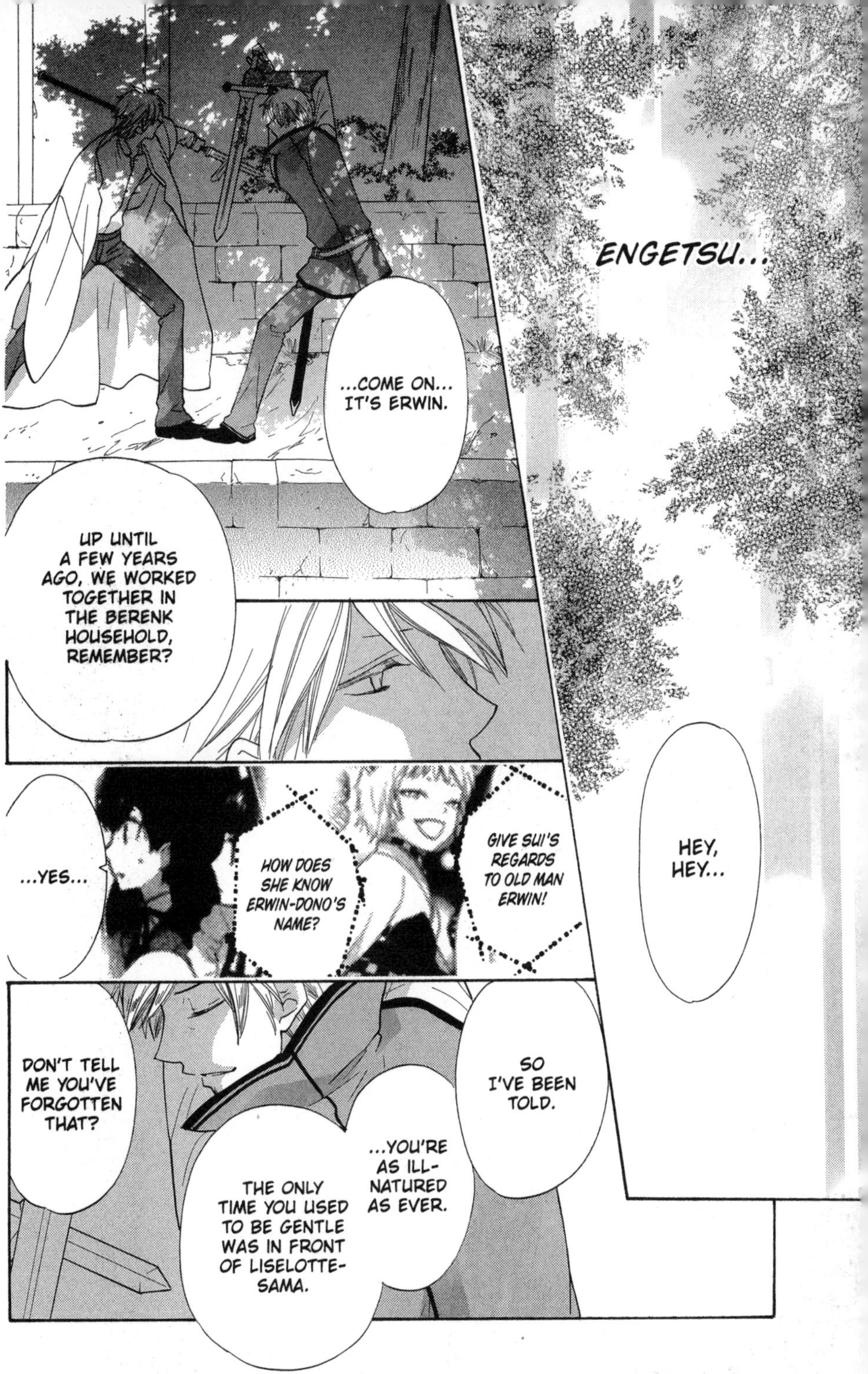
ENGETSU...
HEY, HEY...
...COME ON... IT'S ERWIN.
UP UNTIL A FEW YEARS AGO, WE WORKED TOGETHER IN THE BERENK HOUSEHOLD, REMEMBER?
GIVE SUI'S REGARDS TO OLD MAN ERWIN!
HOW DOES SHE KNOW ERWIN-DONO'S NAME?
...YES...
SO I'VE BEEN TOLD.
...YOU'RE AS ILL-NATURED AS EVER.
THE ONLY TIME YOU USED TO BE GENTLE WAS IN FRONT OF LISELOTTE-SAMA.
DON'T TELL ME YOU'VE FORGOTTEN THAT?

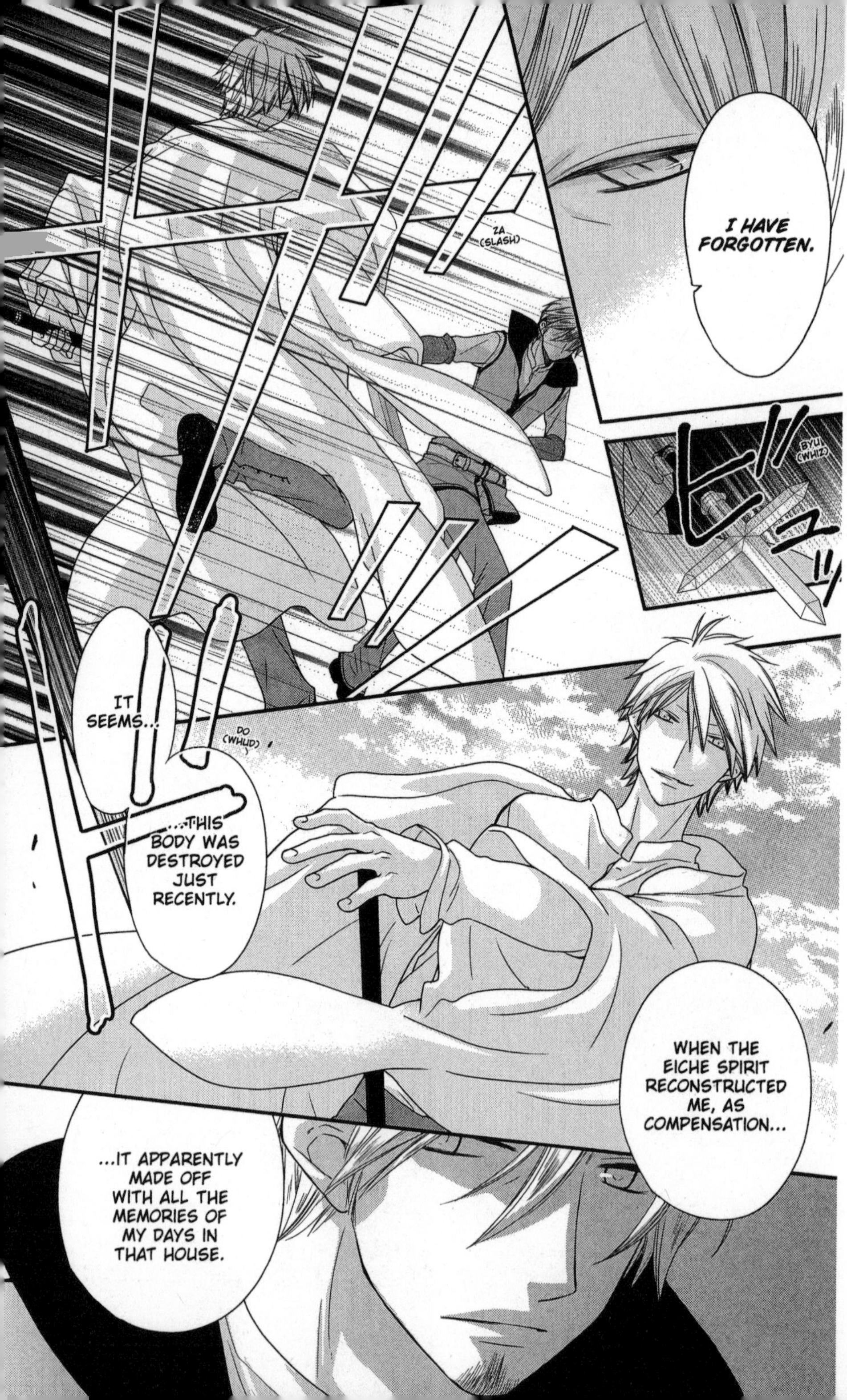
I HAVE FORGOTTEN.
ZA (SLASH)
BYU (WHIZ)
ビュッ
IT SEEMS...
DO (WHUD)
...THIS BODY WAS DESTROYED JUST RECENTLY.
WHEN THE EICHE SPIRIT RECONSTRUCTED ME, AS COMPENSATION...
...IT APPARENTLY MADE OFF WITH ALL THE MEMORIES OF MY DAYS IN THAT HOUSE.

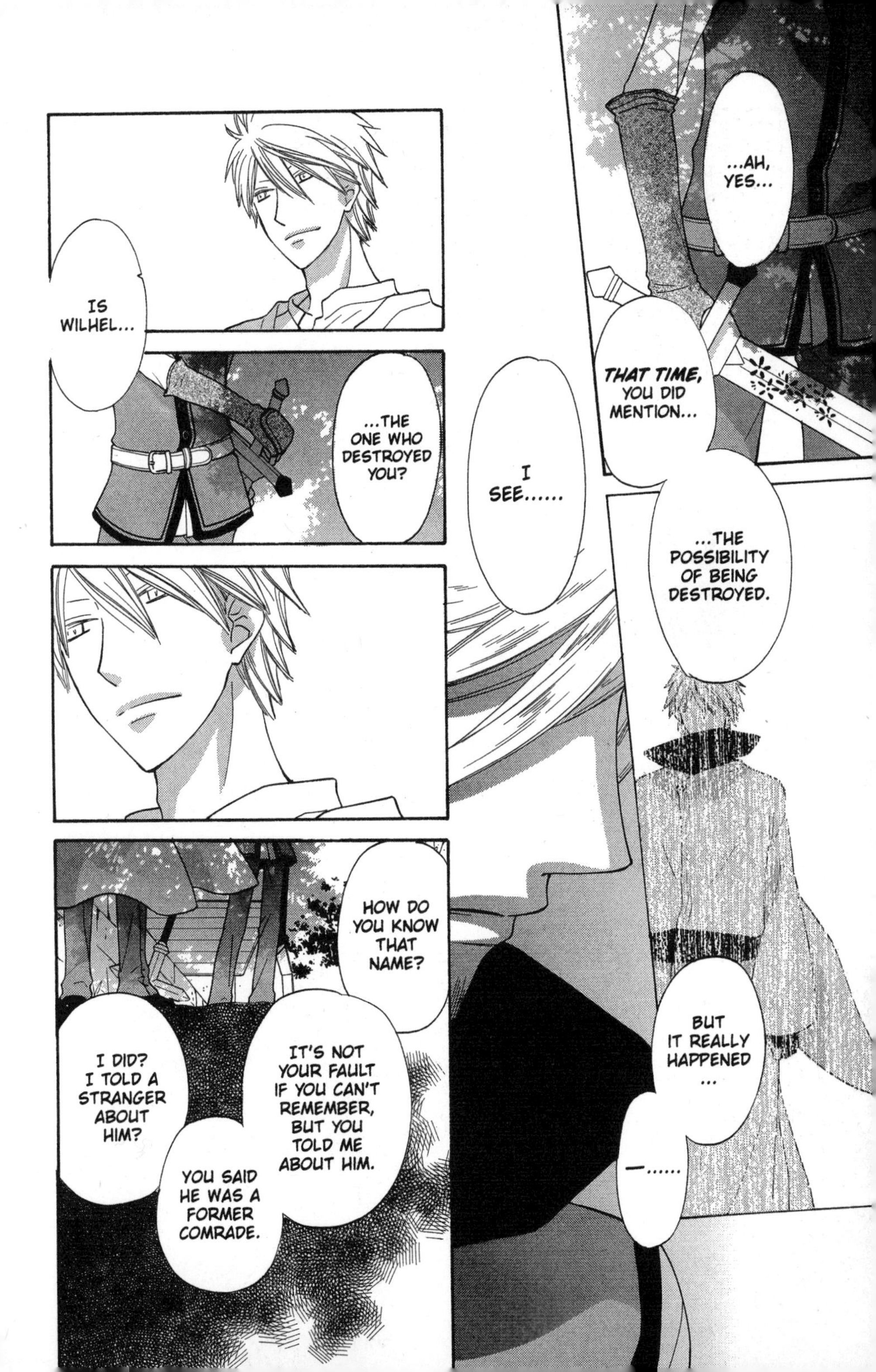
...AH, YES...
THAT TIME, YOU DID MENTION...
...THE POSSIBILITY OF BEING DESTROYED.
I SEE......
BUT IT REALLY HAPPENED ...
—......
IS WILHEL...
...THE ONE WHO DESTROYED YOU?
HOW DO YOU KNOW THAT NAME?
IT'S NOT YOUR FAULT IF YOU CAN'T REMEMBER, BUT YOU TOLD ME ABOUT HIM.
I DID? I TOLD A STRANGER ABOUT HIM?
YOU SAID HE WAS A FORMER COMRADE.

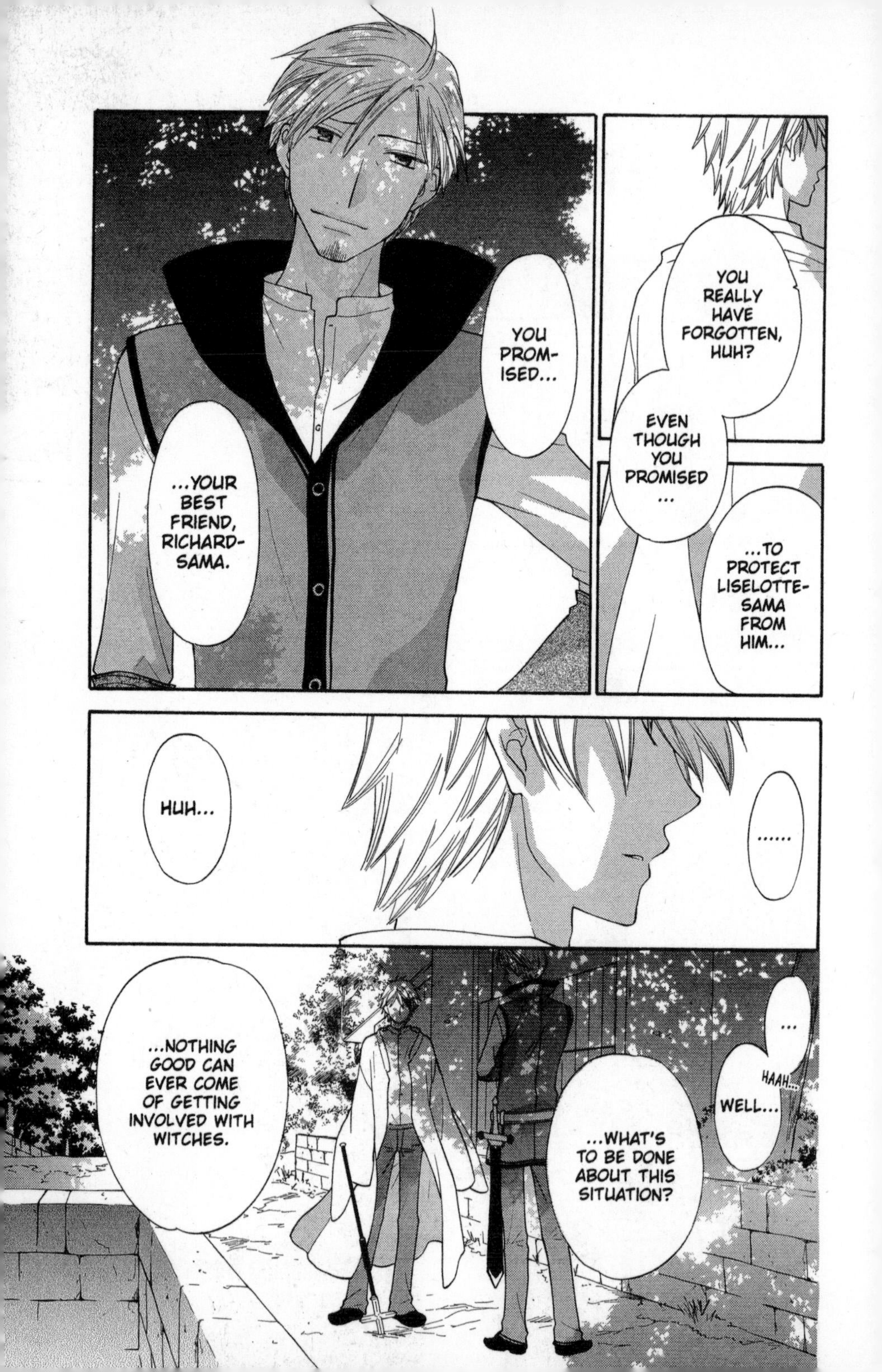
YOU REALLY HAVE FORGOTTEN, HUH?
EVEN THOUGH YOU PROMISED...
...TO PROTECT LISELOTTE-SAMA FROM HIM...
YOU PROM-ISED...
...YOUR BEST FRIEND, RICHARD-SAMA.
......
HUH...
...
HAAH...
WELL...
...WHAT'S TO BE DONE ABOUT THIS SITUATION?
...NOTHING GOOD CAN EVER COME OF GETTING INVOLVED WITH WITCHES.

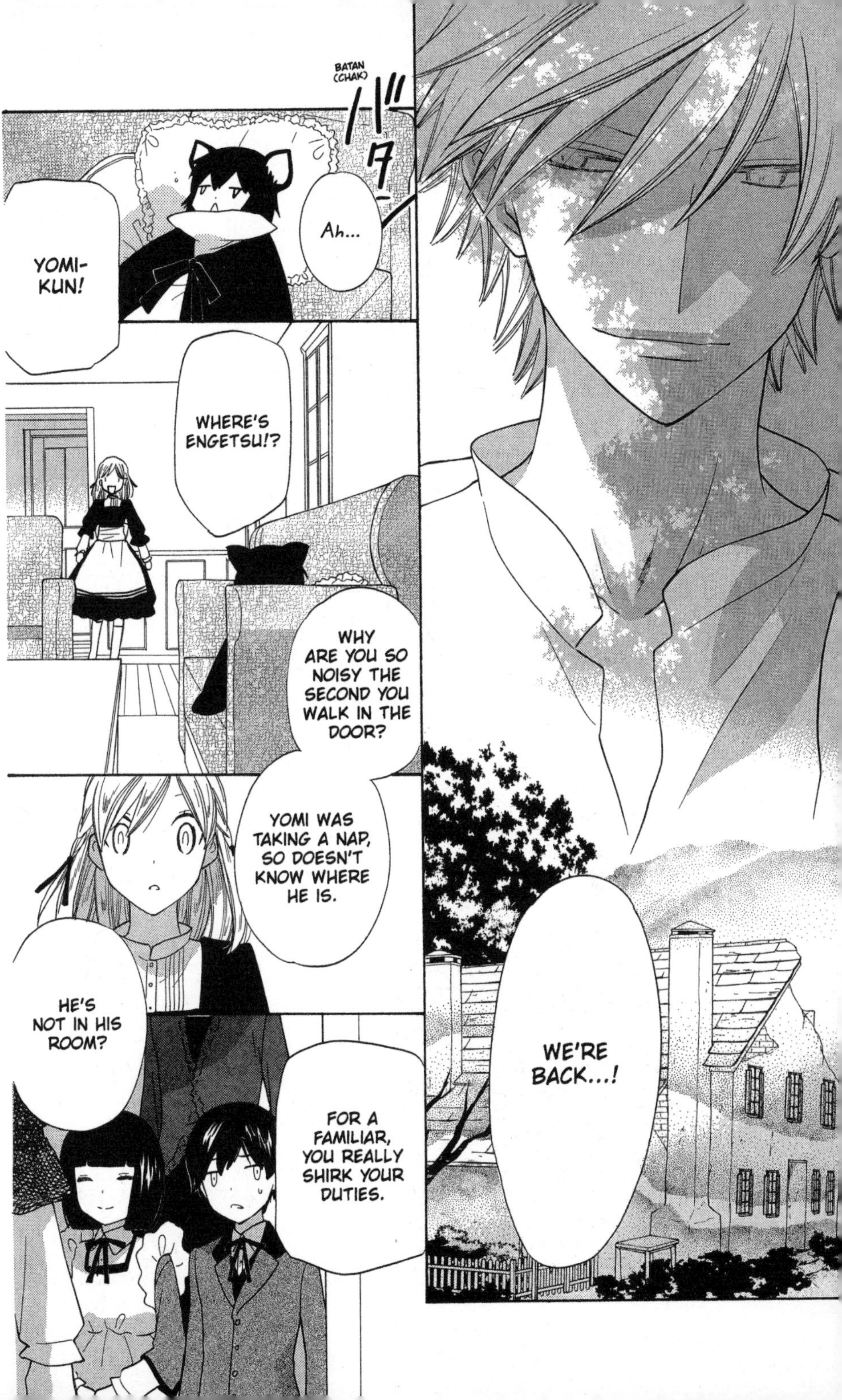
WE'RE BACK...!
BATAN (CHAK)
Ah...
YOMI-KUN!
WHERE'S ENGETSU!?
WHY ARE YOU SO NOISY THE SECOND YOU WALK IN THE DOOR?
YOMI WAS TAKING A NAP, SO DOESN'T KNOW WHERE HE IS.
HE'S NOT IN HIS ROOM?
FOR A FAMILIAR, YOU REALLY SHIRK YOUR DUTIES.

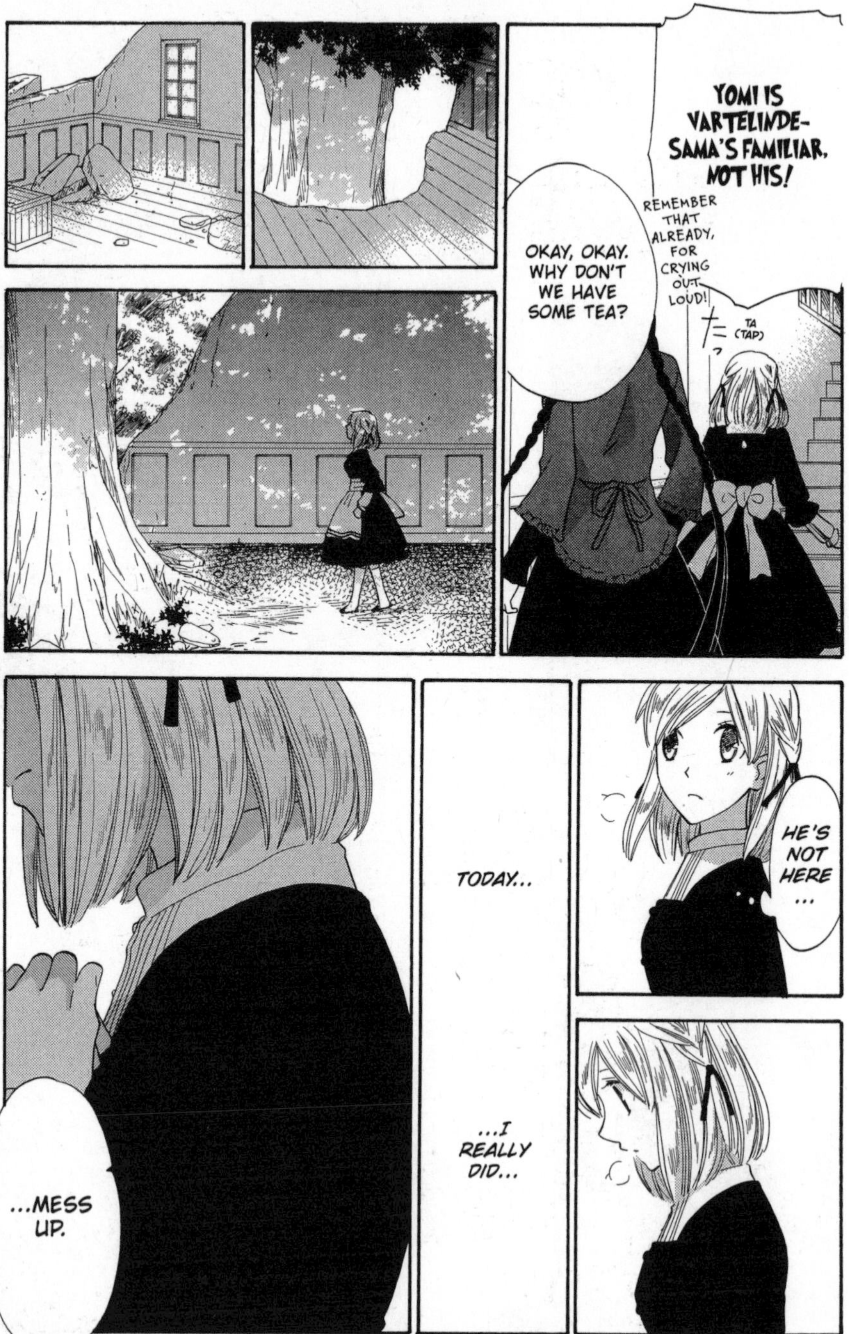
YOMI IS VARTELINDE-SAMA'S FAMILIAR, NOT HIS!
REMEMBER THAT ALREADY, FOR CRYING OUT LOUD!
OKAY, OKAY. WHY DON'T WE HAVE SOME TEA?
TA (TAP)
HE'S NOT HERE ...
TODAY...
...I REALLY DID...
...MESS UP.

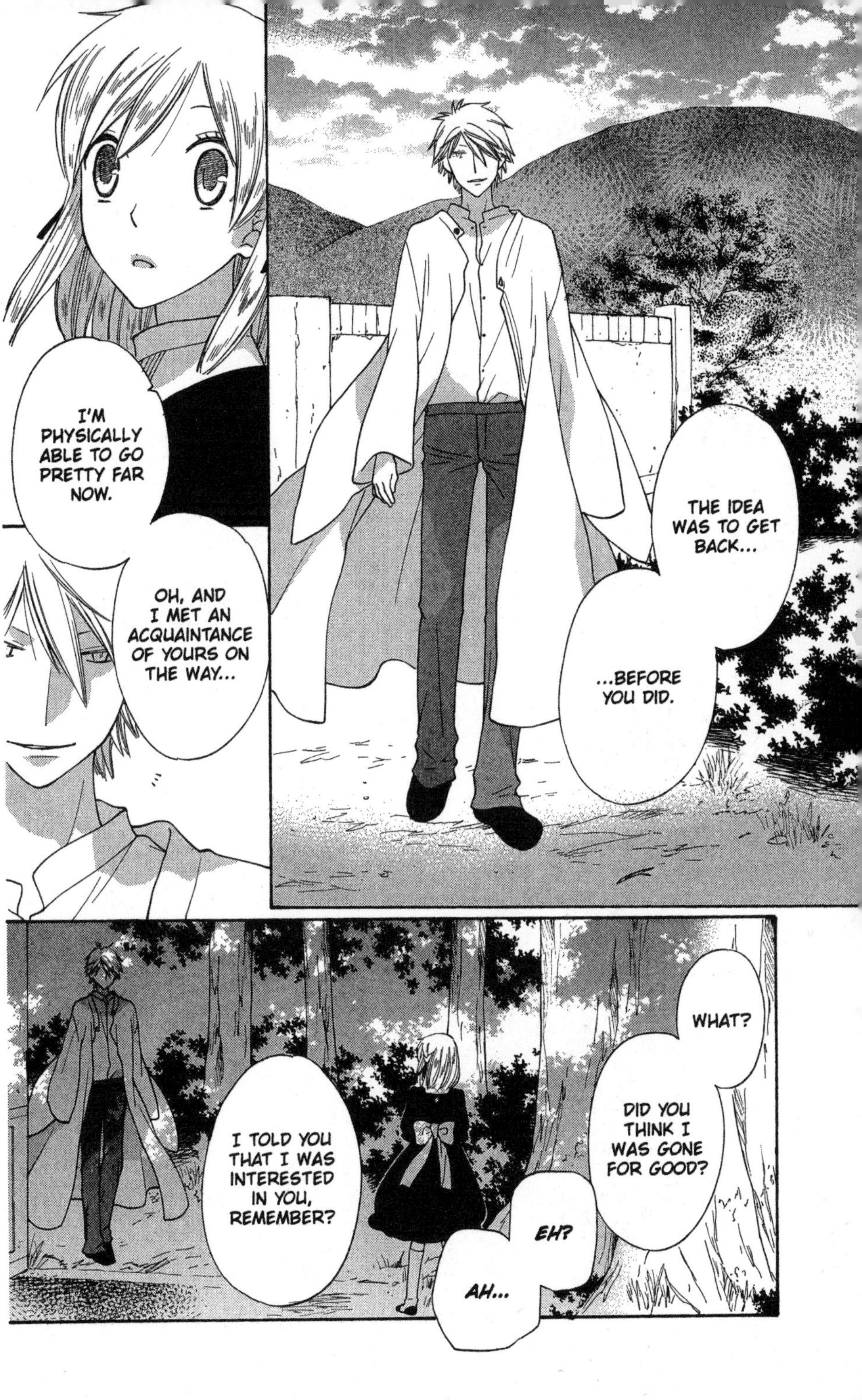
THE IDEA WAS TO GET BACK...
...BEFORE YOU DID.
I'M PHYSICALLY ABLE TO GO PRETTY FAR NOW.
OH, AND I MET AN ACQUAINTANCE OF YOURS ON THE WAY...
WHAT?
DID YOU THINK I WAS GONE FOR GOOD?
EH?
AH...
I TOLD YOU THAT I WAS INTERESTED IN YOU, REMEMBER?

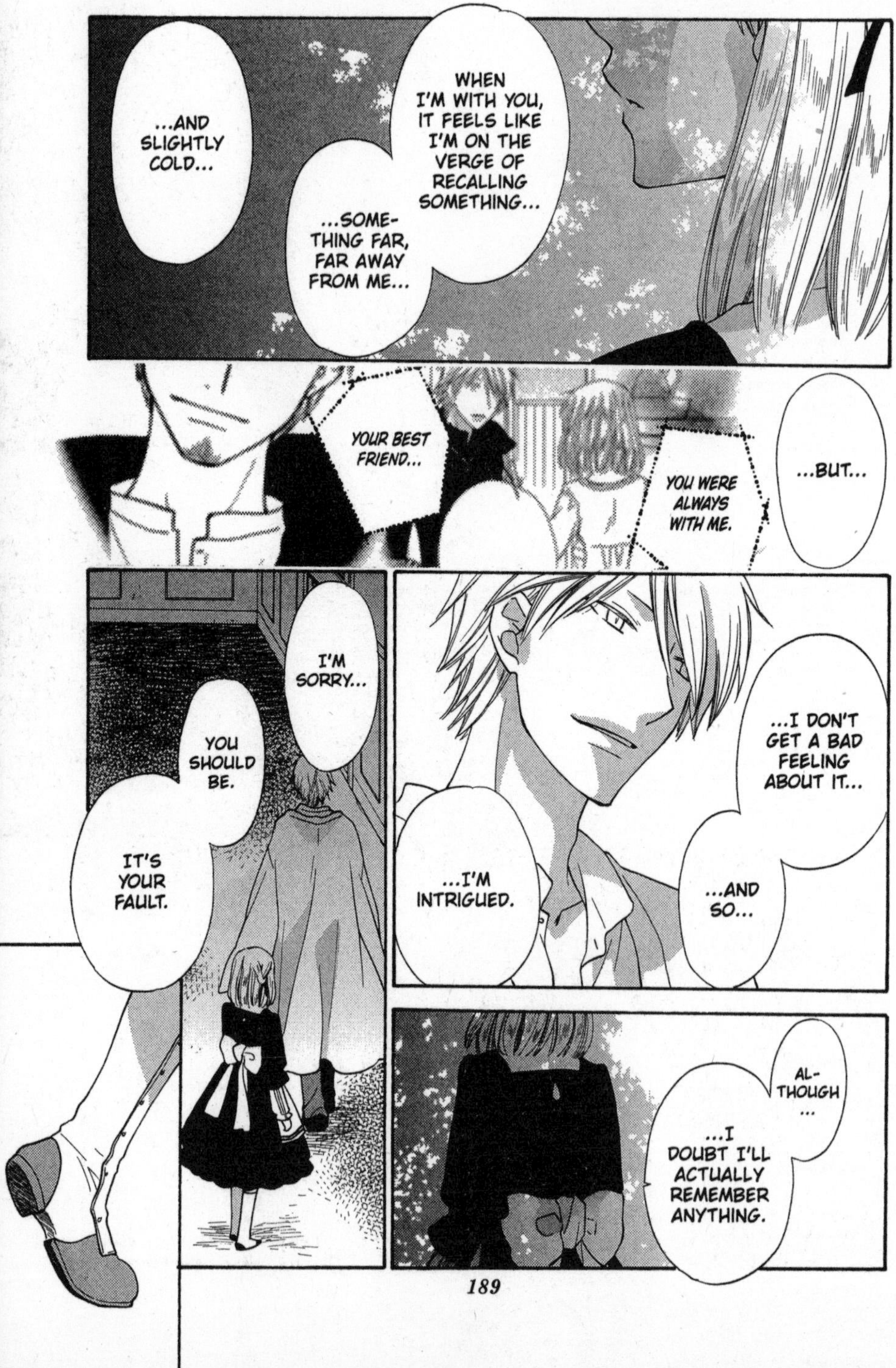
WHEN I'M WITH YOU, IT FEELS LIKE I'M ON THE VERGE OF RECALLING SOMETHING...
...SOME-THING FAR, FAR AWAY FROM ME...
...AND SLIGHTLY COLD...
...BUT...
YOU WERE ALWAYS WITH ME.
YOUR BEST FRIEND...
...I DON'T GET A BAD FEELING ABOUT IT...
...AND SO...
...I'M INTRIGUED.
AL-THOUGH...
...I DOUBT I'LL ACTUALLY REMEMBER ANYTHING.
I'M SORRY...
YOU SHOULD BE.
IT'S YOUR FAULT.

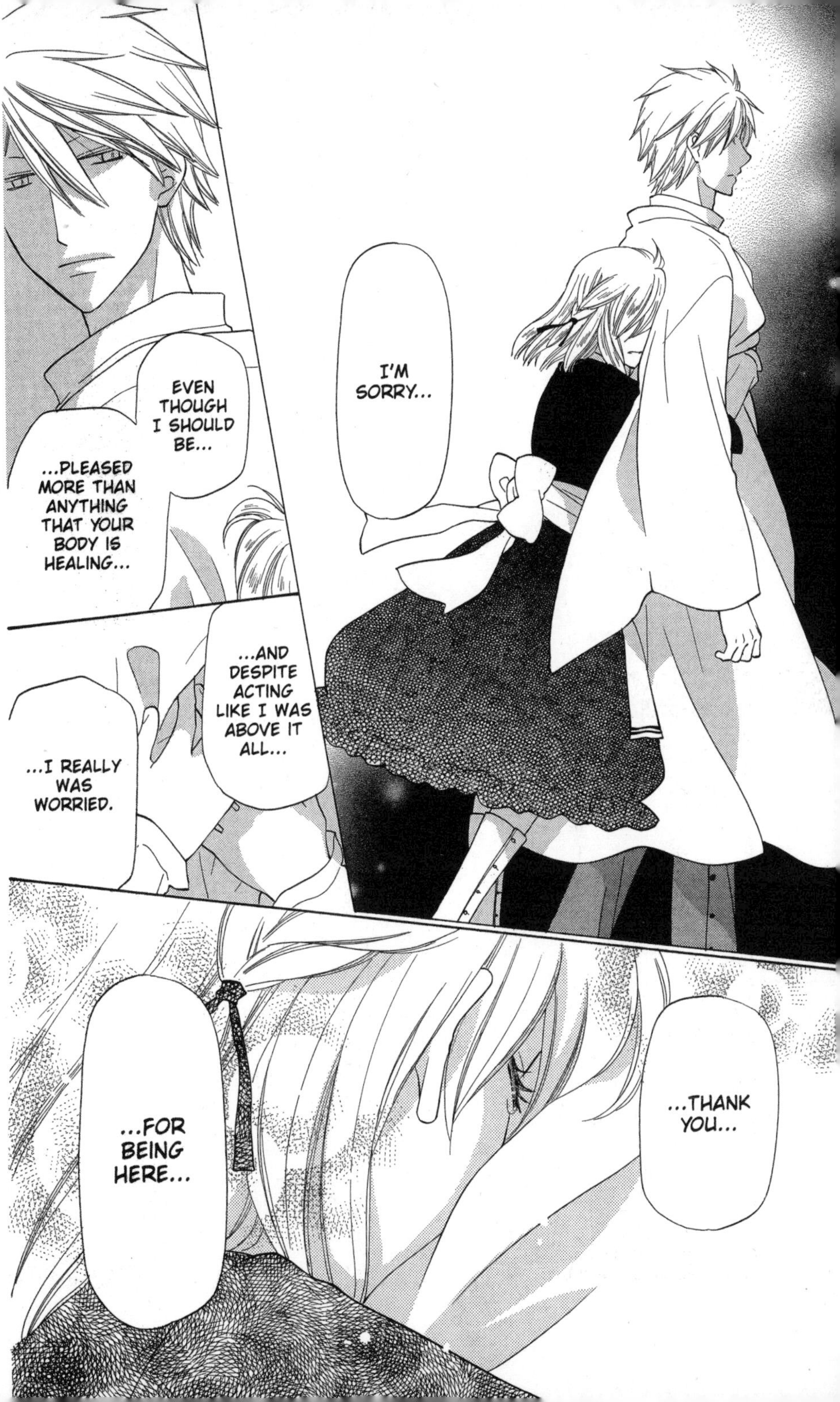
I'M SORRY...
EVEN THOUGH I SHOULD BE...
...PLEASED MORE THAN ANYTHING THAT YOUR BODY IS HEALING...
...AND DESPITE ACTING LIKE I WAS ABOVE IT ALL...
...I REALLY WAS WORRIED.
...THANK YOU...
...FOR BEING HERE...

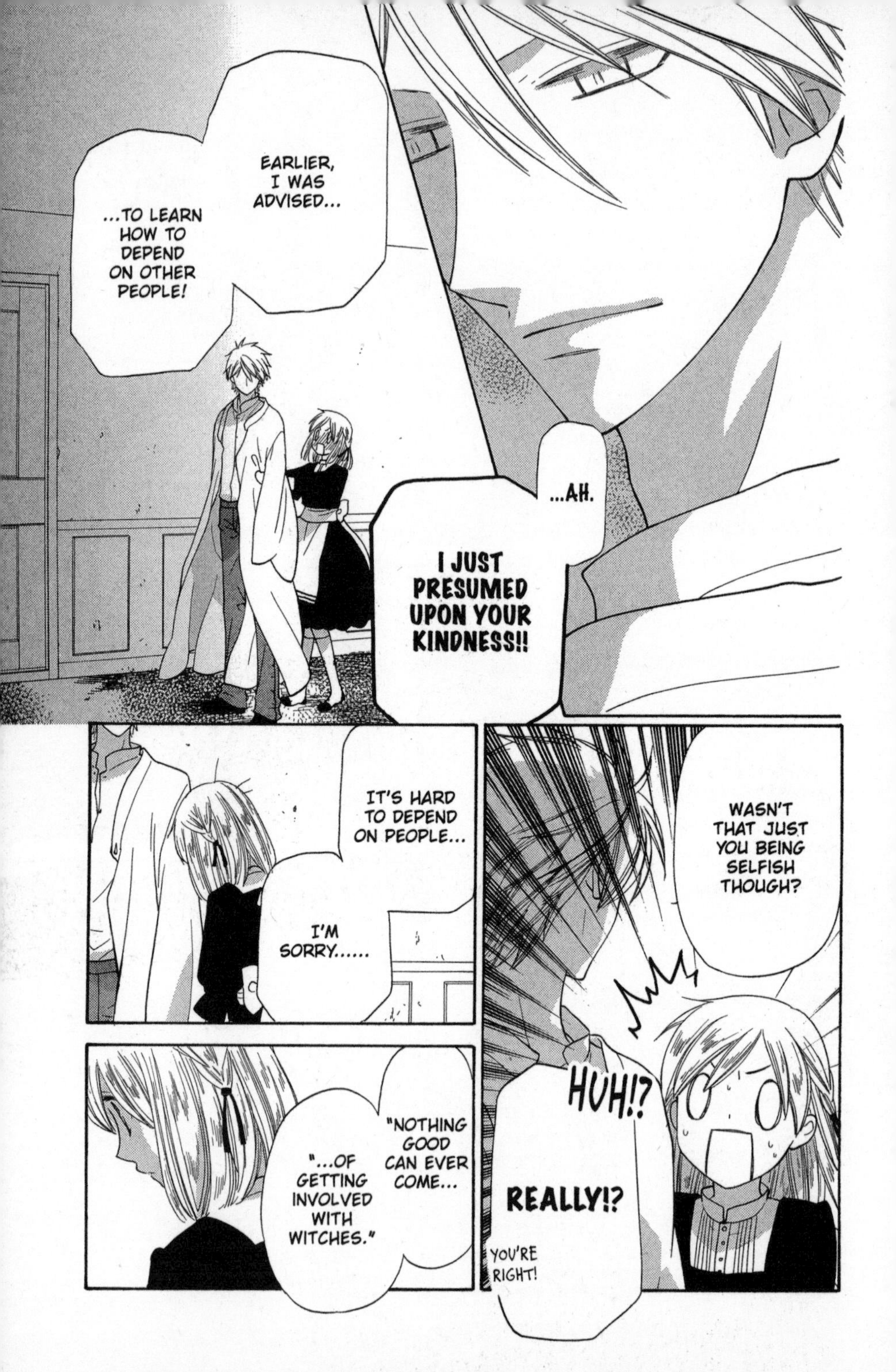
EARLIER, I WAS ADVISED...
...TO LEARN HOW TO DEPEND ON OTHER PEOPLE!
...AH.
I JUST PRESUMED UPON YOUR KINDNESS!!
WASN'T THAT JUST YOU BEING SELFISH THOUGH?
HUH!?
REALLY!?
YOU'RE RIGHT!
IT'S HARD TO DEPEND ON PEOPLE...
I'M SORRY......
"NOTHING GOOD CAN EVER COME...
"...OF GETTING INVOLVED WITH WITCHES."

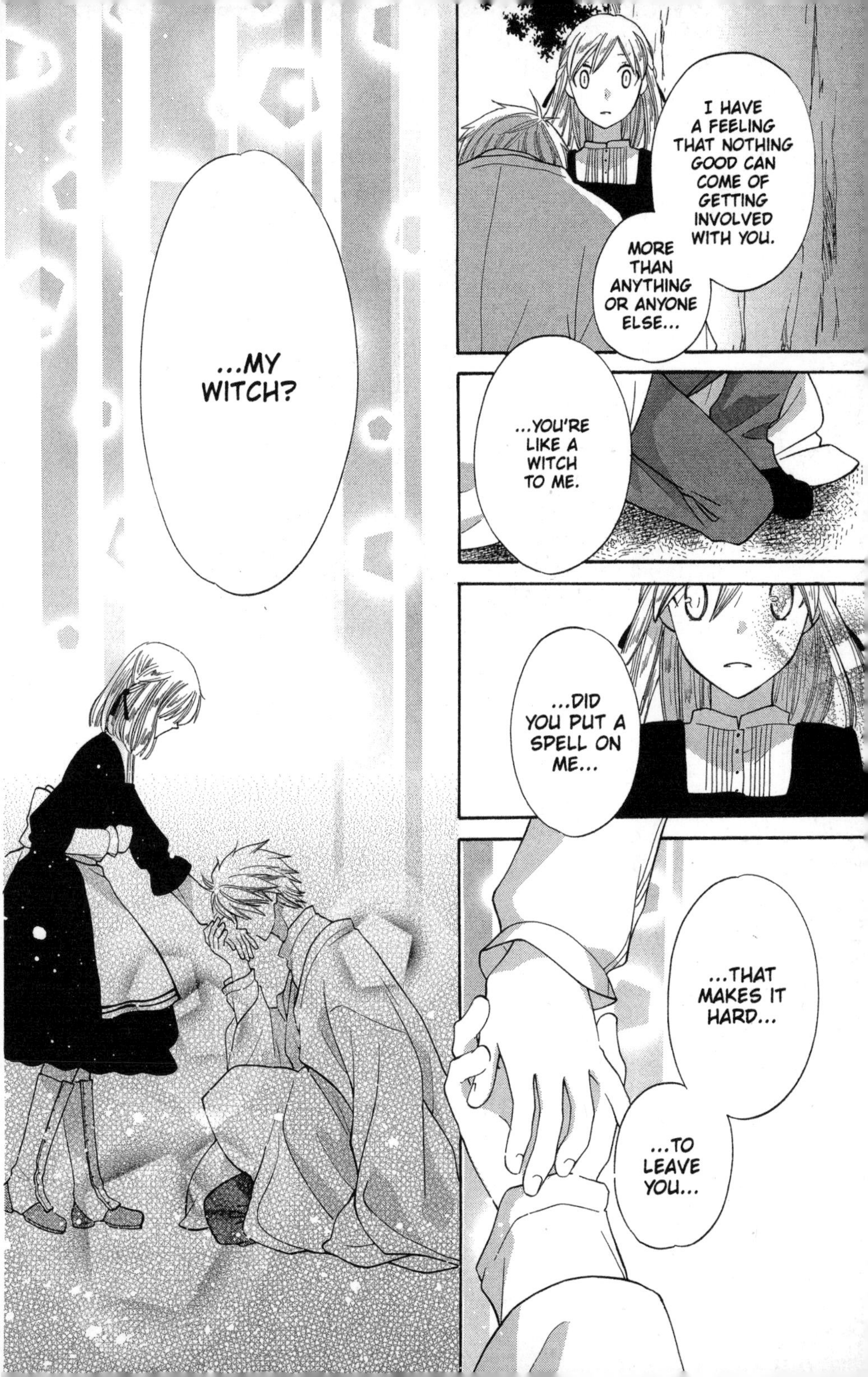
I HAVE A FEELING THAT NOTHING GOOD CAN COME OF GETTING INVOLVED WITH YOU.
MORE THAN ANYTHING OR ANYONE ELSE...
...YOU'RE LIKE A WITCH TO ME.
...DID YOU PUT A SPELL ON ME...
...THAT MAKES IT HARD...
...TO LEAVE YOU...
...MY WITCH?

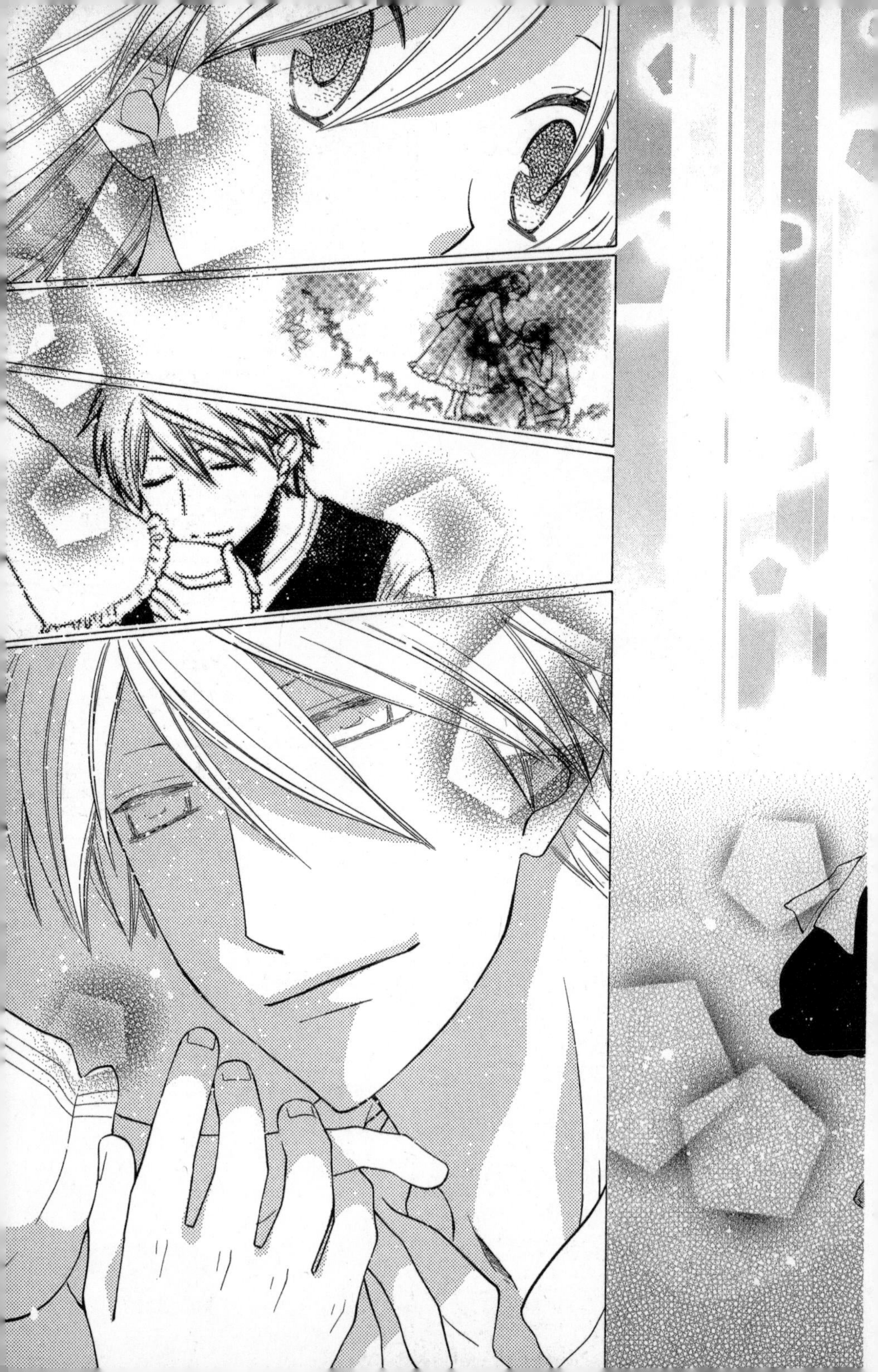

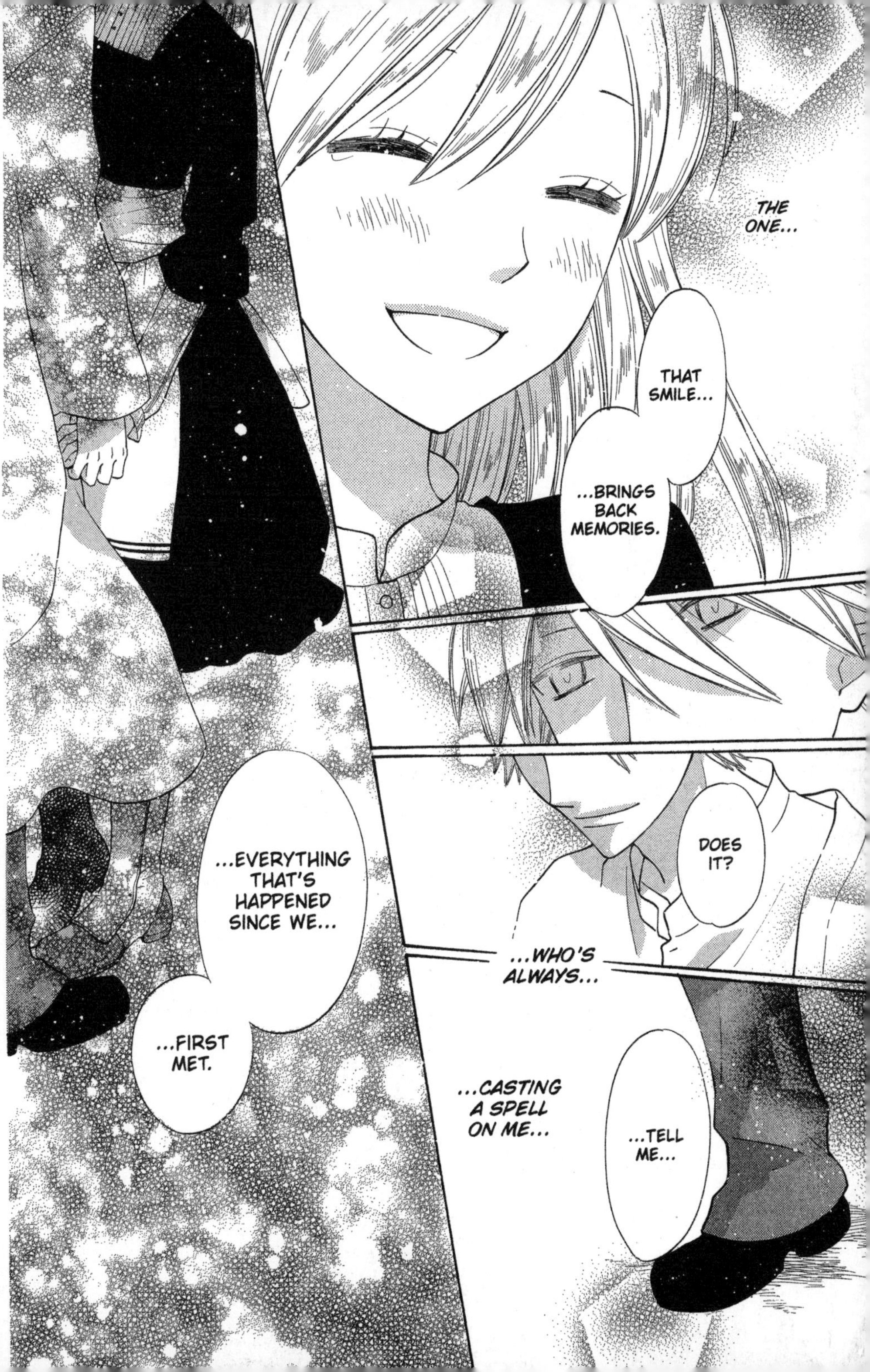
THE ONE...
THAT SMILE...
...BRINGS BACK MEMORIES.
DOES IT?
...WHO'S ALWAYS...
...CASTING A SPELL ON ME...
...TELL ME...
...EVERYTHING THAT'S HAPPENED SINCE WE...
...FIRST MET.

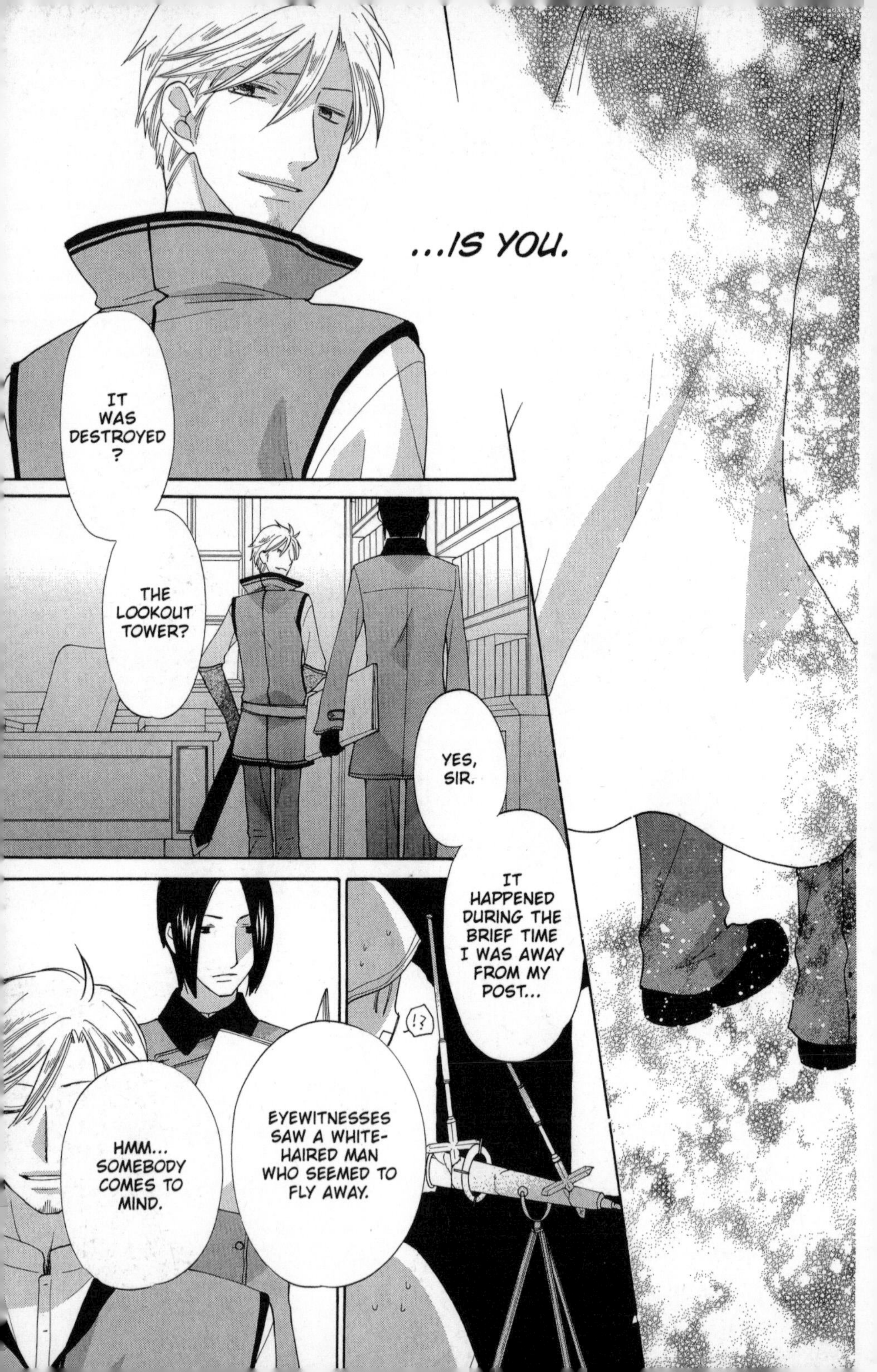
...IS YOU.
IT WAS DESTROYED?
THE LOOKOUT TOWER?
YES, SIR.
IT HAPPENED DURING THE BRIEF TIME I WAS AWAY FROM MY POST...
!?
EYEWITNESSES SAW A WHITE-HAIRED MAN WHO SEEMED TO FLY AWAY.
HMM... SOMEBODY COMES TO MIND.

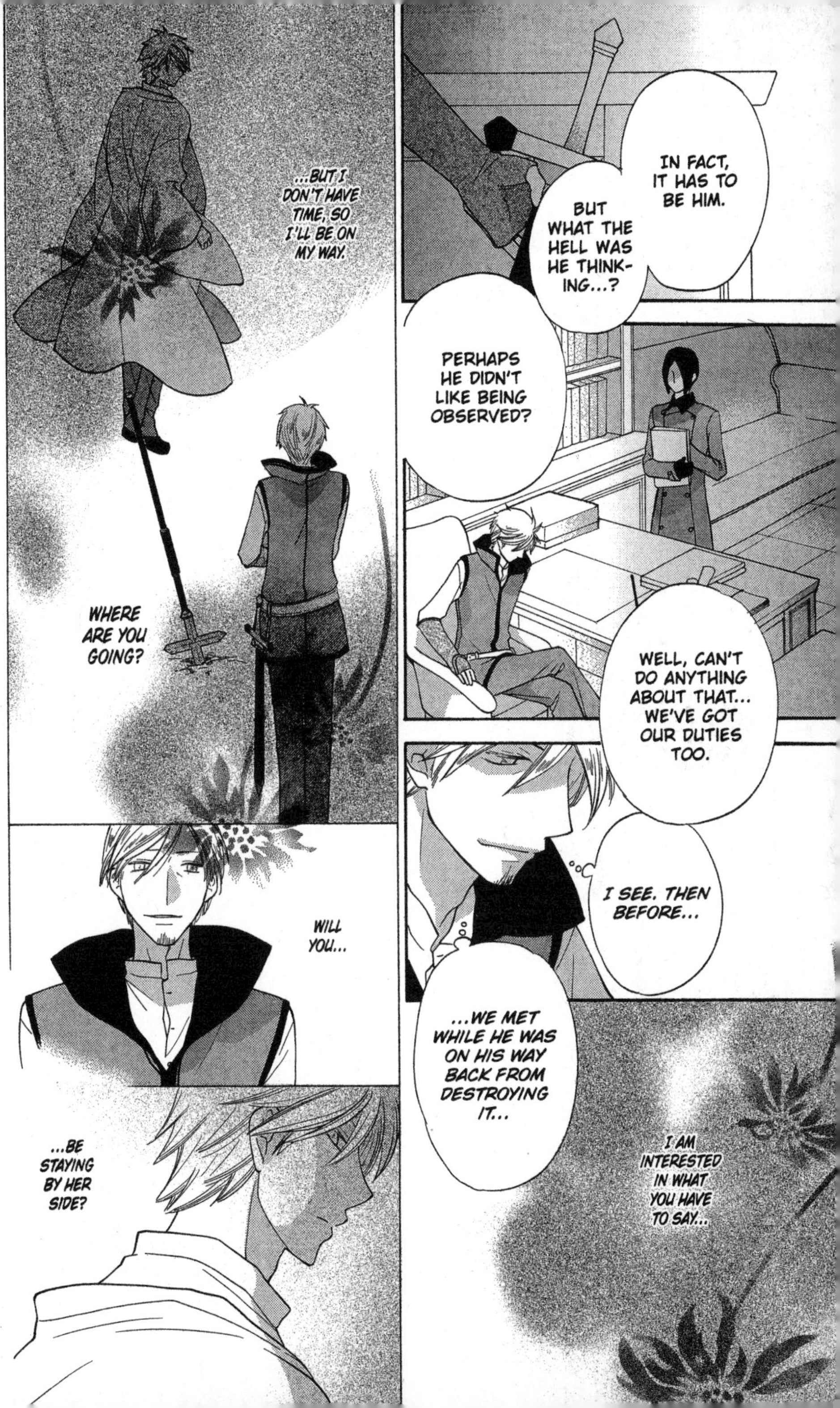
IN FACT, IT HAS TO BE HIM.
BUT WHAT THE HELL WAS HE THINKING...?
PERHAPS HE DIDN'T LIKE BEING OBSERVED?
WELL, CAN'T DO ANYTHING ABOUT THAT... WE'VE GOT OUR DUTIES TOO.
I SEE. THEN BEFORE...
...WE MET WHILE HE WAS ON HIS WAY BACK FROM DESTROYING IT...
I AM INTERESTED IN WHAT YOU HAVE TO SAY...
...BUT I DON'T HAVE TIME, SO I'LL BE ON MY WAY.
WHERE ARE YOU GOING?
WILL YOU...
...BE STAYING BY HER SIDE?

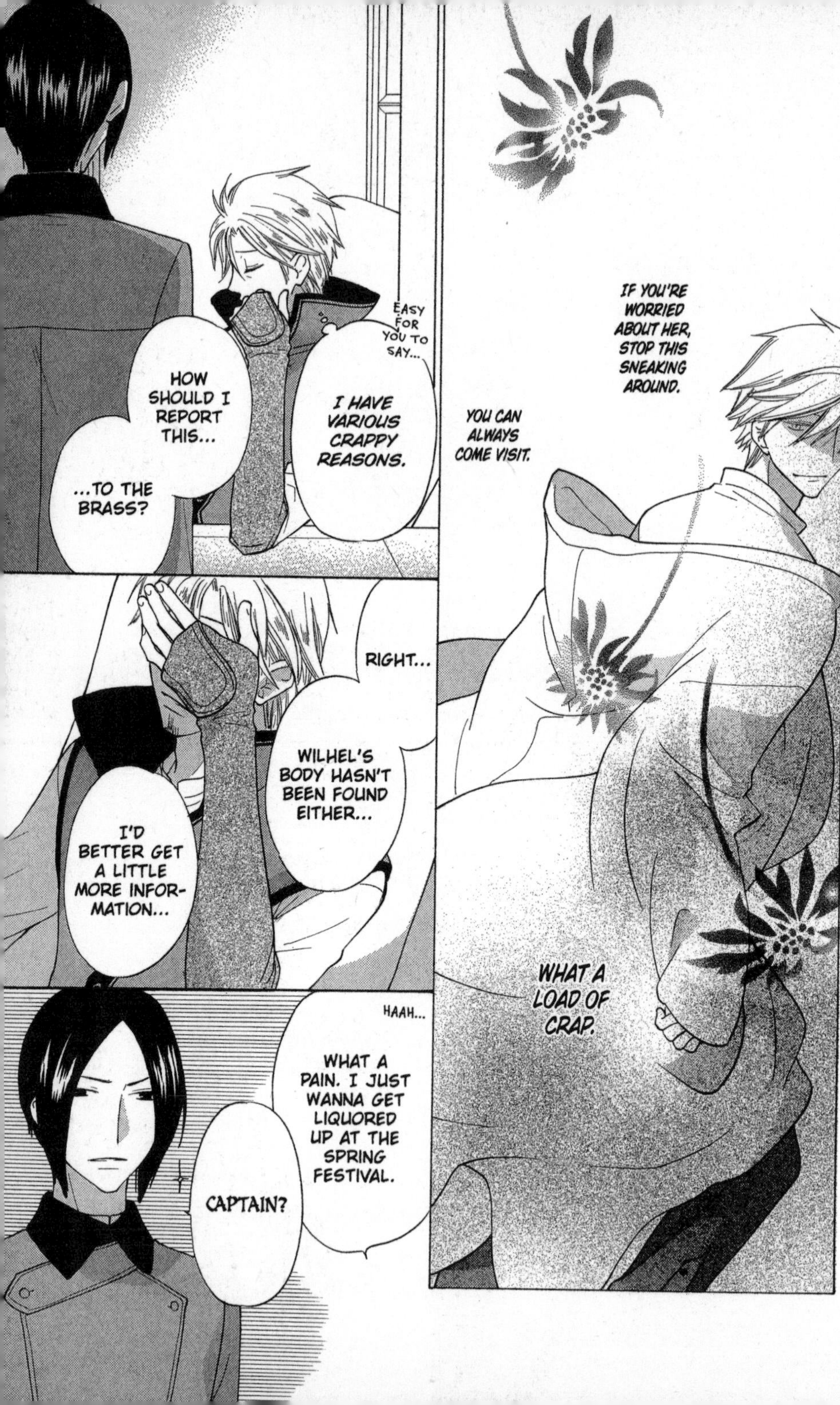
IF YOU'RE WORRIED ABOUT HER, STOP THIS SNEAKING AROUND.
YOU CAN ALWAYS COME VISIT.
WHAT A LOAD OF CRAP.
EASY FOR YOU TO SAY...
I HAVE VARIOUS CRAPPY REASONS.
HOW SHOULD I REPORT THIS...
...TO THE BRASS?
RIGHT...
WILHEL'S BODY HASN'T BEEN FOUND EITHER...
I'D BETTER GET A LITTLE MORE INFOR-MATION...
HAAH...
WHAT A PAIN. I JUST WANNA GET LIQUORED UP AT THE SPRING FESTIVAL.
CAPTAIN?

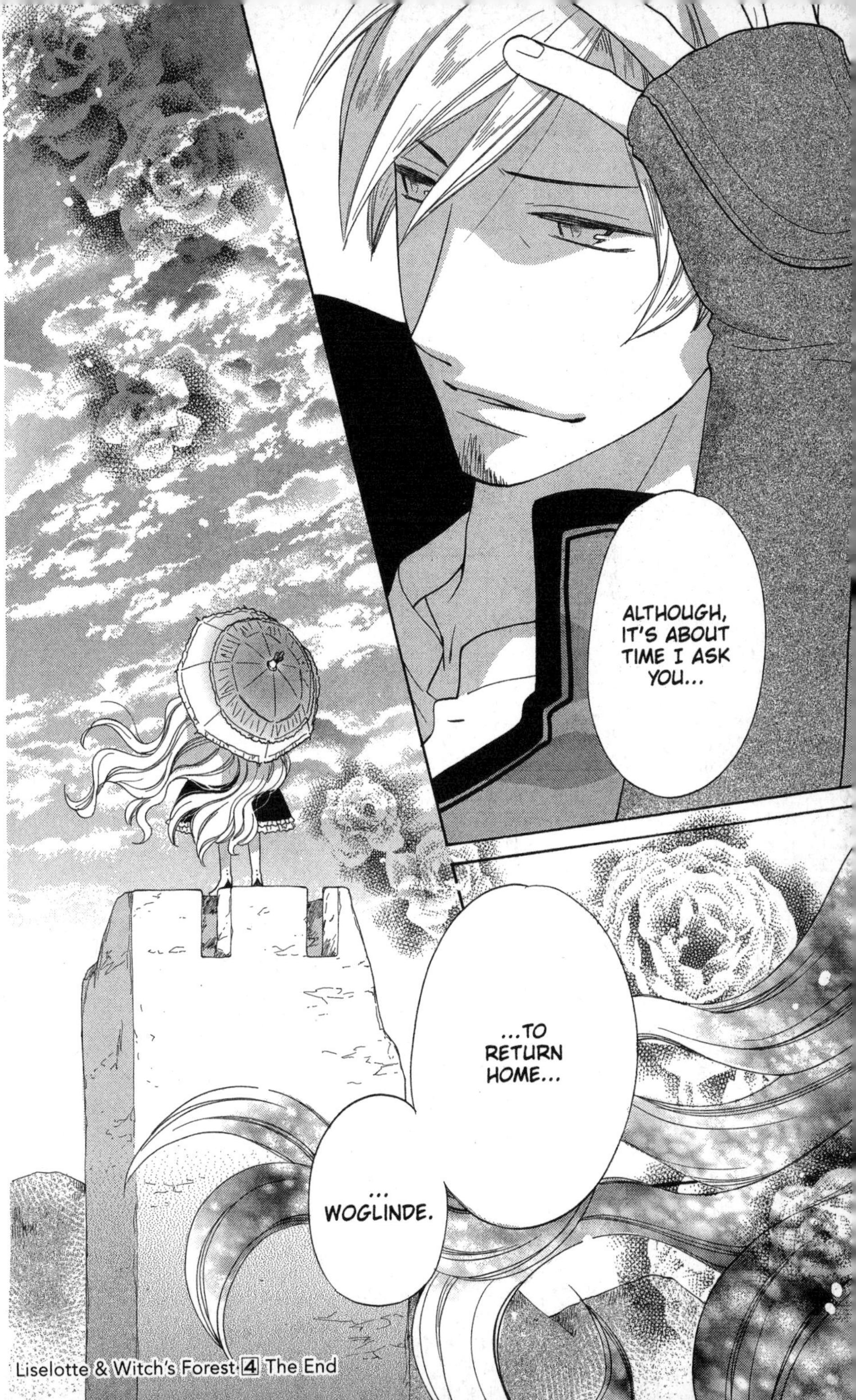
ALTHOUGH, IT'S ABOUT TIME I ASK YOU...
...TO RETURN HOME...
... WOGLINDE.

Liselotte & Witch's Forest 4 The End

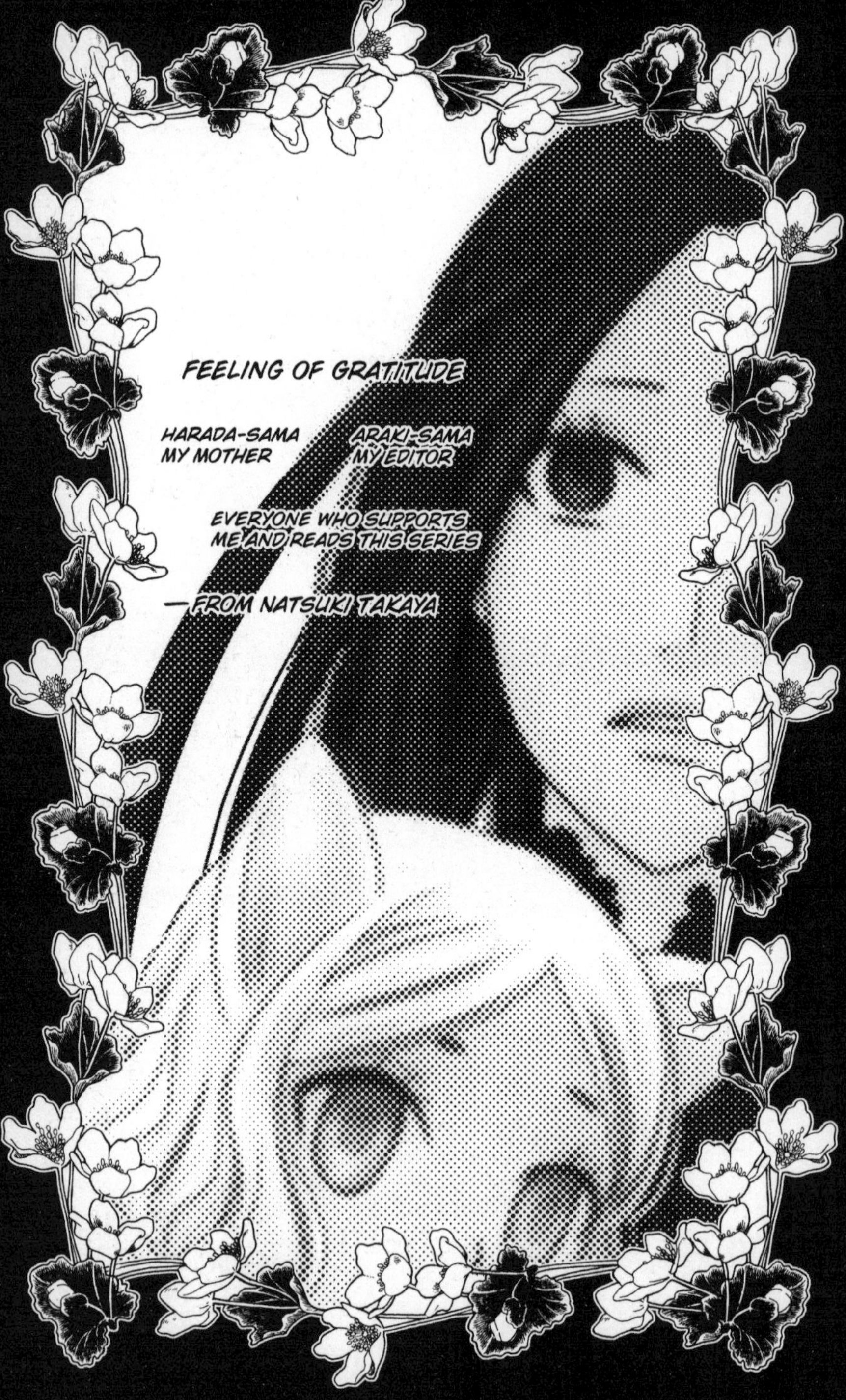
FEELING OF GRATITUDE
HARADA-SAMA
MY MOTHER
ARAKI-SAMA
MY EDITOR
EVERYONE WHO SUPPORTS
ME AND READS THIS SERIES
— FROM NATSUKI TAKAYA

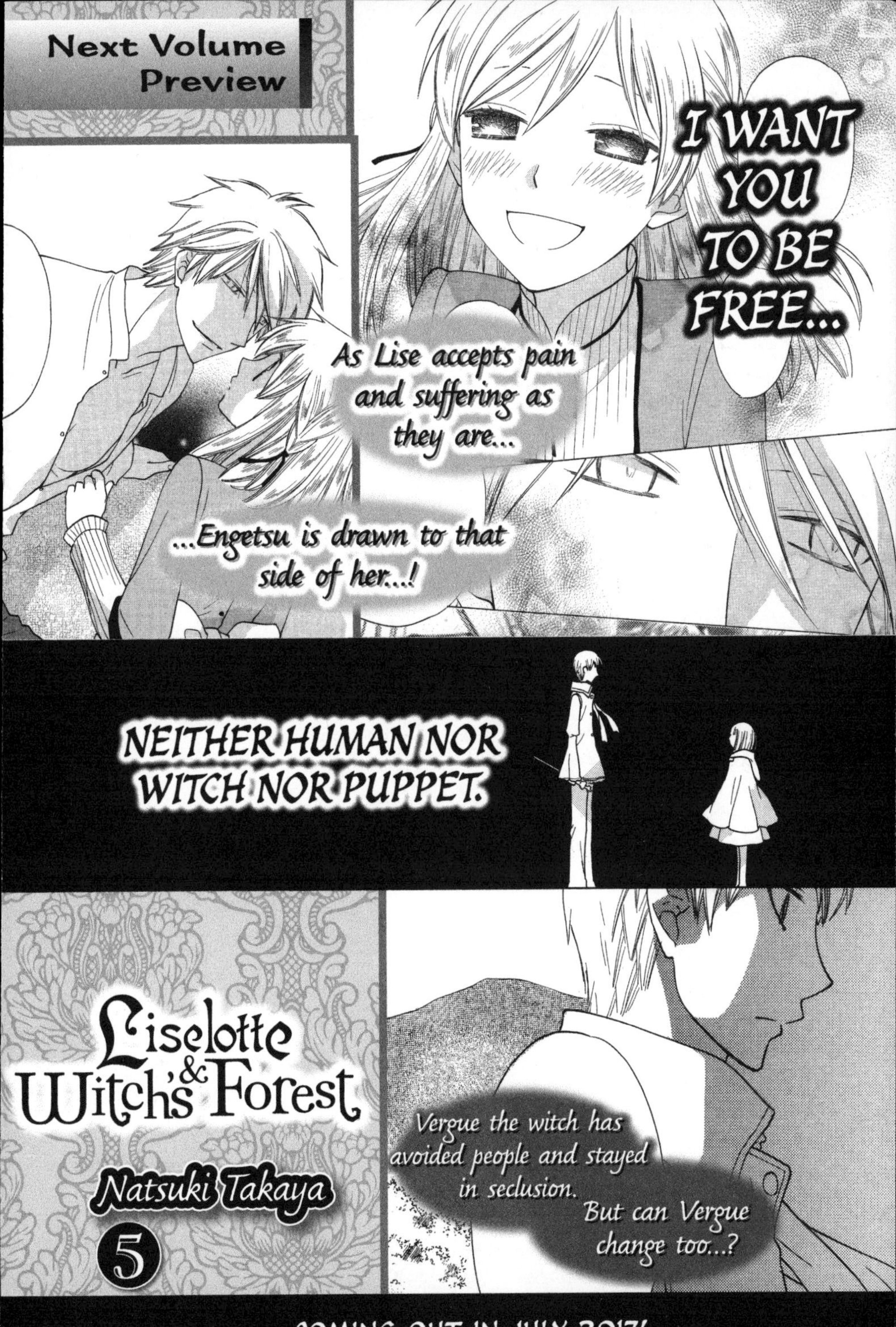
Next Volume Preview
I WANT YOU TO BE FREE...
As Lise accepts pain and suffering as they are...
...Engetsu is drawn to that side of her...!
NEITHER HUMAN NOR WITCH NOR PUPPET.
Vergue the witch has avoided people and stayed in seclusion.
But can Vergue change too...?
Liselotte & Witch's Forest
Natsuki Takaya
5

COMING OUT IN JULY 2017!

TRANSLATION NOTES

COMMON HONORIFICS

no honorific: Indicates familiarity or closeness; if used without permission or reason, addressing someone in this manner would constitute an insult.

-san: The Japanese equivalent of Mr./Mrs./Miss. If a situation calls for politeness, this is the fail-safe honorific.

-dono: A very polite form of address, more formal than *-san*.

-sama: Conveys great respect; may also indicate that the social status of the speaker is lower than that of the addressee.

-kun: Used most often when referring to boys, this indicates affection or familiarity. Occasionally used by older men among their peers, but it may also be used by anyone referring to a person of lower standing.

-chan: An affectionate honorific indicating familiarity used mostly in reference to girls; also used in reference to cute persons or animals of either gender.

Page 143
Woglinde is the name of one of three Rhinemaidens from Richard Wagner's opera *Der Ring des Nibelungen (The Ring of Nibelung)*.

Page 147
Onee-sama is a very polite term for an "elder sister" or an older girl who is not related.

Liselotte & Witch's Forest

Read on for an early look at Volume 5,
coming July 2017!

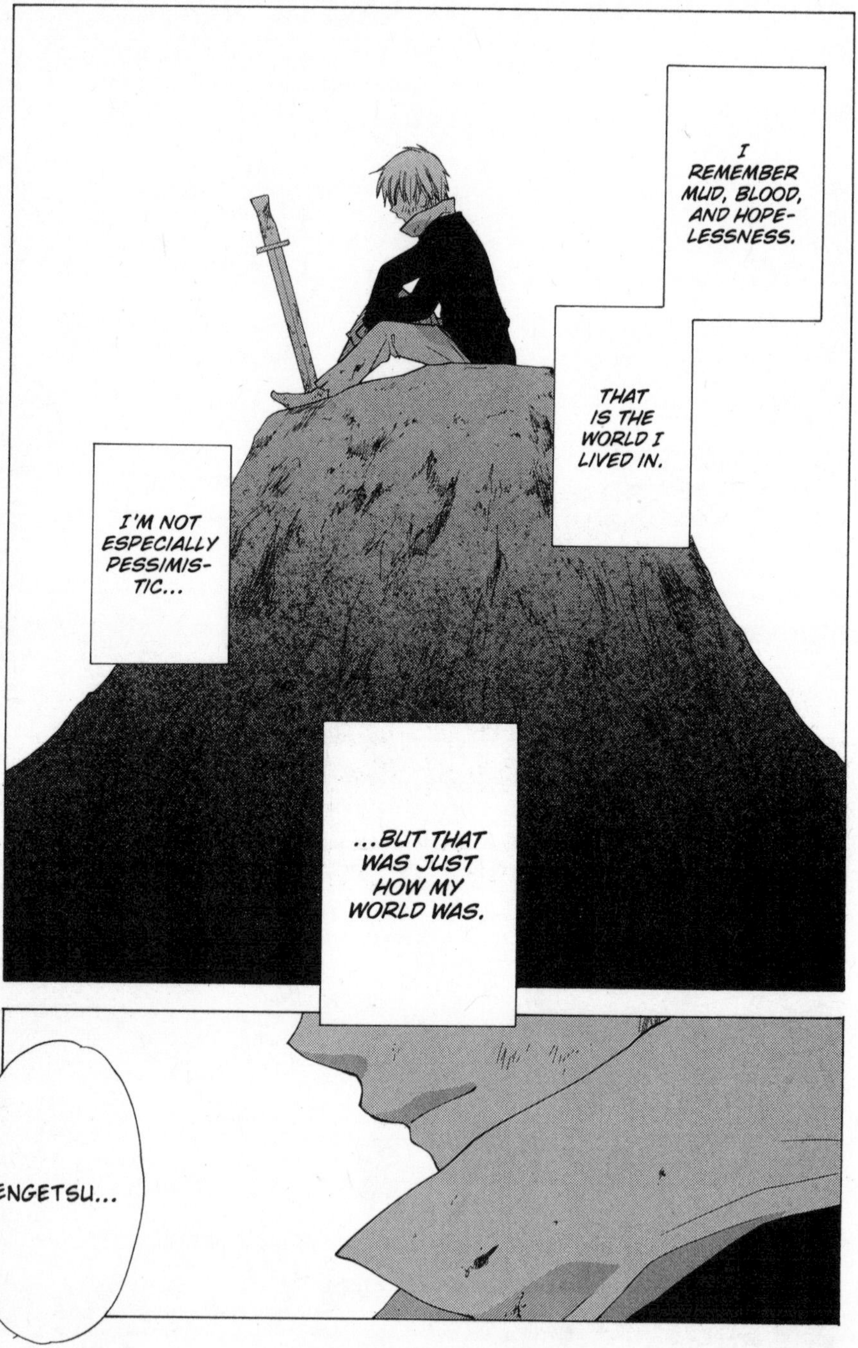
I REMEMBER MUD, BLOOD, AND HOPE-LESSNESS.
THAT IS THE WORLD I LIVED IN.
I'M NOT ESPECIALLY PESSIMIS-TIC...
...BUT THAT WAS JUST HOW MY WORLD WAS.
ENGETSU...

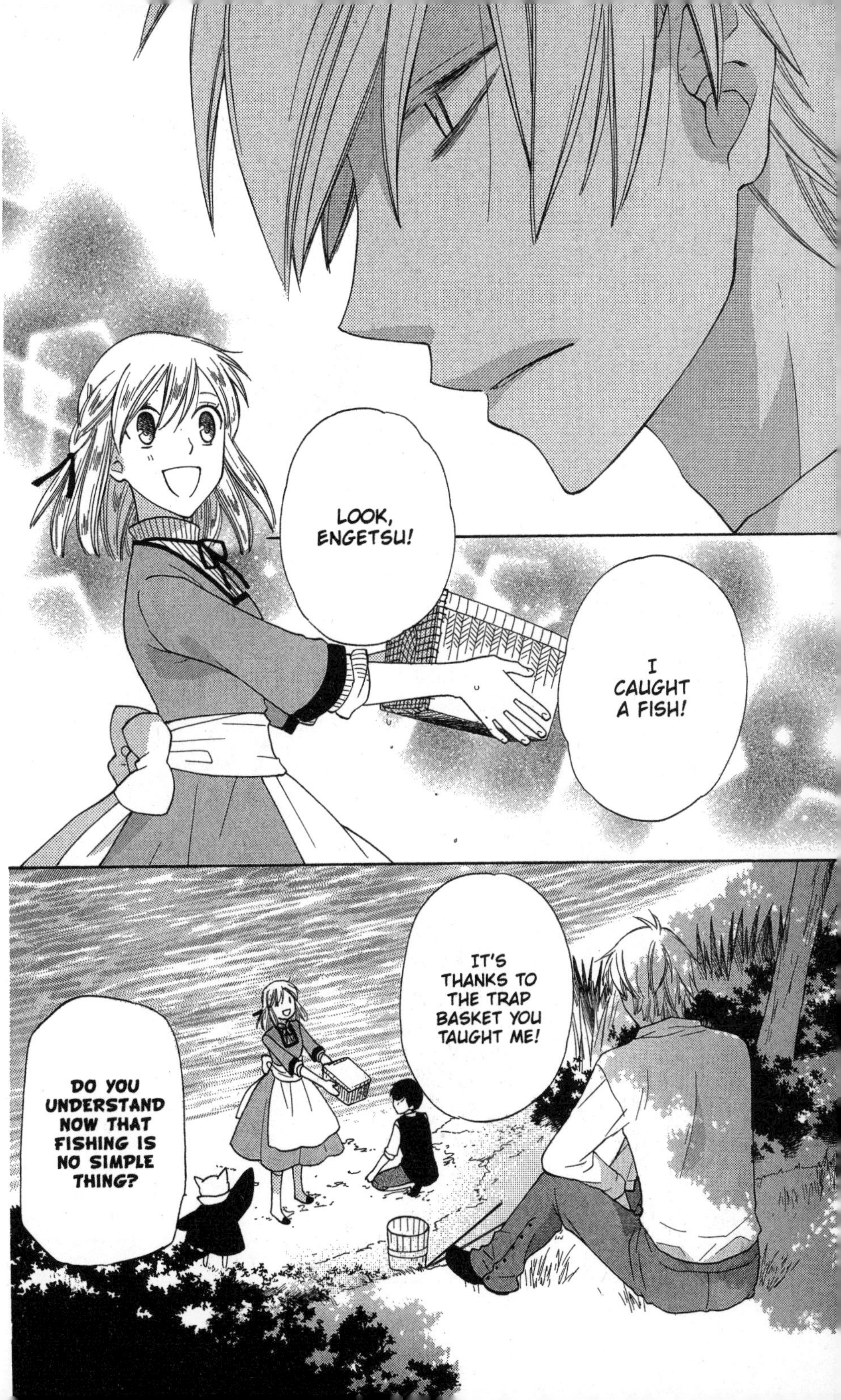
LOOK, ENGETSU!
I CAUGHT A FISH!
IT'S THANKS TO THE TRAP BASKET YOU TAUGHT ME!
DO YOU UNDERSTAND NOW THAT FISHING IS NO SIMPLE THING?

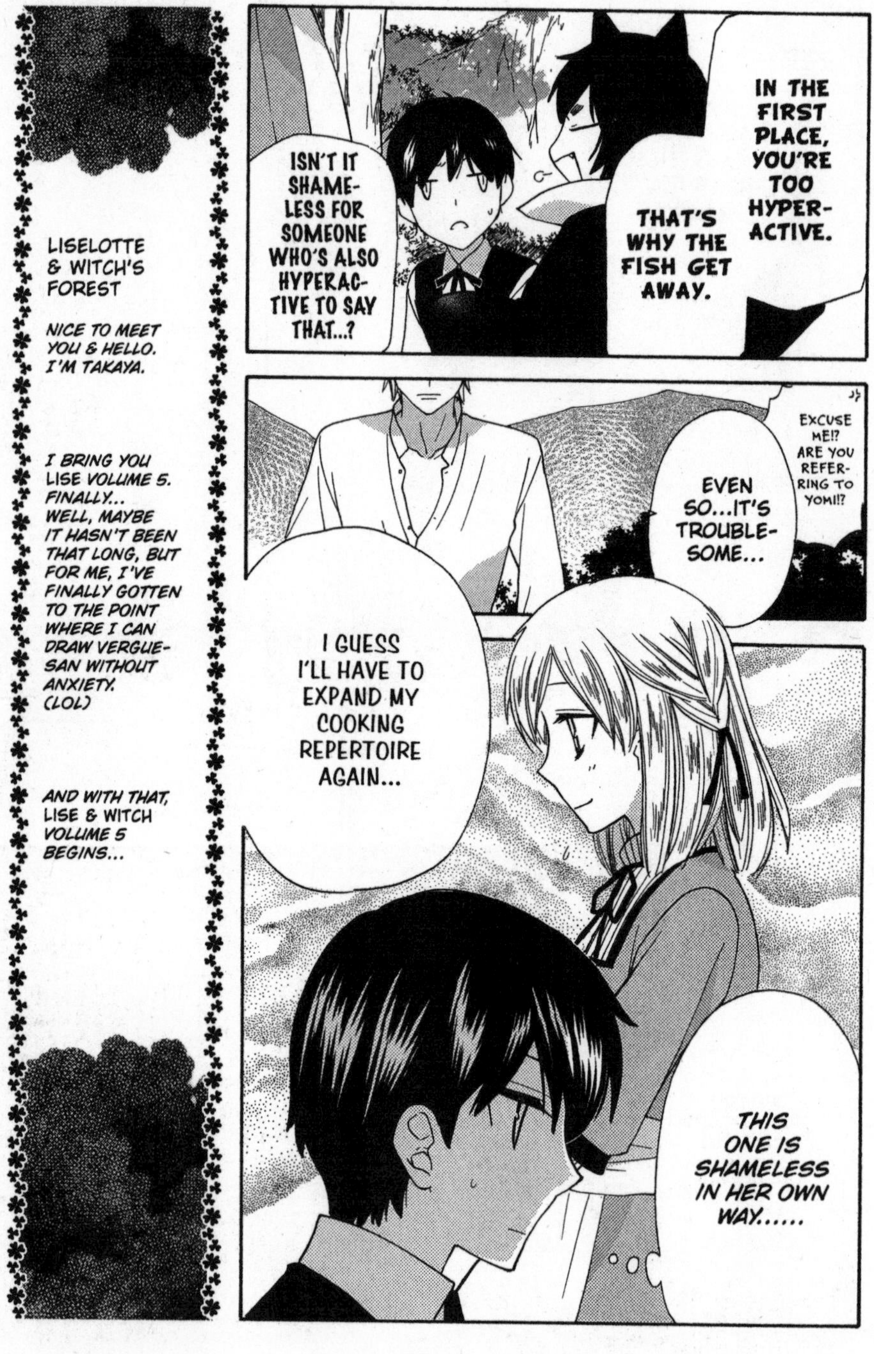
IN THE FIRST PLACE, YOU'RE TOO HYPERACTIVE.
THAT'S WHY THE FISH GET AWAY.
ISN'T IT SHAMELESS FOR SOMEONE WHO'S ALSO HYPERACTIVE TO SAY THAT...?
EXCUSE ME!? ARE YOU REFERRING TO YOMI!?
EVEN SO...IT'S TROUBLESOME...
I GUESS I'LL HAVE TO EXPAND MY COOKING REPERTOIRE AGAIN...
THIS ONE IS SHAMELESS IN HER OWN WAY......

LISELOTTE & WITCH'S FOREST

NICE TO MEET YOU & HELLO. I'M TAKAYA.

I BRING YOU LISE VOLUME 5. FINALLY... WELL, MAYBE IT HASN'T BEEN THAT LONG, BUT FOR ME, I'VE FINALLY GOTTEN TO THE POINT WHERE I CAN DRAW VERGUE-SAN WITHOUT ANXIETY. (LOL)

AND WITH THAT, LISE & WITCH VOLUME 5 BEGINS...

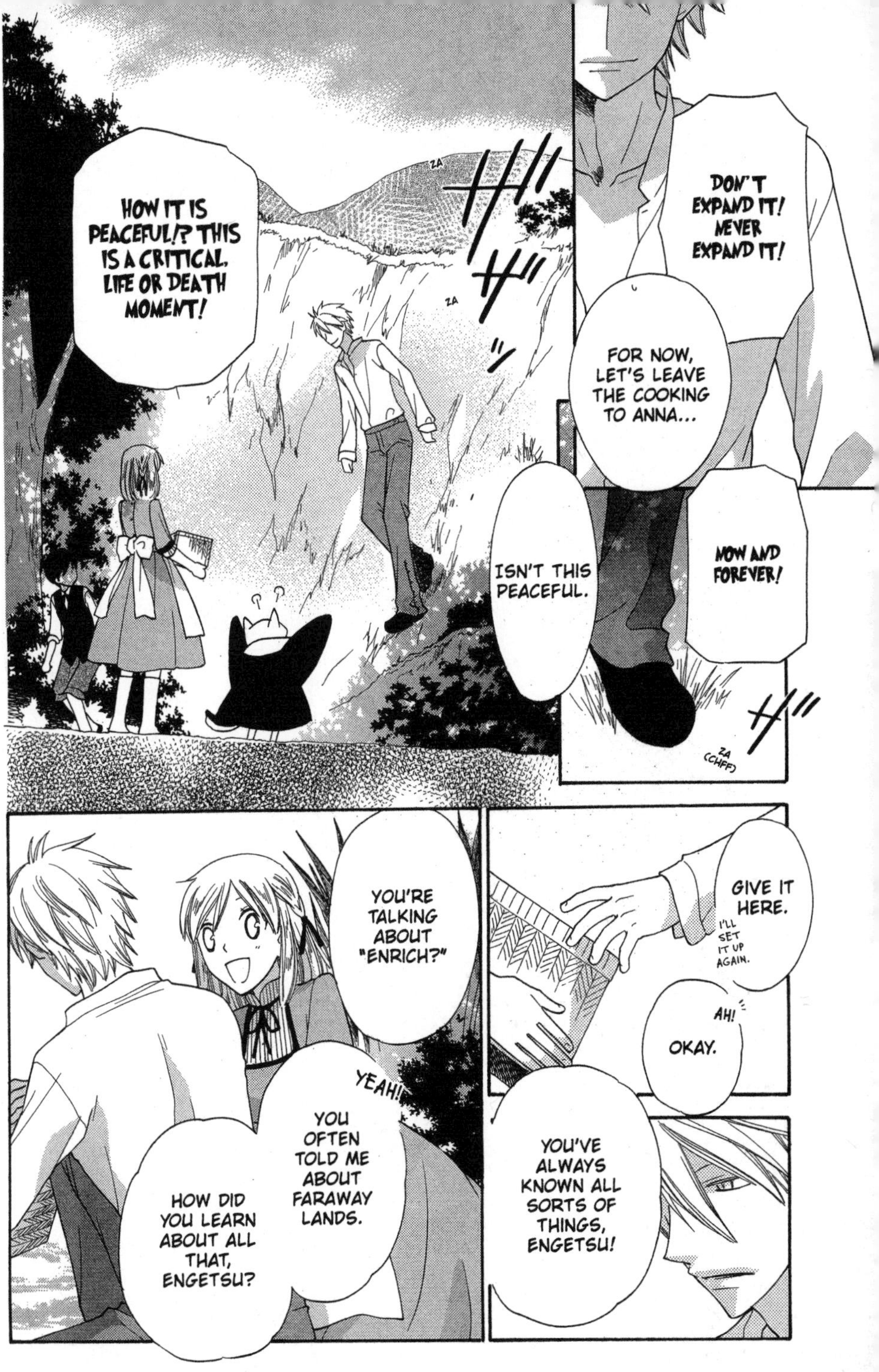
DON'T EXPAND IT! NEVER EXPAND IT!
FOR NOW, LET'S LEAVE THE COOKING TO ANNA...
NOW AND FOREVER!
ZA (CHFF)
ISN'T THIS PEACEFUL.
ZA
ZA
HOW IT IS PEACEFUL!? THIS IS A CRITICAL, LIFE OR DEATH MOMENT!
GIVE IT HERE.
I'LL SET IT UP AGAIN.
AH!
OKAY.
YOU'VE ALWAYS KNOWN ALL SORTS OF THINGS, ENGETSU!
YOU'RE TALKING ABOUT "ENRICH?"
YEAH!
YOU OFTEN TOLD ME ABOUT FARAWAY LANDS.
HOW DID YOU LEARN ABOUT ALL THAT, ENGETSU?

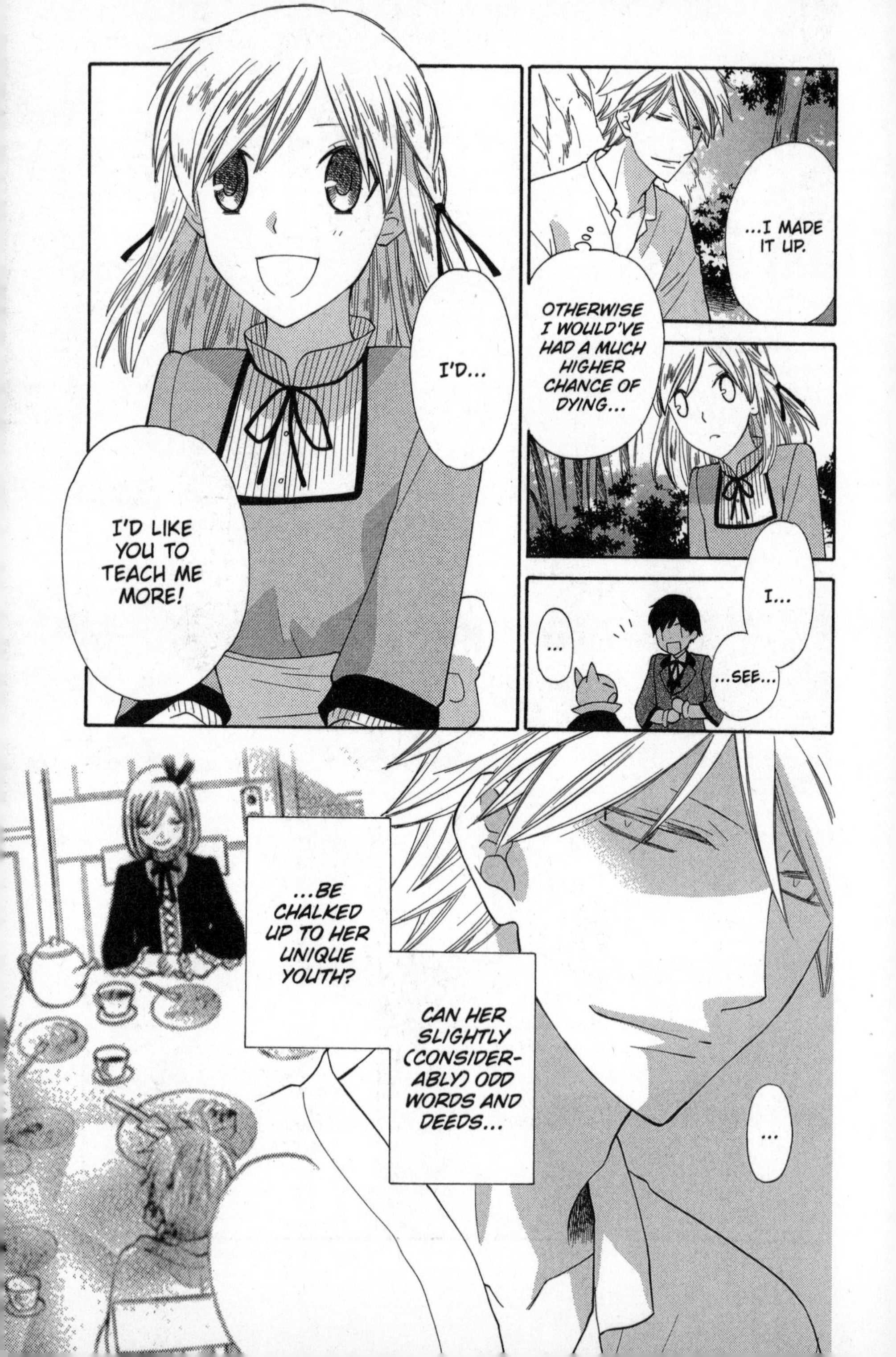
...I MADE IT UP.
OTHERWISE I WOULD'VE HAD A MUCH HIGHER CHANCE OF DYING...
I... ...SEE...
...
I'D...
I'D LIKE YOU TO TEACH ME MORE!
...
CAN HER SLIGHTLY (CONSIDER-ABLY) ODD WORDS AND DEEDS...
...BE CHALKED UP TO HER UNIQUE YOUTH?

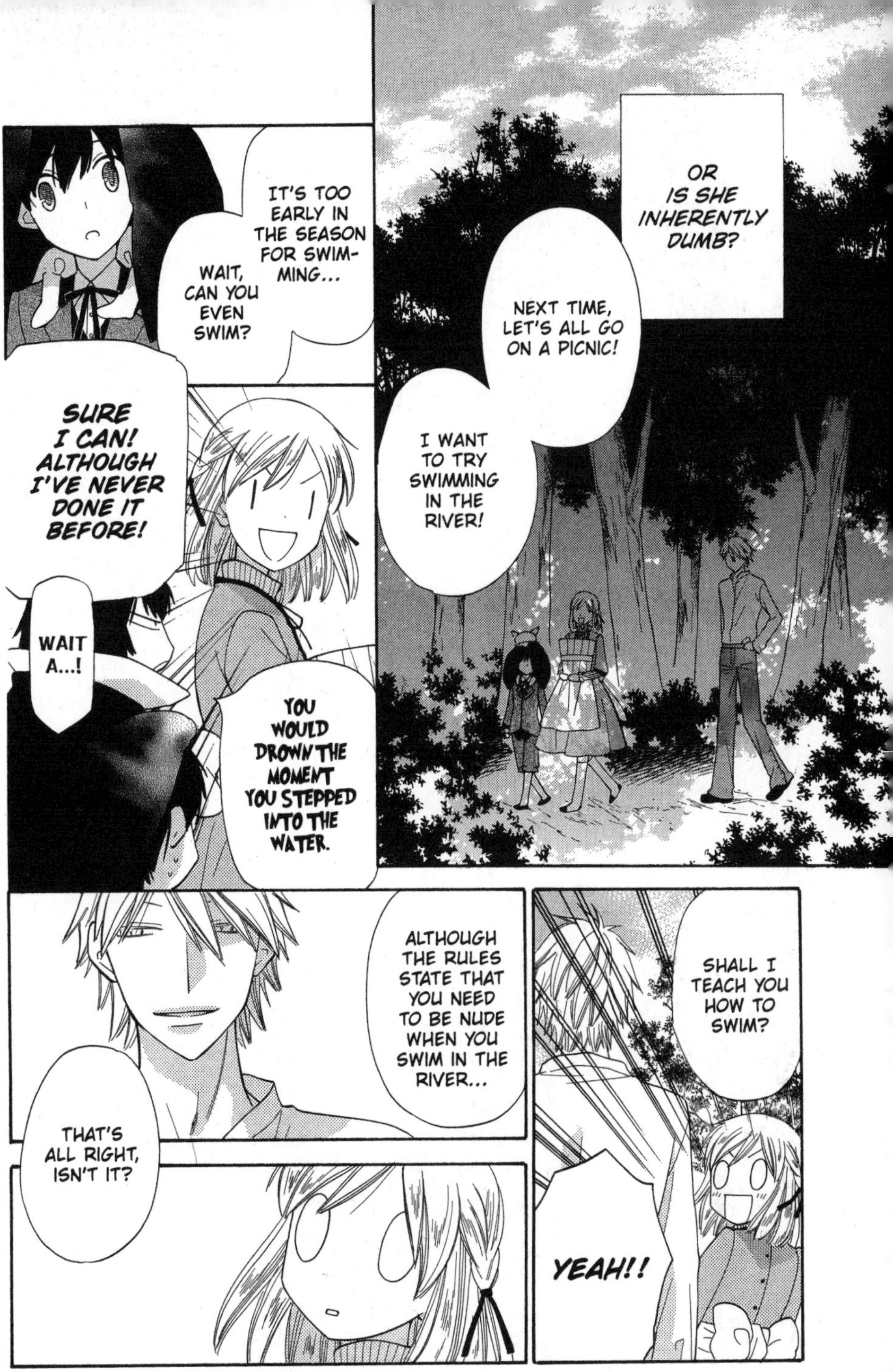

OR IS SHE INHERENTLY DUMB?
NEXT TIME, LET'S ALL GO ON A PICNIC!
I WANT TO TRY SWIMMING IN THE RIVER!
IT'S TOO EARLY IN THE SEASON FOR SWIMMING...
WAIT, CAN YOU EVEN SWIM?
SURE I CAN! ALTHOUGH I'VE NEVER DONE IT BEFORE!
WAIT A...!
YOU WOULD DROWN THE MOMENT YOU STEPPED INTO THE WATER.
SHALL I TEACH YOU HOW TO SWIM?
YEAH!!
ALTHOUGH THE RULES STATE THAT YOU NEED TO BE NUDE WHEN YOU SWIM IN THE RIVER...
THAT'S ALL RIGHT, ISN'T IT?

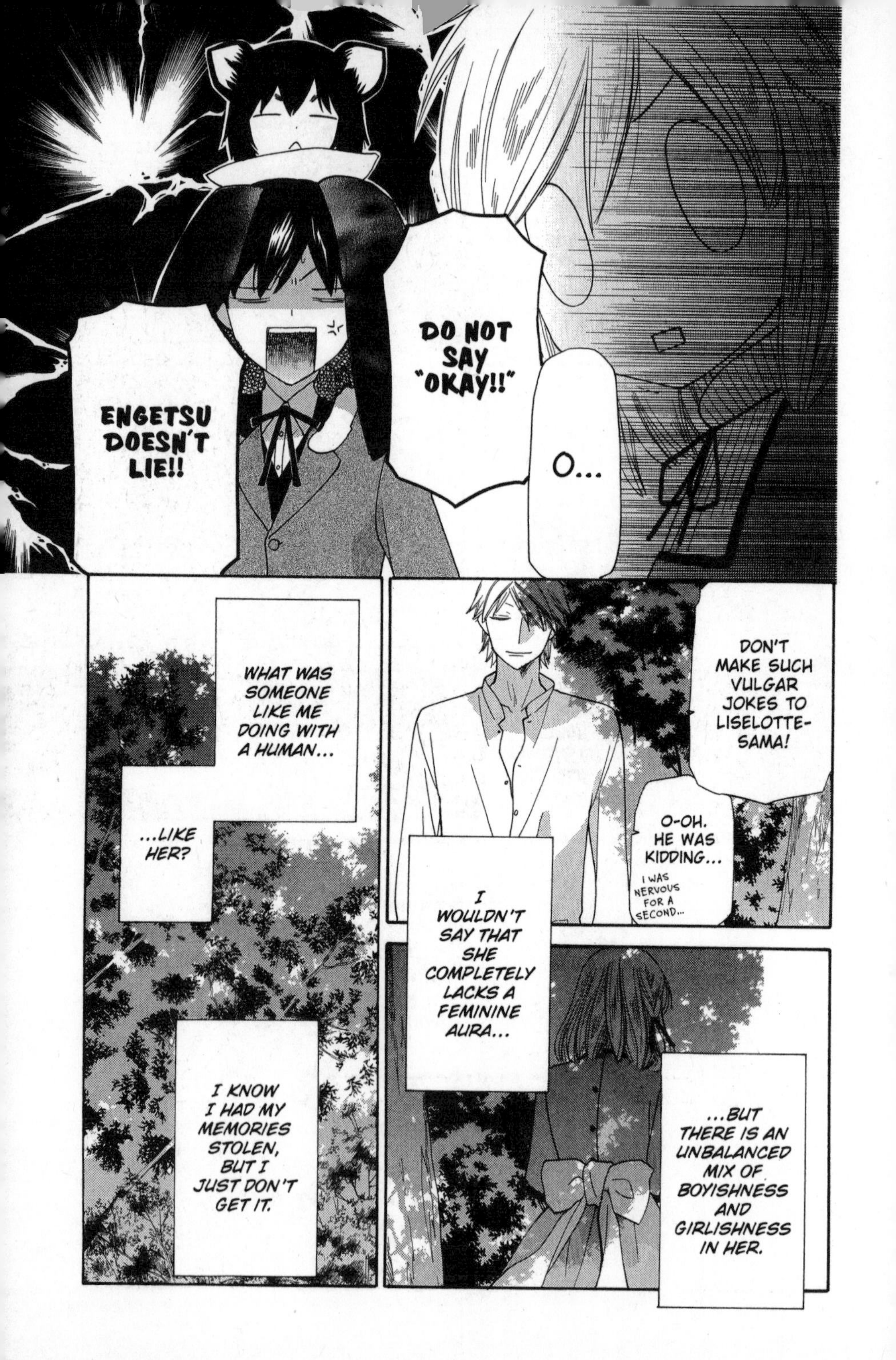
O...
DO NOT SAY "OKAY!!"
ENGETSU DOESN'T LIE!!
DON'T MAKE SUCH VULGAR JOKES TO LISELOTTE-SAMA!
O-OH. HE WAS KIDDING...
I WAS NERVOUS FOR A SECOND...
I WOULDN'T SAY THAT SHE COMPLETELY LACKS A FEMININE AURA...
...BUT THERE IS AN UNBALANCED MIX OF BOYISHNESS AND GIRLISHNESS IN HER.
WHAT WAS SOMEONE LIKE ME DOING WITH A HUMAN...
...LIKE HER?
I KNOW I HAD MY MEMORIES STOLEN, BUT I JUST DON'T GET IT.

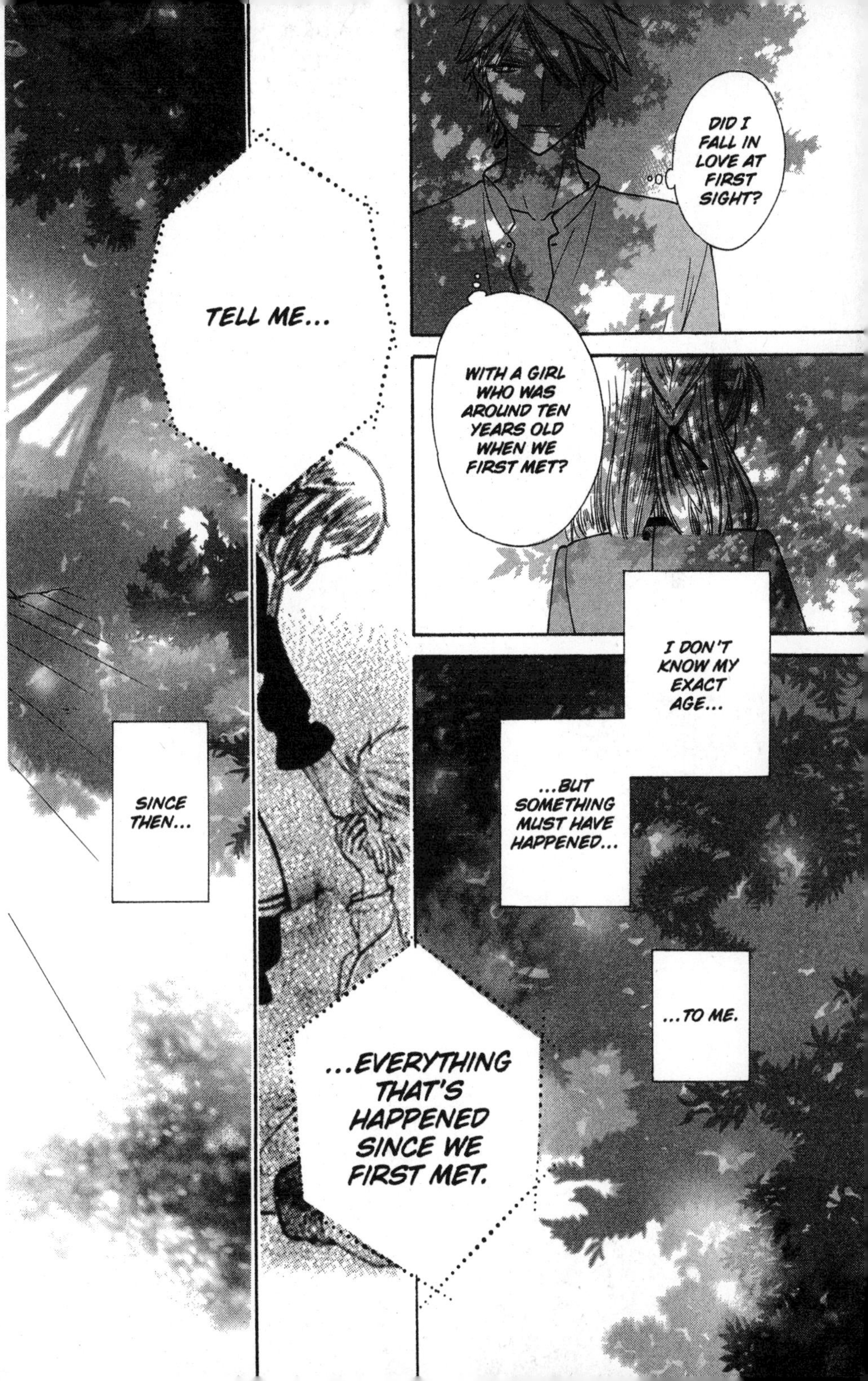
DID I FALL IN LOVE AT FIRST SIGHT?
WITH A GIRL WHO WAS AROUND TEN YEARS OLD WHEN WE FIRST MET?
I DON'T KNOW MY EXACT AGE...
...BUT SOMETHING MUST HAVE HAPPENED...
...TO ME.
TELL ME...
...EVERYTHING THAT'S HAPPENED SINCE WE FIRST MET.
SINCE THEN...

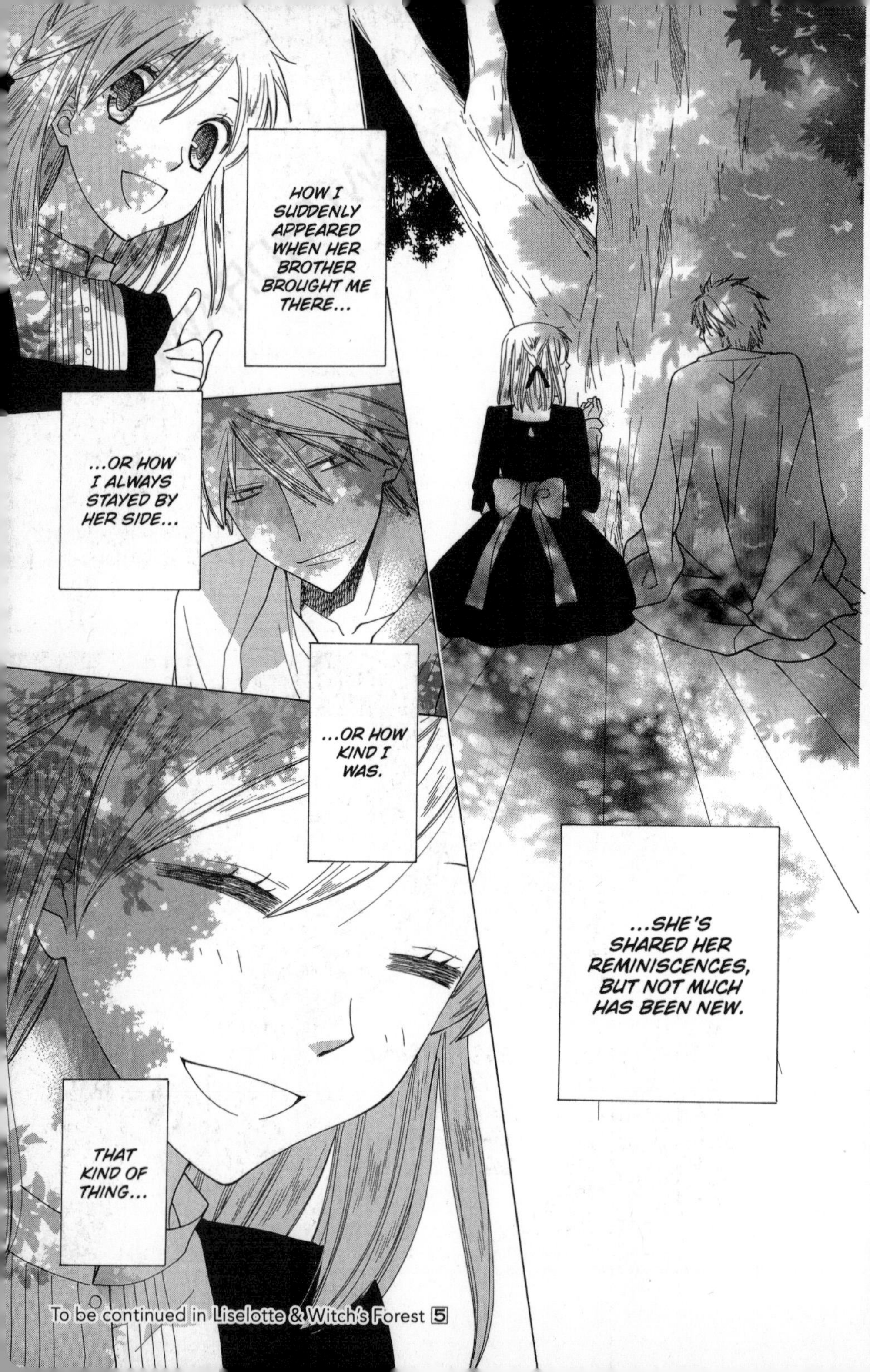
...SHE'S SHARED HER REMINISCENCES, BUT NOT MUCH HAS BEEN NEW.
HOW I SUDDENLY APPEARED WHEN HER BROTHER BROUGHT ME THERE...
...OR HOW I ALWAYS STAYED BY HER SIDE...
...OR HOW KIND I WAS.
THAT KIND OF THING...

To be continued in Liselotte & Witch's Forest 5

P9-ECP-603

WITHDRAWN

Translation: Sheldon Drzka

Lettering: Lys Blakeslee

This book is a work of fiction. Names, characters, places, and incidents are the product of the author's imagination or are used fictitiously. Any resemblance to actual events, locales, or persons, living or dead, is coincidental.

LISELOTTE TO MAJO NO MORI Vol. 4 by Natsuki Takaya
© Natsuki Takaya 2013
All rights reserved.
First published in Japan in 2013 by HAKUSENSHA, INC., Tokyo.
English language translation rights in U.S.A., Canada, and U.K. arranged with
HAKUSENSHA, INC., Tokyo through Tuttle-Mori Agency, Inc., Tokyo.

English translation © 2017 by Yen Press, LLC

Yen Press
1290 Avenue of the Americas
New York, NY 10104

Visit us at yenpress.com
facebook.com/yenpress
twitter.com/yenpress
yenpress.tumblr.com
instagram.com/yenpress

First Yen Press Edition: April 2017

Yen Press is an imprint of Yen Press, LLC.
The Yen Press name and logo are trademarks of Yen Press, LLC.

Library of Congress Control Number: 2016936533

ISBN: 978-0-316-36104-0

10 9 8 7 6 5 4 3 2 1

BVG

Printed in the United States of America